THE DOREEN MASSEY READER

ECONOMIC TRANSFORMATIONS

Series Editors: Brett Christophers, Rebecca Lave, Jamie Peck, Marion Werner

Fundamental to the *Economic Transformations* series is the conviction that "geography matters" in the diverse ways that economies work, for whom they work, and to what ends. The so-called imperatives of globalization, the promises of development, the challenges of environmental sustainability, the dull compulsion of competitive life, the urgency of campaigns for economic rights and social justice – in all of these realms geography really matters, just as it does for a host of other contemporary concerns, from financial-ized growth to climate change, from green production to gender rights, from union renewal to structural adjustment. This major new series will publish on these and related issues, creating a space for interdisciplinary contributions from political economists, economic geographers, feminists, political ecologists, economic sociologists, critical development theorists, economic anthropologists, and their fellow travellers.

Published

The Doreen Massey Reader
Edited by Brett Christophers, Rebecca Lave, Jamie Peck and Marion Werner
Doreen Massey: Critical Dialogues
Edited by Marion Werner, Jamie Peck, Rebecca Lave and Brett Christophers

THE DOREEN MASSEY READER

Edited by

BRETT CHRISTOPHERS
REBECCA LAVE
JAMIE PECK
MARION WERNER

agenda
publishing

First published in 2018 by Agenda Publishing

Agenda Publishing Limited
The Core
Science Central
Bath Lane
Newcastle upon Tyne
NE4 5TF
www.agendapub.com

ISBN 978-1-911116-82-0 (hardcover)
ISBN 978-1-911116-83-7 (paperback)

British Library Cataloguing-in-Publication Data
A catalogue record for this book is available from the British Library

Typeset by JS Typesetting Ltd, Porthcawl, Mid Glamorgan
Printed and bound in the UK by TJ International

CONTENTS

ACKNOWLEDGEMENTS

This volume and its companion, *Doreen Massey: Critical Dialogues*, were spurred by Doreen Massey's untimely passing in March 2016. As we reflected upon her contributions, we lamented that many of Massey's works were relatively difficult to access, and that some had not received the readership and recognition they deserved. Thus began the process of re-reading her many books, articles, and opinion pieces and making the difficult decisions about which to include in this volume.

We would like to thank the many colleagues and former students of Doreen's who sent us recommendations about pieces to consider. We are grateful for editorial assistance from Caitlyn Sears. The process of creating both volumes benefited immensely from the insights and guidance of John Allen, who serves as the literary executor of Doreen's estate. We are also thankful for the support of Agenda Publishing, its managing director, Steven Gerrard, and especially, Alison Howson, who has worked closely and enthusiastically with us on the numerous moving parts of the project. We are indebted to Doreen's sister, Hilary Corton, who graciously granted us permission to reprint the work included here.

Finally, we are so very thankful to Doreen herself for inspiring us with her combination of incisive intellectual analysis, trenchant political critique, and effective social action. We are all the richer for her time with us.

The royalties from both volumes will be donated to charities designated by the Massey estate.

Brett Christophers
Rebecca Lave
Jamie Peck
Marion Werner

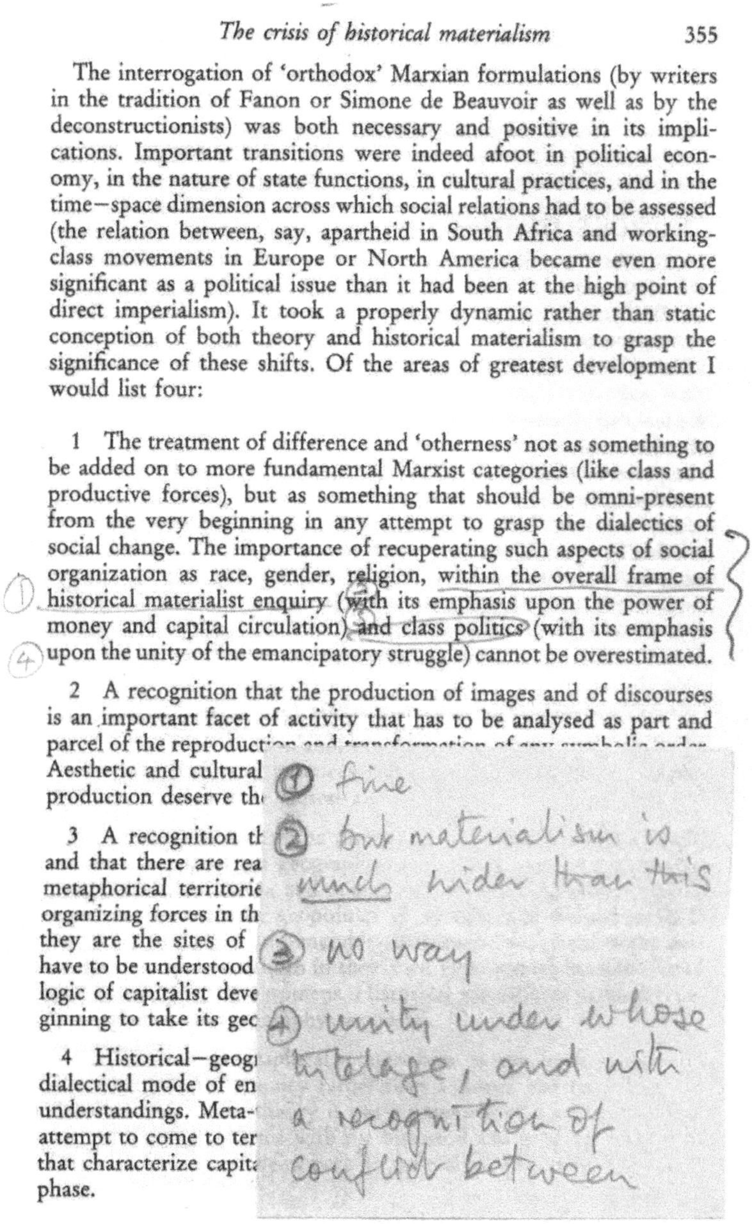

The interrogation of 'orthodox' Marxian formulations (by writers in the tradition of Fanon or Simone de Beauvoir as well as by the deconstructionists) was both necessary and positive in its implications. Important transitions were indeed afoot in political economy, in the nature of state functions, in cultural practices, and in the time—space dimension across which social relations had to be assessed (the relation between, say, apartheid in South Africa and working-class movements in Europe or North America became even more significant as a political issue than it had been at the high point of direct imperialism). It took a properly dynamic rather than static conception of both theory and historical materialism to grasp the significance of these shifts. Of the areas of greatest development I would list four:

1 The treatment of difference and 'otherness' not as something to be added on to more fundamental Marxist categories (like class and productive forces), but as something that should be omni-present from the very beginning in any attempt to grasp the dialectics of social change. The importance of recuperating such aspects of social organization as race, gender, religion, within the overall frame of historical materialist enquiry (with its emphasis upon the power of money and capital circulation) and class politics (with its emphasis upon the unity of the emancipatory struggle) cannot be overestimated.

2 A recognition that the production of images and of discourses is an important facet of activity that has to be analysed as part and parcel of the reproduction and transformation of any symbolic order. Aesthetic and cultural production deserve th

3 A recognition th and that there are rea metaphorical territorie organizing forces in th they are the sites of have to be understood logic of capitalist deve ginning to take its geo

4 Historical—geog dialectical mode of en understandings. Meta- attempt to come to ter that characterize capit phase.

[handwritten annotations:]
① fine
② but materialism is much wider than this
③ no way
④ unity under whose tutelage, and with a recognition of conflict between

Doreen Massey's hand-written annotation of David Harvey's *The Condition of Postmodernity*, the focus of her famous essay "Flexible Sexism" (courtesy of Mark Graham).

CHAPTER 1

OUT OF PLACE: DOREEN MASSEY, RADICAL GEOGRAPHER

Jamie Peck, Marion Werner, Rebecca Lave and Brett Christophers

Doreen Massey changed geography. As a creative scholar, an inspiring teacher, and a restless activist, she initiated new ways of seeing, understanding, and indeed changing the world. She launched critiques, both in the relatively small world of economic geography and the much bigger worlds of social theory and progressive politics, that would prove to be truly transformative; she developed arguments against a host of establishment and orthodox positions that left something better and more productive in their place; she confronted structurally-embedded power relations, most notably of class and gender, while steadfastly resisting political and analytical foreclosure; and she started conversations that continue to resonate and reverberate, not least those around the protean potential of place, even in these challenging times.

"There is no point of departure" is a line that Massey liked to quote from Louis Althusser (1971: 85; Massey 1995c: 351; Featherstone & Painter 2013). For her, it meant that socially-made historical geographies really matter, always and everywhere, and that futures are neither singular nor pre-given. Her own life was a case in point. The product of an "ordinary place" (Massey 2001: 459), a public-housing estate just south of Manchester, Doreen Massey knew where she came from and for that matter, which side she was on. "I'm from the North West [of England] and have lived with, through and kind of in combat with regional inequality [since] my childhood", Massey once explained (Massey with HGRG 2009: 405). Out of the conformity of post-war Britain, Massey fashioned a transformative trajectory not least, she later reflected, by participating in political movements "in the late 60s and the 70s with the emergence of Marxism, feminism, sexual liberation, being part of the GLC [Greater London Council] in the 1980s, or the kind of stuff that has happened more recently", from Chavismo in Venezuela to the Occupy movement in London (*Ibid*: 403, 405; Featherstone *et al.* 2013: 253, 257).

From her adopted home of Kilburn, in North London, she would sometimes commute to work at the Open University with her longtime friend and collaborator, Stuart Hall. The quotidian experience of driving to campus and back served as a reminder to both that one "can never 'go home' ... You can't go back", since neither of them came from "this tract of southeastern England", nor was it possible for them to return to the Jamaica or Manchester of their youth, which of course were not "the same as when we left" (Massey 2000: 230). Walks down Kilburn High Street would evoke for Massey, indelibly, "a global sense of place", quite the opposite of its sometimes parochial, introspective, singular, or static meaning, but instead an open-ended, processual, intersectional, and dynamic sense of place, always in the (re)making (Massey 1991a).

This understanding of place as an emergent constellation, or moving configuration, of social trajectories echoed the way in which Massey sought to problematize connection and difference – not separately but in the same time-space. As she would reflect in relation to her travels (and conversations) with Stuart Hall:

> What the simultaneity of space really consists in, then, is absolutely not a surface, a continuous material landscape, but a momentary coexistence of trajectories, a configuration of a multiplicity of histories all in the process of being made. This is ... part of the delight, and the potential, of space. (Massey 2000b: 229).

That Massey's journey should take her here, all the way from regional science and industrial geography, is a story in its own right. Since there can be no singular point of departure, nor any final moment of closure, our purpose in this chapter is to trace some of the contours and milestones of Doreen Massey's transformative intellectual and political journey. Reassembling the story will require, inevitably, some measure of chronology. But as David Featherstone and Joe Painter wrote in an earlier collection on Massey's career-long contributions, "Any attempt to fit her work into a neat sequential account of geography's recent past ... would be doomed to fail" (Featherstone & Painter 2013: 2). What follows then should be understood less as a sequence of steps or stages, and more as a collection of episodes in the formation of an intellectual and political biography. We begin in Manchester and end in Kilburn. In between, we arc selectively through Massey's paradigm-making interventions in political-economic geography and late-neoliberal politics, through her distinctive interventions in Marxist and feminist theory, seeking to trace along the way some of the contours of her foundational contributions to the understanding of space and spatiality. And it still feels like we are barely scratching the surface ....

OUT OF MANCHESTER

Doreen Massey grew up in a working-class family in the Wythenshawe coun-cil estate in South Manchester, a public housing development that was for a while the largest in Europe (see Massey 2001). Along with many of their neighbours, the Massey family relied upon the state for subsidized housing, free schooling and healthcare. This would be especially important for their eldest daughter, who was born with a calcium disorder that made her bones fragile and subject to breaks throughout her life. "[H]ad there not been a welfare state and the hospitals", Massey later reflected, "I would probably not have survived so well. I really feel in a kind of physical, personal way the need for a welfare state, not as a 'safety net', but just for ordinary people simply to provide a decent life" (Freytag & Holyer 2009: 85). She would take a hardly typical path for a working-class girl from the North, going to Oxford University in the mid-1960s, where not for the first nor indeed last time in her life she would sometimes feel like a "space invader" (see Telegraph 2016: 33; cf. Massey 1994: 185). Somewhat ironically perhaps, given the discipline's overwhelmingly conservative cast at the time, it was through Geography that she discovered her way out, even as she retained an abiding anti-establishment sensibility.

Despite taking a First at Oxford, Massey initially rejected the academic path and instead went to work in the computing department of a market research firm. As she described her thinking later, "The reason I left Oxford not wanting to be an academic was that I'd seen what I thought it meant to be an academic. And I didn't want to be that. So I went into industry – and hated it!" (Freytag & Hoyler 2009: 84). Abandoning the private sector, she began her research career in earnest at the Centre for Environmental Studies (CES), an independent research institute founded by Harold Wilson's Labour Government in 1967 with a remit in spatial planning. Here she would make some of the first moves in what would amount to a radical rethink-ing of industrial and class restructuring. In 1970, Massey returned briefly to Oxford to participate in the UK's first Women's Liberation Movement conference of that era. "From then on", she later reflected, "I have always been involved in feminist movements" (Albet & Benach 2012: 53, editors' transla-tion). Massey would shape and channel her anti-establishment sensibility in productive tension with feminism in the ensuing decades, wary of currents within feminism that tended towards essentialism and narrow identity pol-itics, and always emphasizing the imbrications of class and gender (Albet & Benach 2012: 54). She insisted that "[C]lass and feminism ... [affect] what kind of voice you have; what kind of role you can play, and want to play" (Featherstone *et al.* 2013: 261).

In 1971, Massey was granted a leave from CES to undertake a master's degree in regional science and "mathematical economics" at the University of Pennsylvania in Philadelphia, then a citadel of neoclassical location theory, which she viewed as a "'you ought to know your enemy' kind of thing" (Massey with HGRG 2009: 404). It was here that an extra-curricular visit to the French department provided a quite unexpected introduction to Louis Althusser and to a distinctive (and generative) interpretation of Althusserianism. After Penn, it was not the mathematics of location theory that she pursued, but instead an altogether more radical path. For a while, CES would be an accommodating home for what would prove to be formative work on the political economy of Britain's "regional problem", some of this in collaboration with Richard Meegan (see Meegan 2017). But in 1979, when the incoming Thatcher administration abruptly withdrew funding for the organization, Massey found herself at a crossroads of sorts. Fortunately, at least for the short term, she had a research grant enabling her to work at the London School of Economics, and to make what would prove to be a remarkably catalytic visit to the University of California at Berkeley (Peck & Barnes 2019). It was here, in what was otherwise an especially lean spell for British universities, that an unexpected opportunity arose:

> While I was in California the advertisement came up that offered a post at the Open University and that seemed to me to be a place where it might be possible to be an intellectual, a teacher, a researcher without being at a more formal university, and I applied for that job and I got it. There was a short time to go before I would have been unemployed. So it was either a chair or the dole. (Freytag & Hoyler 2009: 85)

Doreen Massey would spend the next 27 years of her academic career teaching at what many would consider, rather ironically, the most placeless of British universities, the Open University, a distance-learning institution in the infamously anonymous new town of Milton Keynes, where in the context of limited face-to-face contact with students she pioneered innovative ways of "teaching at a distance" (Clarke 2016: 360), not to say engaging across distance.

Massey was on the frontline in some of the signature struggles against Thatcherism, including the miners' strike of 1984–85 and the municipal-socialist project of the Greater London Enterprise Board, events that in retrospect marked an historical inflection point between a regionalist model of labour organization and the ascendancy of the "new urban left". She was also heavily involved in a wide range of intellectual projects, as an early editorial board member of *Capital & Class* and *Red Pepper*, as a co-founder of *Soundings* with Stuart Hall and Michael Rustin, and as the key mover in an extended series of remarkably influential Open University course texts. For many years, Massey was engaged in political struggles in Latin America and South Africa too, as a researcher and activist. And she would devote the later part of her career to a creative and politically-inspiring analysis of why the global financial crisis of 2008 had not led to the collapse of neoliberalism, culminating in a final project in collaboration with Hall and Rustin. Characteristically, what was known as the Kilburn Manifesto could be considered both a product of their (shared) place, as a model of conjuncturally situated political, economic and cultural analysis, and a contribution that resonated and reached significantly beyond that place (see Hall *et al.* 2012; Peck *et al.* 2014). In these, as in so many of her other endeavours, Doreen Massey consistently gave the lie to the idea that the price of theoretical sophistication had to be paid in political irrelevance or incomprehensibility outside (and sometimes even inside!) academia. Similarly, she refused to accept that there should be a dividing line between political and intellectual work.

These were principles that she quite literally embodied. One of the most striking things about Doreen Massey was the contrast between her very small physical stature and her very large personality. Possessed of a radiant smile, ready laughter, and boundless curiosity, she had a notable ability to connect personally and intellectually with those around her. Throughout her life, she moved in academic and political circles dominated mostly by men, and not only rejected but actively challenged the masculinist cultures of both those worlds. "This is a political position, not an essentialization around masculinity, femininity or whatever", she once explained. "But I do find myself amazed by and wary of the ease with which writers make Olympian statements about the age ... [while] standing outside society and describing it and forgetting that we're also within it" (Featherstone *et al.* 2013: 261). Massey never forgot that, despite the enormous influence that her own work would have in geography, in feminism, in social theory, and in left scholarship more generally. She handled this, as she noted in amusement in an interview with graduate students at the University of Kentucky in the early 1990s, by "just carry[ing] on being different!"

> I can't speak like some of these big guys do. If you are five foot one, and you are fair-haired, and you are female, and quite often you can barely see over the podium, then just physically and materially you cannot be imposing in the same way that you can when you are six foot five and have a big male deep voice. The very physicality and materiality of it, as well as the fact that they just take those people more seriously than they take us, starts you off in a different situation. So what I've tried to do is just carry on being different. (Ijams *et al.* 1994: 101)

In what follows, we sketch some of the many generative and inspiring ways in which Doreen Massey carried on by being different, beginning where her scholarly career began, with a transformative critique of industrial location theory.

INDUSTRIAL DISLOCATIONS

Doreen Massey made the first of many field-shaping interventions in 1973, with her practically terminal critique of the science of location theory. "Towards a Critique of Industrial Location Theory", published in the recently-launched radical journal, *Antipode*, marked her uninvited arrival to the male-dominated, white-bread field known at the time as industrial geography. Hers was a nominally "tentative" critique from which the field would never really recover. The journey implied by the article's title did not in the end result in a "march … into a newly-formulated industrial location theory" (Massey 1973: 38, 33), but instead would take a more circuitous route to an entirely different paradigm. Not unlike British industry itself, the field of industrial geography was in a parlous state at the time, dogged as it was by unreflexive strains of empiricism and economism, and falling short in its attempts to account for disorienting patterns of path-disrupting, radical, and often divergent change (see Williams & Thomas 1983; Martin *et al.* 1993).

Critical not only of the epistemological but also the ideological affinities between location theory and neoclassical economics, Massey challenged the prevailing conception of abstract firms operating in abstract space on the grounds both of analytical insufficiency and an evident estrangement from real-world conditions:

> What are emerging as "locational problems," whether intra-urban, interregional or international, are the spatial manifestations of the contradictions of capitalism … spatial development can only be seen as part of the overall development of capitalism. However, it is also true that many of the emerging contradictions of the economic system both take on a specifically spatial form, and are exacerbated by the existence of the spatial dimension. To this end, consideration of "the spatial element" is essential to all effective economic analysis. (Massey 1973: 38-9)

Here, Massey was not only calling into question the plausibility of location theory's claim to a "separate existence", as a project of closed-system theorizing premised on the principles of rational action and general equilibrium, she was also anticipating an entirely different ontology of the economic, together with an understanding of its constitutive spatiality.

The course (and cause) of Massey's work during the 1970s was taking shape. There was a recognition that the disorderly economic conditions of the time – oil crises, deindustrialization, stagflation, industrial-relations strife, anti-immigrant backlash, rising unemployment, the International Monetary Fund's "bailout" of the UK economy, the failure of both Conservative and Labour governments on the altar of economic policy – more than amply confirmed the redundancy of the timid orthodoxy of regional science. More than this, though, they demanded a radical alternative, one that offered analytical purchase on the real-time restructuring of (regional) economies in crisis. A further indicator of Massey's thinking at the time was a book review commissioned by her former boss at CES, Alan Wilson, just a few months after the publication of the *Antipode* article. In a broadly sympathetic but exacting review of David Harvey's *Social Justice and the City*, Massey credited the book for raising questions and problematizing issues "which quite simply *cannot* arise within the normal framework of Anglo-Saxon regional science". The book offered a necessary critique, she continued, albeit an insufficient alternative; it built suggestively on Marxian notions of rent, but less persuasively on the accompanying apparatus of a narrowly-defined class analysis. Overall, she concluded, Harvey's intervention would surely "shake a good many economist-geographers out of their implicit and tautological assumptions" (Massey 1974: 229, 235). Thus, more or less in parallel, Massey and Harvey spurned the trappings and pretensions of positivist geography – with its "trivial notions of causality, [its] idea that a scientific 'law' was something that could be spotted simply through empirical regularity [and with] the mathematics (or the problems in the mathematics) leading the direction of enquiry rather than questions which arose from real world processes themselves" (Massey 1985: 10). The next steps that they would take, however, would be different ones.

Convinced that geography mattered, in a material, political, social and constitutive sense, but deeply sceptical of positivist claims concerning supposedly spatial laws, Massey found in more abstract forms of Marxism both an affinity and an irreconcilable limit. As a member of the editorial board of *Capital & Class* and elsewhere, she had for years been engaged in debates around value theory, dialectics, uneven development and more, but often found these base categories of analysis to be bloodless, "byzantine entanglements" inadequate in political as well as explanatory terms (1995c: 307). As she later reflected, "the way in which I was thinking was definitely influenced, utterly influenced, by Marx", but at the same time, because of its orthodox remit, she "found it very, very difficult to count myself as a Marxist" (Massey with the HGRG 2009: 403, 405). Some of these critical reservations stemmed from Massey's feminism, which shaped her orientations to theory and politics for some time before it was explicitly incorporated into her analytical schema. Initially, then, feminist influences manifested in her reaction against macro-theoretical abstractions that presumed, rather than interrogated, their impact on the world. Neither value, as an abstract category, nor class, understood primarily in economic terms, could explain the lived realities of restructuring (as it would come to be known) observed in particular places and industries. Gender blindness was part of the problem, but there was a wider failure to account for *who* it was that filled the "empty spaces" of so many abstract Marxian categories (cf. Hartmann 1979), and for that matter the different ways in which those empty spaces were filled in different places.

Massey's twin convictions that geography mattered and that Marxian categories must be rendered concrete if they were to furnish analytical and political value were on clear display in her first monograph, *Capital and Land*, coauthored with her CES colleague Alejandrina Catalano (Massey & Catalano 1978). The product of several years of collaborative labour, the book was a trenchant critique of a central pillar of Britain's radically unequal political economy (then, but also now): private landownership. It seamlessly combined theoretical sophistication and empirical exposition, marrying a clear explication of that most abstruse of Marxian demesnes – rent theory – with the first major investigation of patterns of landownership in Britain for over a century, those ownership patterns having remained essentially undocumented since 1873's "Modern Domesday" book, the Return of Owners of Land. The book became a touchstone for scholars of the land question in Britain in the ensuing decades. Its main message – that the social institution of landed property profoundly colours British capitalism – was one that stayed with Massey for the rest of her career (indeed, it was to be explicitly reiterated in the Kilburn Manifesto), although she would not work on land issues again. Instead, her attention turned to what were seen at the time as more pressingly urgent questions – labour, (un)employment, and the political economy of capitalist restructuring.

In collaborative work with Richard Meegan, Massey had been tracking patterns of employment change across dozens of UK industries, in the process uncovering a heterogeneous tangle of sectoral dynamics that belied simplified narratives of the causes of manufacturing job losses and the phenomenon known as deindustrialization. Unpacking what they would call the "anatomy" of job loss meant taking account of a repertoire of causally distinct processes at the sectoral level: in some cases, production systems and employment regimes were being rationalized; in others, they were being reorganized through new waves of technological investment; while elsewhere, the imperative was to drive improvements in productivity by way of intensification (Massey & Meegan 1982). To isolate, analyze and document these distinctive strategies was not to tune out the supposedly steady signal of structural change in favour of cacophonic "noise", Massey and Meegan insisted, nor was it to be diverted by local details or confounding contingencies; instead, it was to theorize generatively with and across difference, to illuminate varied configurations and pathways, and to point to conjuncturally specific stress points and sites of intervention. Crucially, this was not just about wading into the empirical undergrowth and then insisting upon the need for a more granular account; neither was it simply a matter of adding texture while continuing to colour between the lines of big-picture accounts of industrial transformation and uneven development. Instead, these were early steps on the path towards a more deeply relational form of geographical political economy.

When Massey first introduced what was to become one of her signature concepts, the spatial division of labour, she did so "in order to make a point" (1979: 234): the geographically differentiated conditions of production, including for instance the availability and cost of labour, should not be seen as some inert surface across which profit-seeking firms maximized returns. Rather, the relationship between the dynamics of accumulation and the shifting geographies of work and production was one of mutual interaction and adaptation. Beginning, in effect, with just two dimensions – industrial sectors and employment geographies – Massey conjured a vividly three-dimensional understanding of capitalist spatiality, displaying a characteristic combination of complex reasoning and unvarnished exposition. Granting that the orthodox observation that economic activities are distributed systematically in space according to the principle of profit maximization was "correct [but] also trivial", she set out in the space of two paragraphs an alternative (and demanding) remit for political-economic geography:

> What [the orthodox account] ignores is the variation in *the way in which different forms of economic activity incorporate or use the fact of spatial inequality* in order to maximise profits. This manner of response to geographical unevenness will vary both between sectors and, for any given sector, with changing conditions of production ... [There is an] interaction between, on the one hand the existing characteristics of spatial differentiation, and on the other hand the requirements at that time of the particular process of production. Moreover, if it is the case that different industries will use spatial variation in different ways, it is also true that these different modes of use will subsequently produce/contribute to different forms of geographical inequality. Different modes of response by industry, implying different spatial divisions of labour within its overall process of production, may thus generate different forms of "regional problem."

One schematic way of approaching this as a historical process is to conceive of it as a series of "rounds" of new investment, in each of which a new form of spatial division of labour is evolved. In fact, of course, the process of change is much more diversified and incremental (though certainly there are periods of radical redirection) ... In any empirical work, therefore, it is necessary both to analyse this complexity and to isolate and identify those particular divisions which are dominant in reshaping the spatial structure. The geographical distribution of economic activity which results from the evolution of a new form of division of labour will be overlaid on, and combined with, the pattern produced in previous periods by different forms of division of labour. *This combination of successive layers will produce effects which themselves vary over space*, thus giving rise to a new form and spatial distribution of inequality in the conditions of production, as a basis for the next "round" of investment. "The economy" of any given local area will thus be a complex result of the combination of its succession of roles within the series of wider, national and international, spatial divisions of labour.

(Massey 1979: 234–5, emphasis added)

The implications of this remarkably succinct formulation would be far reaching, intellectually and politically. It presaged a style of relational theorizing that did more than transcend the rapidly fading orthodoxy of location theory; it challenged Marxian political economy to engage *and work with* the patterned specificities of industrial restructuring, locality effects, and the complex recombination of class and gender relations, rather than to override them, or to subsume them within reductionist or all-encompassing categories of analysis.

Relational understandings of space and spatiality, in short, were central to Massey's formulations, rather than being secondary to (or derivative of) social processes. This concern with how social processes *take place*, as it were, implied nothing less than a relational ontology. "'Spatial outcomes' are not simply the 'outfall' of restructuring", Richard Meegan (2017: 1287, 1288) has explained, but are constitutively active in shaping successive rounds of investment. And while this is "[o]ften misinterpreted as a geological metaphor of the layering of strata, the notion of the historical layering of rounds of investment spatially is more accurately a metaphor of interaction and articulation." Subsequently, "articulation" would become a hallmark of Massey's approach, initially by way of an Althusserian treatment of the combination of economic, political and ideological forms and practices within regional conjunctures, and then much more expansively, in her influential notion of "relational space" (Massey 1995c: 315–23; Featherstone & Painter 2013: 4–7).

LOCALITY EFFECTS

Massey's foundational arguments concerning the spatiality of capitalism were worked out in extended form, and operationalized too, in *Spatial Divisions of Labour*, a book on which she worked for several years and to which she would return – taking the opportunity to append substantial methodological elaborations – just over a decade later (Massey 1984; 1995c). In its first edition, the book crystalized what was taking shape as the restructuring approach, although in retrospect it may also have represented its zenith (see Warde 1985; Lovering 1989). It carried the burdens of complexity and specificity alongside its mandate for creative conceptualization and active theorization, the explanatory incision and persuasive power of which was not to be matched in the wider research program that followed. Most conspicuously, the somewhat ill-starred "localities" research initiative, a national project funded by the Economic and Social Research Council in the UK and directly inspired by Massey's framework, largely failed to deliver, at least in its own terms. Controversial practically from the outset, the localities research program became the focus for a series of proxy debates around the status of Marxism and postmodernism, the politics of scale, the methodological potential (and limits) of critical realism and structuration theory, and more, not to mention the prosaic, organizational and scientific challenges of managing an expressly polycentric study comprising multiple case-study sites and research teams (see Cochrane 1987; Smith 1987; Bagguley *et al.* 1990).

While initially choosing to remain one step removed from the debates that roiled around the localities initiative – which her work had been instrumental in launching, but in which she had no direct role – Massey continued to support its programmatic rationale. Nationally oriented political debates were only rarely taking account of the diversity of regional and local experiences, she maintained, often asserting the existence of trends and (causal) connections that simply did not hold across scale and space; there were significant limits to explanations of (diverse) local transformations that were crudely pegged to "capitalism in general"; and a host of new social movements and municipal-socialist projects had been seeking to harness "the local" for progressive ends. Empirically, "[s]omething that might be called 'restructuring' was clearly going on, but its implications both for everyday life and for the mode and potential of political organising were clearly highly differentiated and we needed to know how" (Massey 1991c: 269). Theoretically and methodologically, Massey was challenging the conflation of the global scale with supposedly "general" theory claims, or abstraction itself, as well as the false equivalence between the local and the concrete. With a debt to the *Grundrisse*, she insisted on an understanding of the concrete as the synthesis of multiple determinations, pointing out that abstract analysis might just as

11

well focus on small objects as large ones, as it might on the local as well as the global.

Notwithstanding their operational limitations, the locality projects had not been originally conceived as idiosyncratic case studies, detached from broader explanatory frameworks; by design, they had been concerned to explore the spatial constitution of social processes, and the implications – both causal and political – of different, localized configurations of social relations. From the perspective of the localities research program,

> not only was the character of a particular place [understood to be] a product of its position in relation to wider forces (the more general social and economic restructuring, for instance), but also that that character in turn stamped its own imprint *on* those wider processes ... The facts of distance, betweenness, unevenness, nucleation, copresence, time-space distantiation, settings, mobility and differential mobility, all of these affect how specified social relations work; they may even be necessary for their existence or prevent their operation... [The] fact of spatial variation itself, and of interdependence – of uneven development – has major implications. (Massey 1991c: 271–2)

Massey's approach would become synonymous with the slogan "geography matters" (Massey & Allen 1984). While she went as far as to say that "the unique is back on the agenda" (Massey 1985: 19), Massey never displayed any interest in the unmoored pursuit of idiographic detail as an end in itself. To the contrary, her position was that "places [may be] unique but that does not make them inimical to theory" (Graham 1998: 942).

Yet there were influential (mis)readings of *Spatial Divisions of Labour*, and of the rationale for localities research, in which an alleged departure from Marxian theory was equated with a turn not just towards empirics but empiricism (Smith 1986, 1987; Harvey 1987; cf. Scott 2000). David Harvey contended that, "Massey is so anxious to deny structuralist leanings or that the 'logic of capitalist development' has any explanatory power in local settings that all theorising disappears between a mass of contingent labour-management relations in place", asserting that her approach had become "laden down with a rhetoric of contingency, place, and the specificity of history", to the point that the "guiding thread of Marxian argument is reduced to a set of echoes and reverberations of inert Marxian categories" (Harvey 1987: 369, 373). However, there is little in Harvey's critique to suggest (or indeed to recognize) a two-way interplay between the social and the spatial, or for that matter an effort to hold together the general and the particular. Instead, the project was interpreted as a reversal into the cul-de-sac of empirical specificity.

There is no disputing the fact, of course, that *Spatial Divisions of Labour* explicitly grappled with concrete complexity. As Ann Markusen reflected in a symposium convened to mark its enduring contribution, "students sometimes find it difficult to master Massey's book, not because it is densely written – on the contrary it has a light and colloquial tone – but because the analysis is so complex and multifaceted". Massey's response to Harvey's charge that the book was weighed down with contingency and complexity was characteristically forthright: "it certainly was and … I meant it to be!" (Martin *et al.* 1993: 70–1). Far from a repudiation, or retreat from, the concerns of Marxian political economy, Massey had in fact been continuing to employ the classic entry points of the capitalist labour process, the social relations of production, and the problematic of industrial transformation. Operating from – but reaching beyond – this known analytical territory, she had not just illustrated but *elaborated* the working out of processes of uneven development, specifying their (somewhat divergent) sectoral dynamics, and breaking down tendential historical claims in favour of a sharper focus on "layers" of (dis)investment. Not least, her approach was intended to open up and then occupy the space for much less deterministic accounts of place-based conditions and local change. She deftly reworked an Althusserian sense of overdetermination into an alternative conception of spatio-temporal relations, in dialogue with feminist theory and critical realism, by evoking notions such as the "combination of layers", the variable intersection of class and gender relations, the specificities of capitalist class divides and allegiances, and the vagaries of localized politics. Massey's framework put flesh on the bones of sparse formulations like core-periphery and "see-sawing" capital movements, insisting on the irreducibly socio-spatial content of relations that had too often been portrayed mechanistically.

Massey's project in this period, through *Spatial Divisions of Labour* and the remit for locality studies, thus is best understood as a dexterous elaboration of Marxian political economy rather than some radical departure from it. She insisted that theory claims had to be *read through* (and across) conjunctural specificities; theoretical abstractions were not somehow floating above the particular in a "general" sense. Massey's intention had never been to abandon received conceptions of the forces and relations of production or the dialectics of uneven geographical development, but instead to operationalize a framework for mobilizing these relatively abstract formulations *through* the structurally necessary mediations of (industrial) sector and (regional) space. While she did not conceive this work as an escape route from industrial geography, it nevertheless opened the door to quite different ways of thinking – ways of thinking that would soon carry Massey's own work beyond the relatively restrictive problematic of capitalist restructuring.

A VIEW FROM SOMEWHERE

By the end of the 1980s, with the fall of communism and triumphalist "end of history" narratives ringing out from the heartlands of capitalism, geographers and the broader social sciences became immersed in often-fervent disputes over the meaning and status of the watchwords of the time: postmodernism and globalization. Massey had spent the previous decade developing the apparatus of spatial divisions of labour, at least in part, to historicize the restructuring present, to reanimate and contextualize received concepts, and to specify more or less familiar forms of recombination. But as the objective grounds were shifting, Massey now parlayed these conceptual tools derived from her interventions in the far narrower field of industrial geography, along with her poststructuralist and feminist sensibilities, to intervene in these larger debates. Her contributions would unsettle prevailing claims that were often shared by the early boosters and sceptics of globalization about the death of geography, time-space compression, and the global (market) as a scale of "out there" forces and economic predetermination.

These debates benefited immensely from Massey's way of doing theory and being in the world. It is not simply that she critiqued the way that certain academics were validating the global in their work, sometimes echoing the prevailing formulations of corporate and governmental elites, even as they endeavoured to critique capitalism. She also called out the manner in which these universalized arguments were so often decontextualized by jet-setter scholars who seemed to survey (and write about) the world from 30,000 feet, as if to project their own placelessness. Massey argued instead for a more grounded engagement, literally and figuratively. In stark contrast to the "hype and hyperbole" that had become so typical of writing on globalization and postmodernism, she wrote clearly and accessibly, with wry awareness that, "Much of life for many people ... still consists of waiting in a bus-shelter with your shopping for a bus that never comes" (Massey 1992a: 8). She would often share anecdotes about where and how her ideas emerged and how they worked in practice. They might be stories about walking down Kilburn High Road, or sharing a commute with Stuart Hall, or about rounding Lake Windermere in the Lake District. This was how she explained the idea of the global sense of place, for example, and the notion of places as trajectories and multiplicities. Hers was a notion of globalization inseparable from deep commitments to place, but not in some nostalgic or parochial sense; instead, this was a variously more intimate, positional, and political sense of place, imbued always with the recognition of difference. Place was a site of encounter, of engagements with and across difference, globalization being experienced, as a far-from-universal condition, "in here" just as much as "out there".

This kind of view from somewhere had always been a compelling characteristic of Massey's writing and indeed her conceptual outlook, but it would be enriched in new and distinctive ways through her engagements with feminist theory and situated epistemologies, notably the work of Donna Haraway and Sandra Harding, whom she credited with a profound influence on her thinking (Massey 1995c; Albet & Benach 2012). Massey went on to provide object lessons in the power of feminist epistemology and critical spatial thinking in her key interventions of the early 1990s. She put in sharp relief the quite particular privileged positionality of scholars of globalization peddling seemingly universal and generalized claims about the dissolution of the subject, boundaries, and certainties, observing pointedly that,

> Those who today worry about a sense of disorientation and a loss of control must once have felt they knew exactly where they were, and that they had control ... The assumption that runs through much of this literature is that this openness, this penetrability of boundaries is a recent phenomenon. [And yet for the colonized periphery] the security of boundaries of the place one called home must have dissolved long ago, and the coherence of one's local culture must long ago have been under threat.
>
> (Massey 1992a: 9–10)

In her critique of the masculinist gaze exhibited by David Harvey's *Condition of Postmodernity* and Ed Soja's *Postmodern Geographies* in particular, Massey (1991b) exposed the occlusions, exclusions and elisions typical of "unreconstructed" variants of Marxism in human geography. Her critique echoed and built upon key feminist interventions intended to overturn masculinist Marxism across disciplines, including Deutsche (1991), Scott (1988/1999), Hartsock (1987) and Christopherson (1989).

Declaring her sympathy with the overall projects underpinning Soja's and Harvey's books, she challenged their exclusions (not least of swathes of feminist literature) and their apparently unthinking recirculation of supposed universals which "are so often in fact quite particular; not universals at all but white, male, Western, heterosexual, what have you", formulations that also carried broad and deep implications for academic politics, for political representation, and for the practice of political economy:

> Harvey has produced a fascinating, if arguably economistic, exploration of the relation between the definition, production, and experience of space, on the one hand, and modes of production and class formation on the other. But it completely misses other ways, other power-relations, in which space is also structured and

experienced ... This leads to an unnecessarily monolithic view of the modernist period; it shifts the definition of what it was and, by missing out the voices on the margins and in the interstices of what was accepted, it also misses the full force of the critique which those voices, among them feminists, were making of the modernism he does discuss ... After all the feminist debate about representation [including] the directly political critique of modernist representation, it is surely inadequate to put the whole crisis down to time-space compression and flexible accumulation.

(Massey 1991b: 52, 53, 51)

Recognizing that "neither of the authors would want to be thought of as antifeminist", Massey took Harvey and Soja to task for reducing culture and politics to epiphenomena of the mode of production; for positioning class relations "above" other sources and sites of social difference, ascribing overarching or covering status to the former while subordinating or localizing the latter; for normalizing an essentially masculinist analytical gaze; and for universalizing sites and subjects that should always be situated.

ARTICULATING DIFFERENCE

If her intervention into postmodernism was spurred by a principled rejection of masculinist and Western-centric thought, Massey's provocation to imagine "a global sense place" was a timely, and still remarkably relevant, response to the horrors of ethnic cleansing in the former Yugoslavia and the eruptions of nationalist violence across the former Soviet Union (Massey with the HGRG 2009: 417). The equally appalling options of exultant globalism and reactionary ethno-nationalism had fuelled a tendency within progressive and liberal thinking to brand place-based identities as de facto reactionary. Confronting this foreboding conjuncture, Massey countered that local, place-based negotiations of difference were very often fundamental to progressive politics and to democratic struggles more generally. After all, place is one of the arenas in which we "learn to negotiate with others – to learn to form this thing called society", she argued, not least because "a healthy democracy requires, not pacification into conformity, but an open recognition of difference, and an ability to negotiate it with mutual respect" (Massey 2002: 294).

In contrast to readings of the local as a regressive site of restructuring, reactionary elements, and enforced conformity, this is a vision of place as a space of open-ended intersections, of journeys anything but complete:

[W]hat gives a place its specificity is not some long internalised history but a particular constellation of social relations, meeting and weaving together at a particular locus. If one moves in from [a] satellite towards the globe, holding all those networks of social relations and movements and communications in one's head, then each "place" can be seen as a particular, unique point of their intersection. It is, indeed, a *meeting* place. Instead, then, of thinking of places with boundaries around, they can be imagined as articulated moments in networks of social relations and understandings, but where a large proportion of those relations, experiences and understandings are constructed on a far larger scale than what we happen to define for that moment as the place itself … And this in turn allows for a sense of place which is extroverted, which includes a consciousness of its links with the wider world, which integrates in a positive way the global and the local.

(Massey 1991a: 28, original emphasis)

Against a static, bounded and introverted sense of place, Massey argued for a processual understanding of socially structured but always becoming spaces; against deterministic readings of the global as a scale of imperative forces, she insisted on the local as a scale of political vitality and creative potential; against all-encompassing visions of time-space compression, Massey made the case for a more intricate conception of socio-spatial difference. Building from the recognition of multiple identities in (and between) places, her approach was sensitive to the ways in which "power geometries" variously include, exclude, connect, divide, empower and disempower different social groups. This is a reading of place and place identities "constituted *out of* social relations, social interactions, and for [this] reason always and everywhere an expression and a medium of power" implying a conception of place as a "particular articulation [of] power-filled social relations" (Massey 1995b: 284, emphasis added).

The work of constructing an "open", progressive and processual sense of place was for Massey both philosophical and political. It meant supplanting received conceptions of space as inert and empty in favour of a much more disruptive understanding of time-space as a zone of endemic frictions, of both order and chaos (Massey 1992b). Massey sharpened these arguments in dialogue with leading lights of the New Left in the UK, especially Ernesto Laclau, Chantal Mouffe and Stuart Hall. In the early 1980s, they had founded the Hegemony Group, a monthly reading collective that poured over texts by Gramsci, Althusser, Poulantzas and others. It was from her interactions and debates with these figures that Massey became convinced of the necessity for an anti-essentialist politics that dispensed with the dualism of space (as passive) and time (as active), rejecting also the structuralist conceit of grafting social relations onto space as a static, apolitical container.

In her Hettner Lectures in Heidelberg in 1998, Massey proposed a three-fold reconceptualization of space carrying a series of political implications: first, the view of space as "a product of interrelations [and therefore] constituted through interactions" is complementary with an anti-essentialist politics in which identities are always in relational (re)construction; second, since space is a domain of multiplicity and emergence, then it follows that (as feminist and postcolonial theorists have long maintained) stories and visions of the world are multiple too, not singular and universal; and third, because space is "always being made ... never finished [and] never closed", political futures are neither known nor should they be foreclosed (Massey 1999a: 2–3). This amounts to a conceptualization of space that is both theoretically principled and politically open.

Concerned to deconstruct the binaries of orthodox theories, frameworks and formulations in political, conceptual and empirical terms, Massey's work in the 1990s and beyond pushed out in many directions, in part by virtue of an increasing engagement with feminist, postcolonial, poststructural and queer theories (see Massey 1992b, 1994, 1995a, 1999; Henry & Massey 1995). But it would be quite wrong to represent this as a rupture with the reflexive, heterodox Marxism of *Spatial Divisions of Labour* and the restructuring approach (cf. Saldanha 2013). With the benefit of hindsight, Julie Graham would re-read the book as "a founding text in the emerging tradition of poststructuralist economic geography" (Graham 1998: 942; cf. Soja 1987). Massey's (self)-positioning on this score was careful but also quite explicit, plainly stating in the book's second edition that "I do not see Marxist categories as inert", while classifying her approach as "clearly related to historical materialism" (1995c: 312). She acknowledged the continuing salience of Marxist categories while distancing herself from their off-the-shelf, inflexible deployment, (re)stating the case for a non-essentialist analysis of capitalist restructuring. This would seek to cut a path between totalizing metanarratives and the restrictive remit of "local theory", mobilizing a dexterous interpretation of critical realism's layered conception of social reality over "flaccid" acceptance of free-form indeterminacy.

A distinctive handling of articulation was therefore a longstanding methodological feature of Massey's work. While in her work during the 1980s she had been predominantly concerned with circumstances that were "specifically capitalist", neither then nor later did Massey have any time for "deterministic laws, predetermined outcomes or ineluctable stages of history" (1995c: 301–2). After all, tendencies in capitalist restructuring could be immanent even as their realization was – inescapably – contingently conditioned, situationally mediated, and conjuncturally framed, just as local circumstances were emergent in both a causal and a political sense. In other words,

Connection, as well as differentiation, are what it is all about...
It is not necessary, having rejected metanarratives, to reject any
notion of broad (but non-totalising) structures, most especially
if at the same time their multiplicity and complexity is recognised ... Thus, *Spatial Divisions of Labour* rejects metanarratives
... but it does not therefore adopt a position which restricts itself
only to local structures; broad structures, but which are assumed
to be multiple, non-totalising and without pregiven narratives
are acceptable, indeed necessary to the approach ... None of the
structures which are identified need be assumed to have any inexorability in their unfolding. And in the analysis here it is resolutely
assumed that they do not; outcomes are always uncertain, history
– and geography – have to be made.

(Massey 1995c: 303–4, emphasis in the original)

Convinced that "the usual categories of economic geography", including
its privileged object of analysis (industry), were "simply not good enough",
Massey's approach to theory was based on "rigorous conceptualisation",
which would draw upon, without being unnecessarily constrained by,
"previously-achieved understandings of the phenomena in question". Her
methodological preference was to "wrestle with theoretical problems in the
laboratory of an empirical case, rather than simply 'in the abstract', as they
say" (Massey 1995c: 309, 304, 315; Massey & Meegan, 1985). Social scientists, she argued, are routinely confronted by conditions of endemic complexity but this need not imply unprincipled indeterminacy. Political futures,
like social systems themselves, are open but this must not be confused with
the claim that every outcome is equally likely, or that tangential patterns are
beyond specification.

Articulation, in this sense, meant theorizing both with and across difference; it meant theorizing through relations, connections, and interdependencies, while refusing to freeze (or reify) particular combinations. "In
Massey's world", Julie Graham (1998: 942) wrote, "things are related to each
other not primarily through replication or reflection (sameness) but through
articulation – the transformative intellectual and social process of creating
connections and generating in the process unique beings, situations, and
possibilities." At the heart of *Spatial Divisions of Labour* had been an effort
to work a conception of capitalist spatiality from the abstract through to the
concrete, and back again, as a set of spatio-temporal interdependencies and
connections. This was achieved by interrogating a particular "spatial structure" that of intra-firm relations. That left a great deal out, of course, including the relatively familiar territory of *inter*-firm relations as they were being
progressively (re)articulated through markets and networks. As Michael

Storper (1986: 456) had said of the first edition of the book, to focus on the "locational processes that are part of the intracorporate hierarchy ... is to underestimate the complexity of the spatial division of labour". Once attention had shifted, during the 1990s, toward notionally "post-Fordist" dynamics like vertical disintegration, subcontracting and outsourcing, agglomeration economies, interfirm clusters, and industrial districts, many of the substantive arguments in the book were to be overtaken by the restless process of restructuring itself (see Martin *et al.* 1993; Scott 2000). Such is the fate, of course, of so many arguments that take seriously the facts of conjunctural specificity.

In her subsequent reflections, Massey argued for extending the concept of spatial divisions of labour to these novel geographies of industrial districts and inter-firm networks (1995c: 335–9). To do so, however, would have meant foregrounding the chop and churn of uneven development as a principal spatial domain (albeit a contingent and overdetermined one) in the analysis, yet the drift of subsequent work in the field – including in economic geography – augured against such an approach. Indeed, while subsequent work on geographies of agglomeration and global production networks often cited Massey's foundational text, it generally relegated its core concerns to the conceptual background or neglected them altogether (Peck 2016; Werner 2016). Massey opted not to pursue these possibilities herself either, at least not in an explicit way. The same cannot however be said for a second area that she thought offered the possibility, and indeed the necessity, for extending the concept of the spatial division of labour: unpaid labour, or more accurately, "those variable processes through which the paid/unpaid boundary is constructed" (Massey 1995c: 334). Observing ascendant patterns of economic transformation in the global North, not least through her research on gendered divisions of labour in the much-vaunted field of R & D (see Massey *et al.* 1992), and the experiences of structural adjustment in the global South, which was transforming paid jobs into unpaid burdens shouldered primarily by women in the home, Massey argued that any analysis of paid work must incorporate the dynamics of households, gender ideologies, and state practices which shape the moving boundaries between remunerated and unremunerated work in a given conjuncture (1995c: 334–5). This was just one of the ways, Massey later reflected, in which feminist thought influenced the substance and overall project of *Spatial Divisions of Labour*. She maintained that while "gender is essential to the empirical story" in the book, it had not been explicitly positioned "within what was at the time defined as the field of feminist geography"; nevertheless, its style of (relational) theorizing warranted (re)consideration from a feminist standpoint, not least as a contribution to the ongoing project of "re-thinking the way we think" (Massey 1995c: 345, 341, 354).

RELATIONAL SPACE

Massey's response to the first wave of globalization debates in the early 1990s had been to counter with what would eventually become a mainstream critical position: that global space was no less "concrete", no less constructed, than local places; that the global is therefore socially and politically made, not least in *and from* certain places; that simplified and self-fulfilling "impact" models of globalization, which assume vertical relations of scalar domination, are not only misleading but will also tend to constrain and distort political strategies and imaginaries; and that conventional narratives of (neoliberal) globalization represented just one vision of global and transnational politics, against which alternative models could be developed based on principles of egalitarianism, respect, responsibility and democratic deepening. Many of these contentions would be echoed in other strands of critical scholarship and commentary.

Arguably more distinctive, indeed radical, was Massey's parallel rethinking of "the local" in relational terms as a corollary of her critical reading of globalization. Against romanticized or static conceptions of the local, as the scale of essentialized and fixed identities, Massey repeatedly made the case for more processual understandings of space and place as *always* in the making, never closed and never finished. "The character of place is not somehow a product only of what goes on within it, but results too from the juxtaposition and intermixing there of flows, relations, connections from 'beyond' [some of which] may, indeed, go around the world" (Massey 2006: 98). Places, moreover, were anything but a singular category; they always had to be situated in relation to *other* places and scales, and within relations of uneven and combined development. In this context, the political vision that there are other globalizations to be imagined, to be had, not only "prevents us slipping into easy oppositions such as global = bad, local = good", but also "prevents us facing up to neoliberal globalisation simply by retreating into the defensive laager of local place" (Massey 2004b: 98).

This formulation meant that Massey was no less wary of across-the-board versions of horizontalism and the "flat ontologies" that pervaded many nominally poststructuralist accounts (Routledge & Cumbers 2013), than she was of top-down visions of globalism advanced by some orthodox Marxists. Once again, her insistence on places as intersections of multiple relations stemmed from both political and analytical commitments.

> [W]hile we are indeed all discursively subject to a disempowering discourse of the inevitability and omnipotence of globalisation, materially the local identities created through globalisation vary substantially. Not all local places are simply "subject to"

> globalisation. The nature of the resubjectivation required, and of
> the responsibility implied, in consequence also varies between
> places.   (Massey 2004a: 10)

Massey would go on to explore the relational constitution of identity formation both within and between places. She was to become increasingly
convinced that "rethinking identity [could be] a crucial complement to a
politics which is suspicious of foundational essentialism; a politics which,
rather than claiming 'rights' for pre-given identities ... based on assumptions of authenticity, argues that it is at least as important to challenge the
identities themselves and thus – *a fortiori* – the relations through which
those identities have been established" (2004a: 5). It followed that identities and subjectivities are constitutively relational, that they do not precede
(social) interactions in some fixed sense, but are malleable outcomes of those
ongoing interactions (Massey 2006: 92–3). Massey's decisive intervention
was to point out that *spatial* identities were constituted in relational ways as
well, such that they must be understood as "internally complex, essentially
unboundable in any absolute sense, and inevitably historically changing"
(Massey 2004a: 5). As Chantal Mouffe would later reflect, this conceptualization necessitated a spatialized understanding of hegemony; more than this, it
opened up new potential for thinking through counter-hegemonic politics.
Writing against immanent conceptions of "the multitude" as formulated by
Hardt and Negri, Mouffe argued that "to acknowledge the ineradicability of
antagonism implies recognising that every form of order is necessarily a spatialized, hegemonic one, that it constitutes a 'geometry of power'"(2013: 29).

Massey would make her most extensive attempt to elaborate these arguments for an audience beyond geography in the monograph, *For Space*
(2005). The book drew upon an extraordinarily wide range of texts – including French poststructuralism, phenomenology, art criticism, postcolonial
studies, anthropology, geography, feminist theory, and more – to tease out
a series of problems associated with understandings of space as an inert,
static category, developing in its stead an alternative reading of space as a
necessary component of multiplicity and becoming, along with a more open
approach to theoretical and political practice. As Matt Sparke wrote, the
book's title referenced a parallel problematic in Althusser's *For Marx*, even
as it constructed a critique of structuralism's spatial stasis and its entrenched
time-space dualisms (Massey 2005: 40–1; Sparke 2007; see also Saldanha
2013). Rather than proclaim a proper way to be "for space", Massey instead
illustrated the many dead ends and limits to thought enabled by a category
of stasis that permeates Western philosophy which is conventionally given
meaning and circulated as "space". Massey revisited the threefold proposition
on space (as relational, a multiplicity, and in-process) that she had originally

presented in the Hettner Lectures, insisting that this should serve neither as a model nor as a formula but instead as a provocation to critical, progressive theory and politics – jogging them out of the deeply engrained habits of Western thinking that tended to mobilize space towards essentialist, identitarian ends. Her deconstruction of space, here and elsewhere, sought a redefinition and reclamation of the term as necessary to the project of shaping a truly radical politics of identity and place.

In particular, Massey revisited and rejected two common but "evasive imaginations", both of which failed to confront the "challenges of space". Firstly, there was the long-established habit of turning space into time, and geography into history, where "spatial difference [is] convened into temporal sequence" (Massey 2005: 68). Against Rostovian, sequentialist and developmentalist visions of a convergent (global) future, Massey refuted the contention that there is but one way for places to "catch up", since this meant that those positioned "behind" are effectively denied equal standing, quite literally having no space to imagine (let alone take) alternative pathways (Massey 2006: 90). Secondly, there was the practice of thinking of space as a surface, *over* which journeys are made. Against this colonizing imaginary, which also tends to compress multiple histories and geographies into a master narrative-cum-trajectory of modernity, Massey insisted on seeing space and place in terms of constellations, conjunctures, crystallizations and shifting patterns of coexistence, in which space-time exists as a "simultaneity of unfinished, ongoing, trajectories" or "stories-so-far" (Massey 2006: 92; 2005).

These philosophical explorations of space-time were to lead Massey in an additional, somewhat surprising, direction. In collaboration primarily with two physical geographers, Stephan Harrison and Keith Richards, Massey convened a series of conversations to probe the moral, conceptual, and empirical possibilities for bridging the longstanding divide between physical and human geography (Massey 1999b; Harrison *et al.* 2004, 2006, 2008). She had earlier contended that, for all their differences, human and physical geographers shared an imagination of physics as the model science, which had saddled the discipline as a whole with unhelpful and flawed conceptualizations of time, space, and space-time. Against static understandings of space and teleological conceptualizations of time, Massey (1999b: 262) argued that space-time should instead be understood as "relative (defined in terms of the entities 'within' it), relational (as constituted through the operation of social relations, through which the 'entities' are also constituted), and integral to the constitution of the entities themselves (the entities are local time-spaces)". So conceived, this alternative understanding of space-time provided an admittedly abstract but nevertheless potentially generative means to bridge between physical and human geography, building upon the shared concern to explain dynamism, complexity, emergence and process.

In *For Space*, for example, Massey put this relational view of the physical and social to work in the empirical analysis of the landscape of Skidaw, in the Lake District in England, which she saw to be constituted as much by the dynamic physicality of immigrant rocks as of migrant humans (Hinchcliffe 2013). And many other scholars, such as Diane Rocheleau (Harcourt *et al.* 2013), were to find Massey's work an inspiration for the integrated analysis of relations among physical and social systems, grounded in particular places. Although Massey did concede that it can "make your head hurt to think in this way", she argued that it was worth it because, quoting Raper and Livingstone (1995: 364), "the way that spatio-temporal processes are studied is strongly influenced by the model of space and time that is adopted", or as she chose to underscore the point, characteristically, "it matters; it makes a difference" (Massey 1999b: 262).

Massey later offered a unique and highly personal justification for this portion of her intellectual project, and her both/and view of human and physical geography. Already suffering from advanced arthritis, she described her lifelong struggle with a debilitating bone disease. Constant therapy and numerous broken bones had blighted her childhood, a burden shouldered by her parents, especially her mother, who shuttled her in and out of doctor's offices and hospitals. Growing up with a "disability" had shaped a very particular, indeed personal, sense of marginality. As Massey recounted in an interview with Catalan geographers Núria Benach and Abel Albet, "some of my bones have metal pieces, my feet are full of fragments. All told, my body is a major disaster but this disaster has always formed an important part of me, in the sense that each day it poses a small grand challenge. I cannot be exclusively cerebral ... because my body is here each day and, well, it is a very important part of me" (2012: 62, editors' translation). These reflections brought her to the question of norms – of gender and the body – that she had always challenged in her life and in her work. When her physical therapists refused the label "normal", or rejected her qualifications of what she saw as her "good" versus "bad" leg, she felt subjected to what in Foucauldian terms amounted to a strong form of social constructionism. "And it's true, in one way, but in another ... it hurts ... It's pure materiality!" (Albet & Benach 2012: 63). In a characteristic manner, she used the contrast between the lived experience of her aching body and her therapists' descriptions of it as a springboard to reflect on how false dichotomies such as these, between the discursive and the material, continue to mark the divisions between human and physical geography: "we need both at the same time", she concluded.

Massey's life experiences would also be echoed in reflections on the evolution of her theoretical commitments and the tensions between the personal and the political. If Althusser had been Massey's awakening to anti-foundationalism, not least in her invocations of the idea that "there is no point of departure", in her later writing, especially in *For* Space, there were to be stronger affinities to the work of Deleuze and Guattari (1994). Massey (2005) would draw upon the engagements between Deleuze and Guattari and the philosopher Henri Bergson in her explorations of the concepts of multiplicity and becoming – even as she roundly critiqued Bergson for predicating his reading of open ontology on a shallow, fixed treatment of space. Indeed, Massey's former student and Deleuze scholar, Arun Saldanha, argues that it is Deleuze and Guattari's notion of geophilosophy that "comes closest to Massey's philosophical-geographical project" (Saldanha 2013: 50). Yet there were also tensions between Massey's position and the Deleuze–Guattari program. While Massey would embrace the notion of assemblage, especially for its role in facilitating the theorization of more-than-human geographies, she would become increasingly "wary of the 'all is process' view of the world, in so far as it's been translated from a reconceptualization to almost a denial of the existence of 'things' … The body is all process, certainly, but we still have bodies" (Featherstone *et al.* 2013: 255). She expressed similar reservations concerning the widespread use of the notion of "relationality", which too often would be evacuated of the political conundrum that the term had been meant to index:

> The degree to which that conceptual questioning emerged from and was developed within political struggle – including, very importantly, feminist struggles – seems to me to be under-recognised. Many of the explorations of the construction of identity [and] … relational thinking more generally, were importantly first explored in debates within political constituencies – anti-racism, feminism and sexual liberation. It is a great pity when those roots are forgotten; conceptual debate can then lose its urgency and real meaning. The real two-way movement between the conceptual and the political has always, for me, been very important. (Featherstone *et al.* 2013: 260)

Massey steadfastly refused to separate, on the one hand, ontological and epistemological theories of space, and on the other, the political possibilities that were always being opened and foreclosed by contested understandings of space. More than a geophilosophy, then, hers was first and foremost a geography of praxis.

LOCATING RESPONSIBILITY

Massey's commitment to praxis was evident in her work during the miners' strike of 1984–5 and with the Greater London Council; in wide-ranging activities with *Soundings*, as a journal of political commentary and debate; and in projects and collaborations in Nicaragua, South Africa, Venezuela, and elsewhere. It was also manifested in her effort to learn Spanish and French, not simply to translate across languages, but instead to comprehend the different idioms and forms of academic and political debate outside the Anglo sphere (Albet & Benach 2012: 39; see also Vaiou 2017). Never one for the international conference circuit or the trappings of academic celebrity, Massey remained sceptical of scholarly exchange as a detached practice, as an end in itself. This led her to find new ways to interweave theoretical practice with political engagement, becoming a public intellectual even as she bristled at the label. The public meetings convened to debate the collaborative project that was the Kilburn Manifesto – an impassioned plea for a new politics, involving new languages and new alliances – represented Massey in her element, despite her sometimes-faltering health. And in a host of other projects, involving all manner of interlocutors and collaborators, she would continue to explore generative connections between relational thinking, questions of identity, and the politics of responsibility. These would span the sciences, the arts, and the humanities, and they would take her from the corridors of the Open University to Turbine Hall at the Tate Modern, and to Caracas, Venezuela, where the notion of "power-geometries" was adopted by the Bolivarian movement under Hugo Chavez (Massey 2000a, 2009; Eliasson 2013).

The openness that Massey accorded to space, and of place as a space of potential, was never divorced from her preoccupation with its unevenly distributed (and contested) potential, itself continuously reshaped in (mutual) relation to the global and the more-than-local. To the extent to which the generalized dynamics of capitalism, and not only in their globalized and neoliberalized variants, are associated with systematic tendencies toward socio-spatial inequality, it follows that "the local relation to the global will ... vary [along with] the coordinates of any potential local politics of challenging that globalization" (Massey 2004a: 13).

> For in this [alternative] imagination "places" are criss-crossings in the wider power-geometries which constitute both themselves and "the global." In this view local places are not simply always the victims of the global; nor are they always politically defensible redoubts *against* the global. For places are also the moments through which the global is constituted, invented, coordinated, produced. They are "agents" *in* globalisation. There are two immediate implications. First this fact of the inevitably local production of the global means that there is potentially some purchase through "local" politics on wider global mechanisms. Not merely

defending the local against the global, but seeking to alter the very mechanisms of the global itself. A local politics with a wider reach [this represents a different] basis for the recognition of the potential agency of the local ... The second implication of this line of reasoning [is that, if] the identities of places are indeed the product of relations which spread way beyond them ... then what should be the political relationship to those wider geographies of construction? (Massey 2004a: 11)

Massey would go on to explore some of the distinctive power-geometries of this "local production of the global" in her adopted home city of London. In her final monograph, *World City,* she offered a book not so much "about" the place, in the more conventional sense, but rather an extended meditation from, through, and *out of* London, a search for alternative, disruptive, and progressive political-geographical imaginaries, beyond the entrenched hegemony of neoliberal globalism. *World City* positions London as "a crucial node in the production of an increasingly unequal world" (Massey 2007: 8), as a crucible of uneven development, both locally and far beyond the city limits. It is a plea for this epicentre of financialized capitalism to face up to its responsibilities, at home and abroad. The book presents a trenchant critique of New Labour's contradictory embrace of economic competitiveness and social amelioration – epitomized by the Blairite conceit that "while poverty matters, wealth does not" – calling attention to London's simultaneous role as a wealth machine and generator of poverty. The horizons of the book, however, extend far beyond the questions of global-city polarization. Contra the neoliberal construction of cities as competitive agents, engaged in a war of all against all for mobile resources and "assets", Massey develops a relational account of the more-than-local production of economic "success". Yet this was never merely some conventional critique of neoliberalized, global-city urbanism. Beyond some of the established formulations of localism and horizontalism on the left, she reiterates her critique of such defensive formulations of place politics – leaning as they tend to do on received constructions of authenticity and community, and on the idea that localized havens can somehow be constructed, sheltered from out-there forms of globalization – in favour of an "outward-looking politics that seeks to address [the] wider geography of place and to ponder what might be thought of as [its] global responsibilities" (Massey 2007: 176). There is a domestic strain to this argument, for instance where Massey demonstrates the absurdity of the proposition that London-style growth should (or even could) be exported to Britain's provinces, as a solution to a longstanding "regional problem" (see also Allen *et al.* 1998; Amin *et al.* 2000). To the contrary, London-centric growth is seen to be constitutive of this very problem, with the capital itself arguably being the country's *real* "problem region" (John *et al.* 2002; cf. Massey 1979). Transnational extensions of this argument include the suggestion that alternative "geographies of allegiance" might be forged through initiatives providing restitution or reciprocation to those developing countries that effectively subsidize the capital's health service through asymmetrical migration flows of nurses and doctors trained at public expense in countries of the global South.

In 2007, just a few days before the release of *World City*, Massey received an invitation to Venezuela to give a series of lectures and to write a set of essays, including a widely-distributed popular pamphlet that would revisit her notion of power-geometries in the context of the real-time implementation of "21st century socialism" (Massey 2009; Massey with HGRG 2009). She would spend time in dialogue with activists working to form communal councils as part of a broader effort to decentralize state power and to remedy the deep-seated political, economic, and social imbalances that produced and reinforced profound regional inequalities in the country. "My appreciation for the forms and nuances of power was vastly enriched", she reflected, "the concept of power-geometries itself was dynamised – precisely because it was being used in a political *process*" (Featherstone *at al.* 2013: 263, emphasis in the original; see also Massey 2015a). Although Massey had always been politically engaged, the publication of *World City* and her work in Venezuela marked a shift away from what she increasingly saw as abstruse debates within her discipline. She would retire from the Open University in 2009, after almost three decades, but in some respects her intellectual and political activities intensified during her remaining years, especially in the tumultuous context of the global financial crisis and its lingering aftermath.

In what would be her last collaboration with *Soundings* colleagues Michael Rustin and Stuart Hall, the Kilburn Manifesto was an effort to unpack the unfolding crisis and its apparent failure to bring down an increasingly sclerotic neoliberalism. As Massey explained, in the wake of the financial crash of 2008, "today we are sitting here with [UK Prime Minister] Cameron saying that the big problem is the public deficit, and the big state. The economic crisis is partly being solved, at least for the time being, and that is seen as the only problem. The implosion of neoliberal ideology is no longer on the agenda. It's as though they've separated those two instances [the economic and the philosophical] again" (Hall & Massey 2012: 58). The Kilburn Manifesto project involved a series of political events and collaborative writing projects targeted on what were seen, in Gramscian terms, as "antagonisms" in the reigning conjuncture. It included initiatives focused on feminism, generational politics, and race/ethnicity, bringing together social activists, trade unionists, and academics from around the country. The goal was to engage in a process of debate, collaboration, and strategic (re)thinking in order to expose "cracks" or "fissures" in the stubbornly hegemonic ideology of neoliberalism. Amongst other things, this would involve a sustained effort to take apart the notorious "there is no alternative" formulation that since the 1980s had been entrenched as a cornerstone of the neoliberal common sense in Britain, not least to demonstrate that, in Massey's words, this "was a triumph that was engineered" (Peck *et al.* 2014: 2036). In explicating how this common sense was laboriously cobbled together from contradictory elements, the Manifesto and related publications, including columns in *The Guardian* newspaper, sought to develop an alternative narrative aimed at prizing apart political spaces in order to enable "the possibility of thinking a radically different future" (Peck *et al.* 2014: 2039; see also Massey 2013).

Recounting the story of the Kilburn Manifesto project to a packed house at the 2014 annual geography meetings in the United States, a country that she chose rarely to visit, Massey powerfully weaved together her enduring commitments to place-based theorizing, on the one hand, and to forging progressive coalitions for political change on the other. She reminded her audience of the necessary *political* work of relational thinking – the need for a politics of articulation. One of her problematics on this occasion was to grapple with the meaning of "social settlement", understood in the Gramscian sense of how it is that "a glue of ideas, a common sense" is able to articulate, or hold together, seemingly contradictory elements into a conjuncture (Peck *et al.* 2014: 2036). Invoking the tradition of British cultural studies, she insisted that the cultural never "floats free" of the economic, just as the economy, even in its globalized and financialized form, is never disengaged from the cultural and the political, despite attempts to present it otherwise. The task at hand – inseparably analytical and political – is precisely to combine these cultural and economic "instances", and others too, in order to understand the formation of a hegemonic ideology, which after Raymond Williams and Stuart Hall is never fixed or final, but always in the making, always in need of renewal, always contested. When confronting the fracturing hegemony of neoliberalism, she emphasized, it would be necessary to work at the intersection of "constituent power" – which had been on display in movements like Occupy in the wake of the financial crisis – and "constituted power" – efforts to transform the prevailing rules of the game within representative democracy. The latter had been evidenced by the rise of parties like Syriza in Greece, and by the left turn in Latin America. There were even progressive disruptions to politics-as-usual closer to home. In fact, the last blogpost that Massey wrote, for *Soundings*, called on the Left to mobilize around the leadership of Jeremy Corbyn, who had recently been elected leader of the Labour Party in the UK (Massey 2015b). When Massey died, the world – and the British political and academic world in particular – lost a unique chronicler of, commentator on and *participant in* progressive disruptions such as these. She would have been surprised neither by the powerful counter-mobilizations against these breaches of the neoliberal edifice, nor by their resultant mixed fortunes, and would doubtless have carried on tilting at social injustice and its underlying power-geometries in her own inimitable, and different way.

Doreen Massey, we have argued here, changed geography – and in much more than a disciplinary sense. She developed and popularized entirely new ways of thinking and acting geographically, leaving changed worlds behind her. As Roger Lee wrote in one of many obituaries, "She was never prepared to separate theory from the complexity of experience and the possibilities of politics and, in this, Doreen was the epitome of a geographer – wholly aware of the need to understand the multiplicity of relations that interact to shape social and environmental life and of the possibilities for progressive change" (Lee 2016: 311). From her early efforts to rethink and revitalize Marxist categories and her engagements with critical realism, and in her subsequent elaboration of the implications of relational thinking, space as multiplicity, global sense of place, and so many more, Massey always sought to demonstrate the materiality of socio-spatial processes. Throughout her career, she worked to explore the dialectical relations between the material, the social, and the spatial in human geography and far beyond in ways that deftly balanced the structural and the conjunctural, embracing openness and multiplicity while resolutely confronting dominant forms of space and power. Doreen Massey's sense of place was never bounded, restrictive, or limiting; it was where new things could happen, where new alliances could be fashioned, where change could be made. Thankfully, it was one that she shared.

THE BOOK AHEAD

This *Reader* contains 19 of Doreen Massey's texts, of which four were co-authored. We have organised these into sections, the key themes of which all reflect her famous rallying cry: Geography matters! The common thread in the works in Part I is the region; in Part II, it is place; and in Part III, space, although it should go without saying that the boundaries between these sections are hardly fixed or impervious. Brief editorial introductions to each section of the book contextualize the essays and expand upon the varying ways in which these works connect to the central sectional theme.

Our key concern as editors has been to try to capture the breadth of Massey's most important work across the span of her career. This presented a substantial challenge. Her first papers appeared in the late 1960s, when she was employed at the Centre for Environmental Studies; her last publication (Massey 2016) appeared posthumously. (And there was so much that was appropriate about that last piece: it was a review of somebody *else's* work; it was astute and generous; it was on a decidedly political topic, taxation; and it appeared in the journal she co-founded, *Soundings* – she died as the issue was going to press.) Over the course of that near-half-century, Massey wrote prolifically and, as this Introduction has shown, extraordinarily broadly – the careerist option of lifelong specialism and academic turf arrogation was clearly not for her. In attempting to do justice to the full range of Massey's repertoire, we have no doubt missed significant contributions. Nevertheless, having painstakingly revisited her accumulated writings, we are confident that this collection presents a good representation, within the scope of a single volume, of the breathtaking scope and range of Massey's key ideas and arguments; certainly, this collection is the only one than spans her entire scholarly life. It speaks, in short, to those particular intellectual and political debates where Massey's work made, and continues to make, a notable and transformative mark on issues that remain remarkably relevant today.

The texts that we have selected originally appeared in a wide range of venues, both inside and outside Geography, some appearing in academic outlets, while others were addressed to broader public audiences. Thus, in addition to articles from *Environment & Planning D* and *Antipode*, there are texts from *Capital & Class*, *Red Pepper*, *New Formations* and *Socialist Commentary*. And while many of the texts are well known and widely cited, some are not. Academia is a fickle "business" at the best of times – citation need not be correlated with quality, significance, or for that matter influence – and Massey really had no interest in playing the game. Accordingly, several of the texts included in the *Reader* have failed to receive the wide reading and recognition we think they deserve. This might have been because of the relative obscurity of the publication in which they appeared (*Socialist Commentary*, for example); it might have been because the issues in question were not really "academic" ones in the first place (for example, Massey's writing with Hilary Wainwright on the work of miners' support groups); it might have been because the topic subsequently slid off political and scholarly agendas (as it was in the case of the political economy of private landownership in Britain, on which Massey had written in the 1970s). Whatever the reason that some of these texts have to this point flown under the radar, we hope that including them here will help rescue them from the condescension of posterity, a phrase of E. P. Thompson's that she would surely have appreciated.

In all cases, the texts and references remain in the original publication's house style. But we have not reproduced the original texts in their entirety. All have been edited down, and all redactions are clearly indicated. In some cases the redactions are minimal, while in others constraints of space meant that they had to be more extensive. We removed text that overlapped substantively with other chapters in the *Reader*, and also topics that were of interest for audiences at the time of publication but which may have less relevance for readers today, such as particular policy measures or localized disputes. The upside to this necessary process of editing, of course, is that it enabled us to include a wider range of Massey's pieces. The downside is that at points there may be a marginal loss of fluency; where this is the case, we have sparingly added our own words [in square brackets] better to link sections of text separated by redactions. In making these necessary edits, we have been reassured by the fact that nothing we did was likely to blunt the persuasive power of Massey's writing, the reach and resonance of which remains irrepressible.

It would be quite inappropriate, of course, for us to end on a note about the constraints of space. Doreen Massey's work was always about opening up alternatives, new futures and new spaces. The bold style and generative insights even of her earliest contributions are no less compelling today than when they were originally written. And she was always about widening the circle, rather than speaking to narrow constituencies or engaging in academic parlour games. We can only hope that this collection of writings will be read in that same spirit – not least by new generations of readers who may be new to Massey, or less than fully aware of the remarkable scope and depth of her work.

REFERENCES

Albet, A. & N. Benach 2012. *Doreen Massey: Un Sentido Global del Lugar.* Barcelona: Icaria.

Althusser, L. 1971. *On Ideology.* London: New Left Books.

Allen, J., D. Massey & A. Cochrane 1998. *Rethinking the Region.* London: Routledge.

Amin, A., D. Massey & N. Thrift 2000. *Cities for the Many Not the Few.* Bristol: Policy Press.

Bagguley, P. *et al.* 1990. *Restructuring: Place, Class, and Gender.* London: Sage.

Christopherson, S. 1989. "On Being Outside 'The Project'", *Antipode* 21(2): 83–9.

Clarke, J. 2016. "Doreen Massey (1944–1966): Making Geography Matter", *Cultural Studies* 30 (3): 357–61.

Cochrane, A. 1987. "What a Difference the Place Makes: The New Structuralism of Locality", *Antipode* 19 (3): 354–63.

Deleuze, G. & F. Guattari 1994. *What is Philosophy?* London: Verso.

Deutsche, R. 1991. "Boys Town", *Environment and Planning D: Society and Space* 9 (1): 5–30.

Eliasson, O. 2013. "Your Gravitational Now", in D. Featherstone & J. Painter (eds) *Spatial Politics: Essays for Doreen Massey*, 125–32. Oxford: Wiley-Blackwell.

Featherstone, D. & J. Painter 2013. "'There Is No Point of Departure': The Many Trajectories of Doreen Massey", in D. Featherstone & J. Painter (eds) *Spatial Politics: Essays for Doreen Massey*, 1–18. Oxford: Wiley-Blackwell.

Featherstone, D., S. Bond & J. Painter 2013. "'Stories So Far.' A Conversation with Doreen Massey", in D. Featherstone & J. Painter (eds) *Spatial Politics: Essays for Doreen Massey*, 253–66. Oxford: Wiley-Blackwell.

Freytag, T. & M. Hoyler 1999. "'I Feel As if I've Been Able to Reinvent Myself' – A Biographical Interview with Doreen Massey", in D. Massey, *Power Geometries and the Politics of Space-Time*, 83–95. Heidelberg: Department of Geography, University of Heidelberg.

Graham, J. 1998. "Spatial Divisions of Labor: Social Structures and the Geography of Production, by Doreen Massey", *Environment and Planning A* 30 (5): 942–3.

Hall, S. & D. Massey 2012. "Interpreting the Crisis", in S. Davison & K. Harris (eds) *The Neo-liberal Crisis*, 55–69. London: Soundings.

Hall, S., D. Massey & M. Rustin (eds) 2012. *After Neoliberalism? The Kilburn Manifesto*. London: Lawrence & Wishart.

Harcourt, W. *et al.* 2013. "A Massey Muse", in D. Featherstone & J. Painter (eds) *Spatial Politics: Essays for Doreen Massey*, 158–77. Oxford: Wiley-Blackwell.

Harrison, S. *et al.* 2004. "Thinking across the Divide: Perspectives on the Conversations Between Physical and Human Geography", *Area* 36 (4): 435–42.

Harrison, S., D. Massey & K. Richards 2006. "Complexity and Emergence (Another Conversation)", *Area* 38 (4): 465–71.

Harrison, S., D. Massey & K. Richards 2008. "Conversations Across the Divide", *Geoforum* 39 (2): 549–51.

Hartmann, H. 1979. "The Unhappy Marriage of Marxism And Feminism: Towards a More Progressive Union", *Capital & Class* 12 (2): 1–33.

Hartsock, N. 1987. "Rethinking Modernism: Minority vs. Majority Theories", *Cultural Critique* 7: 187–206.

Harvey, D. 1987. "Three Myths in Search of a Reality in Urban Studies", *Environment and Planning D: Society and Space* 5 (4): 367–76.

Henry, N. & D. Massey 1995. "Competitive Time-Space in High Technology", *Geoforum* 26 (1): 49–64.

Hinchcliffe, S. 2013. "A Physical Sense of World", in D. Featherstone & J. Painter (eds) *Spatial Politics: Essays for Doreen Massey*, 178–88. Oxford: Wiley-Blackwell.

Ijams, B., J. Popke & K. Urch 1994."Gender, Space and the Academy: An Interview with Doreen Massey, The Open University", *disClosure* 4: article 9. Available at: https://uknowledge.uky.edu/disclosure/vol4/iss1/.

John, P., S. Musson & A. Tickell 2002. "England's Problem Region: Regionalism in the South East", *Regional Studies* 36 (7): 733–41.

Lee, R. 2016. "Doreen Massey, 3 January 1944 – 11 March 2016", *Geographical Journal* 182 (3): 311–2.

Lovering, J. 1989. "The Restructuring Debate", in R. Peet & N. Thrift (eds) *New Models in Geography, Volume One*, 198–223. London: Unwin Hyman.

Martin, R., A. Markusen & D. Massey 1993. "Classics in Human Geography Revisited: Spatial Divisions of Labour", *Progress in Human Geography* 17 (1): 69–72.

Massey, D. 1973. "Towards a Critique of Industrial Location Theory", *Antipode* 5 (3): 33–9.

Massey, D. 1974. "Social Justice and the City: A Review", *Environment and Planning A* 6 (2): 229–35.

Massey, D. 1979. "In What Sense a Regional Problem?", *Regional Studies* 13 (2): 233–43.

Massey, D. 1984. *Spatial Divisions of Labour: Social Structures and the Geography of Production*. Basingstoke: Macmillan.

Massey, D. 1985. "New Directions in Space", in D. Gregory & J. Urry (eds) *Social Relations and Spatial Structures*, 9–19. London: Macmillan.

Massey, D. 1991a. "A Global Sense of Place", *Marxism Today* June: 24–9.

Massey, D. 1991b. "Flexible Sexism", *Environment and Planning D: Society and Space* 9 (1): 31–57.

Massey, D. 1991c. "The Political Place of Locality Studies", *Environment and Planning A* 23 (2): 267–81.

Massey, D. 1992a. "A Place Called Home?", *New Formations* 17: 3–15.

Massey, D. 1992b. "Politics and Space/Time", *New Left Review* 196: 65–84.

Massey, D. 1994. *Space, Place and Gender*. Cambridge: Polity.

Massey, D. 1995a. "Masculinity, Dualisms and High Technology", *Transactions of the Institute of British Geographers* 20 (4): 487–99.

Massey, D. 1995b. "Thinking Radical Democracy Spatially", *Environment and Planning D: Society and Space* 13 (3): 283–8.

Massey, D. 1995c. *Spatial Divisions of Labour: Social Structures and the Geography of Production*, second edn. Basingstoke: Macmillan.

Massey, D. 1999a. "Philosophy and Politics of Spatiality: Some Considerations", *Geographische Zeitschrift* 87 (1): 1–12.

Massey, D. 1999b. "Space-Time, 'Science' and the Relationship Between Physical Geography and Human Geography", *Transactions of the Institute of British Geographers* 24 (3): 261–76.

Massey, D. 2000a. "Bankside: International Local", in I. Blazwick (ed.) *Tate Modern: The Handbook*, 24–7. London: Tate Publishing.

Massey, D. 2000b. "Travelling Thoughts", in P. Gilroy, L. Grossberg & A. McRobbie (eds) *Without Guarantees: In Honour of Stuart Hall*, 225–32. London: Verso.

Massey, D. 2001. "Living in Wythenshawe", in I. Borden *et al* (eds) *The Unknown City: Contesting Architecture and Social Space*, 458–75. Cambridge, MA: MIT Press.

Massey, D. 2002 "Globalisation: What Does It Mean for Geography?", *Geography* 87 (4): 293–6.

Massey, D. 2004a. "Geographies of Responsibility", *Geografiska Annaler B: Human Geography* 86 (1): 5–18.

Massey, D. 2004b. "The Responsibilities of Place", *Local Economy* 19 (2): 97–101.

Massey, D. 2005. *For Space*. London: Sage.

Massey, D. 2006. "Space, Time and Political Responsibility in the Midst of Global Inequality", *Erdkunde* 60 (2): 89–95.

Massey, D. 2007. *World City*. Cambridge: Polity.

Massey, D. 2009. "Concepts of Space and Power in Theory and in Political Practice", *Documents d'anàlisi Geogràfica* 55: 15–26.

Massey, D. 2013. "Neoliberalism has Hijacked our Vocabulary", *The Guardian*, 11 June. Available at: https://www.theguardian.com/commentisfree/2013/jun/11/neoliberalism-hijacked-vocabulary.

Massey, D. 2015a. "Globalización, Espacio y Poder", in *Memoria del Primer Encuentro de Expertos Gubernamentales en Políticas de Desarrollo Territorial en América Latina y el Caribe*, 9–14. Santiago de Chile: CEPAL, Naciones Unidas.

Massey, D. 2015b. "Why the Corbyn Leadership is Still the Best Hope for Labour", *Soundings blog*, 18 November. Available at: https://www.lwbooks.co.uk/soundings/blog/why-corbyn-leadership-still-best-hope-labour.

Massey, D. (2016). "Tax: a political fault line", *Soundings* 62 (1): 161–3.

Massey, D. & A. Catalano 1978. *Capital and Land: Landownership by Capital in Great Britain*. London: Edward Arnold.

Massey, D. & R. Meegan 1982. *The Anatomy of Job Loss: The How, Why and Where of Employment Decline*. London: Methuen.

Massey, D. with the HGRG [Human Geography Research Group] 2009. "The Possibilities of a Politics of Place Beyond Place? A Conversation with Doreen Massey", *Scottish Geographical Journal* 125 (3/4): 401–20.

Massey, D., P. Quintas & D. Wield 1992. *High-Tech Fantasies: Science Parks in Society, Science and Space*. London: Routledge.

McDowell, L. & D. Massey 1984. "A Woman's Place", in D. Massey & J. Allen (eds) *Geography Matters! A Reader*, 128–47. Cambridge: Cambridge University Press.

Meegan, R. 2017. "Doreen Massey (1944–2016): A Geographer Who Really Mattered", *Regional Studies* 51 (9): 1285–96.

Mouffe, C. 2013. "Space, Hegemony and Radical Critique", in D. Featherstone & J. Painter (eds) *Spatial Politics: Essays for Doreen Massey*, 21–31. Oxford: Wiley-Blackwell.

Peck, J. 2016. "Macroeconomic Geographies", *Area Development and Policy* 1 (3): 305–22.

Peck, J. *et al.* 2014. "The Kilburn Manifesto: After Neoliberalism?", *Environment and Planning A* 46 (9): 2033–49.

Peck, J. & T. Barnes 2019. "Berkeley In-Between: Radicalizing Economic Geography", in T. Barnes & E. Sheppard (eds) *Spatial Histories of Radical Geography: North America and Beyond*. Oxford: Wiley-Blackwell, forthcoming.

Raper, J. & D. Livingstone. 1995. "Development of a Geomorphological Spatial Model using Object-oriented Design", *International Journal of Geographical Information Systems* 9 (4): 359–83.

Routledge, P. & A. Cumbers 2013. *Global Justice Networks: Geographies of Transnational Solidarity*. Oxford: Oxford University Press.

Saldanha, A. 2013. "Power-Geometry as Philosophy of Space", in D. Featherstone & J. Painter (eds) *Spatial Politics: Essays for Doreen Massey*, 44–55. Oxford: Wiley-Blackwell.

Scott, A. 2000. "Economic Geography: The Great Half-Century", *Cambridge Journal of Economics* 24 (4): 483–504.

Scott, J. 1999 [1988]. *Gender and the Politics of History*. New York: Columbia University Press.

Smith, N. 1986. "Spatial Divisions of Labor: Social Structures and the Geography of Production, by Doreen Massey", *Geographical Review* 76 (3): 350–2.

Smith, N. 1987. "Dangers of the Empirical Turn: Some Comments on the CURS initiative", *Antipode* 19 (1): 59–68.

Soja, E. 1987. "The Postmodernization of Geography: A Review", *Annals of the Association of American Geographers* 77 (2): 289–94.

Sparke, M. 2007. "Acknowledging Responsibility *For Space*", *Progress in Human Geography* 31 (3): 395–403.

Storper, M. 1986. "Spatial Divisions of Labor: Social Structures and the Geography of Production, by Doreen Massey", *Progress in Human Geography* 10 (3): 455–7.

The Telegraph. 2016. "Doreen Massey; Geographer Who Examined How Places are 'Socially Constructed'", *The Telegraph*, 21 March. Available at: https://www.telegraph.co.uk/news/obituaries/12200242/Doreen-Massey-radical-geographer-obituary.html.

Vaiou, D. (ed.). 2017. "Special Section: Doreen Massey", *Geographies: A Biannual Review of Spatial Issues* 29 (1): 3–59 [In Greek].

Warde, A. 1985. "Spatial Change, Politics and the Division of Labour," in D. Gregory & J. Urry (eds) *Social Relations and Spatial Structures*, 190–212. London: Macmillan.

Werner, M. 2016. "Global Production Networks and Uneven Development: Exploring Geographies of Devaluation, Disinvestment, and Exclusion", *Geography Compass* 10 (11): 457–69.

Williams, K. & D. Thomas 1983. *Why are the British Bad at Manufacturing?* London: Routledge & Kegan Paul.

PART I

REGION

RESTRUCTURING REGIONS: DOREEN MASSEY ON UNEVEN GEOGRAPHICAL DEVELOPMENT

Brett Christophers, Marion Werner, Rebecca Lave and Jamie Peck

Like several of human geography's other luminaries of the past half-century, Doreen Massey had a deep, career-long interest in the question of uneven geographical development. It was always with her, animating her politics as much as her research practice, from the early 1970s through to the early 2010s. Embracing the challenge of understanding uneven geographical development as a concrete abstraction, Massey approached it by way of iteration between theory and particular empirical and political contexts: it was first and foremost uneven development *in Britain* that exercised her, and her ability to show how her particular conceptualisation of uneven development – which she coined "spatial divisions of labour" – helped explain the consequential particularities of the British case has inspired a generation of economic geographers. Developed in and "of" Britain, the idea of spatial divisions of labour nonetheless could be (and has been) mobilized to illuminate actually-existing economic-geographic realities much further afield. And at its core is the region. Uneven geographical development is, for Massey, a complex, continuous and multi-layered dynamic of *regional restructuring*. This dynamic is the common thread running through the six chapters in Part 1 of this book.

As ever with original thinkers such as Massey, the stimulus to innovative theorization was a realization that existing approaches to understanding the object of interest – in her case, pronounced intra-national spatial variegation in economic processes and outcomes – were simply not up to the task. Most obviously this was true, in Massey's view, of the prevailing economic orthodoxy, neoclassicism, the paradigmatic dominance of which was to be seriously challenged by the modestly titled "Towards a critique of industrial location theory" (Chapter 2). But, significantly, she also thought it was true of the array of heterodox economic approaches that were in circulation during that period – the 1970s – when she began to explore uneven development and to develop her own unique approach to its conceptualization, a process that began in an appropriately grounded way in "Regionalism: some current issues" (Chapter 5; see also Chapter 14).

As Massey saw it, the principal cause of the inadequacy of these various approaches was their weak or simply flawed conceptualization of space. If, as she would later famously insist, geography matters, then neither neoclassicism nor existing heterodoxies adequately showed how or why. Chapter 2 contains Massey's germinal critique of what was, at the time the essay was published (1973), the academic approach most committed to "spatializing" neoclassical economics, namely, industrial location theory; nearly half a century later, it remains one of the most precise and persuasive diagnoses of the problems associated with any attempt to introduce space into mainstream economics' fundamentally aspatial framework. Chapter 5, meanwhile, which was published in 1978, takes to task alternative heterodox approaches. Their common Achilles' heel, Massey claims, is their static and limited perspective on the region. To really get to grips with regional restructuring in the real world, she submits, we need to restructure our conceptualization of the region itself – what it is, how it is constituted, how it gets reproduced.

"Regionalism" (Chapter 5) represents Massey's first sustained attempt to do this and, in the process, to articulate the unique theoretical approach to uneven development elaborated at greater length six years later in her opus, the eponymous *Spatial Divisions of Labour*. Regional restructuring is not just an "outcome" of capitalist accumulation, it is also its medium (and mode) of realization. Massey proposed a remarkably succinct way of understanding this process in terms of distinct rounds of investment, each one associated with a patchwork of regionally-differentiated social economies. Different local conjunctions of specific economic activities, in turn, represented more than a distributional matter, of some jobs being here, others there, but reflected the constitution of social relations. This is the "spatial division of labour". And, crucially, this spatial division of labour is not inert; geography is not "passive." Seeded by one round of economic investment, spatial divisions of labour fundamentally shape, in turn, the nature of the investment that follows in successive rounds. The relationship between economy and space is, in other words, reciprocal. In Chapter 5, Massey shows the power of her conceptual lens by using it to shed light on the massive regional industrial restructuring that was taking place in Britain in the 1970s.

Yet for Massey it was not just an impoverished conceptualization of space that rendered other academic approaches to uneven development inadequate. They had, she thought, at least two other significant shortcomings, and Massey's attempt to redress these deficiencies in her own wide-ranging work on regional restructuring gives it much of its distinctiveness. One of these shortcomings concerned gender. Her work on uneven development always had a feminist component because she recognised that the local spatial division of labour *is* always gendered, and that this gendering substantively influences the nature of subsequent rounds of investment. In South Wales, for example, which was one of her prime examples, a long legacy of heavy industrial investment had created a patriarchal society in which pliable "greenfield" female labour became readily exploitable by newly-arriving electronics firms from the late 1970s. In Chapter 6, "A woman's place?", Massey is writing with Linda McDowell – another pioneer of feminist economic geography – in what would prove to be a formative exploration of the changing articulation of capitalism and patriarchy in four regions of England between the nineteenth century and the late-twentieth century: the northeast, the northwest, inner London, and the Fens of East Anglia. Massey and McDowell show that the challenges with which capitalism has presented patriarchy, and thus the nature of the intersection of class and gender relations, has varied markedly between these different regions and at different moments of their respective histories.

The other key shortcoming of alternative approaches to regional restructuring, in Massey's view, was the lack of agency accorded to labour. Workers did not succumb meekly to exploitation by capital. They mobilized and organized, most notably through unionization; and again, different local forms of unionization affected what capital could and could not do in terms of subsequent rounds of accumulation, thus shaping wider patterns of regional restructuring. In the mid-1980s, primarily in the pages of *Marxism Today*, Massey penned a series of studies of transformations of the geographies of British unionism in the face of the convulsions that Thatcherism unleashed in the nation's working-class heartlands. In Chapter 7 (published in 1989), co-authored with her then graduate student Joe Painter, Massey draws on those studies to provide a "fin de decade" appraisal of the changing geography of British trade unionism that situated this changing geography squarely in the context of a decade of major ongoing regional restructuring.

Underwriting Massey's extraordinary canvas, all the while, was a deep appreciation of the materiality of land, the very soil of all spatial divisions of labour and the terrain on which all regional restructuring plays out. Massey knew that it was not possible to unpack and explain patterns of economic-geographic restructuring without paying due heed to patterns of landownership, least of all in a country such as Britain where no other form of wealth is as heavily concentrated in the hands of the elite. Massey, more than arguably any other observer of British political economy of her generation, knew just how embedded landed interests are in the nation's class structures, economic life, and wealth and income inequalities. In 1978, together with Alejandrina Catalano, she published her first monograph, *Capital and Land: Private Landownership by Capital in Great Britain*. Though it never garnered anything like the attention of *Spatial Divisions of Labour*, it was no less impressive or important an achievement. Its relatively low profile has nothing to do with the quality of the work, and everything to do with the fact that with Britain's abrupt shift to neoliberalism a year after the book was published, the political economy of land in Britain – about which nothing remotely as substantial, illuminating or convincing has been written in the four decades since – was forced off both the political and academic agendas.

In this book we are reprinting two of Massey's shorter pieces on land. Chapter 3, published in 1973, was co-authored with Richard Barras and Andrew Broadbent, who, like Catalano, were colleagues of Massey's at the Centre for Environmental Studies, the think tank at which she worked throughout the 1970s, and the demise of which was precipitated by the incoming Thatcher administration's 1979 decision to withdraw public funding. "Labour must take over land" is an unapologetically political piece. The authors describe the pernicious socioeconomic effects of the prevailing British system of (largely private) landownership, argue that the half measures embedded in the postwar planning system had done little to mitigate these effects, and call instead for full land nationalization. Chapter 4, published in 1977, essentially summarized the arguments of the then-forthcoming *Capital and Land*. It details overall patterns of landownership in 1970s Britain and explains how these had evolved historically. It explores the respective roles of the three main categories of capitalist landowner in Britain in that era – the aristocracy, industrial capital, and finance capital (Massey examined the "financialization" of land, without calling it that, several decades before it became fashionable to do so) – and identifies the primary contradictions generated by each. And, lastly, it renews Chapter 3's call for the nationalization of land: not to end the struggle over land-related issues, but to change the conditions of that struggle.

In short, Massey's works on the political economy of land and regional restructuring gathered in this section are emblematic of her wider oeuvre: politically engaged, deeply rooted in place (in this case, Britain), strikingly original, fundamentally geographic, and powerfully suggestive and generative for other scholars.

CHAPTER 2

TOWARDS A CRITIQUE OF INDUSTRIAL LOCATION THEORY (1973)

I INTRODUCTION

In attempting a critique of a discipline, the fundamental problem always arises that the very concept and definition of disciplines are themselves functions of a particular ideology and epistemology. From the point of view of the critique presented here, the separate existence of an entity called *industrial location theory* is itself open to question. In different ways, many of the classic theories of industrial location have proceeded as though the object of study was an abstract firm – one without effective structural relationships to the rest of the economy. The specific problem of idealised abstraction will be dealt with later. The immediate question is the related one of the presumed separation of spatial behaviour from the economic system as a whole. In fact, of course, the two are intimately related at all levels. In the first place it is rarely valid to retain a complete distinction between the specifically locational decision of the firm and all its other economic decisions. Secondly there is the fact that the nature of a firm's behaviour will be influenced by its position within the total economic structure. And thirdly, at a more aggregated level, the spatial shape of the economy is the result not only of specifically spatial forces, but also of the a-spatial dynamic of the economic system having a spatial manifestation.

It is, then, impossible realistically to treat "the spatial" as a closed system. Certainly industrial location theory does not have an object of its own, and in that sense there could never be an *autonomous* dynamic theory of industrial location. Not all of the work considered here is in contradiction with this view, but the point needs to be borne in mind throughout the following discussion since many elements of the critique spring directly from it.

Nonetheless, there *is* a body of knowledge called "industrial location theory", and the spatial expression of the economic system *does* have to be analysed. Given that, this critique seems a valid exercise to undertake. The bulk of industrial location theory *is* in fact closely related to economics but only in the sense that it derives very directly from neo-classical marginalist economic theory, sharing its ideology, and consequently its epistemological approach.

The threads of industrial location theory covered in this paper fall under four major headings. First, there is a line of development which derives from the initial work of Weber (1909). This centres on the location decision of the individual firm in a known locational environment, where there is no interdependence with the locational decisions of other firms. In contrast, the second group of theoretical studies focuses on small numbers of firms in locationally interdependent situations. Much of this work sprang from an original article by Hotelling (1929).Thirdly, a more "behavioural" approach, stemming from the work of Cyert and March (1963), has recently developed in response both to changing concrete conditions and to contradictions within previous approaches. The fourth theoretical approach considered here is that of August Losch (1954), which was different in that, although it started from an analysis of the individual firm, its prime concern was the examination of potential whole economic landscapes. It was an attempt, essentially, to parallel in spatial terms the economic concept of general equilibrium.

This relationship between location theory and a-spatial neoclassical economics will form one of the themes of this essay. It has influenced the definition of the object for study, the methodology, and the main elements of historical development [...] This element of the critique involves challenging the ideology of the approach as a whole. From "within" that approach, however, a second theme, which will recur throughout the discussion, centres on internal contradictions and problems, particularly those produced by the introduction of the spatial dimension into the a-spatial neoclassical framework. A further contradiction, that between the developments now taking place in location theory and those emerging (in the form of acute socio-economic problems) in the "real world" is dealt with in the final section. Another important theme concerns the pattern of growth of the theory over time. Changes in theoretical structure are brought about in response to the emergence of problems, but the way in which those problems are "seen" determines the nature of the response to them and the consequent theoretic development.

In order for a critique of this nature to be effective, it is necessary for the object of its study to be seen in context. If the perspective of a whole subject is to be examined it is essential to step outside of that perspective. It is only by such a procedure that one can (a) appreciate the nature of the subject for what it is and (b) envisage any possibility of change along the dimension of characteristics which typifies the subject as a whole. A historical approach provides the necessary framework for such an analysis [...] The historical perspective is [...] twofold: firstly to set *theories* in their historical context, and thereby to illustrate both their reactive nature and the role they play in that context; and secondly to see that the approach to industrial location – that is the nature of the theories themselves – should also take industrial location (i.e. its object) in *its* historical perspective.

It is also important to consider carefully the nature of the "space" in which location is taking place. Most industrial location theory deals essentially with some form of "abstract" space. In the case of Losch, for instance, distance is the only quality of space considered as locationally significant. In fact the space of industrial location is the product of a complex historical process. It is also a political and institutional space.

[...]

II ASPECTS OF A-SPATIAL NEO-CLASSICAL ECONOMICS

One of the most familiar modes of attack on neoclassical economics is that which concentrates on the nature of abstraction. Dobb (1940) discusses this in some depth: *Once the formal question of internal consistency is settled, the acceptance or rejection of a theory depends on one's view of the appropriateness of the particular abstraction on which the theory is based.* He goes on to discuss two approaches: *In the first place, one may build one's abstraction on the exclusion of certain features which are present in any actual situation, either because they are the more variable or because they are quantitatively of lesser importance in determining the course of events.* Such abstraction he sees as a necessary and justifiable structural simplification of a reality.

Secondly, however, *one may base one's abstraction [. . .] simply on the formal procedure of combining the properties common to a heterogeneous assortment of situations and building abstraction out of analogy.* As Dobb points out, such distillations of common factors may form such a small part of the mechanics of any one situation that the real structure and motive power is lost. Such can be the case with neo-classical economics. We learn, certainly, of producers and consumers, but not of capitalists, workers, imperialism, and private property. The focus of theory is on an idealism. This approach has been carried over, almost in its entirety, to much of the industrial location theory discussed in this essay.

Moreover, the lack of systemic context, which is one effect of this mode of abstraction, is paralleled by an absence of historical perspective. In most of location theory, as in marginalist economics, the existence of numerous perfectly-competitive profit-maximisers or, alternatively, of an oligopoly, is assumed as given – and consequently (which is the point) unalterable. The dynamic of the system as a whole is ignored. Thus, for instance, although both perfectly-competitive and monopolistic or oligopolistic situations are studied, they are analysed as separate situations, which might obtain perhaps in different places, or in different sectors of the economy. The dynamic relationships between the two, and particularly the development of one from the conditions of the other, are ignored. Static equilibrium is the rule and the aim; internal contradictions and the dynamics of development are not apparent.

Putting together some of the points made above, however, we see that there is contradiction even here. On the one hand there is the pretension to trans-system distillation, on the other there are firm roots in the contemporary economic arrangement. This contradiction arises not because the *particular* abstraction of neo-classical economics is incorrect, but because the whole *concept* of an a-historical formalism of human behaviour is a misapprehension. Behaviour itself is a result of historical conditions and position within the total system at any point in time. Different forms of economic system, and different structural positions within any one such system, will lead to different forms of behaviour. Therefore the critique is not simply either that "economic man", for instance, is an inadequate abstraction, or that there should be a simple transference from analysis at the level of the individual to a 'structural' approach. It is necessary to see behaviour centrally in a historical context, and therefore to have an overall structure containing within it the necessity for the evolution of the *actual* variants in which it exists. Concepts of economic man, and certain theories of the firm, fail to do this in that the starting point for their analysis is an a-historical, self-constitutive subject.

III THE DEVELOPMENT OF MAJOR APPROACHES IN INDUSTRIAL LOCATION THEORY

It is probably fair to say that the whole of industrial location theory lies within one major, overall "paradigm," for, though separate threads of development exist, they have much in common in terms of their epistemological approach and of their function in relation to the economic system of which they are a product. But so-called "paradigms" do not rise and fall in an academic or intellectual isolation. Theories do not develop in a vacuum. Each major approach bears a definite relationship to the material conditions of its age, to the nature of economic organisation, and to the social relations which may be consequent upon those material conditions.

Marginalist economics and its derivative location theory are ideological in the sense that the questions which they ask perform the function primarily of allowing the expression of certain desired "answers". And the *particular* ideology with which they approach the study of capitalism in dominantly a function of social relations. This ideology determines even the definition of the objects studied. Thus neo-classical economics does not talk of surplus value or the rate of exploitation. In consequence it is possible to assume a world of social harmony and commonality of interest. The socially-produced ideology also determines the level of the major focus of interest – the individual firm; the nature of that focus – the exclusive consideration of the point of view of the industrialist rather than that of the working class (profit is the criterion, wages are simply labour costs); and the nature of abstraction – which excludes the concrete power-relations of society.

Since the days of Weber it has not been necessary to adopt another point of view. Minor changes have been made, which will be discussed, but these have been mainly within the context of this overall approach. [...]

Nonetheless, industrial location theory has not followed one continuous stream of development. There have been definite stages and threads in its growth. The rest of this section will briefly elaborate those stages and their role. It is interesting to note the different levels at which criticism, and response to criticism, may occur. The critique in this paper attempts to make fundamental points about the nature of the approach as a whole. When viewed as it were from within the ideology, however, the inadequacies are interpreted differently. Either they will produce minor modifications and sophistications to the given theory, as often as not leading to a cul-de-sac of complexity, or they will stimulate a new line of thought, but still not one which breaks out of the ideological framework.

The brief history which follows attempts to illustrate this development, and its predominant characteristics. Thus, for instance, three levels of critique are described of the initial work of Weber. Firstly, there was the line of development which restricted itself to modification and sophistication of detail in the original approach. Secondly, there was a reaction to more fundamental inadequacies, producing what may be seen as new threads of theoretical development – studies of interdependence, and a more behavioural approach. Thirdly, there is an attempt to show how even those developments are incorrect insofar as they fail to challenge certain assumptions of the analysis.

The Weberian approach

The generally accepted founding father of industrial location theory was Alfred Weber (1909). His analysis was of single firms, and was confined to minimising costs, in the general case specifically transport costs. Weber himself did not formulate the problem in the framework of economic theory, but instead saw it in terms of a physical analogy as a problem of the resolution of various 'location pulls' or 'forces'. Later developments, however, through Isard (1956) and Moses (1958) have shown how Weberian concepts can be incorporated within the existing marginalist substitution analysis.

At the most detailed level of critique, this analysis was judged far too simple, both in terms of the number and complexity of factors which might operate as forces on the location of a plant, and in the fact that too many relationships or states (production coefficients, for instance, and size of output) were taken to be fixed. It was these criticisms which led to further development within this line of theory. And the points are of course perfectly valid within a given context. The fact that the consequent line of development has not greatly increased industrial location theory's ability to understand, or deal with, the real-world situation it faces is not because these criticisms are incorrect, but because they are the wrong ones: the critique was made within too narrow a perspective. Thus a thread of development was produced from Weber's initial analysis. Authors such as Hoover (1937) and Smith (1966) introduced new factors, made some implications explicit, and transformed locational 'forces' into cost *and revenue* surfaces. On the other hand, Predohl started the process of introducing the methods of substitution analysis into the Weberian approach. This was further elaborated by Isard (1956) who, however, kept 'transport inputs' as separate identifiable entities, and thus limited the dimensions of possible substitution. With Moses' (1958) article, this branch of location theory was fully integrated into marginalist economics. Such a line of development thus involved a process of increasing sophistication and detail. Moses in some senses represents the end of the line, for although he did introduce new conceptual approaches from Isard, and his attack was therefore very much a reformulation of the problem, nonetheless his results, showing the total interdependence of the system and the requirement of locational adjustment for every change in any other variable are certainly not useful either in operational application or as a framework for understanding the forces at work in shaping the space-economy. Attempts *have* been made, such as with Smith's (1966) spatial margins, to extract a simplified structure from this approach. But even here the emphasis on the decision of an idealised single firm stultifies the approach as an analytic tool.

Two points should be made at this juncture. First of all, this method of analysis is not without use. Some of the ideas derived from the Weberian approach, for instance, are genuinely important conceptualisations. The second point, however, is indicative of basic problems in the development of location theory as a whole. A considerable amount of the complexity that was finally injected into the Weberian approach was due to the simple introduction of the spatial dimension. In this case the problems arose just because another variable was added but it will be shown later that the attempt to introduce the specifically spatial dimension has rendered some of the easy conclusions of a-spatial economics much more difficult to draw.

It was two other, interrelated, criticisms of Weber which led to the development of *new* strands within the overall context of location theory. They were indeed much more fundamental criticisms, but the way in which they were treated meant that they still did not essentially break out of the existing ideological framework. In the first place, Weber assumed perfect competition. This, however, is at variance with the inclusion of the spatial dimension. There cannot be perfect competition over space. The causes and effects of this fact will be examined in greater detail later, but it should be noted that its implications are important, and that they affect the degree to which location theory can play the same sustaining role as economics. In spite of these implications of the need for a major conceptual re-think, the thread of development to which this realisation gave rise did not produce the jolt to the development of location theory that it might have done. Neither did it have any significant feedback effect on a-spatial economics. Because of the monopolistic element introduced into markets by space the policies of firms are interdependent. An oligopolistic situation prevails. Locational interdependence became the next area for research. Another line of development, closely related, arose from the realisation of the need to relax the assumption of "economic man". This is again a recognition of a genuine inadequacy. However, the alternative "behavioural" approaches which have most commonly been sought reveal a real misapprehension of the reasons why an assumption of "economic man" is incorrect.

Locational interdependence

The interdependence of producers is in part a result of the monopolistic element in their competition. There are two distinct ways such an element of monopoly may enter a spatial economy. In the first place there is that which results from the function of distance itself, and secondly there is the normal a-spatial concept of monopoly as the concentration of capital into a few hands. The development of the branch of industrial location theory which concentrates on locational interdependence was probably to some degree a reaction to both, but certainly much of its stimulus came from the theories of imperfect competition developing in a-spatial economics. And this development in economics was in turn a response to changing real conditions. As a descriptive device, perfect competition was becoming an increasingly unconvincing structure. But although much of the development of theories of locational interdependence was thus undoubtedly an indirect result of the actual monopolisation of capital, with a-spatial economics providing many of the tools of the trade, the resultant theory has focused almost exclusively on certain aspects of that element of monopoly which is solely the result of distance. In fact, very little explicit attention has ever been paid in location theory to the actual monopolisation of capital. In large measure this is once again a result of the essentially static and partial nature of most of that theory. Systemic development is normally excluded from analysis.

Moreover, even the examination of the effect of the element of monopoly conferred by distance has, as mentioned above, been of a fairly restricted nature. The main emphasis has been on individual locational-interdependence situations, examined either through market-area analysis (e.g. Fetter, 1924 and Hyson and Hyson, 1950), or through an approach more allied to game theory (see, for instance, Hotelling, 1929 and Stevens, 1961). These analyses have produced some interesting results, but the *restriction* to this level of detail has prevented the real inferences being drawn. As will be shown below, these affect the whole tenability of Pareto-optimal equilibrium solutions. Furthermore, even within the analysed situations, the actual results in terms of location decisions are usually indeterminate, both in some specific individual situations and as a general characteristic of this class of problems. This point is well made by Chisholm (1971), and is again essentially a result of the monopolistic character of the situation. For while market mechanisms are the controlling force in perfect competition, in situations of imperfect competition it becomes possible for the actors to influence the environment. "Strategies" become important. Given those, the result of any specified game situation may be predictable, but the problem is now that the choice of strategies at this micro level is indeterminate. Increasing complexity of this approach as an analytic tool once again led to a cul-de-sac.

Behavioural alternatives

As should be evident from the preceding discussion, the "behavioural" approach to industrial location developed as the culmination of a number of tendencies. On the one hand, it was a reaction to changing material conditions – in other words to the development of monopoly capital. On the other hand it was also the result of consideration of the effects of space. Assumptions of perfect knowledge, as required by the original Weberian models, are obviously unrealistic as soon as concepts of distance are introduced, while, as pointed out, in a spatial context firms are necessarily locationally interdependent, and consideration of their behavioural strategies therefore becomes important.

In fact, the critique 'from outside the ideology' should be made on very different lines, as will become apparent during the following discussion. This fundamental misconception of the nature of the issues in question meant that once again, although a new "approach" in industrial location studies has emerged, it still contains within it the same fundamental problems.

The reaction to these problems, as they were in fact seen, has taken a variety of forms, which can be characterised (or, more fairly, caricatured) along an axis of which the two poles are purely descriptive behaviouralism and the behavioural theory of the firm. These two approaches are not in practice, of course, often separable, but they do seem to represent possibly conflicting tendencies. This itself signals an emerging central tension in industrial location studies, between the evident need to deal with considerable variety, and the desire to have one central theoretic structure.

At one extreme, descriptive behaviouralism is a simple recognition of variety and will not *of itself* produce a new theoretical formulation. At the other extreme, however, the attempt to develop the theory of *the* firm is just as much a misapprehension of the problem – insofar, that is, as it is an attempt simply to replace one abstract formalism ("economic man") with another ("behavioural theory of the firm").

In other words, we arrive again at the points made in the first two sections of the paper. On the one hand, 'theory' does not have to be represented by a-historical abstraction. On the other, spatial behaviour cannot be isolated from the overall development of the economic system.

General spatial equilibrium

In the last part of this section it is useful to consider the contribution of August Losch (1954). Losch was one of the first people to attempt a spatial counterpart to economic general equilibrium. From an initial even distribution of population he derived from each sector a net of hexagonal markets which fulfilled the zero excess profit conditions. By combining sets of market areas for different goods he produced the well-known sectoral and semi-hierarchical economic landscapes which fulfilled certain welfare criteria such as maximising the number of purchases made locally and minimising the sum of the minimum distances between production sites. The economic system considered explicitly was one of competing profit-maximising firms under conditions of free entry, and with f.o.b. [free on board] pricing. The implication is, therefore, that such a market system can produce the result described.

The ability of the decentralised price mechanism to sustain a general equilibrium solution, and the conformity of the latter with the marginal conditions of Pareto optimality has always been a major weapon in a-spatial economics' armoury of apologetics. The purpose is to prove that a completely decentralised (perfectly-competitive) price mechanism will produce an allocation which is optimal, or, as Bramhall (1969) says in his "An introduction to spatial general equilibrium", it is *an affirmation of the existence of internal control mechanisms in the social order.*

Even in a-spatial economics the assumptions necessary for the derivation of general equilibrium have reached heroic proportions (e.g. see Graaf, 1957), and the implications of the theory of second best and of Arrow's theorem are far-reaching – see Hunt (1972). Nonetheless the introduction of the spatial dimension is critical. Indeed the assumption of much theoretical economics that life takes place on the head of a pin should be regarded as one of its less convincing abstractions.

In the first place some of the assumptions already dubious in a-spatial economics become even less tenable when space is introduced. Thus the whole set of assumptions about economic rationality and perfect knowledge become impossible to maintain over distance, even ignoring, as economic theory traditionally does, any institutional constraints. Even within one city, jobs in the suburbs go unfilled while potential employees remain out of work in the city centre. Similarly, locational inertia prevents the adjustments, which "ideally" are necessary to changes in other variables [....]

Nonetheless, such objections in fact ask only for "realism". They are not theoretical arguments, in that they do not prove any logical impossibility in the attainment through the market of a spatial equilibrium satisfying certain welfare criteria – save of course that to overcome them it is necessary to assume that (continuous) space has no effect. It would still be possible to argue that the market would produce the desired result if only we allowed it to operate 'perfectly'. There are, however, serious *theoretical* problems caused by the consideration of space.

Consider first the specific system designed by Losch, where under a given set of assumptions, profit-maximising firms arrived at an equilibrium satisfying some sort of welfare criteria. [...] Even within this simple framework, however, Mills and Lav (1964) have pointed out a critical inconsistency. Thus, among Losch's assumptions are the following: (i) that the firms are profit-maximisers, and (ii) that the locations are so numerous that the entire space is filled. Mills and Lav show that these two assumptions are not necessarily consistent; that in fact the second is a theorem which should be examined in relation to the first. They proceed to examine it, and find that it will not necessarily always hold. In very similar vein, though much more rarely pointed out, is the problem of the arrangement of the final multi-commodity economic landscape. The idea is that the single commodity sets of hexagonal market areas, having established one point at which they all have a plant, then rotate about this central metropolis until the number of locational coincidences is maximised. Obviously such was not the economic process intended; Losch was explicitly designing an optimal system with normative implications. But as *Palander has shown ... agglomeration economies cannot cause towns to form unless the model postulates some mechanism whereby firms can co-ordinate their choices* (Webber, 1972). In other words, although

Losch's system was in some sense normative, it did nonetheless assume that, given the right conditions, the market economy could produce the desired result. The above arguments show that even within this very restricted formulation this is not necessarily the case. Both of the points above imply a necessity for economic mechanisms of control or co-ordination not included within the model. It is often precisely to *DIS*prove the need for such mechanisms that equilibrium is cited in a-spatial economics.

In fact, of course, the end-state produced by the Loschian equilibrium itself does not fulfil even those welfare criteria acceptable to a-spatial neoclassical economics. F.o.b. prices equal average cost, and delivered price, therefore, exceeds equal average cost, and delivered price, therefore, exceeds marginal cost plus transportation cost. This is again the result of the monopoly element inherent in any discussion of space in these terms. [...] Thus Boventer (1962) writes:

> *The main difficulty in location theory is that in order for a general*
> *equilibrium model to have an optimal solution which the market*
> *or theoretical solution process necessarily approaches and which*
> *fulfils the usual welfare conditions of production, it is necessary to*
> *assume linear homogenous production functions. Indivisibilities*
> *and agglomeration economies, which are basic for locational anal-*
> *yses, in particular for urban analysis, cannot be incorporated in*
> *such a model. If they are included, the substitution principle, if it*
> *is applied at the margin only, loses much of its force and becomes*
> *useless in finding the optimal spatial structure. For this reason, the*
> *marginal principles have to be supplemented by the total condi-*
> *tions of equilibrium.*

And Richardson (1969), writing on a general theory of location, says:

> *Thus, the dilemma is that it is difficult to formulate a determinate*
> *general theory of location without adopting the pedagogic device*
> *of the equilibrium concept, yet if this concept is adopted complica-*
> *tions arise from the probability that general equilibrium is incon-*
> *sistent with the implications of the space economy.*

IV THE SPATIAL DIMENSION, AND CONTRADICTIONS WITHIN ECONOMIC THEORY

Some elements of the relationship in ideology, and hence in epistemology, of industrial location theory to neoclassical economics emerged in the last section. Industrial location theory is thus vulnerable to many of the same criticisms as can be made of that (very vulnerable) subject. For location theory, however, this is only the beginning of the problems. A further line of argument began to emerge in section three, about the crucial nature of the introduction of the spatial dimension into neoclassical economics. In the discussion of Losch, for example, it was shown that his system could not guarantee to produce the equilibrium he described without higher level control mechanisms: that the aggregation of individual decisions cannot be guaranteed to produce the required solution. Moreover, *even if* such a solution were produced, it would not, without very restrictive assumptions, fulfil Pareto optimality criteria. In both these cases, the introduction of the spatial dimension produces internal inconsistencies within the usual body of neoclassical economic theory. The purpose of this brief section is to explore this in more structured form.

In the first place it was seen in the discussion of Moses (1958) how the introduction of space, simply as an extra variable, enormously complicated the analysis and, most particularly, its applicability. With the introduction of a concrete spatial dimension, in fact, the need really does become apparent for a rigorous but structured form of analysis which does not depend on the over-precision of marginalism.

Another way in which the spatial dimension complicates the arguments of economics is through its introduction of an element of monopoly. This has already been mentioned at a number of points and in some detail. Most significantly in the context of this section it was seen how the apparently comforting welfare conclusions of a-spatial general equilibrium become much less easy to draw. This element of monopoly may, however, be illustrated in a variety of ways. In the preceding paragraphs the aspect on which attention was focused was the existence of interdependence between producers. But there are other ways of demonstrating the point, and which link in with other theoretical criticisms already made.

In the first place, each point in space has an absolute quality. Land is not in locational terms an undifferentiated good, and private possession of a parcel of it endows the owner with exclusive rights over a unique entity. The allocation of such a good is therefore critical. This line of argument is of course closely tied to that of rent theory and, to the extent that industrial location theory has managed frequently to remain distinct from that theory, is outside the scope of this paper. The point to be made here is simply that in any integrated (i.e. structural and inter-sectoral) analysis of the spatial arrangement of society at inter-regional level, industrial location theory *cannot* be divorced from (reformulated) rent theory.

The degree of monopoly conferred by space is particularly important to industrial location theory (as opposed, for instance, to residential location) in terms of the control it allows of the area *surrounding* the point of location. In this case it is the in*tra*-sectoral context which is most important; this is the geography of market areas. The level of analysis may be intra-urban, or inter-regional, or international; the point is the same. One of the conditions of perfect competition is that, in equilibrium, consumers will be indifferent between producers – they all charge the same price and their products are indistinguishable. Such conditions can no longer hold when the economy is distributed over space. For that space, and its concomitant distance and transport costs, amount for the consumer to a form of product differenti-ation. The producers may, therefore, raise prices without losing all of their custom, extract monopoly profits, and indulge the more easily in various forms of price discrimination.

Another instance in which the misconceptions of economics become critical when applied to spatial location theory relates to the static and par-tial nature of the conceptual approach. In a-spatial economics the normal restriction to a static view prevents analysis of the dynamic forces within capitalism.

But the restriction is even more crucial in a spatial context, for the spatial and a-spatial concentration of capital may be seen as mutually reinforcing mechanisms. In the first place, the a-spatial concentration of capital itself has spatial effects. Thus Parsons (1972), for instance, illustrates the reinforcement of tendencies to spatial agglomeration which are produced by the increasing dominance of large corporations. On the other hand, space itself may be the active element in the dynamic. In the context of industrial location theory, one of the most important of these "spatial forces" is agglomeration econ-omies. These are, of course, considered by location theory, and considered to be important. But they are usually studied within a conceptual structure which allows their full significance to be missed. In most cases the structure is that of partial analysis, with only one, or at most an oligopolistically small number, of firms being studied. Such is the case with Weberian analysis, for instance. We see the likelihood of individual firms to agglomerate, but do not study the effects of this in terms of the input-output system of eco-nomic activity as a whole. Losch, on the other hand, does consider location at a more aggregate level, and does include the more macro-level effects of (intersectoral only) agglomeration economies. Apart from the other prob-lems already mentioned, however, (including that of the means by which numerous private decision-makers can actually take maximum advantage of agglomeration economies) this approach fails, because of its static equilib-rium nature, to appreciate the cumulative effects of such economies.

Externalities, as a general category which includes agglomeration econ-omies, are not part of the main thread of highly precise mathematical neo-classical economic formulations. This must be a criticism of any theory of the economy. But for location theory/spatial economics this is more than merely some 'aspect' or 'imperfection' ignored. Externalities are, or should be, central to any theory of locational arrangement. Once again the transfer from a-spatial to spatial involves a reinforcement of the inadequacies of neo-classical economics.

These misconceptions and contradictions are not totally ignored in industrial location literature. The contribution of Mills and Lav has already been cited, for instance. There are, moreover, a number of rigorous demonstrations of the deficiencies of the decentralised price mechanism in achieving and maintaining a non-trivial equilibrium solution to certain problems in spatial allocation [...]. Much of this work is, however, given only peripheral attention. [...] If quoted at all, [the central implications of this literature for the standard body of location theory] are usually presented as problems implying a need for modification of the basic theory. *In fact* in many cases they constitute elements of a much more fundamental technical critique.

V CONCLUSIONS: THE PRESENT POSITION

It is appropriate to stress [...] the tentative nature of this critique. Many other approaches, consistent with this one, remain to be covered. Moreover there exist certain threads of location theory (the Dutch analyses of spatial dispersion, for example, and the work on growth pole theory and threshold analysis), omitted here because of not falling within the strict lineage of 'classical' location theory, which are immune to some of the criticisms made here. Nonetheless it is possible to draw a few conclusions from the points made in this essay.

This critique has attempted to demonstrate three main themes. Firstly it shows the confusion implicit in attempting to conceive of a completely autonomous location theory. Similarly, critiques of the standard body of economic theory have concentrated on the economic but non-spatial aspects of the development of capitalism. It is important to understand also the spatial dimension of its development [...]. Secondly, the critique points out that that body of knowledge which is known as industrial location theory suffers from the same idealistic misconceptions as neoclassical economics. It is this overall viewpoint which both determines its object and its form, and enables it to perform a political and ideological function. This function may be articulated through the elaboration of specific constructions which justify the economic system (as can be the case with general equilibrium), through a concentration on individual industrialist rationality and a consequent ignoring of the *effects* of this 'rationality', or through an extreme acceptance of "whatever the locator wants we must provide" (even when it falls in the most non-economic realms of 'psychic income'), an attitude exemplified by much latter-day market-research-type descriptive behaviouralism. Thirdly, this critique has aimed to demonstrate that, even within its own terms of reference, location theory contains fundamental theoretical inconsistencies in relation to 'a-spatial' economics.

Lastly, a major and deepening contradiction emerges from the preceding discussion: there is a widening disparity between the current directions of development of location theory and those of spatial problems (or socio-economic problems with a specific spatial manifestation) in the 'real world.'

We have seen that some of the more recent lines of development in location theory appear to be leading it into a desert of detail – of either the highly mathematical or the behavioural kind. Some of these developments have been discussed. Meanwhile, however, concrete problems are growing worse. Within cities the differentials between central core and suburbs increase; multinational firms make nonsense of policies designed to promote regional equality. Most of the analytical tools available in present industrial location theory are able to explain individual-level decisions as in some way rational, but are helpless in face of the resultant systemic-level *ir*rationality. The fact that planning control is relatively so weak in this sector is only a reflection of the same reverence for the individual capitalist's decision as we find in theoretical industrial location analysis. Our operational regional models recognise the fundamental importance of the industrial base and its intersectoral effects. What are emerging as "locational problems", whether intra-urban, interregional or international, are the spatial manifestations of the contradictions of capitalism.

At this point, the argument has returned to the fact that an autonomous industrial location theory cannot be constituted. Spatial development can only be seen as part of the overall development of capitalism. However it is also true that many of the emerging contradictions of the economic system both take on a specifically spatial form, and are exacerbated by the existence of the spatial dimension. To this extent, consideration of "the spatial element" is essential to all effective economic analysis. But most of existing industrial location theory is placed within an ideology which defines its object and mode of analysis in a way which makes effective analysis impossible.

REFERENCES

Boventer, E. von 1962. "Towards a United Theory of Spatial Economic Structure" PPRSA 10, 163–80. Reprinted in Dean, Leahy and McKee *Spatial Economic Theory*, Macmillan New York 1970.

Bramhall, D. F. 1969. "An introduction to spatial general equilibrium" in Karaska G. J. and Bramhall D. F. *Locational analysis for manufacturing a selection of readings*, MIT Press.

Chisholm, M. 1971. "In search of a basis for location theory" in *Progress in Geography* 2, 111–133.

Cyert, R. M. and March J. C. 1963. *A behavioural theory of the firm*, Prentice Hall.

Dobb, M. 1940. "The trend of modern economics" in *Political Economy and Capitalism*, Routledge and Kegan Paul.

Fetter, F. A. 1924. "The Economic Law of Market Areas" *Quarterly Journal of Economics*, vol 39, 520–29.

Graaff, J. Der 1957. *Theoretical Welfare Economics*, Cambridge University Press.

Hoover, E. M. 1937. *Location Theory and the Shoe and Leather Industries*.

Hotelling, H. 1929. "Stability in competition" EJ vol 39, March 1929 pp 47–57. Reprinted in Dean et al; and in Stigler and Boulding AEA Readings in Price Theory.

Hunt, E. K. 1972 "Economic scholasticism and capitalist ideology" in Hunt and Schwarz (eds.) *A critique of economic theory*. Penguin Modern Economic Readings.

Hyson, C. D. and Hyson W. P. "The Economic Law of Market Areas" *Quarterly Journal of Economics* vol 64 pp 319–24. Reprinted in Dean et al *Spatial Economic Theory* pp 165–169.

Isard, W. 1956. *Location and Space Economy*, MIT Press.

Losch, A. 1954. *The Economics of Location*, Y.U.P.

Mills, E. S. and Lav M. R. 1964. "A model of market areas with free entry" *Journal of Political Economy* vol 72, pp 278–288. (reprinted in Dean, Leahy and McKee).

Moses, L. N. 1958. "Location and the theory of production". *Quarterly Journal of Economics*, 73 No. 2 (also in Dean, Leahy and McKee).

Parsons, G. F. 1972. "The giant manufacturing corporations and balanced regional growth in Britain". *Area* vol 4, 2, 99-103.

Richardson, H. W. 1972. *Regional Economics* Weidenfeld and Nicolson.

Smith, D. M. A. 1966. "A theoretical framework for geographical studies of industrial location" *Economic Geography* 42, 95–113.

Stevens, B. H. 1961. "An application of Game Theory to a problem in Location Strategy". PPRSA 7, 143–158.

Webber, M. J. 1972. *Impact of Uncertainty on Location* MIT Press.

Weber, A. 1909. *Uber don Standort der Industrien*: translated as *Theory of the Location of Industries* (Chicago 1929).

CHAPTER 3

LABOUR MUST TAKE OVER LAND (1973)

with Richard Barras and Andrew Broadbent

In the vastly complex set of problems involved in land policy, it has become fairly clear that half measures are useless. Only a comprehensive approach based on public ownership can produce the practical results needed if we are to make the best social use of land.

It need hardly be stressed that 'the land question' is again at the centre of the political stage. Soaring city centre prices make rational land-use planning virtually impossible, while on the fringes of our urban areas, and in regions of new development, speculators increase the costs of new ventures while returning to the community none of the associated gain in land-values. The objectives of a land policy should be clear. In the first place, speculation in land must come to an end. Secondly, those real increases in the value of land which will nonetheless result from developments which change an area's potential must be recouped for the community. Thirdly, the public should have control over the allocation of land as a valuable scarce resource.

The problem is to design a land policy which can achieve these objectives and at the same time be politically, financially and administratively feasible. In the design of any such land policy, there are certain major questions which must be resolved. These key questions are central to any understanding of the failure of past policies, and critical for the formulation of any future successful approach.

Firstly, much previous discussion has centred around the choice between taxation of increases in the value of land, and outright public ownership. The arguments for the taxation approach include on the one hand that it generates income through securing 'betterment' for the community, and on the other hand that its costs in compensation are zero. Outright ownership, however, can also generate a continuous income through rents. Although this income will admittedly probably at first be smaller because it will have to be set against compensation, the reduction can be minimized by careful phasing of compensation. Moreover, ownership represents a less easily reversible policy, and therefore a more permanent income. Furthermore, the taxation approach suffers from a major disadvantage not shared by outright ownership. This is the crucial question of the level of recoupment of the increase in value. If the whole of this increase is taken by the state through tax, the market in land seizes up altogether. [...] On the other hand, if only a proportion of the increase in value is recouped for the community there is a serious danger of inflation over the whole market as sellers of land push up prices enough to ensure the retention of the previous level of absolute profit. Indeed, with a taxation policy, land remains a commodity for speculative investment. Only with a policy of public ownership (or the unworkable 100% levy) is this misuse of land prevented, and only then can investment funds be freed for other sectors of the economy. One final, very important, consideration again militates in favour of public ownership. For actual ownership endows the public authorities with positive control over the use of land in the area under their jurisdiction. It gives the planning profession a real resource to allocate. Public-sector developments, such as school-building or local authority housing, need no longer be forced directly to buy off the speculators in a situation where the market has been allowed to inflate the price of land. There will still be trade-offs to be made between competing uses for land, but these can be conducted within the public policy-making strategy, not forced into open bargaining with private interests.

The second key question to be faced is whether public ownership should be comprehensive (all land) or only partial. In such cases, 'partial' is usually taken to mean the public ownership of development and redevelopment land (and all that foreseeably developable), within some stated period of time. There are, however, serious arguments against the partial approach. In the first place, it is important not to confuse the need for short-term results in terms, for instance, of better planning and cheaper housing, with a need for a partial approach. The concepts of short-term and partial are in no sense necessarily linked. Indeed, in the use of land, only a carefully worked-out *comprehensive* policy can ensure even short-term results. [...] In the second place, partial policies tied to development fail to make the vital separation between the question of the system of land-tenure and that of the planning machinery and planning powers necessary to achieve short-term strategies. Any system of public ownership which is dependent upon prior planning decisions or planning applications discriminates unfairly between owners of land, setting up in effect a two-class system. Furthermore, a partial policy of public ownership which depended upon administrative designation of areas (for instance, development land) would make planning extremely vulnerable to political influences and pressures from owners. And indeed it would be extremely difficult to devise a rational system for determining where development should take place if the question of development were confused with that of public ownership. Nor is it possible to forecast far enough in advance where major new development will take place [...].

The third major consideration to be faced in the design of any land policy is its financial viability. In this respect, it is important to see the revenue, as well as the cost, side of any policy. Rental policies on publicly-owned land should reflect the costs of acquisition. Furthermore, costs will be crucially dependent upon the means of implementation, the method of compensation (particularly its timing) and the balance between rents and compensation. One thing this does mean, of course, is that a partial policy is not necessarily cheaper.

A last key area for consideration is that of the distinction between land and property. A successful policy would eliminate speculation in the value of *locations*. Such a policy must ensure therefore that this speculation, at the moment largely embodied in land, is not immediately transferred to property. It is, therefore, necessary to define an effective boundary between the property market and the land allocation location-tenure system and institute reinforcing policies for property, such as rent control.

The proposals for land published at the beginning of June in *Labour's Programme for Britain '73* [...] [suggest] that all land designated in structure plans for building, redevelopment and improvement will be taken into public ownership through ten-year rolling programmes, and if necessary, leased (not sold) to developers. The policy thus deliberately makes structure planning the *means* of public ownership. As a partial approach, it is bound to suffer from all the problems outlined above. Structure planners will be forced to decide how much land should be taken over – what is politically feasible and how much it will cost – instead of being able to concentrate on planning the right uses in the right places. Labour's discussion of the policy is heavily concerned with costs and fails to take into account revenue potential in public ownership, and thus it could actually cost more than the comprehensive approach outlined below; it collects very little of the general rise in land values.

In political and electoral terms, the policy is ill conceived. To arm local authorities with apparently arbitrary powers to acquire large amounts of land on planning criteria seems bound to generate mistrust of and opposition to public ownership. Moreover, presumably because of concern over the reaction of owner occupiers, land already used for private housing is omitted entirely. This can only create a two class system, since all new private housing would be leasehold. [...] Overall, this policy, through its discriminatory nature, could become more unpopular than one that can be seen to be comprehensive and fair.

In the search for a satisfactory land policy for Labour over the past twenty-five years the most significant statement of a policy of comprehensive public ownership appeared in *Socialist Commentary* in September 1961. This advocated the public acquisition of the freehold of all land at a single vesting date. Leases were to be issued to all users and rent could be levied progressively over time, varied according to type of user. The terms of the leases would restrict the land to its existing use, so that any change of use would go through the planning machinery in the usual fashion and if accepted a new lease would be issued. An important aspect of the policy was that compensation for the loss of freehold, fixed at existing use value, should be differentially delayed, reducing the financial burden on the scheme at the beginning and ensuring no sudden inflationary effects. However, the mechanism chosen for this phasing was to delay the date of compensation payment until the end of the 'life' of the buildings occupying the land. [...] By confusing the issues of land and property it requires elaborate machinery for 'lifting' buildings, a massive and uncertain exercise that some of the authors of the original policy later conceded made it unworkable. [...]

POLICY FOR LABOUR

In general terms, however, this approach provides a sound basis for an effective comprehensive land policy, and in particular the idea of delayed compensation is crucial but needs to be formulated differently. Working from this, the main points of the suggested new policy for Labour can be set out as follows:

(i) On a single vesting day all land becomes Crownhold and current occupiers automatically acquire Crownhold rights giving full security of tenure. There is an important distinction to be made here between the users and the owners of land at vesting day. Rights should always be given to the users of the land, by-passing those who are owners but not users. However, in order to preserve the necessary distinction between land and property all owners of property, including landlords, must be classified as 'users' of land.

(ii) Crownhold rights should guarantee security of land tenure and continuation of existing use, subject only to the same powers of change as are embodied in the current compulsory purchase machinery. [...]

(iii) Compensation should be assessed on the basis of existing use values at vesting day and the recipient of the compensation should always be the owner of the land at the vesting date.

(iv) For owners who are also users compensation should be delayed until they decided to move or apply for a change of use. This meets the criterion of delayed compensation, but avoids the complex procedure of lifting properties. [...]

(v) Compensation payments should be subject to taxation and could be payable in the form of government bonds. As a general principle it would be preferable for payments to individual owners to be phased through time. [...]

(vi) Policies must be evolved for determining the rents to be charged once land is in public ownership. These will vary according to type of use and location. In general, rents should only be levied once the original owner of the land has started to receive compensation, but for certain specific categories of users such as large property companies rents could be charged immediately after the land becomes crownhold.

What then will be the effects of this policy on major groups in the community? Owner-occupiers will receive compensation for the land when they sell their property. By off-setting this compensation against the land rent on their new property, the policy would have no noticeable effect on them for a considerable period of time. This policy could have its most dramatic and politically telling effect in bringing about a significant reduction in house prices by removing the capital cost of the land. ... With the land element now comprising over one third of the cost of new houses in the South East, a policy of comprehensive public ownership could both eliminate speculation in building land and at the same time bring about a real fall in the price of housing. For those living in private rented accommodation there are two options. The first is to charge land rents to the landlords owning the property and to ensure by strict rent control that these are not passed on to tenants. But if Labour goes ahead with a policy of municipalization of private rented property, the far more satisfactory solution is available of both land *and* property coming under the control of public authorities, amounting to a major extension of the public housing sector.

The politically sensitive issue of security for farmers can be resolved by making leases ensure that the occupants can only be displaced by the same statutory planning procedures as already operate. On the other hand, it will be much easier for new working farmers to set up in operation, since they will no longer have to face the present prohibitive capital outlays for land in today's speculative market. Tenant farmers would become tenants of the state immediately and by appropriate phasing of rental compensation to their former landlords it will be no drain on the financial viability of the policy to ensure that the terms of their new tenancy are more favourable than those of their old. It is important to note that these benefits for the agricultural sector can only be brought about by a comprehensive policy of public ownership.

Lastly, the most crucial financial aspects of the policy concern the commercial sector, and in particular city centre office and retail development. In view of the profiteering that is an intrinsic part of this type of development, it is now politically feasible severely to restrict levels of compensation in this sector. One possibility may be to determine compensation on the basis of the original buying price of the land rather than its current value on vesting day. If commercial rent controls of the type already introduced by the present Conservative government are strengthened their application can ensure that the immediate imposition of substantial rents on land and property companies does not have an inflationary effect by being passed on to tenants. Where the land and property are owned by separate companies, Crownhold rights will be given to the property-owners and the rents paid for the land will automatically accrue to the public authority. The rent from land in commercial uses will be considerably in excess of the phased compensation payments to the original landowning companies, and should become one of the main sources of revenue generated by the policy. This revenue would reflect the location value that is the root cause of the current speculation in city centre land. It is again only possible to ensure that the community as a whole benefits from this value by a comprehensive policy of public land ownership. From a partial policy confined to development and redevelopment land, only a small fraction of this rental income would be recouped.

What, then, does such a policy for land achieve, and how does it relate to the broader political context? The policy framework outlined in the preceding paragraphs represents a positive approach to the ownership and management of land. Building upon past Labour thinking on this issue, it avoids the mistakes of past policies. Politically, its very comprehensiveness ensures that it is non-discriminatory. At the same time, when co-ordinated with other policies needed in their own right, it can protect and be of positive benefit to many of those groups which might normally be wary of such measures.

Moreover, by a suitable co-ordination of costs (compensation) and revenues (rent), such an approach can be not only financially viable, but can enable the long-term accumulation of a capital fund to underpin positive policies of inter-area redistribution and development. [...]

The approach outlined here does not require the creation of any completely new structure for the administration of land as a public resource. It can be tied naturally to the existing hierarchy of planning machinery at local and regional levels. Indeed, this machinery can thus be transformed and given more positive powers of allocation, planning and pricing. And it will be possible for the locational structure of our cities and regions more accurately to reflect public policy decisions rather than socially inappropriate market criteria.

CHAPTER 4

THE ANALYSIS OF CAPITALIST LANDOWNERSHIP: AN INVESTIGATION OF THE CASE OF GREAT BRITAIN (1977)

I

The boom and collapse of the land and property market in the early 1970s in Great Britain revealed a lack of knowledge and understanding of the present nature of private landownership by capital. The reaction of 'the left' (including that of the present author) to the events of that period was confused. One possible interpretation was to write off the political battle [...] as just one more victory for industrial capital, in this case against the moribund remains of something called 'landed property'. This latter, it was vaguely suspected, quite possibly still had feudal connections but was now virtually extinct, and certainly posed no major difficulties for capital. The problem with this interpretation – apart from incorrect assumptions of association between aristocracy, landownership and feudalism – was that it failed to answer the question of what role private landownership now plays in the British social formation. The assumption in fact appeared to be that landownership now played no structural role. But events themselves belied that view. [...] The existing pattern of private landownership clearly was having contradictory repercussions on the wider processes of accumulation and of the reproduction of social relations. A common alternative view recognized the existence of such structural contradictions but attributed them to something variously entitled 'the property sector' and 'landed capital'. The difficulty of this interpretation was that the definition and nature of this landed interest, and consequently of its specific economic and political effects, were left unanalysed.

The research from which this paper stems was concerned to analyse both the present nature of private landownership by capital in Great Britain, and also the effects of such private landownership on a social formation dominated by capitalism.[1] This paper will indicate some of the results of that

---

1   The full results of this research are presented in Massey and Catalano (1978).

enquiry and will also make some points on the interpretation of struggles over, and changes in, the form of landownership in such a social formation. [...] [It contains] a brief outline and analysis [...] of the present forms of land-ownership by private capital in Great Britain, and of their relative importance. An overall theme stresses [...] [the significance of structural social relations and] the empirical study of such relations in concrete social formations [...]. It is argued that analysis along these lines will enable identification of the different forms in which private landownership by capital may present con-tradictions to the process of accumulation, and further that, although these contradictions may change in nature, they cannot under capitalism be simply overcome by the replacement of one system of landownership by another. [...]

II

[...]

In order to approach the questions posed by the events of the early 1970s as to the present nature and effects of private landownership in Great Britain, it is necessary to examine such landownership in terms of the specific forms it takes as a social relation. It is argued that these different forms of land-ownership reflect their different locations within the structure of the overall social formation. [...]

While, as will be argued, the demise of the old landed interest in Great Britain is not yet complete, its former coherence does not continue on the same basis today as it did even in the nineteenth century. This change has not simply been in the breakdown of the dominance of a former landed 'group' and of the distribution of the basis of that dominance (the land) amongst the general populace. At the most trivial level, there has been no such general redistribution.[2] Moreover, the extension of ownership has not been a simple extension of the same type of landownership and its attendant implications.[3] Nor could it be; the old type was dependent precisely on not being extended.

---

2   Inland Revenue figures on the distribution of wealth among private individuals in the UK show that, although land is now never the main form of wealth in any wealth bracket (not surprising in a social formation dominated by capitalism), the importance of land as a form of wealth (in both percentage and ranking terms) increases in general with increasing total wealth, that no form of wealth is as differentially concentrated into the top wealth bracket (over £200,000), and that land is the form of wealth that the least wealthy have the least access to (see Massey and Catalano, 1978, chapter 1). (In these figures 'land' does not include land incorporated with buildings, land held by persons but in company or trust form, and land held through shareholdings.)

3   That is, huge privately owned estates, much of which were let out on a tenancy basis.

What has happened with the decline of these old estates during the last century is that new forms of landownership, and of relation to the land, have developed and/or expanded. The uses of land have changed, both within and between urban and non-urban sectors, and there have been shifts in the nature of the rent relation in different branches of the economy.

Landownership in Great Britain is a capitalist institution. The ownership of land is no longer a crucial relation of production; it does not in itself imply any control over the process of production. Rental payments, similarly, are specifically capitalist, and correspond to the same changes in the nature of the relations of production. Feudal rent was the form taken by the dominant relation of production, the form of appropriation of surplus labour. Capitalist ground rent, on the other hand, represents an intervention in the distribution of surplus value. Feudal rent arises directly from the condition of exploitation of labour; capitalist rent arises from the secondary conditions of competition between individual capitals. This does not imply, however, that capitalist ownership of land has exactly the same implications in its nature and effects, whatever the group of agents involved. It is suggested here that there are three distinct types of landowners. They differ from each other in terms both of the relations of landownership, and of the role of that landownership within the overall structure of the social formation. The prime aspect of this distinction relates to the role of landownership in the general situation of the different groups of agents, that is, the part played by the ownership of land in the overall political, ideological and economic position and role of the groups. This characteristic reflects a second: the nature of the relation between that form of landownership and the social formation as a whole. Together, these features determine the distinctly different places and ways in which particular forms of private landownership may throw up contradictions in the development of a dominantly capitalist social formation. The argument so far has indicated that an assessment of the effect of landownership by capital within a dominantly capitalist social formation demands analysis on the basis of such types.

The first of the three types of bourgeois landownership identified we have called 'former landed property'.[4] In descriptive terms, this type is represented by a number of groups of agents, including the landed aristocracy, the landed gentry (primarily in England), the Church of England, and the Crown Estates. Our search of secondary sources of data indicates that, although certainly

---

4   It should be stressed that all that is presented here is notes on the different nature of each of these types. In particular, little attention is paid to the relation of landownership to the other purely economic interests and roles of each group and to the specific roles of each in the different 'sectors of land use'. These themes are developed in detail in Massey and Catalano (1978).

declining, this group still owns nearly 40% of the total land area of Great Britain. Of this, about three quarters is in the hands of the landed aristocracy, a category including some two hundred titled families owning very large estates and a few owning smaller remnants. It also includes the Queen as an individual. Within this category, a small group of ducal families holds a dominant position – Westminster (with estates in London and other towns, agricultural land in England, and estates in Scotland), Beaufort (primarily agricultural), and Northumberland (vast acreages now primarily agricultural but once providing huge returns on mineral rights). In acreage terms, the landholdings of former landed property are predominantly rural, but three of the four groups identified above – the landed aristocrats, the Church and the Crown Estates – also have important urban estates.

As a form and pattern of landownership, this type results from the specific nature of the transition from feudalism to capitalism in most of Great Britain. The development of this pattern was related to the early establishment of capitalism in agriculture in Great Britain, in which the direct producers were separated from the land and capitalist tenant farming established with hired wage labour, but where the land continued to be owned in large, tenanted estates. It should be emphasized that it is the pattern and class-structure of this type of landownership which is here in question, and *not* the particular agents involved. This is true particularly of the landed aristocracy.[5] In the cases of the Church and the Crown Estates, on the other hand, the institutional agents are themselves a product of the pre-capitalist period.

This relation to capitalism as the dominant mode of production influences the specificity of this type as a form of landownership. For although the nature of the landownership of this group is certainly articulated within the dominant capitalist mode of production, it is still not what one might call 'purely capitalist' landownership. Land for this group is not one sector for investment, like any other, chosen simply on the basis of its potential economic return and with no commitment beyond that. For them, in any case, it is rare for capital to have been invested in landownership. Thus, for all of the four groups referred to above (landed aristocracy, gentry, Church and Crown Estates), the ownership of land is an integral part of a wider social role, in which considerations other than 'return on capital invested' are of real importance. This wider role influences the nature of the economic relation to landownership. Although true for each of them, the way in which this operates is slightly different in each case. For both the aristocracy and the gentry, 'landownership' is not a question simply of owning land, but of owning specific tracts of land with which they have a historical connection. Moreover,

---

5   The book by Massey and Catalano (1978) goes to some lengths to divest 'the landed aristocracy' of their personal feudal connotations.

for the landed aristocracy landownership is also firmly related to a particular conception of social relationships, primarily a paternalistic tenancy relationship with the farmers and householders on their estates. Thus, for instance, Perrott (1968, 156–7) writes of the tendency of the nobility to own land abundantly or not at all, a tendency which 'means that the nobleman expects to have an estate big enough to allow him to live on rents paid by tenants rather than on primarily farming the land himself'.[6] Few aristocratic families, in other words, hang on with only a home farm; the loss of a tenantry usually signifies the end of their role as landowners. The landed gentry, on the other hand, which in the past has developed few interests and therefore economic supports beyond its estates and country duties, tends to remain. But though the gentry are in this way reduced to being owner-farmers, the commitment to specific pieces of land, and the inherited social duties which define their place within country life, mean that for them, too, landownership retains connotations of social relations which go beyond, and significantly differentiate them from, the interests of purely industrial capital.

For the Church of England also, the economic relation to landownership takes on a specific form as a result of its wider social role. Its tax status as a charity, for instance, both provides useful exemptions, and imposes restrictions. The Church Commissioners are unable in law to charge their assets, and never work on borrowed money (Property and Investment Review, 1975). They are therefore not subject to problems of gearing and have therefore been rather less vulnerable in the recent setbacks in the property market. In turn, however, this increases their need to raise money for further developments to increase income from sale of existing assets. There are even constraints imposed by the Church's concept of 'morality'. To some extent this limits the options for investment – the Church took no part in the hotel boom of the early 1970s, for instance.

Fourth, for the Crown Estates economic considerations are tempered by its having no liabilities to meet. Its revenues go to the consolidated fund of the Treasury, the duty of the Crown Commissioners being to 'maintain and enhance its value and the return obtained from it, but with due regard to the requirements of good management'. This relative lack of financial pressures has meant that it has adopted a more conservative attitude towards its land management, and, as with the Church and aristocracy, its economic room for maneuver is even further limited by the 'historic' nature of much of the property associated with its landownership.

For all four groups, it is true both that 'pulling out of land' would involve more than economic considerations, and that the nature of their more purely

---

6　This, of course, is a conception of landownership directly based on the nature of the establishment of capitalism in agriculture in Great Britain.

economic relation to land is heavily affected by broader social/ideological considerations.

Finally, the position of this pattern of landownership as an adaptation to capitalism means that for these owners land is the basis for other activities. They are farmers, or timber-growers, or urban developers, because they own land, and not the other way round.

The other two types of landownership must now be dealt with speed-ily, and mainly by comparison with the first. The second type, 'industrial landownership', is in fact not really landownership as such. For this group, the ownership of land is neither the result of selecting sectors for invest-ment nor the basis of a separate economic or other function. Land in this case is owned because it is a condition of production. The economic rela-tion to landownership is consequently dominated by considerations of the relevance of particular characteristics of land to the process of production. [...] This type of landownership comprises the bulk of industrial capital,[7] including ownerfarmers. It also includes the construction industry, though more detailed analysis (Massey and Catalano, 1978, chapter 5) indicates that this industry holds a special position, straddling the contradiction between landownership and industrial capital.

The third type, 'financial landownership', is, like the second, a form of landownership more directly a product of the already-dominant capitalist mode of production. Unlike the second type, however, this is landowner-ship 'as such'; it is distinguished from that of former landed property by the fact that it operates completely within capitalist terms. This means simply that land (and property) ownership *is* just another sector to invest in. The group includes property companies, pension funds and insurance compa-nies. Although there are, certainly, differences among them in the relation to landownership, all are purely the economic relations of capitalism to a sector for investment of money capital. Of course these institutions may not actually shift their money from sector to sector in immediate response to short-term variations in return. But this will be because of the precise nature of their holding, perhaps because it is held as a long-term asset, or because of fears of altering the overall market situation. For these groups their ideo-logical context is related to their present economic function, which includes landownership, and does not, as in the case of former landed property, place constraints on that function. Finally, where landownership is part of other activities (such as property development), it is neither the historical raison d'être for those other activities (as in the case of former landed property) nor simply a necessary condition (as in the case of industrial capital's landown-ership); it is an integral part of those activities.

---

7   The major part of manufacturing industry in Great Britain owns the land on which the productive sections of its activity are located.

III

This division of bourgeois landownership into three structurally distinct groups indicates that no one catch-all category of landed capital – that is, no single coherent fraction of capital based on the ownership of land – can be said to exist.[8] This does not mean, however, that the existence and structure of private landownership has ceased to have any effects on the development of capitalism in Great Britain. Indeed, the examination of this structural division into different types is an important aid in the analysis of those effects. [...] [Historical] shifts between these forms may in part represent attempts to overcome impediments to the accumulation process posed by the existing type of landownership. [...] [However], although the specific contradiction posed by an existing form of landownership may thereby be overcome, the form which takes its place will come in its turn to pose its own, and different, contradictions. Given this, it is a mistake to argue that conflicts over landownership are all a fundamentally similar struggle with 'landed capital' or, the opposite point of view, that 'rent is inevitable under capitalism and that is all there is to it'. Such conclusions obscure differences and problems. First of all, they obscure the specific nature of the effects of different types of landownership in particular historical periods within the development of a capitalist social formation. Secondly, and consequently, they obscure the significance of changes in the form of landownership.

An example may help to illustrate a number of the points being made here. Until the inter-war period in Great Britain agricultural production took place primarily on a tenancy basis, with landownership overwhelmingly in the hands of the former landed property group. The first and major change which occurred in this pattern – the growth of owner-occupation – was an integral part of the effort to increase productivity in agriculture. In 1919 only 11% of agricultural land was owner-occupied (Sutherland, 1968); today the figure is around 50% (Clayton *et al.*, 1967). Over the same period, output rose considerably and employment in the sector declined sharply. The key to the resultant increases in productivity was mechanization, in other words an increase in the technical composition of capital. The very considerable impact of production change on the composition of capital even over the latter part of this period is indicated by the fact that 'as a share of farm *expenses*, labour fell from 42% in 1948–6 to 20% in 1965–6 (even though individual) wages rose sharply' (Pollard, 1969, 410, section 3, emphasis as in original, our parentheses).

---

8   The three groups, and especially the two groups of 'landowners as such', are also distinct at the political and ideological levels, with different means of political representation, ideological bases and involvement in political battles. The question of the class nature of the different groups of landowners is dealt with more fully in Massey and Catalano (1978).

Such an increase in technical composition, however, demanded consider-able investment in constant capital, and tenancy as a form of landownership presented a barrier to that necessary process of investment. Evidence from the present period (see, for instance, Harrison, 1967; Estates Gazette, 1976a and 1976b; Country Landowners Association, 1976)[9] gives a clear indica-tion of the significant difference in rates of investment between farms under owneroccupation and those operated on a tenancy basis. Together with the aggregate-level correspondence between investment rate and change in tenurial form this corroborates the interpretation that the move towards owneroccupation was a significant factor in the improvement in the flow of capital into agriculture. The tenure change was, moreover, encouraged by the state (see, for instance, Pollard, 1969).

The progressive shift away from former landed property towards land-ownership by industrial capital was, therefore, bound up with the inability of the former type of ownership to cope with the demands for investment. This change itself, however, had contradictory effects. The spread of owner-occupation also represented a process at variance with the general development of capital – it established a decentralized system, with a rather larger number of smaller individual capitals within agriculture. This aspect of the new form of landownership created problems in its turn. Investment in agriculture has certainly increased relative to the previous position, but pres-sures exist for it to increase still further. Further increases in productivity, however, require not only flows of capital into agriculture but also increases in the size of farm.[10] Existing forms of private landownership pose a barrier to this latter process in two ways. Owner-occupation itself poses a barrier, since the dominance of individual proprietorship means that such farmers have too little capital and too little borrowing potential to make the process of concentration easy (Harrison, 1967, gives extensive evidence on this). The size of farm *is* increasing within the owner-occupied group, and a process of centralization is occurring, but progress is slow. The problem is, moreover, exacerbated by the existence of the third type of landownership – financial landownership. With owneroccupation farming (industrial landownership) the only way to expand a farm is for the owner to buy land. However, since the Second World War the price of farm land has risen far faster than have farm incomes (see, for instance, Munton, 1976; Clayton *et al.*, 1967; OECD, 1970); in other words the rise in land prices has been due to factors other than changes within agricultural production. The point is that whereas a

---

9 This, and other empirical evidence referenced in this paper, is analysed in detail in Massey and Catalano (1978).

10 This had not been a crucial requirement for increases in productivity in the interwar period – see Pollard, 1969.

combination of owner-occupation and subsequent unforeseen rises in land prices might indicate a retention of profits which could be reinvested in agricultural production, if this rise in land prices is not a result of changes in agricultural production it represents neither profits surplus to the original land-price nor, consequently, an ability to invest either in more land or in further mechanization. Although, therefore, those owneroccupiers who bought their land in the inter-war period, or before prices began to rise so steeply, almost certainly did not pay a price which reflected what in fact turned out to be the true rental stream, the subsequent rise in land prices constitutes not a lowering, but a reinforcement, of the barrier to investment. And, of course, a major contributor to the recent steep climb in land prices has been the increased intervention in the market of the financial landownership form (see, for instance, Estates Gazette, 1976b; Munton; 1976).

Even though the purchases by financial institutions and property companies have been small in acreage terms, the effect on prices has been considerable. This is so for a number of reasons. First, in agriculture, land prices can change quickly because of the low annual turnover of land (currently about 1½ to 2% per annum – see Sandford, 1976), and the supply of land for sale is not responsive to changes in land prices (Munton, 1976). A growing demand by such institutions can therefore quickly push up prices. Second, this effect on prices is heightened precisely by the fact that the new demand is dominated by the financial landownership form. For the concern of that landownership form in its acquisition of agricultural land has been rather more in the stability of that land as a capital asset over the longer term than in the immediate potential for production or current rent levels. As such, the entry of this form of landownership into the market has increased the divergence between price and agricultural income and raised the barrier to investment. [...]

This briefly sketched example serves to illustrate both the relation of historical shifts in landownership patterns to the contradictions thrown up to the process of accumulation, and the fact that neither the establishment of industrial landownership, in the shape of owner-occupation farming, nor the increasing dominance of the financial landownership form, heralded the elimination of such contradictions. It was also clear, however, that the different forms of landownership posed distinctively different contradictions. Moreover, differentiation occurred even, in this example, within a single branch of production (agriculture). Neither can the cause of these contrasts between the contradictions be reduced to descriptive explanations such as 'tenurial form'. Tenancy is the dominant tenurial form both where agricultural land is owned by former landed property and where it is owned by agents in the financial type of landownership. But the problems caused by landownership were different in each case. In the case of former landed property the problem was that certain aspects of the tenancy relation itself (e.g. security, lease-length, etc.) held down the rate of investment on existing farm units. In the case of financial landownership the situation was more complex. On the one hand, the entry of financial landownership raised land prices and indirectly reduced the possibilities for an increase in productivity by making more difficult any expansion in farm-size. On the other hand, it may be precisely the further intervention of this landownership form which constitutes one method of overcoming this difficulty, both because of its greater access to money capital [...] and because it can overcome the problems of individual proprietorship and build up multilocational, risk-spreading, farmholdings. Finally, it should be noted that in all cases these effects went beyond the simply distributional to affect the structure of the process of accumulation itself.

IV

Finally, although it is not possible here to produce anything like an analysis of the current situation in Great Britain, a few brief comments are in order. A preliminary point concerns the question of which of the three types is at present central to issues of landownership – and it seems clear from our analysis that it is the financial form. First, it is financial landownership which is establishing its dominance precisely in those sectors of land use (agricultural and tertiary) where there are the most significant changes in the form and pattern of landownership. This is most obvious in the tertiary sector where the financial form dominates landownership directly. But even more significant is the fact that it is precisely where the financial form of landownership is dominant that are found the most explicit political struggles. The most obvious of these [...] is that within major city-regions. In the cities, although the absolute amount of land owned by the groups comprising this landownership type is small, none the less precisely because this *is* financial landownership it dominates the shape of the land market. This is possible because it is only financial landownership which is solely concerned with the maximization of return on land as such. The dynamic created through this form of landownership has been partly responsible for the spatial problems of urban areas [...]. Such problems cannot be 'explained' as a case of aggregate-level irrationality resulting from capitalist 'anarchy'. They are a specific effect of a particular form of landownership. An agglomeration, with the locational advantages it entails, can be an advantageous condition of production. It cannot, however, be reproduced by an individual industrial capital (see, for example, Topalov, 1973). For landowners, however, the very development of an agglomeration may increase the differential profits which can be intercepted, since land is now more highly specified in terms of locational advantages. In effect, to one monopolizable condition of production, land, is added another, the locational advantages of agglomeration. Under the domination of financial landownership, the appropriation of these potential rents will be maximized, and will thereby produce locational change. The result of the operation of financial landownership on the metropolitan form is once again to produce conflicts with the process of accumulation.

Urban landownership can also more directly disturb the process of value production. Much rent on urban land is charged on non-productive activities, but this can itself place private landownership in an indirectly antagonistic position with industrial capital. In such sectors of land use as banking capital, there may well be differences in profitability between locations. [...] However, the services provided by banking capital are 'paid for' by charges on the surplus value produced by industrial capital. The absolute level of such charges is determined, not directly by value-relations (since there is no process of value-production in the activities of banking capital), nor by a mechanistic economic 'model', [...] but by a struggle with industrial capital over surplus value 'already' produced. Overall increases in rents may therefore be passed back in the form of these charges on the productive sector. Moreover, [...] [any] overall increase in rents which is passed back on the industrial sector has no necessary relationship to the structure of value-production in that sector, and may therefore have disruptive implications on that production.

A number of comments arise immediately. First, it is evident again that the contradictions posed by landownership are specific to the particular forms of ownership involved. Second, in this case too, the effects of the pattern of landownership on the process of accumulation clearly go beyond the simply distributional. Finally, it is clear once again that the increasing importance of landownership in what we have termed its financial form by no means implies an end to the problems posed by landownership.

Indeed, it is arguable that the problems raised by this form of landownership may be more intractable than those posed, for example, by former landed property. The reason for this is again bound up with the relation of the form of landownership to the structure of the social formation. Former landed property as a type is dominated by groups of landowners which are, in economic and political terms, increasingly peripheral to the dynamic capitalist development. In a sense, therefore, problems posed by that form of landownership may be more easily attacked. Financial landownership, however, is increasingly dominated by banking capital,[11] and banking capital is both

---

11 Once again, in a paper of this length, this must remain more or less an assertion. The supporting argument would include, for instance, reference to the growing role of financial institutions as direct landowners, and the increasing real subordination of property companies to banking capital.

central to the process of capitalist accumulation and an integral and important element in the power-bloc represented in the state. What the increasing role of banking capital may do, therefore, rather than removing the problems of landownership, is to make more difficult any attempts by capital to overcome those problems.[12]

[...]

V REFERENCES

Clayton, D., Harrison, A. and Hill, B. 1967: Capital taxation and land ownership in England and Wales: a preliminary assessment. *University of Reading, Department of Agricultural Economics, Miscellaneous Studies, No. 44.*

Country Landowners Association 1976: *Land price survey: England and Wales.*

Estates Gazette 1976a: Land ownership expenses: Ministry inquiry. *Estates Gazette* 27 (February 28), 670.

----- 1976b: For the country practitioner. *Estates Gazette* 237 (March 20), 872-3.

Harrison, A. 1967: Farming change in Buckinghamshire. *University of Reading, Department of Agricultural Economics, Miscellaneous Studies, No. 43.*

Massey, D. B. and Catalano, A. 1978: *Capital and land: private landownership by capital in Great Britain.* London: Edward Arnold.

Munton, R. J. C. 1976: An analysis of price trends in the agricultural land market of England and Wales. *Tijdschrift voor Economische en Sociale Geografie* 67, (4).

OECD 1970: *Capital and finance in agriculture.* Paris: OECD.

Perrott, R. 1968: *The aristocrats.* London: Weidenfeld and Nicolson.

Pollard, S. 1968: *The development of the British economy 1914-67* (second edition). London: Edward Arnold.

Property and Investment Review 1975: Analysis. *Property and Investment Review* December.

Sandford, C. 1976: Inflation, taxation, landownership. *Estates Gazette,* 13 March, 789–93.

Sutherland, D. 1968: *The landowners.* London: Anthony Blond.

Topalov, C. 1973: *Capital et propriete fonciere.* Paris: Centre de Sociologie Urbaine.

---

12 It should be stressed that this refers only to a possibility. In fact, one of the results of the empirical enquiry into landownership was to indicate the tenacity of former landed property and the continued importance of their landholdings. Moreover, former landed property is defending a form of landownership which is basic to the existence of a group as such. Most (though not all) of the agents of financial landownership would be relatively unaffected in their form by the removal of land as a sector for investment. It is none the less the case that financial landownership and banking capital have so far strongly defended their interests in land.

CHAPTER 5

REGIONALISM: SOME CURRENT ISSUES (1978)

SOME DEFINITIONS AND THEMES

The term 'regionalism' is a very inadequate one. Recent discussions in the CSE Working Group, however, failed to come up with anything that was both more accurate and less than a paragraph long. For the purposes of this survey, 'regionalism' is taken to refer to the analysis of intra-national spatial differentiation. Its concern is to study the mechanisms by which the process of accumulation generates uneven spatial development, and the effects of such unevenness on the development of a national social formation and particular areas within it. The scale is intra-national in the sense that it is at this level at which the spatial unevenness which is the focus of attention *occurs*. This does not mean, however, that such differentiation is *produced* solely by mechanisms defined at the national or intra-national level. Spatial unevenness in the process of accumulation, within a social formation, may just as well be dominantly the product of mechanisms operating at an international scale. The object of study, however, is spatial uneven development and its effects within a national economy. Such effects may occur at any spatial level within the social formation, from inequalities between major regions to patterns of growth and decline of particular cities (1).

The process of accumulation within capitalism continually engenders the desertion of some areas, and the creation there of new reserves of labour-power, the opening up of other areas to new branches of production, and the restructuring of the territorial division of labour and class relations overall. The geographical distribution of population is typically far more than a general tendency to agglomeration superimposed on a "territorial division of labour, which confines special branches of production to special districts of a country" (*Capital* 1, p.353), as occasionally implied by Marx. Even in those few areas where particular branches of production *have* entirely dom-inated the economy, it is not possible simply to assume that such areas will be the same as others equally so dominated. It is more than the branch of production which determines the characteristics of a region. Thus Gervais, Servolin and Weil (1965) distinguish three types of agricultural region in France, a distinction based primarily on the nature and stage of articulation of capitalism with peasant production, and on the dominant form of class relations (quoted in Lipietz, 1977, pp.48–52). Such differences in the econo-mies and class structures of particular areas may also be associated with sig-nificant differences in political relations. The resulting picture of 'regions' and of 'inter-regional relationships' is thus enormously complicated. The purpose of work within regionalism is to understand the formation, nature and effects of this spatial differentiation.

Why, however, should socialists be interested in the analysis of this aspect of uneven development? Briefly, the fact and the form of spatial differentia-tion can affect both political and economic development. The levelling-out of employment rates between regions figured in the UK National Plan as a means of increasing the available labour-force; in Italy regional disparities are argued to have been beneficial for accumulation (Secchi, 1977). Analysis of spatial differentiation can therefore be an important component simply in understanding the working of an economy.

But there are also much more immediate political reasons. Most obvi-ously, analyses of uneven regional development can contribute to the debate on regional separatist movements. More generally, however, the present cri-sis is affecting different parts of the country in different ways and to different degrees. Such spatial differentiation can frequently operate in a divisive way in the working class. When faced with massive declines in local industry and jobs, community groups and unions have frequently fought as though the problem was one of and for their area. This, of course, is the way in which the 'problem' is represented by capital, and it has two main repercussions. First, it sets workers of one area against those of another in a chase after available jobs, for instance. The prime recent example of this has been the attempt to portray the inner cities as having lost out to the State-assisted peripheral regions. Here an important part of the work within regionalism can be to show the relation between the disparate problems and struggles of different parts of the country. A second repercussion of 'regional problems' is that localised economic problems are often understood as stemming from the supposed inadequacies of the particular areas and its people. The Red Paper on Scotland attributes some of the problems of Scotland to a shortage of local entrepreneurs (see Firn, 1975); the White Paper on Inner Cities of the present Labour Government lays much of the blame for the present decline of those areas on their inhabitants' lack of (appropriate) skills. A prime aim of studies in regionalism is to combat this spatial definition of phenomena and to analyse and point to the real causes of such disparities.

The purpose of this survey is to present some of the issues currently pre-occupying analysis within regionalism. However, because work in this field is as yet rather disparate (indeed coherent debates are only just now beginning to emerge), the paper has as an aim also to formulate some major lines of implicit contention and to argue for a particular approach to analysis. Many of the debates hinge on methodological issues, but their implications go way beyond methodology. Such issues include: whether or not one starts analysis from pre-given regions; the potential or otherwise of the regional analysis of Stuart Holland; the possibility of 'borrowing' formulations from underdevelopment theory. It is primarily around questions such as these that the structure of the paper is organized.

APPOACHES TO ANALYSIS

The concern, then, has been how to formulate approaches which enable analysis of the complexity of spatial differentiation; how to go beyond general references to 'uneven development'. The present section briefly indicates a number of approaches which have been attempted, each of which has yielded insights and information, but each of which also has its problems.

Abstract formulations and general laws

There have been a number of attempts to derive general propositions concerning the spatial form and development of the capitalist mode of production. First, the possibility has been investigated of elaborating a 'law of value over space' (see, for example, Hein (1976), Lipietz (1977)). At different levels of analysis, both these authors reject such mechanisms and proportionalities. Indeed Lipietz interprets the absence of any regulatory economic mechanisms over space as a fundamental reason for State intervention in the geographical organisation of capitalism [...]. A rather different attempt at the formulation of general statements about the geography of capitalism has been to propose a characterisation of the system's component parts. Thus, Castells (1977) defines the urban as the space of capitalist consumption, the region as the space of production. Such attempts have in general been roundly criticised (Harloe, (1978) and Sayer (1977)), primarily as abstract and arbitrary.

Thirdly, there are a number of writings which propose a necessary tendency within capitalism towards spatial centralisation, not only of control, over the process of production, but of production itself. Such conclusions have a degree of empirical backing and an apparent radicalism, and are clearly stimulated by a desire to counter the conclusions of equality which emerge from neo-classical theory (see Holland, 1976; Purdy, 1977; Castells, 1977). Marx, too, was inclined to see an inevitable tendency under capitalism towards spatial concentration (see *Capital,* volume 1, p.352 and *Grundrisse,* p.587, both quoted in the discussion in Harvey, 1975). But, apart from their dubious theoretical status, the vulnerability of such ahistorical generalisations has become apparent in face of the recent tendency for the regional decentralisation of production (see later, and criticisms in Mellor (1975), Harloe (1978) and Massey (1976)). Empirically, neither the neo-classical nor the 'centralisation' school is correct. Though apparently opposed, they share the same problem of substituting for historical analysis predictions derived from an a-historical formal model.

Given its political importance, the work of Stuart Holland merits a little more elaboration. Holland's (1976) argument is that a tendency to regional inequality is intrinsic to capitalism but that it has until recently been off-set, primarily by State action. The present dominance of multinationals has undermined this ability of the State since these firms are able both to play off States against each other and to locate in the Third World, thereby ignoring the peripheral regions of metropolitan countries. The tendency to regional inequality has therefore re-emerged. Empirical evidence to the contrary is seen as an exception, merely 'disguising' the underlying trend (p.57). This is not in any way a class analysis, and indeed, by concentrating on regional rather than class relations, it has potentially divisive implications. Equilibrium theory is simply replaced by an elaboration of Myrdal and Perroux; in order to account for the previous invisibility of the claimed empirical tendency, State regional policy has to be interpreted as unambiguously directed towards regional equality; the State is umpire between capital and the public interest – a role it would again play in Holland's proposed policy solution; present regional problems are in fact interpreted as the result, not of capitalism, but of a 'meso-economic sector' which, with its super-profits, has broken free from economic imperatives – again an important proposition since it enables the proposed solution of nationalised forms acting differently from their private competitors (2).

Holland's work does not, then, provide a jumping-off ground for analyses of spatial differentiation, nor even of the regional problem, though it has certainly raised some important empirical issues and highlighted the political significance of certain aspects of spatial uneven development. Its frequent acceptance as 'Marxist' – or at least as the best we've got – should be a stimulus to further work.

Approaches 'borrowed' from underdevelopment theory

Few of the Marxist classics treat the subject-matter of regionalism to more than a passing reference (cf, for instance, the comments of Harvey, 1975, p.274). This lack of forebears has produced a sense of unease, an important effect of which has been a tendency to adopt methods of analysis developed at 'other spatial scales'. In particular this is true of work at the international level, in imperialism and underdevelopment. However, this paper will argue that, while much may be gleaned from such analysis for the study of spatial differentiation within a social formation, it is *not* possible simply to transplant them to 'a lower level of spatial disaggregation'. The relations between nation states within world imperialism are not to be equated with 'interregional relations' within a nation.

First, there are empirical differences between nation states and their constituent 'regions'. These include, for instance, monetary unification and trade and customs policies (see, eg, Hechter, 1975). More fundamentally, the State as a focus for class relations is usually less strong at regional level than national (Lipietz, 1977). These are, of course, tremendous generalisations, and great variation exists in the degree to which such differences hold, but, as we shall see, they are indicators of potential problems in any simple transference of theories derived at the international level to problems of intra-national spatial differentiation.

A second, and related, implication of such transference is that there is a general problematic of 'the spatial', of which the basic idea is that geographical differentiation and 'inter-areal relations' at one scale are simply those of another scale writ large, or small. As Anderson (1975) points out, in such a problematic "spatial form and scale are considered in the abstract, forgetting that we are dealing with *social* divisions of territory and socially different types of territorial division" (p.15). The object of analysis is not arbitrary divisions of 'space' as such.

Thirdly, and most importantly, the theories discussed in the present section tend on the whole in their application at international level to take nation states as objects given to analysis. Whether or not this is correct at an international level, this paper will argue that 'regions' are *not* necessarily pre-given to the study of intra-national spatial differentiation. Considerable debate exists on this, and as will be seen there are a number of different approaches to the problem. This paper will argue that regions must be constituted *as an effect of* analysis; they are thus defined in relation to spatial uneven development in the process of accumulation and its effects on social (including political) relations. Thus the analysis of the production of uneven development does not imply a pre-given regionalisation.

81

This is not to say, however, that there can never be reasons for analysing the place, within the overall process of spatially uneven development, of an already-specified region. The recent growth of 'regional nationalism' has inevitably brought such questions to the fore. For this to be a valid procedure, however, there has to be a clear reason for taking the regions as given. To take an example, what is the basis for analysing 'East Anglia' in terms of its 'interregional relations'? As far as I am aware, there is no significant and specifically East Anglian social or political force. And if indeed East Anglia is a coherent entity in terms of economic criteria, this should be the result of analysis and not assumed from criteria and boundaries constructed in some other area of investigation. This point will be taken up again later.

There is another theme which underlies much of the work discussed in this section [...]. This concerns the presence, or not, within regions of metropolitan capitalist countries, of pre-capitalist forms. The implications of most of the work reported here is that no such forms exist. [...] Only Lipietz (1975; 1977), writing in France, presents argument and empirical evidence for the opposite point of view. The issue is of course far broader than the problems of regional analysis, and stems from underlying theoretical and political positions.

Finally, it should be stressed that the theories of underdevelopment referred to here are all subject to debate and criticisms in relation to their application at international level. It is beyond the scope of this paper to deal with those debates. All that will be referred to here are those points which concern their use at regional level.

In one of the more thoughtful attempts to use *dependency theory,* Carney, Hudson, Ive and Lewis (CHIL) (1975) draw "on this body of theory... to suggest certain characteristic features of underdeveloped regions in the way Szentes (1971) has done for countries, and 'test' them against our British case study – the North East" (of England) (p.144). They argue "that the temporary externalisations of economic contradictions that characterised an imperial phase of capitalist development are, in some capitalist societies, and especially France and the United Kingdom, being replaced, in part, by attempts to contain them internally" (p.157). Their argument involves analysing the contradictory place of the North East where "the basis of profitability ... historically has involved depression of wages as they enter into costs of production, and/or the reproduction of a large reserve army of unemployed" (p.149), in an overall economy "the basis of (which) lies in high real wages and high demand for consumer goods within the domestic market, and on capitalist consumption and State expenditure to prevent realisation crises re-emerging whilst allowing continued capital accumulation" (p.149).

In another example, Carter (1974), in a discussion of bourgeois analyses of the Scottish Highlands, uses Frank (1970) to challenge the typical view of that region as the 'archaic' sector of a dual economy.

Significantly, at the empirical level the debates about this approach do reflect the problem of switching objects of analysis, from international to interregional. This is particularly the case in relation to class structure. CHIL, in their paper on N.E. England, talk of an "indigenous bourgeoisie" and advocate the use of Frank's work to explain how the local bourgeoisie has become increasingly controlled from outside the region (pp.153–4). Considerable scepticism of this position is expressed in Anderson (1975) and in a discussion reported in Harloe (1975, p.166). [...] [Such] matters are clearly empirical questions. Mellor (1975) who severely criticises (on empirical grounds) the use of dependency theory, herself gives evidence of regional class distinctiveness within both working class and bourgeoisie.

Closely related to dependency theory are the concepts of *unequal exchange*. Lipietz (1977) and Sayer (1977) both examine the usefulness of this approach, and the concepts are referred to in a number of other studies. The positions follow those of Emmanuel (1972; 1975) and Amin (1973; 1976) with Lipietz's approach integrating concepts of 'external articulation' and 'unequal exchange in the broad sense' (spatial differentiation in the distribution of industries with high and low organic compositions), and 'integration' and 'unequal exchange in the narrow sense' (based on spatial differentiation of wage levels) with Rey's (1973) concepts of stages in the process of articulation to capitalism of non-capitalist modes.

[...] Sayer (1977) follows Emmanuel in arguing that "unequal exchange in the narrow sense is unlikely to take place *within* countries unless there is some institutionalised differentiation of wages within each sector (eg, apartheid)". In fact, it is not clear that such a statement can be made *a priori*, but anyway the evidence for its empirical validity or otherwise is not unambiguous.

Empirical criticism is also made of unequal exchange in the broad sense. This is that, while the usual notion of this form of unequal exchange would have low organic composition sectors in the peripheral regions, high organic composition sectors in the 'central areas', and consequently a flow of value (with profit-equalisation) from periphery to centre, in fact one of the characteristics of recent industrial investment in intranational peripheral regions in Western Europe and the USA has been its high degree of capital-intensity relative to that of the centre. Thus Sayer refers to "some interesting and possibly counterintuitive spatial and structural changes [...] and perhaps surprising inverse relationship between regional income and capital investment per employee" (p.6). (3)

The opposite point of view is put by Lipietz (1977). For him, unequal exchange in the broad sense represents the articulation of different modes, or different stages of modes, of production (see, for instance, pp.58, 61), but its *effect* is one of the bases for regional inequality of wages typified in the phase of integration and implying unequal exchange in the narrow sense.

Moreover, it is as an empirical question of unequal exchange in the *narrow* sense that Lipietz raises current tendencies of manufacturing investment (pp.58–59). Here, however, the problem is not the specification of the mechanism of unequal exchange but simply a worry as to why the inequality of wages has not provoked the equilibrating reaction to be anticipated from the simple equation form (i.e. why do capital intensive plants form a significant proportion of the production processes presently being established in peripheral areas?).

[...]

The third line of work which tries to formulate regional questions in an 'imperialism' framework is that which uses the *internal colony* model. We refer here only to attempts to apply the approach to regions within metropolitan capitalism. Hechter's (1975) discussion of the British Celtic fringe is probably the best-known example. Hechter's own approach is not squarely within the Marxist tradition, and although he uses terms such as mode of production, this tends to refer to rural/urban differences rather than to class relations and modes of appropriation of surplus labour. His work has, however, been influential amongst Marxists and non-Marxists, and particularly within the nationalist movements. Lovering (1977) provides a detailed discussion and critique of the use of concepts of internal colonialism within Plaid Cymru. His criticisms include the loose and incorrect use of the term 'exploitation', the conception of the State as a deliberate conspiracy, and the lack of empirical evidence for many of the claims of the proponents of the model – in terms, for instance, of class structure, and net flows of resources.

Finally, the use of all three of these approaches either implies or encourages an analysis of the production of spatial differentiation which starts from pre-defined regions (a characteristic, as we have seen, related to their original, international contexts). All the authors are aware of this problem and its implications, but it is difficult, using such approaches, to escape them. [...] The analyses of Wales referred to by Lovering [...] do have a reason, at least at the political level, for starting with a predefined region. Yet, as Lovering points out, the divisions and dependencies within Wales are comparable to those between Wales and England. Where there are such dislocations between 'political' and economic regionalisations, that itself may be an important phenomenon to analyse.

[...]

Lipietz (1977) is aware throughout of these problems (see, for example, pp.25–26), and his regions and inter-regional relations *are* therefore the product of his analysis. But even in Lipietz's work problems arise when linking regions defined in terms of their histories to regions defined in terms of their relation to the presently-emerging spatial division of labour. Clearly there is no necessary one-to-one correspondence between the two and it may not therefore be appropriate to start (as Lipietz tends to) from a spec-ification of the first for an analysis of the second. Such change over time in the 'regionalisation' of a social formation may involve a radical restructuring both in the 'shape' of the spatial variation and in the nature of the use made by capital of any given form of differentiation. In fact, what Lipietz is doing here is to handle implicitly a change in regional structure which we would argue should be made explicit in the framework of explanation.

From accumulation to spatially uneven development

The approach which is suggested here begins from the process of accumu-lation and analyses the production of spatially uneven development without any pre-specified regionalisation of that space. From analyses of accumula-tion, it produces concepts of geographical organisation in terms of the spatial division of labour.

We take as starting-point the historically-dominant processes of produc-tion, and define the uneven geographical distribution of the conditions for accumulation in relation to those processes. In general terms, this means beginning with those elements of accumulation which both have an effect on the rate of profit and are unevenly spatially distributed (Hein, 1976; Regional Social Theory Group, 1978). It is the fact that regional inequality is specified in relation to the evolving characteristics of production which makes this not an externally-provided regionalisation.

In any given period, new investment in economic activity will be geo-graphically distributed in response to this pattern of spatial differentiation. But the nature of this response may vary. The term "spatial division of labour" is meant to refer to the *way* in which economic activity responds to geo-graphical inequality in the conditions of accumulation – the particular kind of use made by capital of such inequality. This will differ both between sectors and, for any given sector, with changing conditions of production. The term does not, therefore, refer to a division between regions.

The nature of capital's response to spatial unevenness is itself a product of the interaction between the existing characteristics of spatial differentiation and the requirements at any time of the dominant process of production. This interaction is important – not only does production shape geography, the historically-evolved geographical configuration (both the fact of spatial differentiation and its particular nature) has its influence on the course taken by accumulation. Thus, for instance, it may be precisely the fact of spatial separation which enables the preservation for a longer period than otherwise of certain conditions of accumulation – low wages and lack of militancy may be easier to ensure (for capital) in isolated areas dependent on one or two individual capitals. In turn, the preservation of such conditions may influence the kind of technological changes pursued by capital.

It should also be stressed that the forms of spatial differentiation relevant to the process of accumulation are by no means confined to 'the purely economic'. The degree of organisation and militancy of the labour force are well-recognised 'location factors' even within neo-classical industrial location theory. What such location theory does not recognise, of course, is that it is the specific form taken by class relations which determines these conditions. Such relations may be the basis for the lack of organisation of the labour force (Mandel, 1963, gives a detailed example of this from Flanders). Again, specific relations of land-ownership may prevent what would otherwise be the best location for a particular production process (Lipietz, 1975). State regional policies (which themselves may be a response to economic and local political conditions) may also be influential.

One schematic way of approaching this as a historical process is to conceive of it as a series of rounds of new investment, in each of which a new form of spatial division of labour is evolved. In fact, of course, the process of change is much more diversified and incremental, though certainly there are periods of radical redirection. In general, however, any new form of spatial division of labour will typify only the more advanced sectors of production, and may well vary between each sector. Between rounds, in other words, conditions will change. They will do so as a result of the combination of 'more purely spatial' changes with those in the requirements of production. First, the process of accumulation may be affected by changes in relative location through developments in transport and communication. The pressure towards improvements in these derives from the requirement both to cut costs of production and to reduce the time of circulation (*Grundrisse*, pp.533–538; see also Harvey, 1975). The effect is that "the relative differences (in distances) may be shifted about by the development of the means of transportation and communication in a way that does not correspond to the geographical distances"... a fact "which explains the deterioration of old and the rise of new centres of production because of changes in communication and transportation facilities" (*Capital*, 2, p.253). Such shifts in the spatial surface produce changes in the relative competitive positions of individual capitals, in the relative prices of different commodities, in methods of production, etc. At a more aggregate level, they will change the relative competitive position of branches of production in whole regions, and even transform the conditions in a particular region to being favourable to a branch of industry not yet located there.

Second, changes in the characteristics of accumulation may occur either in the production requirements of specific branches – and therefore in their locational requirements (see e.g. Dunford, 1977; Massey, 1976) – or in the balance between branches of production with different locational demands. In either case, a different regional distribution of production will result.

This new distribution of economic activity, produced by the evolution of a new division of labour, will be overlaid on, and combined with, the pattern produced in previous periods by different forms of spatial division. The combination of successive layers will produce effects which themselves vary over space, contributing to a new form and geographical distribution of inequality in the conditions of production, as a basis for the next round of investment. A spatial division of labour is therefore not equivalent to a 'regionalisation'. It is suggested, on the contrary, that the social and economic structure of any given local area will be a complex result of the combination of that area's succession of roles within the series of wider, national and international, spatial divisions of labour.

[...]

So far, the discussion of the approach which starts from accumulation has concentrated on the response of capital to spatial differentiation. The second, and equally important, stage is the analysis of the effects of that response. This will be taken up in a later section. For the moment, we use this general approach to present some of the changes in regional economic patterns at present going on in the U.K.

AN EMERGING FORM OF THE SPATIAL DIVISION OF LABOUR

For reasons of space, this section can only be indicative, but it seems important to present at least the main features of what appears to be emerging as a new form of intra-national spatial division of labour, and one which characterises certain expanding branches of production, such as electronics.

Briefly, then, the characteristics of production which underlie this new use of space include: the increasing size of individual capitals and the related features of a smaller number of larger plants in direct production (Dunford, 1977), complex units of production – e.g. chemical/petro-chemical complexes (Castells and Godard, 1974; Dunford 1977), the division of production into autonomously-functioning stages which can be also separately *located* (Lipietz, 1977; Massey, 1976), and the increasing separation within individual capitals of the function of overall control (Lipietz, 1977). Within production too there have been major changes – in particular the recent apparent acceleration of deskilling of direct work alongside an increase in research and development. Finally, the role of the State is typically of growing importance both in financing major individual projects (Castells and Godard, 1974; Blietrach and Chenu, 1975) and in the provision of 'regional infrastructure'.

Where such changes take place in an intranational context in which there is marked spatial differentiation in wage levels of direct workers, in levels of skill, in degree of organisation of the labour movement, and in the degree of presence of, for instance, banking and commercial capital, a new form of geographical organisation is arising. Such is the case in most countries of Western Europe and North America.

One use by capitals of such spatial differentiation is increasingly based on the geographical separation of control and R & D functions from those direct processes of production still requiring skilled labourers and of these in turn from mass-production and assembly work requiring only semi-skilled labour-power. (It should be noted that this is not some ideal-type model, but simply a form frequently found amongst presently-leading sectors.)

This third stage of production is increasingly located in areas where semi-skilled workers are not only available (since they are everywhere), but where wages are low, and where there is no tradition – at least among these workers – of militancy. Typically this will involve the incorporation of workers with no previous experience of capitalist relations of production – drawn either from the remnants of pre-capitalist modes, from the collapse of a previously-dominant industrial branch (in which case it will be the women, not the workers employed in the former specialisation, who will be employed) or from areas where workers (again mainly women) do not become totally dependent on (nor organised around) capitalist production relations (e.g. seaside resorts with seasonal self-employment in tourism). Although the introduction of these factories into such (frequently depressed) areas is hailed by the State as beneficial, (4) its positive effects may be minimal. Wages and skills remain low, and it is not even necessarily the case that much new employment will result: one of the major characteristics of such factories is that they have few local links and stimulate little locally in terms of associated production (the Italians label them 'cathedrals in the desert'). A good example in the UK is given by Carter (1974) in his analysis of the Highlands. Some of these plants may themselves be relatively labour-intensive (such as electronics assembly), others employ very few workers (steel and chemical complexes are typical examples).

The 'second-stage' of production is typically located in the old centres of skilled work – primarily nineteenth century industrial towns and cities: the critical characteristic of this stage, however, is its decreasing (quantitative) importance. More and more, standardisation and automation are enabling capital to be locationally freed from its old ties to skilled labourpower. It is the link between such changes in the production process and the possibilities open to capital as a result of the spatial differentiation of labour-power (together, of course, with the collapse of other sectors, characterised by a different spatial division of labour and formerly based in the cities) which is behind much of the present industrial decline of the inner cities (see Community Development Project, 1977; Massey and Meegan, 1978). In such sectors as electronics, it appears that this rung in the spatial division of labour is fast disappearing and that a simple dichotomy is emerging between the city-regions (rather than the inner cities) of the core, and the peripheral regions. Thus, changes in the labour-process as a result of competition, the use by capital of spatial differentiation; and the reconstitution of the working class, here go hand in hand. The fact of geographical differentiation in the wages, skills, and organisational strength of the working class both influences the form of, and enables, particular developments in accumulation. The fact of the spatial basis of the organised strength of skilled labour-power both encourages spatial decentralisation from those bases when capital's dependence upon skill decreases, and thereby enables a much more effective undermining of the strength of the working class (5).

Finally, the central metropolitan regions (such as London, Paris) are typified by the presence of control functions, research, design and development, and by the significant presence of managerial and technical strata (it is this presence, rather than the absence of manual work, which is distinctive).

A number of points should be quickly made to round off this brief description. First, the pattern which has been described is an intra-national division of labour, but the precise form which it takes within any one nation will be determined also by the place of that nation itself within the international division of labour. [...] Second, this is thus a very different *form* of spatial division of labour from, for instance, sectoral specialisation. Its economic repercussions are also different – regions at the 'bottom' end of the hierarchy, for instance, are placed in direct competition with countries in the Third World. [...] Finally, it is clear that the latest form of the spatial division of labour is establishing not only a different form of use by capital of spatial differentiation, but also a new shape of geographical 'regionalisation'.

THE EFFECTS OF SPATIAL DIFFERENTIATION IN THE PROCESS OF ACCUMULATION

The analysis of the evolution of a new spatial division of labour is, however, only the first stage in the study of spatial differentiation. It is next necessary to analyse the way in which this new use of space is combined with the geographical pattern of previous uses. It is the effects of this combination which produce both the distinctive characteristics of local areas, and the overall pattern of regional variation in a social formation.

First, there are the effects on any particular geographical location or area. Some examples of direct effects have already been referred to, but there are broader implications. Thus, taking initially just the economic level, the presently-emerging spatial division of labour does not character-ise every branch of production. It arises from the combination of certain newly-dominant features of the process of production with a spatial config-uration formed as a result of previously-dominant features. The 'new spatial division of labour' described here is therefore one (a) which is a feature pri-marily of new and advanced sectors of production, and (b) which is articu-lated with an inherited, and different, form of spatial division. New branches of production may be introduced, affecting the conditions of production of established local industry; large inter-regional or multinational capital may enter an area previously the preserve of local firms. This process of combina-tion will therefore produce effects which go beyond the direct implications of the locational strategies of capital, and which will possibly produce precisely that regional specificity which a number of the analyses referred to earlier (and which started from a regional base) have correctly been trying to grasp.

Moreover, these effects are not confined to production. They will include, for example, locally-differentiated effects on class structure (Lipietz, 1977, p.85, Lewis and Hudson, 1977, are good examples). Gramsci's work also con-tains a number of comments on and analyses of this aspect of the impact of spatially-differentiated accumulation: Turin is "the proletarian city, *par excel-lence*" ... "precisely because of this powerfully united character of the city's industry" (in *The Historical Role of the Cities*, Gramsci, 1977), and similar analyses are made of Milan, Piedmont, and the city-countryside relationship. Mandel (1963) analyses the formation of the 'two proletariats' of Belgium as a result of the distinct economic development of the regions of Wallonia and Flanders. As is clear from both Gramsci and Mandel, such processes may also imply a potentially politically significant spatial differentiation in forms of class struggle. Castells (1977, ch.14) makes similar points in relation to 'urban social movements'.

It is the combination of effects such as these which produces the com-plex form of spatial variation which is the empirical phenomenon with which regional analysis is faced. This paper has argued so far that the *causes* of such complex differentiation can not be explained adequately by starting from any pre-given regionalisation. However, the examination of the resultant pattern of accumulation, and of its effects, may well require some method of spatial summary, and this may include the identification of 'regions'. Considering that it is so central, there is relatively little debate on 'the concept of a region' (either its possibility or its nature). One of the clearest positions is that of Lipietz (1977) who insists on the dominance, in the definition of any such entity, of distinctive social relations based pri-marily on the geographically-differentiated articulation of capitalism with pre-capitalist modes (see, for instance, pp.33, 26; and Lipietz, 1975, p. 419).

[...] [Such] a position, also held by others in specific analyses, is disputed at both empirical and political levels. [...]

[A] different question which can be raised against Lipietz's definition concerns not whether the *particular* criterion is appropriate but whether there is any point in attempting to establish *any* criteria for universal application. It may be that regional specificity and coherence may be established on a variety of different bases – though 'class relations' in a general sense will evidently be a dominant component. Mandel's (1963) work on Belgium again provides a good example. Having begun from an analysis of the process of accumulation in relation to Belgium as a whole, he analyses the spatially-differentiated form that this takes, and the impact of this in turn on class relations (see above). His analysis is that Wallonia and Flanders are distinct in terms of date of industrialisation, the nature (branch, size, etc.) of industry, the degree of urbanisation and the nature of internal spatial organisation, and in terms of language, culture and religion, and politics – in relation both to nationalism and socialism. It emerges clearly not only that spatial separation has been very important in the construction of these characteristics of the Belgian national social-formation, but also that the integration between form of accumulation and politics and ideology, and the effect of that, clearly warrants the identification within the country of two distinct regions.

It should not be assumed, however, that in every spatial analysis of a national capitalist economy such divisions will always emerge so clearly, nor that they necessarily cover the total geographical area of the state. Such a 'regionalisation' should not be forced on unwilling evidence. At the economic level, for instance, the combination of successive spatial divisions of labour may not produce in any sense coherent economies. It has already been mentioned that Lipietz's regions switch from those constructed through historical analysis (and which are based on the articulation of modes of production) to those characterised on criteria (primarily type of labour-power) relevant to an analysis of the present spatial division of labour. 'Region' may mean many things – in this case both a coherent spatial entity in terms of social relations and a geographical disaggregation on the basis of a single economic variable. Lipietz's is a perfectly feasible procedure so long as the different status of these regional types is fully recognised. Moreover, it is possible to summarise and analyse the effects of geographical differentiation without the construction of coherent regions. In the UK over the last decade or so, for instance, a definite change has been taking place in the form, composition and geographical distribution of the reserve army of labour. Some aspects of this have already been referred to (e.g. the decline of the 'inner cities'). This is an important phenomenon to recognise and to analyse but it is not necessary therefore to define, say, inner cities, as 'regions' the coherence of which extends beyond the distribution of this aspect of accumulation. In such cases, different geographical bases may well be appropriate for the analysis of different phenomena.

Finally, whether or not coherent regions may be defined from the analysis, the rationale for any particular form of geographical summary should be related to its usefulness in analysing the *effects* of such differentiation. These effects will occur not only at the local level (as already discussed) but also as a result of the impact of the fact and form of spatial differentiation on the development of the social formation as a whole. A number of studies have been produced analysing this impact, in both economic and political terms. One point which emerges clearly from them is that no *a priori* assumptions should be made as to whether such effects are problematic or positive for capital. There is some tendency to assume that severe spatial inequality is necessarily a problem for capital, that regional policy is designed to cope with these negative effects, but that it is continually subordinated to the more pressing demands of accumulation. At certain historical periods this is undoubtedly true (examples include the UK in both the 1930s and 1963), but spatial inequality may also be functional. Both aspects appear in Secchi's (1977) study which emphasises the role of territorical inequality in both periods of growth and the crises of the Italian economy. Secchi carries this analysis through to the political implications of the spatial pattern, particularly in relation to systems of intercapitalist alliances. Garofoli (1975b) takes up the same themes. Carney, Lewis and Hudson (1977) examine the contradictory effects in the UK of the inter-war geographical specialisation in Departments I and II. They argue that: "The crucial restraint on the continued accumulation of capital in the Department II industries of the South was the depressed conditions of consumption in those areas dominated by Department I production". Yet at the same time: "One of the conditions for the success of Department II production in the South was that a large mass of skilled labour was thrown out of work in the North and so acted as a reserve army sustaining reductions in production costs in the South by their presence and sustaining production needs for labour-power by their migration south" (p.58). Again, of course, such effects have more than simply economic implications. Mandel's article (Mandel, 1963) examines the very important political repercussions of Belgium's patterns of regionalisation, this time in terms of the labour movement.

IN CONCLUSION

This review has been something of a mad dash through a disparate and sometimes confusing field of work. It is hoped, however, that a number of points have been established. First, that there is such a field of study as regionalism, with a valid general object. Second, that within that field there are a number of very different stages of analysis and distinct questions. In particular, attention has been focused in this paper on the difference between the production of spatial unevenness, the effects of that unevenness, and the fortunes of particular regions. It is argued here that these must be carefully distinguished, both in terms of the questions being asked and in terms of the direction of causality involved. Finally, spatial differentiation can have important effects, both on the development of a national capitalist economy, and on the course of political struggle.

NOTES

[...] Much help was received in writing this survey from discussion in the CSE Regionalism Group, and in the Editorial Committee of *Capital and Class*, and in particular from detailed comments by James Anderson, Mick Dunford, Mike Geddes, John Harrison, Jim Lewis, Richard Minns, Diane Perrons and Andrew Sayer.

(1) For reasons of space the present review has a very restricted scope. It is confined in its empirical basis, and to some extent in its propositions, to metropolitan capitalist countries, and it has had to omit consideration of a number of very closely related fields of work, in particular analysis of nationalism, and of the burgeoning debate specifically on 'urbanism'. Neither has there been room to consider the literature on state intervention in this field, particularly regional policy.

(2) A number of these points are elaborated further in Anderson, 1977.

(3) Earlier in the same article Sayer examines the difficulties of using measures of capital intensity to indicate organic composition. It is clear, however, that he is referring to a real phenomenom in terms of the direction of differentials in organic composition. It is also the case, of course, that the workers in the different regions are applying labour power of different skills, etc. (value).

(4) Such developments are also frequently attributed to regional policy – which may well have encouraged them, but not in any sense against the trend of the changing requirements of accumulation. It is interesting to note that those who hold to the 'inevitable spatial concentration' model of capitalism, are also forced to attribute such developments solely to the effectiveness of state intervention.

(5) Spatial separation and differentiation can also be important elements in more immediate strategies, either of individual capitals (for which geographical mobility may enable total changes in production which might otherwise be fought by the unions on-site) or of State policy (the way in which inner city workers have been set against those of peripheral regions is a good recent example).

REFERENCES

Amin, S., 1973, *L'Échange inégal et la loi de la valeur*, Anthropos - IDEP Paris.

Amin, S., 1976, *Unequal development*, Harvester.

Anderson, J., 1975, "The political economy of urbanism: an introduction and bibliography", Department of Urban and Regional Planning, Architectural Association.

Anderson, J., 1977, *Stuart Holland's regionalism: reformism reheated*, paper presented to CSE Regionalism Working Group, mimeo.

Bettelheim, C., 1972, Appendix I *Theoretical Comments*, in Emmanuel (1972).

Bleitrach, D., and Chenu, A., 1975, "Aménagement: régulation ou aggravation des contradictions sociales? Un exemple: Fos-sur-mer et l'aire métropolitaine marseillaise".

Brenner, R., 1977, The origins of capitalist development: a critique of neo-Smithian Marxism. *New Left Review*, vol. 104, pp.25–92.

Carney, J., Hudson, R., Ive, G. and Lewis, J., 1975, "Regional underdevelopment in late capitalism: a study of the North East of England" in Masser, I. (ed.) *Theory and practice in regional science*, Pion, London.

Carney, J., Lewis, J. and Hudson, R., 1977, "Coal combines and interregional uneven development in the UK" in: Massey, D. B. and Batey P. W. J. (eds) London Paper in Regional Science, vol. 7, *Alternative Frameworks for analysis*, Pion, London.

Carter, I., 1974, "The highlands of Scotland as an underdeveloped region" in: E de Kadt and G. Williams (eds), *Sociology and Development*, Tavistock Publications, pp.279–311.

Castells, M., 1977, *The Urban Question*, Edward Arnold.

Castells, M. and Godard, F., 1974, *Monopolville: l'enterprise l'etat, l'urbain*, Mouton.

Community Development Project, 1977, *The Costs of Industrial Change*.

Dunford, M. F., 1977, "Regional policy and the restructuring of capital", Sussex University: Urban and Regional Studies, Working Paper 4.

Emmanuel, A., 1972, *Unequal Exchange: a study of the imperialism of trade*, New Left Books.

Emmanuel, A., *et al*, 1975, *Un débat sur l'éxchange inégal*, Maspero, Paris.

Firn, J., 1975, External control and regional policy, in *The Red Paper on Scotland*, edited by Gordon Brown.

Frank, A. G., 1970, *Latin America: Underdevelopment or Revolution*. Monthly Review Press, New York.

Garofoli, G., 1975a, Produttività del lavoro e salari: uni analisi dei differenziali intersettoriali ed interregionali, *Archivio di Studi Urbani e Regionali*, no.3–4, pp.97–123.

Garofoli, G., 1975b, Un' analisi critica della politica di riequilibrio regionale in Italia: il caso del Mezzogiorno, *Archivio di Studi Urbani e Regionali*, no. 34, pp.165–183.

Gervais, M., Servolin, C., and Weil, J., 1965, *Une France sans Paysan*, Le Seuil, Paris.

Gramsci, A., 1977, "The historical role of the cities", in *Selections from political writings*, 1910-1920. Lawrence and Wishart.

Harloe, M. (ed), 1975, "Proceedings of the conference on urban change and conflict", Centre for Environmental Studies, Conference Papers 14.

Harloe, M., 1978, "Marxism, the state and the urban question: Critical notes on two recent French theories", in: Crouch, C. (ed), *British Political Sociology Yearbook*.

Harvey, D., 1975, "The geography of capitalist accumulation: a reconstruction of the Marxian Theory", *Antipode*, vol. 7, No.2, pp.9–21 (also in Peet, 1977).

Hechter, M., 1975, *Internal colonialism: The Celtic fringe in British national development, 1536–1966*, International Library of Sociology, Routledge and Kegan Paul.

Hein, W., 1976, "The accumulation of capital on the world scale, the nation state and uneven development; Outline of a theoretical approach", Paper to CSE Working Group on the Neocolonial State, mimeo.

Holland, S., 1976, *Capital vs. the Regions*, Macmillan Press.

Lee, R., 1977, "Regional relations and economic structure in the EEC" in: Massey, D. B. and Batey, P. W. J. (ed), London Papers in Regional Science, vol. 7, *Alternative Frameworks for Analysis*, pp.19–38.

Lipietz, A., 1975, "Structuration de l'espace, problème foncier et aménagement du territoire", *Environment and Planning*, A, vol.7, pp.415–425.

Lipietz, A., 1977, *Le capital et son espace*, Maspero: Economie et Socialisme, 34.

Lovering, J., 1977, "The theory of the 'internal colony' and the political economy of Wales", mimeo.

Mandel, E., 1963, "The dialectic of class and region in Belgium", *New Left Review*. vol.20, pp.5–31.

Marx, K., *Capital*, Lawrence and Wishart.

Marx, K., *Grundrisse*, Penguin.

Massey, D. B., 1976, "Restructuring and regionalism: some spatial effects of the crisis". Paper presented to CSE Working Group on Regionalism. Centre for Environmental Studies, Working Note 449.

Massey, D. B., and Meegan, R. A., 1978, "Restructuring vs. the Cities", *Urban Studies*, vol.15, No.3.

Mellor, R., 1975, "The British Experience: combined and uneven development" in: Harloe, M. (ed), 1975.

Purdy, D., 1977, "Review of Holland's 'Capital vs. the Regions' and 'The Socialist Challenge'" *Capital and Class*, No.1.

Regional Social Theory Group, 1978, "Accumulation, the regional problem and nationalism" in: P. W. J. Batey (ed) London Papers in Regional Science, vol.8, Pion, London.

Rey, P-P., 1973, *Les alliances de classes*, Maspero, Paris.

Sayer, A., 1977, "The law of value and uneven development: some problems and possibilities for analysis". Paper presented to the Regional Social Theory Group, Regional Science Association, Lanehead Workshop, July. Mimeo.

Secchi, B., 1977, "Central and peripheral regions in a process of economic development: The Italian case" in: Massey, D. B. and Batey, P. W. J. (eds), London Papers in Regional Science, vol.7: *Alternative Frameworks for Analysis*, Pion, London.

Szentes, T., 1971, *The political economy of underdevelopment*, Akademiai Kiado, Budapest.

CHAPTER 6

A WOMAN'S PLACE? (1984)

with Linda McDowell

The nineteenth century saw the expansion of capitalist relations of production in Britain. It was a geographically uneven and differentiated process, and the resulting economic differences between regions are well known: the rise of the coalfields, of the textile areas, the dramatic social and economic changes in the organization of agriculture, and so forth. Each was both a reflection of and a basis for the period of dominance which the UK economy enjoyed within the nineteenth-century international division of labour. In this wider spatial division of labour, in other words, different regions of Britain played different roles, and their economic and employment structures in consequence also developed along different paths.

But the spread of capitalist relations of production was also accompanied by other changes. In particular it disrupted the existing relations between women and men. The old patriarchal form of domestic production was torn apart, the established pattern of relations between the sexes was thrown into question. This, too, was a process which varied in its extent and in its nature between parts of the country, and one of the crucial influences on this variation was the nature of the emerging economic structures. In each of these different areas 'capitalism' and 'patriarchy' were articulated together, accommodated themselves to each other, in different ways.

It is this process that we wish to examine here. Schematically, what we are arguing is that the contrasting forms of economic development in different parts of the country presented distinct conditions for the maintenance of male dominance. *Extremely* schematically, capitalism presented patriarchy with different challenges in different parts of the country. The question was in what ways the terms of male dominance would be reformulated within these changed conditions. Further, this process of accommodation between capitalism and patriarchy produced a different synthesis of the two in different places. It was a synthesis which was clearly visible in the nature of gender relations, and in the lives of women.

This issue of the synthesis of aspects of society within different places is what we examine in the following four subsections of this chapter. What we are interested in, in other words, is one complex in that whole constellation of factors which go to make up the uniqueness of place.

We have chosen four areas to look at. They are places where not only different 'industries' in the sectoral sense, but also different social forms of production, dominated: coal mining in the north-east of England, the factory work of the cotton towns, the sweated labour of inner London, and the agricultural gang-work of the Fens. In one chapter we cannot do justice to the complexity of the syntheses which were established in these very different areas. All we attempt is to illustrate our argument by highlighting the most significant lines of contrast.

Since the construction of that nineteenth-century mosaic of differences all these regions have undergone further changes. In the second group of sections we leap ahead to the last decades of the twentieth century and ask 'where are they now?'. What is clear is that, in spite of all the major national changes which might have been expected to iron out the contrasts, the areas, in terms of gender relations and the lives of women, are still distinct. But they are distinct in different ways now. Each is still unique, though each has changed. In this later section we focus on two threads in this reproduction and transformation of uniqueness. First, there have been different changes in the economic structure of the areas. They have been incorporated in different ways into the new, wider spatial division of labour, indeed the new international division of labour. The national processes of change in the UK economy, in other words, have not operated in the same way in each of the areas. The new layers of economic activity, or inactivity, which have been superimposed on the old are, just as was the old, different in different places. Second, however, the impact of the more recent changes has itself been moulded by the different existing conditions, the accumulated inheritance of the past, to produce distinct resulting combinations. 'The local' has had its impact on the operation of 'the national'.

THE NINETEENTH CENTURY

Coal is our life: whose life?

Danger and drudgery; male solidarity and female oppression – this sums up life in the colliery villages of Co. Durham during much of the nineteenth century. Here the separation of men and women's lives was virtually total:

men were the breadwinners, women the domestic labourers, though hardly the 'angels of the house' that featured so large in the middle class Victorian's idealization of women. The coal mining areas of Durham provide a clear example of how changes in the economic organization of Victorian England interacted with a particular view of women's place to produce a rigidly hierarchical and patriarchal society. These villages were dominated by the pits and by the mine owners. Virtually all the men earned their livelihood in the mines and the mines were an almost exclusively male preserve, once women's labour was forbidden from the middle of the century. Men were the industrial proletariat selling their labour power to a monopoly employer, who also owned the home. Mining was a dirty, dangerous and hazardous job. Daily, men risked their lives in appalling conditions. The shared risks contributed to a particular form of male solidarity, and the endowment of their manual labour itself with the attributes of masculinity and virility. The shared dangers at work led to shared interests between men outside work: a shared pit language, shared clubs and pubs, a shared interest in rugby. Women's banishment from the male world of work was thus compounded by their exclusion from the local political and social life.

Jobs for women in these areas were few. Domestic service for the younger girls; for married women poorly paid and haphazard work such as laundry, decorating or child care. But most of the families were in the same position: there was little cash to spare for this type of service in families often depending on a single source of male wages. For miners' wives almost without exception, and for many of their daughters, unpaid work in the home was the only and time-consuming option. And here the unequal economic and social relationships between men and women imposed by the social organization of mining increased the subordinate position of women. A miner's work resulted in enormous domestic burdens for his wife and family. Underground work was filthy and this was long before the installation of pithead showers and protective clothing. Working clothes had to be boiled in coppers over the fire which had to heat all the hot water for washing clothes, people and floors. Shift work for the men increased women's domestic work: clothes had to be washed, backs scrubbed and hot meals prepared at all times of the day and night. [...]

These Durham miners, themselves oppressed at work, were often tyrants in their own home, dominating their wives in an often oppressive and bullying fashion. They seem to have 'reacted to [their own] exploitation by fighting not as a class against capitalism, but as a gender group against women – or rather within a framework of sex solidarity against a specific woman chosen and caged for this express purpose' (Frankenberg, 1976, p. 40). Men were the masters at home. Here is a Durham man, who himself went down the pits in the 1920s, describing his father:

> He was a selfish man. If there was three scones he'd want the
> biggest one. He'd sit at the table with his knife and fork on the
> table before the meal was even prepared... Nobody would get the
> newspaper till he had read it.
>
> (Strong Words Collective, 1977, pp. 11–12)

Thus gender relations took a particular form in these colliery villages. National ideologies and local conditions worked together to produce a unique set of patriarchal relations based on the extreme separation of men's and women's lives. Masculine supremacy, male predominance in every area of economic and social life became an established, and almost unchallenged, fact. Patriarchal power in this part of the country remained hardly disturbed until the middle of the next century.

Cotton towns: the home turned upside down?

The images of homemaker and breadwinner are of course national ones, common to the whole of capitalist Britain, and not just to coalfield areas. But they were more extreme in these regions, and they look a particular form; there were differences between the coalfields and others parts of the country.

The cotton towns of the north-west of England are probably the best-known example from, as it were, the other end of the spectrum, and a major element in this has been the long history of paid labour outside the home for women. It is often forgotten to what extent women were the first labour-force of factory-based, industrial capitalism. 'In this sense, modern industry was a direct challenge to the traditional sexual division of labour in social production' (Alexander, 1982, p. 41). And it was in the cotton industry around Manchester that the challenge was first laid down.

Maintaining patriarchal relations in such a situation was (and has been) a different and in many ways a more difficult job than in Durham. The challenge was nonetheless taken up. Indeed spinning, which had in the domestic organization of the textile industry been done by women, was taken over by men. Work on the mule came to be classified as 'heavy', as, consequently, to be done by men, and (also consequently) as skilled (Hall, 1982). The maintenance of male prerogative in the face of threats from women's employment, was conscious and was organized. [...] But if men won in spinning, they lost (in those terms) in weaving. The introduction of the power loom was crucial. With it, the factory system took over from the handloom weavers, and in the factories it was mainly women and children who were employed. This did present a real challenge:

The men who had been at the heads of productive households were unemployed or deriving a pittance from their work whilst their wives and children were driven out to the factories.

(Hall, 1982, p. 24)

Nor was 'the problem' confined to weavers. For the fact that in some towns a significant number of married women went out to work weaving meant that further jobs were created for other women, doing for money aspects of domestic labour (washing and sewing, for example) that would otherwise have been done for nothing by the women weavers. Further, the shortage of employment for men, and low wages, provided another incentive for women to earn a wage for themselves (Anderson, 1971).

The situation caused moral outrage among the Victorian middle classes and presented serious competition to working-class men. There was 'what has been described as "coincidence of interests" between philanthropists, the state – representing the collective interests of capital – and the male working class who were represented by the trade union movement and Chartism – which cooperated to reduce female and child labour and to limit the length of the working day' (Hall, 1982, p. 25). In the same way, it was at national level that arguments about 'the family wage' came to be developed and refined as a further means of subordinating women's paid labour (for pin money) to that of men's (to support a family). The transformation from domestic to factory production, a transformation which took place first in the cotton towns,

provoked, as can be seen, a period of transition and re-accommodation in the sexual division of labour. The break-up of the family economy, with the threat this could present to the male head of household, who was already faced with a loss of control over his own labour, demanded a re-assertion of male authority.

(Hall, 1982, p. 27)

Yet in spite of that reassertion, the distinctiveness of the cotton areas continued. There were more women in paid work, and particularly in relatively skilled paid work, in the textile industry and in this part of the country, than elsewhere:

In many cases the family is not wholly dissolved by the employment of the wife, but turned upside down. The wife supports the family, the husband sits at home, tends the children, sweeps the room and cooks. This case happens very frequently: in Manchester alone, many hundred such men could be cited, condemned to domestic occupations. It is easy to imagine the wrath aroused

101

among the working-men by this reversal of all relations within the family, while the other social conditions remain unchanged.

(Engels, 1969 edn, p. 173)

This tradition of waged-labour for Lancashire women, more developed than in other parts of the country, has lasted. Of the early twentieth century, Liddington writes 'Why did so many Lancashire women go out to work? By the turn of the century economic factors had become further reinforced by three generations of social conventions. It became almost unthinkable for women *not* to work' (1979, pp. 98–9).

And this tradition in its turn had wider effects. Lancashire women joined trade unions on a scale unknown elsewhere in the country: 'union membership was accepted as part of normal female behaviour in the cotton towns' (Liddington, 1979, p.99). In the nineteenth century the independent mill-girls were renowned for their cheekiness; of the women of the turn-of-the-century cotton towns, Liddington writes: 'Lancashire women, trade unionists on a massive scale unmatched elsewhere, were organized, independent and proud' (1979, p. 99). And it was from this base of organized working women that arose the local suffrage campaign of the early twentieth century. 'Lancashire must occupy a special place in the minds of feminist historians. The radical suffragists sprang from an industrial culture which enabled them to organize a widespread political campaign for working women like themselves' (p. 98).

The radical suffragists mixed working-class and feminist politics in a way which challenged both middle-class suffragettes and working-class men. In the end, though, it was precisely their uniqueness which left them isolated – their uniqueness as radical trade unionists *and* women, and, ironically, their highly regionalized base. [...]

The rag-trade in Hackney: a suitable job for a woman?

But there were other industries in other parts of the country where women were equally involved in paid labour, where conditions were as bad as in the cotton mills, yet where at this period not a murmur was raised against their employment. One such area was Hackney, dominated by industries where sweated labour was the main form of labour-organization.

What was different about this form of wage relation for women from men's point of view? What was so threatening about women working? Hall (1982) enumerates a number of threads to the threat. The first was that labour was now *waged* labour. Women with a wage of their own had a degree of potentially unsettling financial independence. But Lancashire textiles and the London sweated trades had this in common. The thing that

102

distinguished them was the spatial separation of home and workplace. The dominant form of organization of the labour-process in the London sweated trades was homeworking. The waged-labour was carried out in the home; in Lancashire, birthplace of the factory-system, waged-labour by now meant leaving the house and going to the mill. It wasn't so much 'work' as 'going out to' work which was the threat to the patriarchal order. And this in two ways: it threatened the ability of women adequately to perform their domestic role as homemaker for men and children, and it gave them an entry into public life, mixed company, a life not defined by family and husband.

It was, then, a change in the social *and the spatial* organization of work which was crucial. And that change mattered to women as well as men. Lancashire women did get out of the home. The effects of homeworking *are* different: the worker remains confined to the privatized space of the home, and individualized, isolated from other workers. Unionization of women in cotton textiles has always been far higher than amongst the homeworking women in London.

[...]

Thinking back to the contrast between the coalfields and the cotton towns and the relationship in each between economic structure and gender relations and roles, it is clear that the difference between the two areas was not simply based on the presence/absence of waged labour. We have, indeed, already suggested other elements, such as the whole ideology of virility attached to mining. But it was also to do with the *kind* of work for women in Lancashire: that it was factory work, with machines, and outside the home. In the sweated trades of nineteenth-century London, capitalism and patriarchy together produced less immediate threat to men's domination.

There were other ways, too, in which capitalism and patriarchy interrelated in the inner London of that time to produce a specific outcome. The sweated trades in which the women worked, and in particular clothing, were located in the inner areas of the metropolis for a whole variety of reasons, among them the classic one of quick access to fast-changing markets. But they also needed labour, and they needed cheap labour. Homeworking, besides being less of an affront to patriarchal relations, was one means by which costs were kept down. But costs (wages) were also kept down by the very availability of labour. In part this was a result of immigration and the vulnerable position of immigrants in the labour market. But it was also related to the predominantly low-paid and irregular nature of jobs for men (Harrison, 1983, p. 42). Women in Hackney *needed* to work for a wage. And this particular Hackney articulation of patriarchal influences and other 'location factors' worked well enough for the clothing industry.

But even given that in Hackney the social organization and nature of women's work was less threatening to men than in the cotton towns, there were still defensive battles to be fought. The labour-force of newly arrived immigrants also included men. Clearly, were the two sexes to do the same jobs, or be accorded the same status, or the same pay, this would be disruptive of male dominance. The story of the emergence of a sexual division of labour within the clothing industry was intimately bound up with the maintenance of dominance by males in the immigrant community. They did not use the confused and contradictory criteria of 'skill' and 'heavy work' employed so successfully in Lancashire. In clothing *any* differentiation would do. Phillips and Taylor (1980) have told the story, of the establishment of the sexual division of labour in production, based on the minutest of differences of job, changes in those differences over time, and the use of them in whatever form they took to establish the men's job as skilled and the women's as less so.

Rural life and labour

Our final example is drawn from the Fenlands of East Anglia, where the division of labour and gender relations took a different form again. In the rural villages and hamlets of nineteenth-century East Anglia, as in the Lancashire cotton towns, many women 'went out to work'. But here there was no coal industry, no factory production of textiles, no sweated labour in the rag trade. Economic life was still overwhelmingly dominated by agriculture. And in this part of the country farms were large, and the bulk of the population was landless, an agricultural proletariat. The black soils demanded lots of labour in dyking, ditching, claying, stone-picking and weeding to bring them under the 'New Husbandry', the nineteenth-century extension of arable land (Samuel, 1975, pp. 12, 18). Women were an integral part of this agricultural workforce, doing heavy work of all sorts on the land, and provoking much the same moral outrage as did the employment of women in mills in Lancashire. [...] The social and spatial structure of the rural communities of this area also influenced the availability and the nature of work. Apart from work on the land, there were few opportunities for women to earn a wage. Even if they did not leave the village permanently, it was often necessary to travel long distances, frequently in groups, with even more serious repercussions in the eyes of the Victorian establishment:

> The worst form of girl labour, from the point of view of bourgeois respectability, was the 'gang' system, which provoked a special commission of inquiry, and a great deal of outraged commentary, in the 1860s. It was most firmly established in the Fen districts of East Anglia and in the East Midlands. The farms in these parts tended to be large but the labouring population was scattered ...

> The labour to work the land then had to be brought from afar,
> often in the form of travelling gangs, who went from farm to farm
> to perform specific tasks.   (Kitteringham, 1975, p.98)

There are here some familiar echoes from Lancashire. And yet things were different in the Fens. In spite of all the potential threats to morality, domesticity, femininity and general female subordination, 'going out to work' on the land for women in the Fens, even going off in gangs for spells away from the village, does not seem to have resulted in the kinds of social changes, and the real disruption to established ways, that occurred in Lancashire. In this area, women's waged-labour did not seem to present a threat to male supremacy within the home. Part of the explanation lies in the different nature of the work for women. This farm labour was often seasonal. The social and spatial organization of farmwork was quite different from that of factory work, and always insecure. Each gang negotiated wage rates independently with the large landowners, the women were not unionized, did not work in factories, were not an industrial proletariat in the same sense as the female mill workers in the cotton towns. Part of the explanation too, as in the colliery villages, lies in the organization of male work. Men, too, were predominantly agricultural labourers, though employed on an annual rather than a seasonal basis, and like mining, agriculture work was heavy and dirty, imposing a similar domestic burden on rural women.

[...]

WHERE ARE THEY NOW?

What is life like in these areas now? Have the traditional attitudes about women's place in the home in the heavy industrial areas survived post-war changes? Have Lancashire women managed to retain the independence that so worried the Victorian middle class? In this century there have been enormous changes in many areas of economic and social life. The communications revolution has linked all parts of the country together, TV, radio, video and a national press have reduced regional isolation and increased the ease with which new ideas and attitudes spread. Changes in social mores, in the role of the family, in the labour process of domestic work, increased divorce rates and a rapid rise in women's participation in waged-labour between the Second World War and the end of the seventies have all had an impact. And yet, we shall argue here, regional differences remain.

There are, as we said in the introduction, two threads which we shall follow in this process of the reproduction of local uniqueness. The first concerns the geographically differentiated operation of national processes. Over

40% of the national paid labour-force in the UK now consists of women: a vast majority of them married. One of the consequences of this growth of jobs 'for women' has paradoxically been both an increase and a reduction in regional differences. The gender division of labour is changing in different ways in different areas, in part in response to previous patterns. Regional disparities in the proportion of women at work are closing, but the corollary of this, of course, is that the highest proportions of new and expanding jobs are in those very regions where previously few women have been involved in waged-labour. The four regions are being drawn in different ways into a new national structure of employment and unemployment. We cannot here attempt to explain this new spatial pattern. One thing we do hint at, though, is that the form of gender relations themselves, and the previous economic and social history of women in each of these places, may be one, though only one, thread in that explanation.

The areas, then, have experienced different types of change in their economic structure. In many ways the growth of jobs for women has been of greater significance in the north-east and in East Anglia than in the cotton towns or in Hackney. But that is not the end of the story. For those changes have themselves been combined with existing local conditions and this has influenced their operation and their effect. The impact of an increase in jobs for women has not been the same in the Fens as it has been in the coalfields of the north-east. This, then, is the second thread in our discussion of the reproduction of local uniqueness.

In the rest of this chapter we try to show the links between past and present patterns, how changing attitudes to women and men's roles at work and in the family in different parts of the country (themselves related to previous economic roles) both influence and are influenced by national changes in the nature and organization of paid employment over time. The present gender division of labour in particular places is the outcome of the combination over time of successive phases. Space and location still matter. The structure of relationships between men and women varies between, and within, regions. Life in inner London is still not the same as in the Fenlands, in the coalfields of the north-east, as in the textile towns round Manchester. The current division of labour between women and men is different, paid employment is differently structured and organized, and even its spatial form varies between one part of the country and another.

Coal was our life?

The decline of work in the pits is a well-known aspect of post-war economic changes in Britain. How have the men and women of the north-east reacted to this decline in their traditional livelihood? Have the changes challenged or strengthened the traditional machismo of the north-eastern male? What is happening in the north-east today in many ways recalls some of the images – and the social alarm – generated by the cotton towns a hundred years earlier. It is now in the north-east that homes are being 'turned upside down' and patriarchy threatened by women going out to work. At the beginning of the 1960s, still something less than a quarter of all adult women in the old colliery areas worked outside their homes for wages. The figure has more than doubled since then. And part of the explanation lies in the local distinctiveness, the uniqueness of these areas that has its origins in the nineteenth century. The women of this area have no tradition of waged-labour, no union experience. It was, of course, these very features that proved attractive to the female-employing industries that opened branch plants in increasing numbers in Co. Durham in the sixties and seventies.

The new jobs that came to the north-east, then, were mainly for women. They were located on trading estates and in the regions two New Towns built to attract industrial investment and also to improve housing conditions. The women who moved into the New Towns of Peterlee and Washington provided a cheap, flexible, untrained and trapped pool of labour for incoming firms. And added to this, the loss of jobs for men together with the rent rises entailed by a move to new housing pushed women into the labour market.

Male antagonism to the new gender division of labour was almost universal. Outrage at women 'taking men's jobs', pleas for 'proper jobs', an assumption that the packing, processing and assembly line work that loomed even larger in the economic structure of the area was an affront to masculine dignity: 'I think a lot of men feel that assembly work wouldn't be acceptable; they'd be a bit proud about doing that type of work in this area. North East ideas are ingrained in the men in this area' (Lewis, 1983, p. 19). These assumptions appear to be shared by the new employers: 'we are predominantly female labour orientated ... the work is more suited to women, it's very boring, I suppose we're old-fashioned and still consider it as women's work ... the men aren't interested'.

[...]

Industry in the country?

How has life changed in the Fens? In some ways, continuity rather than change is the link between the past and present here. For many women, especially the older ones, work on the land is still their main source of employment. [...] Not much different from their grandmothers and great-grandmothers before them. Gangs are still a common feature and the nature of fieldwork

107

has hardly changed either. Flowers are weeded and picked by hand. Celery and beet are sown and picked manually too. And this type of work is considered 'women's work'. It is poorly paid, seasonal and backbreaking. Male fieldworkers, on the other hand, have the status of 'labourers', relative permanence and the benefits associated with full-time employment. And they are the ones who have machinery to assist them.

Life *has* changed though. Small towns and rural areas such as the Fens have been favoured locations for the new branch plants and decentralizing industries of the sixties and seventies. Labour is cheap here – particularly with so few alternatives available – and relatively unorganized. Especially for younger women, the influx of new jobs has opened up the range of employment opportunities. It provides a means, still, both of supplementing low male wages, and of meeting people – of getting out of the small world of the village.

[...]

It seems that the expansion of industrial jobs 'for women' has had relatively little impact on social relations in the rural Fens. In part, this is to do with the local conditions into which the jobs were introduced: the impact back of local factors on national changes. The Fenland villages today are still Conservative – politically and socially. Divorce, left-wing politics, women's independence are very much the exception. [...] Gender relations in East Anglia apparently have hardly been affected by the new jobs, let alone 'turned upside down'.

A regional problem for women?

The contrast with the cotton towns of Lancashire is striking. Here, where employment for women in the major industry had been declining for decades, was a major source of female labour, already skilled, already accustomed to factory work, plainly as dexterous as elsewhere. And yet the new industries of the sixties and seventies, seeking out female labour, did not come here, or not to the extent that they went to other places.

The reasons are complex, but they are bound up once again with the intricate relationship between capitalist and patriarchal structures. For one thing, here there was no regional policy assistance. There has, for much of this century, been massive decline in employment in the cotton industry in Lancashire. Declines comparable to those in coalmining, for instance, and in areas dominated by it. Yet the cotton towns were never awarded Development Area status. To the extent that associated areas were not designated on the basis of unemployment rates, the explanation lies at the level of taxes and benefits which define women as dependent. There is often less point in signing on [for unemployment benefits]. A loss of jobs does not necessarily show up, therefore, in a corresponding increase in regional unemployment. Development Areas, however, were *not* designated simply on the basis of unemployment rates. They were wider concepts, and wider regions, designated on the basis of a more general economic decline and need for regeneration. To that extent the non-designation of the cotton towns was due in part to a more general political blindness to questions of women's employment.

So the lack of regional policy incentives must have been, relatively, a deterrent to those industries scanning the country for new locations. But it cannot have been the whole explanation. New industries moved to other non-assisted areas – East Anglia, for instance. Many factors were in play, but one of them surely was that the women of the cotton towns were not, either individually or collectively in their history, 'green labour'. The long tradition of women working in factory jobs, and their relative financial independence, has continued. In spite of the decline of cotton textiles the region still has a high female activity rate [...] [T]he women of the cotton towns are now facing very different changes from those being faced by the women of the coalfields. Here they are not gaining a new independence from men; to some extent in places it may even be decreasing. Women's unemployment is not seen to 'disrupt' family life, or cause TV programmes to be made about challenges to gender relations, for women do the domestic work anyway. Having lost one of their jobs, they carry on (unpaid) with the other.

Hackney: still putting out

What has happened in Hackney is an intensification of the old patterns of exploitation and subordination rather than the superimposition of new patterns. Here manufacturing jobs have declined, but the rag trade remains a major employer. The women of Hackney possess, apparently, some of the same advantages to capital as do those of the coalfields and the Fens: they are cheap and unorganized. [...] In Inner London, moreover, the spatial organization of the labour-force, the lack of separation of home and work, strengthens the advantages: overheads (light, heat, maintenance of machinery) are borne by the workers themselves; workers are not eligible for social security benefits; their spatial separation one from another makes it virtually impossible for them to combine to force up wage rates, and so on.

So given the clear advantages to capital of such a vulnerable potential workforce, why has there been no influx of branch plants of multinationals, of electronics assembly-lines and suchlike? Recent decades have of course seen the growth of new types of jobs for women, particularly in the service sector, if not within Hackney itself then within travelling distance (for some), in the centre of London. But, at the moment, for big manufacturing capital and for the clerical-mass production operations which in the sixties and seventies established themselves in the Development Areas and more rural regions of the country, this vulnerable labour of the capital city holds out few advantages. Even the larger clothing firms (with longer production runs, a factory labour process, locational flexibility and the capital to establish new plant) have set up their new branch plants elsewhere, either in the peripheral regions of Britain or in the Third World. So why not in Hackney? In part the women of Hackney have been left behind in the wake of the more general decentralization, the desertion by manufacturing industry of the conurbations of the First World. In part they are the victims of the changing international division of labour within the clothing industry itself. But in part, too, the reasons lie in the nature of the available labour. Homeworking does have advantages for capital, but this way of making female labour cheap is no use for electronics assembly-lines or for other kinds of less individualized production. The usefulness of this way of making labour vulnerable is confined to certain types of labour process.

The influx of service jobs in central London has outbid manufacturing for female labour, in terms both of wages and of conditions of work (see Massey, 1984, ch. 4). But working in service jobs has not been an option available to all. For women in one way or another tied to the home, or to the very local area, homeworking in industries such as clothing has become increasingly the only available option. Given the sexual division of labour in the home, homeworking benefits some women: 'Homework when properly paid, suits many women: women who wish to stay at home with small children, women who dislike the discipline and timekeeping of factory work and wish to work at their own pace' (Harrison, 1983, p. 64). [...] The involvement of all members of a family in homework or working as a team in small family-owned factories is not uncommon, especially among ethnic minorities. For small companies the extended family may be essential to survival:

> the flexibility comes from the family: none of their wages are fixed. When times are good, they may be paid more. When they are bad, they are paid less. They get the same pay whether their hours are short or long.   (Harrison, 1983, p. 63)

The fact that women are employed in the context of an extended family is important not only in the organization of the industry but also for the lives of the women themselves. They may have a wage, but they do not get the other forms of independence which can come with a job. They do not get out of the sphere of the family, they do not make independent circles of friends and contacts, nor establish a spatially separate sphere of existence. Within the family itself the double subordination of women is fixed through the mixing in one person of the role of husband or father with that of boss and employer.

But it is not that there have been no changes in recent decades for the homeworkers of Hackney. They too have been caught up in and affected by the recent changes in the international division of labour. The clothing industry of London in the second half of the twentieth century finds itself caught between cheap imports on the one hand and competition for labour from the better working conditions of the service sector on the other. The clothing firms with the ability to do so have long since left. For those that remain, cutting labour costs is a priority, and homeworking a means to do it. So an increasing proportion of the industry's work in the metropolis is now done on this social system while the amount of work overall, and the real wages paid, decline dramatically. For the women who work in this industry there is thus more competition for available work, increasing vulnerability to employers and intensification of the labour process. And this change in employment conditions brings increased pressures on home life too, though very different ones from those in the north-east, or the Fens. For these women in Hackney their workplace is also their home.

[...]

Low wage, non-unionized workers in Hackney are competing directly with the same type of low-technology, labour-intensive industries in the Third World. But it is precisely the history of the rag trade in Hackney, the previous layers of economic and social life, that have forced this competition on them. The intersection of national and international trends, of family and economic relationships, of patriarchy and capitalism have produced this particular set of relationships in one area of Inner London.

REFERENCES

Alexander, S. (1982) 'Women's work in nineteenth-century London: a study of the years 1820–50', pp. 30–40 in E. Whitelegg *el al.* (eds.), *The Changing Experience of Women*, Martin Robertson, Oxford.

Anderson, M. (1971) *Family and Structure in Nineteenth-Century Lancashire*, Cambridge University Press, Cambridge.

Engels, F. (1969 edn) *The Conditions of the Working Class in England*, Panther, St Albans.

Frankenberg, R. (1976) 'In the production of their lives, man (?)... sex and gender in British community studies', chapter 2, pp. 25–51 in D. L. Barker and A. Allen (eds.), *Sexual Divisions and Society: Process and Change*, Tavistock, London.

Hall, C. (1982) 'The home turned upside down? The working class family in cotton textiles 1780–1850', in E. Whitelegg *et al.* (eds.), *The Changing Experience of Women*, Martin Robertson, Oxford.

Harrison, P. (1983) *Inside the Inner City,* Penguin, Harmondsworth.

Kitteringham, J. (197S) 'Country work girls in nineteenth-century England', Part 3, pp. 73–138, in R. Samuel (ed.), *Village Life and Labour,* Routledge and Kegan Paul, London.

Lewis, J. (1983) 'Women, work and regional development', *Northern Economic Review,* no. 7. Summer, pp. 10–24.

Liddington, J. (1979) 'Women cotton workers and the suffrage campaign: the radical suffragists in Lancashire, 1893–1914', chapter 4, pp. 64–97, in S. Burman (ed.), *Fit Work for Women,* Croom Helm, London.

Massey, D. (1984) *Spatial Divisions of Labour: Social Structures and the Geography of Production,* Macmillan, London.

Phillips, A. and Taylor, B. (1980) 'Notes towards a feminist economics', *Feminist Review,* vol. 6, pp. 79–88.

Samuel, R. (197S) *Village Life and Labour,* Routledge and Kegan Paul, London.

Strong Words Collective (1977) *Hello, are you working?* Erdesdun Publications, Whitley Bay.

CHAPTER 7

THE CHANGING GEOGRAPHY OF TRADE UNIONS (1989)

with Joe Painter

INTRODUCTION

Recent years have been tough for the trade unions. Headline after headline has proclaimed their imminent demise, their irrelevance to changing occupational and industrial structures and to supposedly transformed ideologies. They have come under political onslaught. Given all of this, they have survived remarkably well.

The emerging evidence of a stabilisation in their position, at least in numerical terms, itself says something about the causes of the problems. Trade union membership has not declined because of some autonomous ideological shift away from unionism, or more generally away from collectivism and towards individualism (Gallie, 1987). On the contrary, there is some evidence that those who remain in trade unions today are more consciously trade unionist than previously. Given the political climate, being a trade union member is possibly more of a political statement than it was when, in the then major sectors of the economy, taking up trade union membership was almost a reflex action.

The bulk of the recent decline in trade union membership has resulted from a straightforward loss of jobs, a process concentrated in the more unionised sectors, and from people going out of union membership when moving jobs to sectors where unions have been less successful in gaining an organisational foothold (Gallie, 1987). These two processes are associated mainly with the massive recession in the early eighties and with very long term structural changes in the economy, particularly changes in the labour process and in the occupational structure of the workforce. To these problems can be added an extraordinarily hostile government bent on attack. With hindsight, the first factor (the recession) seems to have been the cause of all the headlines, but it will probably be the other two phenomena (the long-term 'structural changes' and the political onslaught) which ultimately will be seen to have posed the bigger challenges. We shall look at these in the sections which follow.

Table 7.1 shows the clear shift from growth to decline in total membership of all unions between the 1970s and 1980s. This has not been reversed. But the real collapse took place in the recession years between 1980 and 1983, which fits at aggregate level with Gallie's findings. Since then, when manufacturing in particular suffered very badly, the year-on-year losses have been reduced. Furthermore, the most recent results confirm a far better performance for a range of unions even than in the middle of the decade. The GMB (General, Municipal, Boilermakers and Allied Trades Union), for example, gained over 2,000 members in the last quarter of 1987, while the Union of Shop, Distributive and Allied Workers (USDAW), the National and Local Government Officers' Association (NALGO) and the Union of Construction, Allied Trades and Technicians (UCATT) all showed membership gains of between 1.1 and 2.3 per cent in 1987 as a whole [...]

But if the unions have survived (just) the worst of the recession, they nevertheless face major challenges from various (related) sources.

Table 7.1 Changes in trade union membership, 1974–85

Year	Total number of members	Union members as a % of the workforce[2]	% change in membership over previous year
1974	11.8	46.6	+2.7
1975	12.2	47.9	+3.6
1975[1]	12.0	47.2	
1976	12.4	48.5	+3.0
1977	12.8	50.1	+3.7
1978	13.1	50.7	+2.1
1979	13.3	51.1	+1.3
1980	12.9	49.5	−2.6
1981	12.1	46.6	−6.5
1982	11.6	44.8	−4.2
1983	11.2	41.6	−3.1
1984	11.0	39.9	−2.2
1985	10.7	38.4	−2.5

Figures relate to December of each year, to the UK and all trade unions.

Notes: 1. In 1975, 31 organisations were no longer considered to be trade unions. There are thus two sets of figures for 1975, one with these organisations and one with them excluded.

2. Includes unemployed.

Source: Central Statistical Office 1988.

The recession of the early 1980s was arguably an accentuation of many structural economic changes which had been underway for some time. They have involved: major shifts between sectors of the economy; changes in the work process leading to changes in the occupational structure of the work-force; a transformation in the gender composition of the employed population; and a growth of part-time work.

The current Government's onslaught has been launched against this background. In this chapter we shall look mainly at the sectoral shifts and at some elements of the political attack. In both, 'geography' has been an important part of what has been going on.

THE CHALLENGE OF A CHANGING STRUCTURE

There were definite geographical bases to the trade union movement in Britain in the immediate post-war years. The pattern largely reflected the geography of industry and a particular industrial structure. This was a trade union movement based on a capitalism which was overwhelmingly urban, and where different parts of the country retained their individual industrial specialisms.

During the period of post-war growth, through to the end of the 1950s, the broad outline of this geography was largely reinforced. But since then it has changed quite radically: while some unions have grown rapidly in new regions, there has also been a massive decline in many areas of former strength.

The new geography of union membership is more widely-distributed, both overall and within individual unions. The heartlands of the trade union movement have declined relatively and absolutely. There has been decentralisation to new areas. The growth of new sectors in the economy has produced threats and opportunities for trade unions. It has enabled the development of new, more widely dispersed trade unions, and it has seen the rise of non-unionism in particular areas, industries and sections of the work-force. This in turn suggests the emergence of new potential trade unionists.

The decline of the heartlands[i]

In the immediate post-war years trade union membership in Britain was concentrated in the cities and in particular regions of industrial concentration. Many individual unions, especially those organised in specific industries, were overwhelmingly based in just one or two parts of the country. In 1951, for example, nearly half of NUTGW's (National Union of Tailors and

Garment Workers) membership was in London, Leeds and Manchester, and half of NUFLAT's (National Union of Footwear, Leather and Allied Trades) members in the shoe industry were in the East Midlands. Some unions were even more geographically concentrated: the Association of Textile Workers (ATW) was exclusively confined to North West England, and the NUM (National Union of Mineworkers) was synonymous with the coalfields.

These are all unions which organised in specific industrial sectors, and their geography mirrored that of the industries in which they were based. But other unions, even though they might spread across much of manufacturing industry, were still overwhelmingly concentrated in the main industrial areas of nineteenth and early twentieth century British capitalism. The ABU (Amalgamated Engineering Union) and its forebears is a classic example. In this earlier period half its members were in five areas: London, Lancashire, Birmingham-Coventry, South Wales and the Glasgow-Paisley area.

We refer to these geographical bases as the unions' 'heartlands'. They varied between unions. In some areas a single union might organise most trade unionists – the coal and textile areas are the most obvious examples. Elsewhere the heartlands of the different unions overlapped to form bases of trade unionism more generally, especially in the cities. Since the 1960s these various heartlands have been seriously eroded. In part, this loss reflects the decline in total membership of unions which were almost entirely confined to particular areas, but it is also the result of differential patterns of loss and gain. Most notably the old bases of membership in these unions have seen the greatest proportional reduction, although the timing has varied considerably between unions.

[...] In the AEU [Amalgamated Engineering Union], for instance, the shift in balance has been quite dramatic. In 1951, 3,500 more members of the then AUEW [Amalgamated Union of Engineering Workers] were in the old base areas than in the rest of the country. However, by 1979 the situation was reversed and the areas which had once been the union's periphery had 120,000 more members than the old heartlands. Moreover, this shift was dramatically reinforced through differential patterns of decline after 1979. Between 1979 and 1981, total membership of the AUEW fell by 17 per cent, but the decline in the heartland area was 22 per cent.

Not all unions were so geographically concentrated in the early post-war years. Membership of general unions, such as the then GMWU (General and Municipal Workers' Union), and unions in sectors more directly related to population distribution (mainly service sector unions such as USDAW), was much more widely dispersed, though with a numerical bias towards the cities which strengthened the urban concentration of the union movement as a whole. Trends even within these unions are reinforcing the tendency towards a more dispersed geography. In 1961, 28 per cent of the GMWU's membership was in the urban areas of the North West and its London and Eastern region, and only 20 per cent was in the whole of the North and Scotland. By 1979 these magnitudes had been almost reversed. A similar shift happened within USDAW.

So the trade union movement is confronted with the absolute and relative decline of many of its former bases of strength. In itself this is some kind of loss of identity, of history.

Why has it happened?

To some extent the shifts in the geography of these unions reflect organisational changes within the unions themselves. There have been mergers, amalgamations, and changes in recruitment strategy. But more importantly there have been major changes in the sectoral composition, technology and geographical organisation of industry itself.

There seem to be three crucial components of these changes:

1. The decline of older industries: First there has been straightforward industrial decline as the deindustrialisation of Britain has spread through successive generations of industry [...] Among the first to decline were old labour-intensive and characteristically female-employing consumer goods industries. Increasing imports and a wider international reorganisation of production had dramatic effects on the clothing, shoe and textile industries and consequently on NUTGW, NUFLAT and the ATW.

The decline of other industries, for instance engineering, began in the 1960s and 1970s, taking with it sizeable chunks of unions such as the AUEW. Finally, deindustrialisation has also affected the geography and internal composition of the more general unions. The decline of the EETPU (Electrical, Electronic, Telecommunication and Plumbing Union) in Merseyside, Humberside, South Wales and London between 1974 and 1983 is related to the fall in membership in the older manufacturing sections of the union. Similarly, the decline of the then GMWU in London, especially in the 1960s is associated with the steady destruction of that city's manufacturing base.

2. The search for cheaper labour: There have also been geographical shifts in response to intensifying competition. Within Britain, a differential pattern of change has seen the net decline of the major conurbations and net gains in the smaller towns and the peripheral areas.

The changing geography of the NUTGW clearly shows this process [...] [with a] changing balance between the NUTGW's original geographical base and the rest of the country from the early 1950s to the early 1980s. The old base shows continuous decline but, before 1979, there was absolute growth

117

in membership in other regions. The clothing industry, trapped between low-cost imports and rising competition for labour in its established locations, relocated elsewhere – the North, Scotland, parts of Yorkshire and Humberside, Northern Ireland, the South West, East Anglia and the outer South East – in search of cheaper labour.

[...]

3. *Changes in the production process*: There have also been considerable changes in the technology of production. The introduction of automated and computerised equipment has often reduced the numbers of skilled manual workers while increasing the numbers both of technicians and of relatively unskilled 'machine minders'. This process has been yet another to affect detrimentally the older 'craft' unions within manufacturing.

Increased automation has helped managers to introduce new forms of production organisation. Working practices common in Japanese industry are used as models. The need to cut costs and respond rapidly to changing product markets has led to efforts to increase the functional, numerical and time flexibility of workforces. Quality circles and workplace councils have been established in a few plants. These developments, if they become widespread, could weaken workplace trade unionism, by bypassing traditional forms of union organisation like shop stewards' committees, and by emphasising the role of the individual and the small team rather than the collective workforce.

New practices may be introduced in the context of investment on greenfield sites, in some cases by foreign (including Japanese) companies. Such changes may be associated with the introduction of single-union agreements. The Japanese car manufacturer Nissan started production at its Sunderland plant in July 1986 after reaching a single-union agreement with the ABU. There are just two grades of shop-floor workers at the plant, compared with the heavily demarcated plants characteristic of traditional British manufacturing. In fact reports suggest that no more than 7 per cent of workers at the plant have actually joined the AEU (*Financial Times*, 1988).

Such changes may also be introduced in existing plants, although they may be resisted by established trade unions. This happened in the disputes at Ford and General Motors in early 1988, where the unions managed to reduce what they saw as the damaging effects of the changes for their members.

Finally, these developments are sometimes associated with locational change or investment on a new site, particularly in an area or to a workforce with a lower level of unionisation. For instance companies establishing electronics plants in South Wales have actively avoided areas with strong traditions of unionisation associated with coal mining, and have preferred un-unionised women workers to their more heavily unionized counterparts (Morgan and Sayer, 1984).

Indeed, once again, geographical mobility can make life easier for management, especially where technological change implies potentially disruptive changes in the work process, skill definitions and the social composition of the workforce.

This is clear not only from the changing balance between unions representing different types of workers, but also in the changing membership composition even of individual unions. Within the GMB there has been a dramatic rise in female membership. Feminisation often reflects the downgrading of skills. And in the GMB it has been greatest in those areas, particularly Development Areas, to which there has been decentralisation. Since the 1960s the proportion of women members in the North, Scotland and South Wales has risen faster than anywhere else. But more importantly feminisation also reflects changes in sectoral composition within the union (from shipbuilding to local government and food and drink for instance). The point is that together they have brought about significant changes in both the internal composition and the geography of the union.

The growth of new sectors

Shifts in the wider sectoral structure of the economy are reflected in the aggregate figures for unionisation in different sectors. Over a period of ten years, the best-unionised sectors of the economy have seen the largest reductions in employment (Table 7.2). As well as the relative growth and decline as people join and leave the workforce, people changing jobs (for example from transport to wholesale distribution, a not-impossible move) are likely to be going from more to less unionised sectors.

Table 7.2 Employment change and union density by industry

Sector	Change in employment 1976–86	Union density 1984 (%)
Banking, insurance and finance	+709,000	43
Business and other services	+383,000	21
Hotels and catering	+211,000	21
Wholesale distribution	+162,000	32
Energy and water	−61,000	88
Transport	−123,000	85
Metals and mineral products	−290,000	68
Vehicles and transport equipment	−322,000	81
Metal goods and mechanical engineering	−493,000	55

Union density measures the proportion of the relevant workforce belonging to a trade union.

Source: Labour Research Department 1987.

Sectoral changes in the economy have also seen the growth of new unions, in particular the white collar unions both within and outside the public sector. Both the initial geography of these unions and subsequent developments have reinforced the changes outlined in the previous sections.

Take first the public sector unions. By their very nature most of them have been spread across the country. Moreover their growth has been associated with a shift in the balance of their membership from the conurbations to surrounding regions. For NALGO, between 1951 and 1983 the gains in membership outside the London, West Midlands and North West conurbations were greater than those within them [...] For NUPE (National Union of Public Employees) regional membership data, which is only available for dates after 1970, shows a similar pattern. Between 1971 and 1983 the share of membership in the unions' 'periphery' of the North, South West and Wales increased from less than 7 per cent to over 20 per cent.

There are a number of reasons for the changing geography of the public sector unions. First, there are important geographical differences in union traditions. In the case of NUPE's health service membership, union officials pointed out that it is generally more accepted and expected for nurses, for instance, to join a union in Scotland than it is in some other areas. A second factor, which promotes dispersion, is the general decentralisation of population from conurbations. Third, there have been significant changes in the allocation formulae applied by central government in distributing resources among regions, involving greater emphasis on public services in 'problem' peripheral regions.

Taken together, the increase in membership of the public sector unions (between 1951 and 1983 NALGO and NUPE together grew by over a million, over half this increase occurring after 1970) and the increasingly dispersed nature of the unions highlights their growing weight in the new geography of the trade union movement as a whole. More recent figures indicate that the combined memberships of NALGO, NUPE and the other major health union, COHSE (Confederation of Health Service Employees) grew by 6 per cent between 1976 and 1986, ten years which have otherwise been very difficult for the unions.

White collar unions in the private sector were more concentrated than those in the public sector, but not as concentrated as the craft or industrial unions. These unions too have become more evenly distributed. For the then AUEW-TASS (Technical, Administrative and Supervisory Section) between 1951 and 1982 the proportion of the membership in London and Manchester declined, and although that for the West Midlands increased, so did the proportional share for the South West and South Wales, Northern Ireland and Southern England.

[...]

120

These rapid changes in sectoral structures and labour processes have been accompanied by changes in the workforce. An increasing proportion of workers are women – the feminisation mentioned earlier – especially women working part-time [...] A crude sectoral analysis of the changing workforce illuminates these trends. Firstly, manufacturing has collapsed: 7.9 million people were employed in manufacturing in Great Britain in 1971, but by December 1986 this figure had fallen to 5.1 million (Central Statistical Office, 1987; Department of Employment, 1988). By far the largest proportion – some 93 per cent – of manufacturing employment remains full-time, and the proportion of jobs held by women has stayed virtually static, at just under 30 per cent.

By contrast, service sector employment has risen steadily, from 11.3 million in 1971 to 14.3 million in December 1986. A much greater proportion of jobs are now part-time: 32.1 per cent in 1986, compared to 23.5 per cent in 1971. The proportion of jobs done by women has risen from 49.5 per cent to 54.6 per cent over this period and, of the 7.8 million women employed in services in 1986, 49.1 per cent were part-time; the corresponding proportion in 1971 was 39.2 per cent (Central Statistical Office, 1987; Department of Employment, 1988). These figures conceal important differences between public and private sector services, but the broad picture is of a declining manufacturing sector providing full-time jobs, mostly for men, and a growing service sector providing some full-time jobs for men and a mixture of full- and part-time jobs for women [...]

These changes have posed challenges and offered opportunities to the trade unions. By and large, trade unionism has in the past been male-dominated. Women workers have been less well unionised than their male counterparts, and positions of power in unions, even in those like NUPE with large female memberships, have tended to be occupied by men.

The increase in part-time and temporary working is also a source of new challenges for trade unions. Because part-timers tend to spend less time at work than full-time colleagues (not as obvious as it seems, since 'part-time work' may involve full-time hours but only part-time rights) they have less contact with each other and with their potential union. The strength of collective organisation is thus already undermined by the nature of the employment contract. Temporary workers may also be less inclined than permanent workers to join a union, as they may not see their job as a long-term relationship requiring the support of traditional trade unionism.

The location of many new jobs away from old regions of union strength adds a geographical challenge to the others. With little local union or labour-movement culture to draw on, workers in expanding regions like the South East, East Anglia and the South West must develop from scratch a familiarity with the ideas and practices of trade unions.

121

Many unions are responding to these challenges. For example, the TGWU (Transport and General Workers' Union) has launched a 'Link-up' campaign to recruit part-time and temporary workers, while the GMB is actively trying to improve its appeal to women and minority groups through a vigorous equal opportunities policy. [...]

Whether these campaigns can be successful remains to be seen, particularly given the difficulties of organising in the growth sectors like leisure, tourism, financial services and high technology manufacturing (*The Independent*, 1988), but the unions have at least accepted the challenge.

THE POLITICAL ATTACK

It is in this context that the Thatcher Governments have launched their attack on trade unions. Long-term 'structural' changes cannot be separated from the impact of the politics of the current Government. These structural changes are not immutable, nor is the Government's onslaught independent of the economic context in which it occurs. These economic and political developments are conditioned by each other.

Firstly, many of the policies of this Government have hastened the long-term changes described above. Its monetarism, and its prioritisation of finance over manufacturing, and of high-technology over traditional industries, have all reinforced the problems faced by the sectors in which unions have historically been strongest. The accentuated move towards service employment, especially in the private sector, has had parallel effects.

Secondly, a number of the Government's wider policies seem to be motivated as much by a desire to break up bases of union strength as by more explicitly expressed aims. The Government's dislike of local authorities is evident, and is based on a recognition of the ability of some Labour councils to become foci for mobilising opposition [...] But it is also true that the local public sector also represents some of the more coherent remaining bases of trade union influence and membership. The attack on local authorities, the resultant cutbacks in their services and in particular measures such as competitive tendering are also attacks on NUPE and NALGO. Similarly with the health service – the Government's intense dislike of COHSE and (again) NUPE is well known and is at least one element in the strategy of breaking up, by one means or another, public sector provision.

Thirdly, moreover, the Government seems to have been both clearly aware of the long-term changes in the economy and acute enough to focus its attacks and attention on key points within those changes. Furthermore, on a number of occasions the geographical dimension has been a key element in the situation.

This is neither new nor unique to this government. We saw examples earlier of companies using locational change and choice against trade unions, and in the 1960s and early 1970s when such decentralisation was at its height, regional policy helped facilitate such moves. Again, national energy strategy over decades has in part been conditioned by fear of the potential power of the NUM. And it was clearly seen as strategically important to keep the newly developing off-shore oil industry as free as possible from trade union power and influence.

Nonetheless the Thatcher Government has been particularly precise in its selection of targets. The degree of planning which went into the miners' strike, and the care with which the battle was selected and provoked, has been documented elsewhere (Beynon, 1985). This was a strategic attack on a crucially symbolic part of the trade union movement [...] and was also an attack on one of the heartlands mentioned previously. The mining regions were not just highly unionised areas; they were, indeed still are, bases for an ideology and a way of life in many ways utterly opposed to Thatcherism. The one significant field where this was not true was Nottinghamshire and the potential for division which this provided, combined with differences in at least short-term economic futures, was fully exploited. It was an early demonstration of Margaret Thatcher's acute geographical sense!

This geographical sense is being demonstrated again with the attack on urban areas and their local authorities. After the coalfields, the major urban areas are among the most important of the geographical bases of resistance. Moreover, while the membership of public sector unions has become more depressed in recent decades, they retain very large memberships in the big cities, and these unions are among the fastest growing in the country. In the general context of decline their proportionate numerical significance has increased enormously. Indeed, although figures to prove this point are impossible to come by, it seems likely that most trade unionists in many of the larger urban areas in this country are now in a fairly small number of increasingly strong, and often belligerent, public sector unions. In that context, inner-city policy, together with the policies on local government, education and health, can be interpreted as attacks on one of the few strengthening bases of trade unionism, sectorally and geographically.

There have been other instances of 'seizing the moment' (and the place) too. There seems little doubt that Government enthusiasm for certain forms of foreign inward investment in former Development Areas (the North East, Scotland, Wales) owes not a little to the perceived effect it might have on industrial relations in British industry more widely. Nissan's investment in the North East is an obvious example, and although it has certainly not produced an immediate revolution in the labour process and labour-management relations throughout the British car industry, it has had its imitators. More widely, Nissan's location in the North East, a region formerly renowned for its highly unionised sectors, shows just how far moods have been changed by years of high unemployment and sheer desperation for jobs. In the 1960s and early 1970s many firms decentralised to these so-called 'peripheral' regions in search of female labour, assuming that such labour would be both cheap and relatively uncontaminated by the trade union history of the region. On many occasions the male workforce of the region was avoided. This may now be less true as a result of the combination of continuing high unemployment, a new generation of male labour, and a new-found political confidence among elements of management. The way in which the British Government backed a US multinational (Ford) against British trade unions over the proposed investment in Dundee shows the importance attached to this particular element in the tussle over the future of trade unionism.

But most new investment is going into the outer-outer metropolitan area of the South East. And it is in this area, held up by the Government as the image of the future, that union densities are lowest and falling fastest among key sections of the workforce. One significant bundle of sectors here, though by no means the most important in terms of numbers, is grouped around 'high technology'. The relative decline in importance of big corporate research laboratories, in contrast to the increase in smaller detached outfits, the relative power of scientists and technologists in these labour markets (reinforced by nationally inadequate training and a high degree of concentration in one region), and a rhetoric (and sometimes a reality) of participation and control in smaller high technology units, have produced an atmosphere dominated by competitive individualism and utterly antipathetical to trade unionism. Conditions in a key growth sector are thus particularly difficult for trade unions. They were certainly made worse by the government's banning of trade unionism at GCHQ (Government Communications Headquarters) in the heart of the M4 corridor. With so much high-technology industry in the region dependent upon military expenditures, the point is unlikely to have been missed by those competing for government contracts.

As a final example, there is Docklands, a massive development crucial to the Government's strategy for Britain's place in the international division of labour of the twenty-first century – this time as a financial centre with London as one of the few world cities. Yet this development is in an area once highly unionised, an important base of the TGWU, and indeed one of the places where general unionism was born. Of course the new economic activities are not about employing the local people. Nonetheless some of them will be employed in a variety of mainly servicing capacities. And it has clearly been crucial to keep 'the unions' out. [...]

CONCLUSION

Recession, longer-term economic changes, and an immediate political offensive (to which one might add a changing – in some cases radicalizing – wider political climate), have presented immense challenges to British trade unionism. The problem posed by the recession was the sheer speed and intensity of change; the longer term changes pose challenges of working out new ways of organising, in new sectors, among new groups in new places; and the political attack is over the very existence, and the *terms* of existence, of a meaningful trade union movement.

Geography has been integral to all this. At the broadest level, the geographical shifts imply a major change in local conditions of organisation. The new areas and regions are different from the old. The 'heartlands' are not the bases that they were. By no means all the areas of numerical strength were areas of militancy, still less of political radicalism. The dominance of localities by single industries and single unions can as easily lead to paternalism and class complicity (and concepts of the economy of 'our region') and to the weakening of trade unionism, as to independent union strength. But some of them were the geographical heart, symbolically and organisationally, of the movement. In different ways this has been true of some of the coalfields, and of the complex of car-industry-related unions in the West Midlands. Different again have been the cities. Lane (1982) has written of the rich texture and diversity of the network of unions which made the cities so good for (certain forms of) organisation. And, inevitably, because they were home to so many of these unions, the cities have been hit particularly hard. [...] If one city stands out as having suffered from declines in almost all these unions, it is London. The timing and rate of decline has varied between unions but the combined effect is startling. Moreover, the very process of change can itself present difficulties, as old established centres of organisation become more marginal, at least in numerical terms, to a union's strength, and new areas begin to assert their increased weight. What is more, the membership in the new areas is being built up, not in a post-war boom, but in a period of restructuring. Combine this with all the other changes that are going on within the unions – shifts in the balance between unions, shifts in the balance of skills and industries, and shifts in gender composition – and one can understand feelings of uncertainty, even a loss of identity. We may mourn or celebrate these changes, but they are certainly a lot to cope with.

Moreover, geographical shift has not just produced new problems for unions to deal with, and new conditions to organise in; it has also been actively used as a weapon against trade unions. The current use of greenfield sites as locations in which to restructure labour processes and industrial relations is just the latest phase in capital's use of 'geography' against labour.

125

Yet things are not entirely gloomy. In simple numerical terms the situation has stabilised since the recession. And other evidence, of a more qualitative and political nature, indicates that the union movement is not to be written off. The results of ballots on closed shops and on political funds have been positive. A report on pay deals pointed to the 'sheer resilience of collective organisation' and argued that no-strike and single-union deals had had little impact on the vast majority of pay negotiations (Incomes Data Services, 1987; see also Kelly, 1987). Indeed both IDS and Kelly note that some recent changes, such as strike-ballot legislation and certain forms of agreements about flexibility in the labour process, can be turned into strengths for trade unions. Certainly the 1988 Ford strike indicated, as the plants began to be affected across Europe, the potential vulnerability of tightly-integrated multi-plant networks operating on just-in-time systems, without the changes in culture and social relations needed to support those systems (Sayer, 1986).

It seems unlikely that there is anything irretrievably anti-union in the new growth areas. Defence of public sector services, with its links to consumers and its base in communities, often dominating the union movement in urban areas in the north, is one potential base of a different sort. There are interesting comparisons to be drawn and lessons to be learned, from the new areas of growth. While Scotland's Silicon Glen is renowned for its extremely low levels of unionism, electronics factories in South Wales are much more likely to be organised. There are differences between the industrial structures, to be sure, but there are more similarities, and the contrast in levels of unionism is instructive since it indicates that there is little that is inevitable. Although the old heartlands (in terms of location, sector and segment of the workforce) now seem in retrospect to have provided good conditions for organising, they did have to be built up in the first place.

NOTE

[i] This and the following two sections are based on a previous article by Doreen Massey and Nicholas Miles (1984).

REFERENCES

Beynon, H. (ed) (1985) *Digging Deeper: Issues in the Miners' Strike*, London: Verso.
Central Statistical Office (1987) *Social Trends*, London: HMSO.
Department of Employment (1988) *Employment Gazette*, April.
Financial Times (1988) 'Single union car plant has AEU membership of 7%', 26 April.

Gallie, D. (1987) 'Patterns of similarity and diversity in British urban labour markets: trade union allegiance and decline', paper presented to the Sixth Urban Change and Conflict Conference, University of Kent, Canterbury, 20–23 September.

Incomes Data Services (IDS) (1987) *IDS Report 505*, London: IDS.

Independent, The (1988) 'Shop staff present crucial challenge', 3 May, p. 5.

Kelly, J. (1987) *Labour and the Unions*, London: Verso.

Lane, T. (1982) 'The unions: caught on an ebb tide', *Marxism Today*, September, pp.6–13.

Massey, D. and Miles, N. (1984) 'Mapping out the unions', *Marxism Today*, May, pp.19–22.

Morgan, K. and Sayer, A. (1984) 'A modern industry in a mature region: the remaking of management-labour relations', *Urban and Regional Studies Working Paper 39*, University of Sussex.

Sayer, A. (1986) 'New developments in manufacturing: the "just-in-time" system', *Capital and Class*, 30, pp.43–72.

PART II

PLACE

RECONCEPTUALIZING PLACE: DOREEN MASSEY ON RELATIONAL GEOGRAPHICAL PROCESSES

Rebecca Lave, Brett Christophers, Marion Werner and Jamie Peck

With nationalist, anti-immigrant, and white supremacist politics again on the rise, Massey's writing from the 1990s and early 2000s is strikingly, almost painfully relevant today. Her distinctively geographic entrance point into these debates was through re-envisioning place. In Massey's analysis, place is not a static, bounded, homogenous territory to be defended against incursion, but instead the interconnected product of relations stretching across multiple scales, interlinking us in relations of tension and solidarity. In the chapters in this section, Massey builds on this conceptualization of place as process (Chapter 9) to reframe the geographical roots of identity (Chapter 10), re-envision the bases of political solidarity (Chapter 8), examine the contested boundaries between home and work (Chapter 11), redirect the left's critique of globalization (Chapter 12), and propose a powerful re-imagining of citizenship and the importance of 'care at a distance' (Chapter 13).

Massey's re-envisioning of place as a constellation of social, economic, and cultural relations stretched across space, some restrictive and some enabling, is common to all the chapters in this section, but is theorized most explicitly in Chapters 9 and 10: "Power-geometry and a progressive sense of place" and "A place called home?". As she conceptualizes it, the uniqueness of a particular place comes not from a bounded, internally nurtured, singular identity, but from the specificity of its linkages to other places and scales as they accumulate and interact over time. Individual places are extraverted: linked to the wider world and knit together out of multiple identities (Chapter 10). The global, national, and local scales which can seem so distinct, she argues, are in fact shaped and co-constituted not only by flows and interconnections of capital and labour, but also of meaning, culture and ideas. Crucially, different individuals, groups, and places have very different relations to these interconnections. Some create them, some are stuck with them; some benefit from them in ways that weaken others' ability to do so (Chapter 9).

One of Massey's key points in these chapters is that the uniqueness of place stems not from homogeneity, but from multiplicity and heterogeneity. Acknowledging differences along axes of race, class, gender, and colonial history is one of the most characteristic aspects of her work. But so too is the recognition of solidarities that can bridge those differences via linked oppressions and shared geographies (Chapter 8). For Massey, place is, "one of the arenas where people (of all ages) learn to negotiate with others – to learn to form this thing called society" (Chapter 13: 199). Yet she also consistently points out the real contradictions that complicate these negotiations. The way forward, she argues, is not to paper over differences but to acknowledge and "fac[e] up to them", as no genuine alliance can be built through simple addition of interests (Chapter 8: 146). Put differently, in Massey's work we see a clear-eyed, consistent recognition that there are no linkages without tensions. Differences matter. But those differences can serve to broaden the base of solidarity, rather than necessarily undermining it, if they are confronted.

This simultaneous attention to difference and interconnection is clearly visible in her work at a variety of scales, from her microscale analysis of the construction of masculinity and home/work boundaries in the British high-tech sector (Chapter 11), to her turn in the early 2000s to the politics of globalization (Chapters 12 and 13). In "Masculinity, dualisms and high technology" (Chapter 11), Massey analyzes the mutually reinforcing, inherently gendered dualisms that structure labour in high-tech economies, pointing out that the path to effective resistance is not reinforcing one pole of the dualism (as in the attempts of some individual men to defend home from the incursions of work), but in collective action to relink the poles and deconstruct these patriarchal dichotomies.

In a similar move at a far larger scale, Massey argues that local/global dichotomies are deeply unhelpful for critiquing globalization in two succinctly and accessibly argued pieces for popular audiences: "The geography of power," initially published in *Red Pepper* (Chapter 12), and in "Globalisation: what does it mean for geography?" written for the British Geographical Association, which serves primary and secondary school geography instructors in the UK (Chapter 13). In the first of these short chapters, Massey argues that the left's dualistic critique of globalization must change to reflect the deep interconnections between local and global scales, and the fact that there is nothing inherently progressive or repressive about either. In the second, she eloquently encapsulates this period of her work and her arguments about place, globalization, and the role of geography as a field. The key here is her call for us to take responsibility not simply for the historical relations, such as colonialism and slavery, that make us what we are, but also for the geographical relations that shape the conditions of our lives.

Taken together, the chapters in this section illustrate a number of central characteristics of Massey's thought, including her transformative critique of economism, her consistent intertwining of intellectual and political work, and the striking compassion that accompanied all of this work.

One of the many ways in which Massey's approach foreshadowed wider transformations in the field was her refusal, as an economic geographer, to accept narrowly economistic explanations. Nothing in these chapters can be explained by capitalism alone; ethnicity, gender, histories of colonialism, flows of ideas all powerfully shape the world we live in and how we experience it. As she succinctly puts it in Chapter 9 (150), "there is a lot more determining how we experience space than what 'capital' gets up to". Thus she has little patience with analyses that limit materialist analysis to economics and capitalist class relations, a theme that can be found in Parts 1 and 3 as well.

Another theme of Massey's work clearly illustrated in this section is the inseparability of intellectual and political work. The conjoined political and intellectual impact of her work comes across on a number of different registers. Most obviously, Massey focused on topics with clear and ongoing political relevance, from the miners' strike (Chapter 8) to the World Trade Organization protests (Chapter 12), from gendered divisions of labour (Chapter 11) to anti-immigrant movements (explicitly in Chapter 13, and powerfully implicit in Chapters 9 and 10). More unusually, particularly for a critical human geographer, Massey emphasized the political impacts of academic prose and its accessibility (or more accurately, its *inaccessibility*) to popular audiences (Chapters 10 and 15). She argued that if we wish to substantively change the world, our analyses must be intelligible outside of academia. And she very much walked that talk, writing clearly and eloquently, and regularly reaching outside of academic venues entirely (as in Chapters 12 and 13).

The third long-term theme of Massey's writing illustrated in this section is her striking combination of clear-eyed critique and compassion. Massey was totally unwilling to let us (or herself) off the hook for the ferocious inequalities of our world, but she had enormous sympathy for how we all got on that hook in the first place, and for the struggle to remove ourselves from it. She was willing to make the uncomfortable point that her white male comrades' discomfort with postmodernity and time-space compression was a reflection of their own class and gender privilege (Chapters 9, 10 and 15). But she was equally willing to point out her own culpability, and the ways in which "our relative mobility and power over mobility and communication entrenches the spatial imprisonment of other groups" (Chapter 9: 152). Moral and conceptual critiques are clearly linked in all of the chapters in this section (and indeed across Massey's career). And yet those critiques both highlight, and are driven by, the notable breadth of Massey's compassion. Her clear sense of kinship and solidarity with others extends globally to immigrants stuck in interrogation rooms at Heathrow, women fetching water in rural Africa, residents of favelas in Rio, white male tech workers striving to participate more equally in reproductive labour, and unemployed coal miners, among many others. This compassion is consistently expressed through, or perhaps derived from, recognition of connections across space and place, the ties that bind the global and the local. As Massey noted, her analyses were always deeply geographic because this is ultimately the dimension of coexistence, in the sense that thinking spatially means thinking of the relations with others, beyond ourselves (Chapter 12).

As we attempt to intervene in today's perilous politics, to find our own mixture of critique and compassion, Massey's call for a geography of care is enduringly relevant: "Could we not consider a different geography of care and responsibility? We might think of it as an ethics, a politics, of connectivity rather than of nested territories. Specifically we could open up a bit more *the question of (the possibility of) responsibility and care at a distance*" (Chapter 13: 201).

CHAPTER 8

BEYOND THE COALFIELDS: THE WORK OF THE MINERS' SUPPORT GROUPS (1985)

with Hilary Wainwright

The miners' strike seems to epitomize those aspects of the labour movement and class politics that certain interpreters have found 'old fashioned', sectional and, by implication, bankrupt. Male manual workers, the old working class with a vengeance, fighting to save jobs in what is officially described as a declining industry, stateowned and located in isolated declining regions. And yet around this struggle a massive support movement has grown up – almost unreported – with as broad a social and geographical base as any post-war radical political movement.

THE COALFIELDS

The social structure of the mining communities reflects the industry which is their livelihood: lack of white-collar jobs, their proletarian nature, the overwhelming dominance of male, manual labour. The regions are distinctive in other ways too. They are predominantly white; they are socially conservative; traditional sexual divisions of labour – woman as homemaker, man as bread-winner – have been deeply ingrained and only recently begun to break down.

Their politics have been workplace-based. They are the fiefdoms of one of the most important unions in labour movement history, symbolizing – at least for men – the old strengths of a solidarity born of mutual dependence at work, and the reliance of a whole community on a single industry. The themes of discipline and collectivism run deep and strong in the political atmosphere. These are regions owned, regulated, fed and watered by the central state. The industry is nationalized, high proportions of the inhabitants live on state subsidies, and for an alternative to work in the pit they appeal to state regional policy. They have voted Labour for years, through thick and (mainly) thin. And the local state, for ages too, has been in the hands of the Labour Party right wing. They are the heartlands of labourism. What this means is that the strike is taking place in some of the most self-enclosed and socially homogeneous regions of the country. And indeed that geography is part of the rationale and the character of the strike. The one-to-one relationship between community and coal, at least for male employment, has been one of the bases of its solidarity. Levels of militancy have been in part related to dependence on the industry (this, it should be noted in passing, is a nice boomerang of that 1950s 'anti-regional policy' of keeping alternative employment for men out of the coalfields). And that dependence on a single industry has also been one of the bases for the struggle going beyond the workplace, to become an issue of community survival. Again there is some kind of relationship: it is the coalfields most affected by the reconstruction of the 1950s and 1960s, for instance by new workers moving in from other areas, and therefore the more recently constituted communities, which have been least solid in the strike. Geographical coherence therefore has been an element of strength but its corollary – geographical separation – has potentially been an isolating factor.

Put these social and geographical characteristics together and the strike could easily be seen as an old politics, slogging away in its own redoubts, far away from where 'the rest of us' live. And indeed, several commentators on the left (as well as the right) have seen it in those terms. The last gasp of the old labour movement, in its decaying heartlands, isolated, sectional, macho, and with little resonance beyond its regions, its unions, and – of course – what they call the 'hard left'.

SUPPORT FROM ELSEWHERE

What has actually happened has been quite different. One of the most stunning aspects of the strike has been that in many ways it has not remained locked within those characterizations. With trade union leadership at sixes and sevens, their creaking structures, and their lack of credibility, unable to lead any response, and with party political leadership embarrassed by the whole affair – in spite of, maybe because of, all this heavy-footed inertia – there has sprung up a completely different way of organizing support, indeed an expansion of what the concept of support means. 'The grass roots', people of all sorts, previously politically active and not, have just got on with it. Often in the most unexpected ways and places, support networks have been organized, fundraising events launched, and distribution systems established.

THE CITIES

Some of the strongest support has come from Labour's other base – and Thatcher's other opposition – the big cities. What the cities share with the coalfields – apart from Labour MPs – is industrial decline and the feeling that they have been singled out for attack. The Prime Minister knows the geographical bases of her enemies. In the cities, in addition to economic devastation, the assault comes in the form of rate-capping and the proposed abolition of the GLC [Greater London Council] and the Metropolitan Counties.

In other ways, however, the cities and the coalfield regions are very different from each other. In the cities there is generally a great mix of industries, including services, and a variety of jobs. Many of those in work are on low pay, in casual occupations, working in small firms, and in many areas levels of unionization are low. There is a different kind of physical dereliction. In the middle of all this lives an enormously diverse population; in many cities ethnic minorities, gay and lesbian communities, women's groups and 'alternative' networks of many kinds form an important element. The tradeunion movement is also different from that in the coalfields. Here its very industrial variety has been the basis for a tradition of local links and networks. Public sector and white-collar unions are especially important.

All this in recent years has begun to spawn a politics quite distinct from coalfield labourism. It is often anarchistic, socially adventurous, with a commitment to politics outside the work-place as well as within. It is the radical, as opposed to the labourist, end of the labour movement – if you like; a different kind of trade unionism in uneasy combination with an alliance of the dispossessed.

And yet, in spite of these contrasts, the support from the cities has been massive. On Merseyside there are fourteen support groups, which between them have sent off £1 million so far (a *million* pounds – from a city itself in desperate poverty), and that's not including work-place collections, and new groups are still being formed. There are normally fifty to sixty miners out in the city centre. From Birmingham support goes to South Wales, and also to other more local coalfields. From London it has gone to Kent, South Wales, Staffordshire and the North East; individual boroughs and support groups of various sorts have twinning arrangements with pits in many different coalfields. There are people with buckets, collections of food, on high streets everywhere, an anarchy of support groups and what appear to be a number of different attempts to form umbrella organizations.

[...]

The nature of the support from the cities reflects the characteristics of the conurbations, and grows out of a constellation of very varied connections people have made. Movingly, impressive support has come from those who

137

are themselves experiencing industrial dereliction. Liverpool 8 (Toxteth) was one of the first places on Merseyside to spawn a support group: 'it grew up literally overnight at the end of April'. The support group in Kirkby, a 1950s outer-city council area shattered by economic collapse, has achieved a fifty per cent response to its door-to-door collections. In London, people in the areas round the Royal Docks have set up the Durham-Docklands Miners' Support Group. On an early visit they took £750 with them to the North East. As they handed over the cheque to the Durham Women's group 'there were tears in their eyes – and ours'. The secretary of the Docklands Group recalls: 'It was the derelict villages that shook me. You could see how much they depended on the pit. The villages without a pit were dead. New factories had once been built but they've been closed long since. We know from the experience of what happened to us what will happen to them'. The Docklands, like the coalfields, was a community dependent on a single dominant economic focus. The slogan of the Durham-Docklands Miners' Support Group is 'Don't let the mines go the same way as the docks'.

Support comes, too, from the trade unions in the cities. In Liverpool although some of the work-place collections seem to have been slower to build up momentum there are now contributions from most factories. The body plant at Ford, Halewood gets about £1,000 every fortnight and the PTA plant between £900 and £1,300 every week. The collections are for different, specific needs each time, so people know how they are helping. In London a vast variety of branches, chapels and work-place communities have regular collections, have adopted pits, and organize special appeals and events. Support has been especially strong in Fleet Street, Inner London local authorities, the Civil Service, hospitals and schools.

Perhaps the most notable of all has been the support from marginalized and oppressed groups. The Labour party women's section is central to the organisation of support in Merseyside. AfroCaribbean groups, Cypriot groups, the Asian community and Turkish people have contributed and organized support. [...] On Merseyside it's unemployed people who keep the co-ordinating centre going for the support groups. And centres for the unemployed are often the physical base for the support organizations. In Southampton, Cardiff, Manchester, York, Glasgow and Edinburgh there are 'Lesbians and Gays Support the Miners' groups. [...]

And finally the left-wing local authorities themselves play a part, though necessarily circumscribed by red (i.e. blue) tape. Both City and County Councils are part of Merseyside's Trade Union Labour Party Campaign Committee, a central part of the support activity. In London Ken Livingstone chairs the 'Mineworkers' Defence Committee' set up to co-ordinate support from the different political groups, and in Camden and Islington women from Kent were given mayoral receptions. [...]

THATCHERLAND

Most unexpected of all has been the support which has come from the outer-metropolitan and more rural stretches of south and east England. Electorally this has been Thatcher's strongest base [...] It is not an area without its problems. Here too older manufacturing industry is in decline (the railways at Swindon for example), and unskilled school leavers have little to look forward to other than unemployment or a job at a routine repetitive end of a service industry (insurance perhaps), or one of the much vaunted high-tech growth industries. But the dominant image at least is affluence, confidence, prosperity. Unemployment is below the national average, both jobs and people are moving into the area, and there are high proportions of the new middle class and their social accoutrements – the gin-and-Jaguar belt.

Much has been made in recent political speeches about the increasing gap between North and South. It is a political and ideological divide as well as an economic one. And yet, during this strike, thousands of people from such unlikely sounding places as Borehamwood (Cecil Parkinson's seat) and Rottingdean not only contributed to the Christmas Appeal for the miners and their families, but also wrote letters saying why, expressing their support, and urging the miners to go on. St Albans and Wivenhoe have become renowned, through media coverage, for their organization, activity and generosity. It would be wrong to pretend that this stretch of the country had suddenly turned radical. The very high proportion of Christmas letters which came from Thatcher country may well have been precisely a result of the relative lack of more organized campaigning in such areas. Contributors to the Appeal expressed a strong desire to dissociate themselves from the popular image of satisfied southerners: 'Even in rural Somerset there is support and admiration for *our* miners' stated one.

[...]

But support has not been confined to donating money and writing letters. There has also been, even in these parts of the country, the development of active support groups with direct involvement in the strike. Two examples may help to illustrate what is happening.

Cambridge is one of the hearts of high-tech land. It is set in a basically Tory area, but the town has a hung council and Labour local control (which has had its advantages – such as getting a licence for collecting). The university has always resisted the development of manufacturing industry, so there is no major manual trade-union base. Its Labour Party is large – the result, perhaps of the social nature of the town – for the bulk of the membership comes from the white-collar and intellectual sections, those who live in the terraced houses of the centre, rather than from the small outer-council estates, though the latter do vote solidly Labour. [...] Cambridge has twinned with Blidworth and Rainworth, two pit villages in Nottinghamshire where only a minority came out on strike. [...]

Milton Keynes is a very different bit of the British sunbelt. Not ancient academic spires, but Britain's biggest new town. Like most new towns Milton Keynes shares one thing with Cambridge – the lack of a major tradition of manual-labour trade unionism. When they began the support group the organizers reflected on this and were cautious about how much support they would raise – 'It's a strange place Milton Keynes, it's not like an old labour movement area. It's not like Liverpool and places ... it's bred into them in Liverpool'. In the event, a major organization has been established, drawing together all kinds of local groups and individuals including 'lots of people completely new to politics'. Milton Keynes Miners' Support Group began through the trades council and is based in the Unemployed Workers' Centre. Between 150 and 200 people are associated with it, not all coming to meetings, but available to provide meals, accommodation and help. People are there as individuals, but very important links have been established with Afro-Caribbean Club, the Sikh Society, the large local Peace Group and the Ecology Party. [...] Milton Keynes today supports South Derbyshire and contributes to Cannock, Staffs. [...]

All this activity, in the cities, in Thatcherland and throughout the country has been far more than simply giving aid to some distant struggle. It has had an integral relation to the strike. A typical comment, this one in fact from Liverpool, runs 'there is a constant flow of information about the strike ... people feel really involved in the strike ... it doesn't feel like charity. When miners arrive they are immediately put to work. They feel involved in the organization, part of the same movement, rather than the recipients of charity'. And in Milton Keynes there is a keen awareness that although one of the areas it supports has only a small minority out on strike, aid there is vital for the strike as a whole – 'those few strikers are vital. Keeping them able to stay out stops the NCB [National Coal Board] being able to say any area is back completely'. So all this organization and support is essential, and the people involved see that; they have a strategic sense of what they are involved in.

EXPLANATIONS

What has led such diverse groups of people to feel that this strike, however geographically and socially distant, concerns and involves them? There is no single explanation but there are several common themes. They crop up in letters sending donations, in conversations during street collections, in discussions about why a particular group is giving an unexpected amount of support.

RESONANCE

A recurring theme is the resonance – sometimes based on sympathy, sometimes on respect, on fond memories or past friendships and family connections – which the miners have with people of every region and nearly every social group. The letters to the national Christmas Appeal express this resonance most vividly.

Many letters recall experiences of the generosity of the miners and their families. A retired social worker writes: 'I worked in the coalfields for seventeen years. I know how quickly miners responded to the appeals for help from those who were less fortunate than themselves. They most certainly do not deserve the abuse that flows from those who know so little about them'. Two pensioners from Herne Bay remember: 'the wonderful friendship shown to us in Derbyshire. For me it was a lonely soldier during the war, training amongst strange people and far from home. For my wife it meant being offered a refuge for two very young children. We never forgot how our buckets of coal came to us after that'. [...]

A COMMON CAUSE AGAINST THATCHER

The pent-up hostility expressed towards Thatcher is overwhelming, whatever people's views on the strike itself. 'Anti-Scargill, anti-all violence but above all *anti-Thatcher*. Good luck' says, one Home Counties' contributor to the Christmas Appeal. 'Thank God for the NUM [National Union of Mineworkers], at least one union has the guts to stand up to her' writes a contributor from Hastings, expressing a view of many who feel that the NUM is taking on a common enemy. 'As a civil servant', another man wrote starkly, 'I feel that your cause is ours, if you fail we all fail'.

Street collectors found a similar sense of common cause. During a first collection in Milton Keynes an unemployed man with a family gave £10 after cashing his giro [benefit cheque]. 'You can't afford to give that much surely?' said the collector. 'I can't afford not to', was the response.
[...]

In Toxteth, Brixton, Chapeltown in Leeds and other inner-city areas where blacks are in a majority, an understanding of what it is like to live under police occupation lies behind the strong feelings of support. [...]

FINDING ALLIES

But the wholehearted and enthusiastic involvement of all kinds of women's groups, Labour Party women's sections, women's peace groups, and childcare campaigns, in the industrial action of a notoriously male-chauvinist union is not based just on antiThatcherism. Their involvement has been inspired by the power and confidence of the women in the mining communities.

The response of the Enfield women's peace group in London sums it up: 'We were inspired by the women. We wanted to show them that they weren't alone, that we need each other. Our links with the women in Cannock have helped to overcome our isolation and sense of powerlessness'. The involvement of the women had helped people outside the coalfields to understand the community issues at stake.

The people who set up the Durham-Docklands support group illustrate this. Eddie Corbett explains: 'Before I met the women (from Durham) I'd felt sympathetic to the miners but I didn't really want to be involved. I saw them collecting outside tube stations and thought of them just as trade unionists. After hearing the women and their stories of hardship and the police I understood it was families and communities at stake.' It was then that he and the other[s] made the connection between their fight for democratic control over their community against a non-elected government quango, the London Docklands Development Corporation and the miners' defence of their communities against the government-appointed NCB. 'They are fighting the same regime, the same undemocratic process as we are.'
[...]

POLITICAL CATALYSTS

There are some elements, then, of an explanation for the extraordinary widespread support which exists for the miners, behind the media picture of an isolated and sectorial strike. But an adequate explanation must include the driving forces behind the initial formation of the larger support groups. In most cases, town or city-wide support groups have been initiated by trades councils or local Labour Parties, with socialists outside the Labour Party providing important support. The impetus to create support groups was more than trade-union solidarity. Memories of the 1972 and 1974 miners' strikes provide a powerful image, a source of great expectations. When the miners take action, governments fall. At the beginning there was a strong sense of the miners' power to break Thatcher's grip. It was not that people wanted to leave it to the miners; it was rather a feeling that Thatcher would find it difficult if another front was opened up, especially in the coalfields. In the cities, campaigning alliances were already forming to fight abolition [of the metropolitan councils] and rate-capping [measures to restrict the spending of local councils]. There was a feeling that at last a trade-union battalion, the most militant, had gone into action. As the strike developed and the other big battalions held back, not so big now, as the women became an organized force and the strike increasingly became a strike about communities, the significance of the support groups became clearer. It seemed increasingly that their work was crucial to the miners' power and their chances of success. Personal links and the adoption of pits created a momentum of their own. A new, or at least more confident, do it yourself politics flourished out of necessity.

FORMS OF ORGANIZATION

That phrase 'out of necessity' comes up again and again as people explain the work of their support groups. It helps to explain the form that the support movement takes. Out of necessity, the support movement has started from existing organizations and resources. Picking up whatever in the old structures suited their urgent purpose. They grew from whatever organizations could be most rapidly geared into action, from networks of friends, to tightly organized NGA [National Graphical Association] chapels. They used whatever resources were available from church halls to county halls, from the Labour Party's duplicator [copy machine] to the WRP's [Workers Revolutionary Party] newsletter. Out of necessity the initial organizations have moved outwards to extend support.
[...]

CO-ORDINATION

In most towns and cities there are miners' support groups that play a co-ordinating role, organizing big functions, rallies, concerts, etc. In the larger cities the co-ordinating meetings also play an important role in sorting out some of the problems which arise within groups, between groups and in relations with strike centres. As we have already said these groups have usually been initiated through the local Labour Party or trades councils. All left parties are normally involved, though the Socialist Workers Party was a latecomer to the support groups, and initially chose its own forms of direct support for the strikers. Everyone comments on the unique degree of cooperation between political groups.
[...]

TWINNING AND THE DISTRIBUTION OF FOOD

Connections of personal friendship, political commitment, and material sustenance between the support groups and the pits are the energy supply of the support movement as much as the life-blood of the strike.

Take Cambridge for instance. They've organized holidays for miners' families; there was a massive exercise at Christmas with, amongst much else, an individually chosen present and collection of stocking-fillers for each child (over two hundred of them); there's at least one trip a week from Cambridge to Notts, and there have been long and short visits, both ways. 'We've had speakers down from them and spoken ourselves up there. We've picketed, had women pickets, worked in the kitchens, gone to the Cash and Carry, looked after the children, joined in parties, pub sessions and gigs'.
[...]

PREACHING TO THE UNCONVERTED

Just as groups have improvised to find the best way of distributing the support, so they have tried all kinds of ingenious ways of collecting funds and putting across their arguments. Individuals have been buying and selling British Telecom shares and sending the proceeds to the Christmas Appeal. Greenham Women have marched from pit heads to nuclear power stations, giving out leaflets and holding meetings on the way to make the connection between the case against nuclear power and the miners' demands. The most impressive thing about this aspect of the work of the support groups is the emphasis on reaching out to the uncommitted. It is as if all the heart-searching about the left being stuck in a ghetto, shop-floor leaders being out of touch with their members and so on, has produced an almost evangelical commitment to win support on the street, in the pubs, on the shop floor and in door to door collections. In Kirkby for instance the support group has leafletted each house at least three times and visited at least once. Few election campaigns could better that! Its political importance is that arguments are reaching people, independently of the media.

The forms of organization in the support movement, and in the mining communities are an extraordinary combination of traditional labour-movement structures with the open, campaigning styles of CND [Campaign for Nuclear Disarmament] and the women's movement. The women in the mining communities have played perhaps a leading role in inspiring the support movement. And their relationship with the NUM nationally as well as locally sets the example for this combination. In a sense their organization and its importance is sustaining the strike and extending support has given a new legitimacy to the demands of women outside the coalfields for real power within labourmovement organizations. [...]

CONCLUSIONS

Whatever the outcome of the strike, labour movement politics will never be the same again. There will no doubt be attempts to block, if not stamp out, the new initiatives that cut across so many traditional procedures and hierarchies. It will be a struggle to consolidate and develop the improvised democracy, produced inside the coalfields and beyond, by the strike.

But the pressures to continue the process of change will be strong. Through the strike and the support movement many people new to political involvement have become experienced, effective speakers, expert organizers and confident socialists. A lot has been learned. Amongst these new activities a gut anti-Thatcherism has begun to be more precisely articulated to win a positive belief in another way of organizing society.

This is partly the result of learning about the problems of other groups. Miners, for instance, learned through their visits to the cities of the problems of racism. As one Nottingham miner put it 'I'd never been racist, I don't think, but I'd never really understood it before.' Support groups in the rural south learnt from the solidarity and collectivism of the mining areas, from 'the steadfastness and sheer courage up there,' as one of the Cambridge group told us. Travelling and exchange visits across the country are an important source of power. Usually it is only the leadership that has an overview of what is going on. Moreover these visits help create unity at the base, across the old structures. They have also created connections between different, previously quite separate, sections of the working class; cleaners fighting privatization in London speaking on one platform at miners' meetings, miners from Nottingham joining the picket line at Addenbrooks Hospital in Cambridge; miners promising to join the people of Docklands in action to stop a businessmen's airport. Finally, there has been a learning of an immensely practical sort; learning to manage thousands of pounds on behalf of hundreds of people; facing up to the real problems of building an alternative welfare system, a system of distribution according to need. Such experience leaves more than memory.

The support groups we have talked to in most detail already have plans for the future. In Cambridge, they want to find a way of consolidating the network into a more permanent organization after the strike is over. In Liverpool they feel they have established a strong organization which they will need again and won't let collapse. In Milton Keynes they are already planning a 'trade-union month' as part of an attempt to strengthen the unions there.

One of the most politically decisive experiences of many who have been part of the support movement is that they have tried the traditional hierarchies and leadership of the labour movement and found them severely wanting. The lack of political leadership has been most important. It has been the failure of some of the Labour Party's Parliamentary leaders to get across the economic and social arguments for the mining communities which has created the vacuum that the support groups are trying to fill. Even now the parliamentary leadership seems to be making little attempt to give effective national backing to the support movement or even draw media attention to its size and scope.

But instead of wasting time passing resolutions calling on the leadership to do the things that will never materialize, people in the localities have, on the whole, just got on with it. [...]

In much of their work many support groups illustrate in practice the kind of movement we need to build in order to achieve socialism: A commitment to change through building up democratic power at the base, in the factories and in the communities; a breaking down of the traditional, inhibiting boundary between politics and trade unionism; a sense of local strength and identity which at the same time is not parochial; a commitment to a non-sectarian but principled form of unity, in which different political tendencies are respected and work together; an emphasis on reaching out, a confidence that radical demands can be popular if they are argued for.

It would be wrong to pretend that all this has happened without problems. In all this activity there have of course been tensions; tensions between different political perspectives and groups, conflicts between the new-found strength of women and the powerbases previously established as male, suspicions of the white left on the part of some black groups. But constructing links between groups, between areas, between issues can never be achieved without tensions. There are real contradictions between the multiple issues which have become linked to the support network during the strike and no genuine democratic 'alliances' could ever be built without recognizing and facing up to them. In this context the strength of the support networks is precisely that 'alliances' have been built in the course of real, day-to-day, political action. These are not 'links' established simply by writing out lists of policies, nor are they a 'common programme' negotiated between party leaders.

We are not claiming the world. But nonetheless something radically different has emerged out of a movement in support of what was seen as an 'old' struggle. Many thought this impossible. They have argued that the left must move with the times – that 'old-fashioned' class struggles are doomed to isolation, without resonance or relevance to present-day socialist policies. Behind this argument is an equation of class politics, on the one hand, and the existing institutions of the labour movement on the other. To make such an equation leads to an incorrect assessment of the political choice before us, as one between industrial muscle and the new social movements. The existing institutions of labour *are* old fashioned and sectional. But what the miners' strike has shown is that these institutions can be superseded and challenged without abandoning class politics. It has shown that it is not a question of *either* industrial action *or* the new social movements, nor is it one of just adding the two together. What is important is a recognition of a mutual dependence and a new openness to influence, of the one upon the other. What this strike has demonstrated is a different direction for class politics. New institutions can be built through which 'class politics' can be seen as more than simply industrial militancy plus parliamentary representation. [...]

CHAPTER 9

POWER-GEOMETRY AND A PROGRESSIVE
SENSE OF PLACE (1993)

TIME-SPACE COMPRESSION AND THE GEOMETRIES OF POWER

Much of what is written about space, place and postmodern times emphasizes a new phase in what Marx once called 'the annihilation of space by
time'. The process is argued, or more usually asserted, to have gained a new
momentum, to have reached a new stage. It is a phenomenon which Harvey
(1989) has termed 'time-space compression'. And the general acceptance that
something of the sort is going on is marked by the almost obligatory use in
the literature of terms and phrases such as speed-up, global village, overcoming spatial barriers, the disruption of horizons and so forth.

Yet the concept of time-space compression remains curiously unexamined. In particular, it is a concept which often remains without much social
content, or with only a very restricted, one-sided, social content. There are
many aspects to this. One is, of course, the question of to what extent its
current characterization represents very much a Western, colonizer's view.
The sense of dislocation which so many writers on the subject apparently
feel at the sight of a once well-known local street now lined with a succession of cultural imports – the pizzeria, the kebab house, the branch of
the middle-eastern bank – must have been felt for centuries, though from a
very different point of view, by colonized peoples all over the world as they
watched the importation of, maybe even used, the products of, first, European
colonization, maybe British (from new forms of transport to liver salts and
custard powder); later US products, as they learned to eat wheat instead of
rice or corn, to drink Coca-Cola, just as today we try out enchiladas.

But there are just two points which it seems particularly important to
raise in the current context. The first concerns causality. Time-space compression is a term which refers to movement and communication across

149

space. It is a phenomenon which implies the geographical stretching-out of social relations (referred to by Giddens (1984) as time-space distanciation), and to our experience of all this. However, those who argue that we are currently undergoing a new phase of accelerated time-space compression usually do so from a very particular view of its determination. For Jameson and for Harvey these things are determined overwhelmingly by the actions of capital (Jameson 1984; Harvey 1989). For Harvey it is, in his own terms, time space and money which make the world go round, and us go round (or not) the world. It is capitalism and its developments which are argued to determine our understanding and our experience of space. This is, however, clearly insufficient. There are many other things that clearly influence that experience, for instance, ethnicity and gender. The degree to which we can move between countries, or walk about the streets at night, or take public transport, or venture out of hotels in foreign cities, is not influenced simply by 'capital' [...] [but also by a] complex mix of colonialism, ex-colonialism, racism, changing gender relations, and relative wealth. Harvey's simple resort to 'money' alone could not begin to get to grips with the issue. (Incidentally, of course, the example also indicates that 'time-space compression' has not been happening for everyone in all spheres of activity.) In other words, and simply put, there is a lot more determining how we experience space than what 'capital' gets up to. Most of the arguments so far around time-space compression do not recognize this. Moreover, to argue for this greater complexity is not in any way to be anti-materialist, it is simply not to reduce materialism to economism.

The second point about the inadequacy of the notion of time-space compression as it is currently used is that it needs differentiating socially. This is not just a moral or political point about inequality, although that would be sufficient reason to mention it: it is also a conceptual point. Imagine for a moment that you are on a satellite, further out and beyond all actual satellites; you can see 'planet earth' from a distance and, rare for someone with only peaceful intentions, you are equipped with the kind of technology that allows you to see the colours of people's eyes and the number on their number-plates. You can see all the movement and tune-in to all the communication that is going on. Furthest out are the satellites, then aeroplanes, the long haul between London and Tokyo and the hop from San Salvador to Guatemala City. Some of this is people moving, some of it is physical trade, some is media broadcasting. There are faxes, e-mail, film-distribution networks, financial flows and transactions. Look in closer and there are ships and trains, steam trains slogging laboriously up hills somewhere in Asia. Look in closer still and there are lorries and cars and buses and on down further and somewhere in sub-Saharan Africa there's a woman on foot who still spends hours a day collecting water.

Now, I want to make one simple point here, and that is about what one might call the *power-geometry* of it all; the power-geometry of time-space compression. For different social groups and different individuals are placed in very distinct ways in relation to these flows and interconnections. This point concerns not merely the issue of who moves and who doesn't, although that is an important element of it; it is also about power in relation *to* the flows and the movement. Different social groups have distinct relationships to this anyway-differentiated mobility: some are more in charge of it than others; some initiate flows and movement, others don't; some are more on the receiving end of it than others; some are effectively imprisoned by it.

In a sense, at the end of all the spectra are those who are both doing the moving and the communicating and who are in some way in a position of control in relation to it. These are the jet-setters, the ones sending and receiving the faxes and the e-mail, holding the international conference calls, the ones distributing the films, controlling the news, organizing the investments and the international currency transactions. These are the groups who are really, in a sense, in charge of time-space compression; who can effectively use it and turn it to advantage; whose power and influence it very definitely increases. On its more prosaic fringes this group probably includes a fair number of Western academics.

But there are groups who, although doing a lot of physical moving, are not 'in charge' of the process in the same way. The refugees from El Salvador or Guatemala and the undocumented migrant workers from Michoacán in Mexico crowding into Tijuana to make perhaps a fatal dash for it across the border into the USA to grab a chance of a new life. Here the experience of movement, and indeed of a confusing plurality of cultures, is very different. And there are those from India, Pakistan, Bangladesh and the Caribbean, who come halfway round the world only to get held up in an interrogation room at Heathrow.

Or again, there are those who are simply on the receiving end of time-space compression. The pensioner in a bedsit in any inner city in this country, eating British working-class-style fish and chips from a Chinese take-away, watching a US film on a Japanese television, and not daring to go out after dark. And anyway, the public transport's been cut.

Or – one final example to illustrate a different kind of complexity – there are the people who live in the favelas of Rio; who know global football like the back of their hand, and have produced some of its players; who have contributed massively to global music; who gave us the samba and produced the lambada that everyone was dancing to a few years ago in the clubs of Paris and London; and who have never, or hardly ever, been to downtown Rio. At one level they have been tremendous contributors to what we call time-space compression; and at another level they are imprisoned in it.

This is, in other words, a highly complex social differentiation. There is the dimension of the degree of movement and communication, but also the dimensions of control and of initiation. The ways in which people are inserted into and placed within 'time-space compression' are highly complicated and extremely varied. It is necessary to think through with a bit more conceptual depth, a bit more analytical rigour, quite how these positions are differentiated. Moreover, recognition of this complexity raises the important issue of *which* condition of postmodernity we are talking about – *whose* condition of postmodernity?

More immediately, two points arise from these considerations. The first raises more directly questions of politics. If time-space compression can be imagined in that more socially formed, socially evaluative and differentiated way, then there may be the possibility of developing a politics of mobility and access. For it does seem that mobility and control over mobility both reflect and reinforce power. It is not simply a question of unequal distribution, that some people move more than others, some have more control than others. It is that the mobility and control of some groups can actively weaken other people. Differential mobility can weaken the leverage of the already weak. The time-space compression of some groups can undermine the power of others. This is well established and often noted in the relationship between capital and labour. Capital's ability to roam the world further strengthens it in relation to relatively immobile workers, enables it to play off the plant at Genk against the plant at Halewood. It also strengthens its hand against struggling local economies the world over as they compete for the favour of some investment. But also, every time someone uses a car, and thereby increases their personal mobility, they reduce both the social rationale and the financial viability of the public transport system – and thereby also potentially reduce the mobility of those who rely on that system. Every time you drive to that out-of-town shopping centre you contribute to the rising prices, even hasten the demise, of the corner shop. And the 'time-space compression' which is involved in producing and reproducing the daily lives of the comfortably-off in first-world societies – not just their own travel but the resources they draw on, from all over the world, to feed their lives – may entail environmental consequences, or hit constraints, that will limit the lives of others before their own. We need to ask, in other words, whether our relative mobility and power over mobility and communication entrenches the spatial imprisonment of other groups.

A politics of mobility might range over issues as broad as wheelchair access, reclaiming the night and the streets of cities for women and for older people, through issues of international migration, to the whole gamut of transport policy itself. Conceptualizing space, mobility and access in a more socially imaginative way, and abandoning easy and excited notions of generalized and undifferentiated time-space compression, might enable us to confront some of these issues rather more inventively.

The second point is simply a question. Why is it that for so many of the academics who write about time-space compression, who are in relative control of their new mobility and means of communication, who jet off to (or from) Los Angeles to give a paper on it, does it generate such feelings of insecurity? Harvey (1989), for instance, constantly writes of vulnerability, insecurity and the unsettling impact of time-space compression. This question is important less in itself than because, as will be argued in the next part of this chapter, it seems also to have generated in them, as a counter to all this insecurity, a very particular (and unprogressive) sense of place.

A PROGRESSIVE SENSE OF PLACE

Those writers who interpret the current phase of time-space compression as primarily generating insecurity also frequently go on to argue that, in the middle of all this flux, one desperately needs a bit of peace and quiet; and 'place' is posed as a source of stability and an unproblematical identity. In that guise, place and the spatially local are rejected by these writers as almost necessarily reactionary. Space/place is characterized, after Heidegger, as Being; and, as such, as a diversion from the progressive dimension of Time as Becoming (see Harvey (1989); and Massey (1991) for a critique of this position).

There are a number of serious inadequacies in this argument, ranging from the question of why it is assumed that time-space compression will produce insecurity, through the need to face up to – rather than simply deny – people's need for attachment of some sort, whether through place or anything else. It is also problematical that so often this debate, as in the case of Harvey, starts off from Heidegger, for if it had not started off from there, perhaps it would never have found itself in this conceptual tangle in the first place.

None the less, it is certainly the case that there is at the moment a recrudescence of some problematical senses of place, from reactionary nationalisms to competitive localisms, to sanitized, introverted obsessions with 'heritage'. Instead of refusing to deal with this, however, it is necessary to recognize it and to try to understand what it represents. Perhaps it is most important to think through what might be an adequately progressive sense of place, one which would fit in with the current global-local times and the feelings and relations they give rise to, and one which would be useful in what are, after all, our often inevitably place-based political struggles. The question is how to hold on to that notion of spatial difference, of uniqueness, even of rootedness if people want that, without it being reactionary.

There are a number of distinct ways in which the notion of place which is derived from Heidegger is problematical. One is the idea that places have single essential identities. Another is the idea that the identity of place – the sense of place – is constructed out of an introverted, inward-looking history based on delving into the past for internalized origins. [...]

Another problem with the conception of place which derives from Heidegger is that it seems to require the drawing of boundaries. Geographers have long been exercised by the problem of defining regions, and this question of 'definition' has almost always been reduced to drawing lines around a place. I remember some of my most painful times as a geographer have been spent unwillingly struggling to think how one could draw a boundary around somewhere like 'the East Midlands'. Within cultural studies, some of the notions of 'cultural area' sometimes seem equally to entail this problematical necessity of a boundary: a frame in the sense of a concave line around some area, the inside of which is defined in one way and the outside in another. It is yet another form of the construction of a counterposition between us and them.

And yet if one considers almost any real place, and certainly one not defined primarily by administrative or political boundaries, these supposed characteristics have little real purchase. Take, for instance, a walk down Kilburn High Road, my local shopping centre. It is a pretty ordinary place, north-west of the centre of London. Under the railway bridge the newspaper-stand sells papers from every county of what my neighbours, many of whom come from there, still often call the Irish Free State. The postboxes down the High Road, and many an empty space on a wall, are adorned with the letters IRA. The bottle and waste-paper banks are plastered this week with posters for a Bloody Sunday commemoration. Thread your way through the often almost stationary traffic diagonally across the road from the newsstand and there's a shop which, for as long as I can remember, has displayed saris in the window. Four life-sized models of Indian women, and reams of cloth. In another newsagent I chat with the man who keeps it, a Muslim unutterably depressed by the war in the Gulf, silently chafing at having to sell the *Sun*. Overhead there is always at least one aeroplane – we seem to be on a flight-path to Heathrow and by the time they're over Kilburn you can see them clearly enough to discern the airline and wonder as you struggle with your shopping where they're coming from. Below, the reason the traffic is snarled up (another odd effect of time-space compression!) is in part because this is one of the many entrances to and escape-routes from London, the road to Staples Corner and the beginning of the M1 to the north. These are just the beginnings of a sketch from immediate impressions but a proper analysis could be done, of the links between Kilburn and the world. And so it could for almost any place.

Kilburn is a place for which I have a great affection; I have lived here many years. It certainly has 'a character of its own'. But it is possible to feel all this without subscribing to any of the Heideggerian notions of 'place' which were referred to above. First, while Kilburn may have a character of its own, it is absolutely not a seamless, coherent identity, a single sense of place which everyone shares. It could hardly be less so. People's routes through the place, their favourite haunts within it, the connections they make (physically, or by phone or post, or in memory and imagination) between here and the rest of the world vary enormously. If it is now recognized that people have multiple identities, then the same point can be made in relation to places. Moreover, such multiple identities can be either, or both, a source of richness or a source of conflict. Second, it is (or ought to be) impossible even to begin thinking about Kilburn High Road without bringing into play half the world and a considerable amount of British imperialist history. Imagining it this way provokes in you (or at least in me) a really global sense of place. Third, and finally, I certainly could not begin to, nor would I want to, define it by drawing its enclosing boundaries.

So, at this point in the argument, get back in your mind's eye on a satellite; go right out again and look back at the globe. This time, however, imagine not just all the physical movement, nor even all the often invisible communications, but also and especially all the social relations. For as time-space compression proceeds, in all its complexity, so the geography of social relations changes. In many cases, such relations are increasingly stretched out over space. Economic, political and cultural social relations, each full of power and with internal structures of domination and subordination, stretched out over the planet at every different level, from the household to the local area to the international.

It is from that perspective that it is possible to envisage an alternative interpretation of place. In this interpretation, what gives a place its specificity is not some long internalized history but the fact that it is constructed out of a particular constellation of relations, articulated together at a particular locus. If one moves in from the satellite towards the globe, holding all those networks of social relations and movements and communications in one's head, then each place can be seen as a particular, unique point of their intersection. The uniqueness of a place, or a locality, in other words is constructed out of particular interactions and mutual articulations of social relations, social processes, experiences and understandings, in a situation of co-presence, but where a large proportion of those relations, experiences and understandings are actually constructed on a far larger scale than what we happen to define for that moment as the place itself, whether that be a street, a region or even a continent. Instead then, of thinking of places as areas with boundaries around, they can be imagined as articulated moments in networks of social relations and understandings. And this in turn allows a sense of place which is extra-verted, which includes a consciousness of its links with the wider world, which integrates in a positive way the global and the local.

This is not a question of making the ritualistic connections to 'the wider system' – the people in the local meeting who bring up international capitalism every time you try to have a discussion about rubbish-collection – the point is that there are real relations with real content, economic, political, cultural, between any local place and the wider world in which it is set. [...]

These arguments, then, highlight a number of ways in which a progressive concept of place might be developed. First of all, it is absolutely not static and in no way relates to the Heideggerian view of Space/Place as Being. If places can be conceptualized in terms of the social interactions which they tie together, then it is also the case that these interactions themselves arc not static. They are processes. One of the greatest one-liners in Marxist exchanges has for long been 'ah, but capital is not a thing, it's a process'. Perhaps this should be said also about places; that places are processes, too. [...] Second, places do not have to have boundaries in the sense of divisions which frame simple enclosures. 'Boundaries' may, of course, be necessary – for the purposes of certain types of studies for instance – but they are not necessary for the conceptualization of a place itself. Definition in this sense does not have to be through simple counterposition to the outside; it can come, in part, precisely through the particularity of linkage *to* that 'outside' which is therefore itself part of what constitutes the place. This therefore gets away from that association between penetrability and vulnerability. [...] But why, then, does settlement so often have to be characterized as 'enclosure' (Robins 1991: 12; Emberley 1989: 756)? For it is this kind of characterization that makes invasion by newcomers so threatening. A notion of places as social relations, on the other hand, facilitates the conceptualization of the relation between the centre and the periphery, and the arrival of the previously marginal in the (first-world-city) centre (although it should be pointed out, since it is usually forgotten, that some alien others – women – have been living there for a long time).

Third, clearly places do not have single, unique 'identities'; they are full of internal differences and conflicts (Massey 1991). [...]

Fourth, and finally, none of this denies place nor the importance of the specificity of place. The specificity of place is continually reproduced, but it is not a specificity which results from some long, internalized history. There are a number of sources of this specificity – the uniqueness of place (Massey 1984). There is the fact that the wider relations in which places are set are themselves spatially internally differentiated. *Contra* some of the debate within cultural studies, globalization does not entail simply homogenization. Indeed, the globalization of social relations is yet another source of (the reproduction of) geographical uneven development, and thus of the specificity of place. [...] Further, the specificity of place also derives from the fact that each place is the focus of a distinct *mixture* of wider and more local social relations and, further again, that the juxtaposition of these relations may produce effects that would not have happened otherwise. And, finally, all these relations interact with and take a further element of specificity from the accumulated history of a place, with that history itself conceptualized as the product of layer upon layer of different sets of linkages both local and to the wider world. [...]

It is a sense of place, an understanding of 'its character', which can only be constructed by linking that place to places beyond. A progressive sense of place would recognize that, without being threatened by it: it would be precisely about the *relationship* between place and space. What we need, it seems to me, is a global sense of the local, a global sense of place.

REFERENCES

Emberley, P. (1989) 'Places and stories: the challenge of technology', *Social Research* 56 (3): 741–85.

Giddens, A. (1984) *The Constitution of Society*, Cambridge: Polity Press.

Harvey, D. (1989) *The Condition of Postmodernity*, Oxford: Basil Blackwell.

Jameson, F. (1984) 'Postmodernism, or the cultural logic of late capitalism', *New Left Review* 146: 53–92.

Massey, D. (1984) *Spatial Divisions of Labour: Social Structures and the Geography of Production*, Basingstoke: Macmillan.

––– (1991) 'The political place of locality studies', *Environment and Planning A*, 23: 267–81.

Robins, K. (1991) 'Prisoners of the city: whatever could a postmodern city be?', *New Formations* 15: 1–22.

CHAPTER 10

A PLACE CALLED HOME? (1992)

In the debates about such concepts as 'home', 'place', 'location-locality', identity and sense of place and so on, one of the prime contributions of geographers so far, and most particularly of economic geographers, has been to provide a kind of backcloth, more precisely an economic rationale, for some of the senses of dislocation, fragmentation and disorientation that are currently being expressed by so many.

The argument is that we are living through a period (the precise dating is usually quite vague) of immense spatial upheaval, that this is an era of a new and powerful globalization, of instantaneous worldwide communication, of the break-up of what were once local coherencies, of a new and violent phase of 'time-space compression'.

It is certainly true that these things are going on. The world economy, and the local, regional and national economies (if one can still indeed talk of such things) which make it up, look very different from the way they looked, say, as the world emerged from war in 1945.

I CHANGES IN THE WORLD ECONOMY

The changes even in the last twenty years have been enormous. They are characterized in a variety of ways: as a move from organized to disorganized capitalism, from modern to postmodern, from industrial to post-industrial, manufacturing to service, from Fordist to post-Fordist. The frequency of use of the prefix 'post' indicates the prevailing uncertainty about the positive shape of the new (and indicates also, therefore, the fact that it is open to contestation), but one of the key processes universally agreed to be at the heart of it all is globalization. In spite of all the rhetoric (and to some extent the reality) of small firms and of individual entrepreneurship, of flexibility, niche-marketing and decentralization, of the potential importance of local economies and of economies of scope rather than scale, the reality is that within the economic system power is related to size.[1] The key movers within the world economy remain the multinational, now increasingly transnational and global, corporations, and their power is increasing.[2] The internationalization of capital is a process with old roots, but in recent decades it has increased in intensity and scope and changed in its nature. The total flow of international direct investment (that is, investment directly into production facilities, from one country to another) increased by about 15 per cent *per annum* (in current US dollar terms) through the 1970s, more than trebled overall between 1970 and 1980, and has continued to increase, in spite of slowdowns and looming crises in the world economy, since then.[3] The form which this investment takes has also shifted. The earliest important form of capital export was aimed at obtaining raw materials for processing and production 'back home'. Later the investment in processing and production was itself done overseas, to capture foreign markets, to get round tariff barriers and trade restrictions, and so forth. This is the form which is still, in volume terms, most significant today. More recently, however, capital export has also been into production overseas, but not to serve the markets in which the production is located, but for re-export, either to the home country or to third markets. Here, the stimulus behind the push to multinationalization is the ability to take advantage of the specificities of conditions of production (whether these be cheap labour, lack of unionization, or the availability of particular skills and cultural traditions).

It is important to recognize what these forms of capital export represent. They are more than the increasing spatial reach of a particular group of companies, though of course they *are* that. But they are also – and more helpfully – understood as the stretching out of different kinds of social relationships over space. And that means also the stretching out over space of relations of power, and of relations imbued with meaning and symbolism. It is not just, in the rather straightforward economic cases which we have just been discussing, that capitalist relations of production have been exported. It is that they have taken on a new spatial form. Accumulation, through the extraction of surplus, takes an internationalized form. And, in each of the three cases mentioned above, it does so in a different way, whether that be through the internationalization of the supply of raw materials, through the

---

1 K. Robins, 'Tradition and Translation: National Culture in its Global Context', in J. Comer and S. Honey (eds), *Enterprise and Heritage*, Routledge, London 1991.

2 N. Thrift, 'The Geography of International Economic Disorder', in D. Massey and J. Allen (eds), *Uneven Re-Development: Cities and Regions in Transition*, Hodder and Stoughton in association with the Open University, London 1988.

3 *Ibid.*

multiplication of basically similar branch plants or a particular corporation in a range of countries to sell to their local markets, or through the organization of different plants in different countries each producing, according to their own 'comparative advantage', components to be assembled into a global product to be exported elsewhere. Each of these cases represents a different 'spatial structure of production',[4] a different way in which capitalist social relations of production may be stretched over space. The most recent, quite newly emerging, form of spatial structure is that of the 'global corporation' – a massively multinationalized entity, frequently incorporating not only the above forms of international spatial structure but others as well, which spans a vast variety of sectors of production (both manufacturing and services) and which is organized not so much from a centre in one country from which the tentacles of relations of power spread out to others, but on a more truly international basis, with a global profits strategy, a view of a world divided for this purpose into regions, each with their own operational headquarters, and with – this is as yet a tendency on the horizon rather than a fully-fledged achievement – no particular country called 'home'.

For most companies, however, there is still an identifiable national origin and in that sense a clear geographical 'direction' to the flows of foreign direct investment. But the geography of these flows has been changing and becoming more complex.[5] While before 1970 it was US corporations which incontrovertibly dominated, both in size and in number, this is no longer so clearly the case. Before 1970, more than two-thirds of foreign direct investment was accounted for by US multinationals; today the figure is way below half. Japan, (West) Germany and Canada have grown in importance as sources of foreign investment and the number of multinationals based in the 'South' has increased. The bulk of the flows remains between first world countries, but with the big change that there is now significant foreign investment *into* the USA, and from first world countries to a handful of 'developing' economies.

The final big change has been the massively increasing internationalization of finance, and of services more generally. [...] [G]lobalization has been deepened in recent years, to penetrate into ever more sectors of national and regional economies.

Little of this would have been possible without new technologies of communication, of image-processing and transmission and of information systems.[6] And it is the internationalization of some of these systems themselves

---

4   D. Massey, *Spatial Divisions of Labour: Social Structures and the Geography of Production*, Macmillan, Basingstoke 1984.

5   Thrift, *op. cit.*

6   D. Morley and K. Robins, 'Spaces of Identity: Communications Technologies and the Reconfiguration of Europe', *Screen*, vol. 30, no. 4, Autumn, 1989, pp. 10–34.

which brings home most clearly the fact of the globalization of the inputs to daily life. The burgeoning communications empires of a handful of corporations (Paramount, Sony, Disney) and individual 'players' (Murdoch, Berlusconi, Bertelsmann), and the oft-quoted example of CNN are at the focus of it all. Their own national identities become confused or irrelevant (Murdoch operates far from his home shores; Sony takes over companies like CBS and Columbia Pictures, for long regarded as part of – and certainly important influences on – US identity). Powerful forces for forging a sense of what is 'home' are produced by capital which comes from somewhere else entirely. Their messages flow across old earth boundaries in ways in which no national government can easily prevent. There is emerging, it is argued, a new 'global space of electronic information flows'.[7] And complex and intersecting as it is, there are again – as in the case of manufacturing, services and finance – clear, broad geographies of power. Once again, the presence of the US is dominating. [...] The link between culture and place, it is argued, is being ruptured.

Before we evaluate the reality of all this, and the implications that are drawn from it for the meaning of home and locality, there are a few important points which ought to be registered. Thus, globalization can in no way be equated with homogenization. The spanning of the globe by economic relations has led to new forms and patterns of inequality not simply to increasing similarity. Even the 'global products', apart from the obvious and perhaps too often quoted examples of Coca Cola and McDonalds, penetrate different national markets in different ways. Their globality, and the consequent ability of companies to produce them on a mass scale, comes from their finding numerous different niche-markets in all corners of the earth. The companies can thereby combine economies of scope (variety in the range of their production) with economies of scale. Moreover, along with the chaos and disorder which characterizes the new relations there is also a new ordering of clear global-level hierarchies. The few global cities which dominate the world economy, such as New York, London and Tokyo, do so because they are the foci, the points of intersection, of vast numbers of these 'social-relations-stretched-over-space', and because they are at the end of those relations where power is lodged. There is clearly emerging a global hierarchy as social and economic power seem inexorably to be increasingly geographically centralized. And these forms of organization extend down below the national, to the regional and the local. Regional and local economics are increasingly locked in, not so much to national economies, but directly to the world economy. Indeed it becomes ever more doubtful how valid it is to speak even of coherent national economies in some cases, but certainly of

---

7   *Ibid.*

subnational ones. Local, regional and national are increasingly drawn into, and constituted by, a logic which exists at international level. Thus there is a series of tensions: a world characterized on the one hand by complexity and potential disorder, but on the other hand very clear and consistent directions in the geography of power; and the continuance of geographical diversity but one formed, not so much out of a home-grown uniqueness, as out of the specificity of positioning within the globalized space of flows.

There are also, within the wider context of globalization, some counter-tendencies. It is argued that certain characteristics of the post-mass-production flexible specialization lend themselves to the development of relatively coherent and internally networked local economies. [...]

[W]hatever the importance of these new localisms – and it *is* disputed – they are occurring in a context of a truly major re-shaping of the spatial organization of social relations at every level, from local to global. Each geographical 'place' in the world is being realigned in relation to the new global realities, their roles within the wider whole are being re-assigned, their boundaries dissolve as they are increasingly crossed by everything from investment flows, to cultural influences, to satellite TV networks. Even the different geographical scales become less easy to separate – rather they constitute each other: the global the local, and vice versa. Moreover, as distance seems to be becoming meaningless, so relations in time, too, are altered. Before the 1970s companies made major investment decisions every few years and received prices once a year; exchange rates changed roughly every four years, interest rates perhaps twice a year. All this now seems incredibly slow and ponderous. [...] It is this combination of changes in our experience of space and time which has given rise to the powerful notion that the age we are living in is one of a new burst of 'time-space compression'.

II POSTULATED IMPLICATIONS – AND SOME RESERVATIONS

Moreover, it is argued that this new round of time-space compression has produced a feeling of disorientation, a sense of the fragmentation of local cultures and a loss, in its deepest meaning, of a sense of place. The local high street is invaded by cultures and capitals from the world over; few areas remain where the majority of industry is locally owned; places seem to become both more similar and yet lacking in internal coherence; home-grown specificity is invaded – it seems that you can sense the simultaneous presence of everywhere in the place where you are standing. Conceptualized in terms of the geography of social relations, what is happening is that the social relations which constitute a locality increasingly stretch beyond its borders; less and less of these relations are contained within the place itself.

It has indeed clearly unnerved a lot of people. There is much talk of post-modern geographies of fragmentation, depthlessness and instantaneity. [...] Baudrillard speaks of delirium and vertigo in the face of a world of images and flows. Harvey argues that the disorientation of present times is giving rise to a new – and in his view almost necessarily reactionary – search for stability through a sense of place.[8] Robins writes that 'the driving imperative is to salvage centred, bounded and coherent identities – placed identities for placeless times'[9] Jameson calls for cognitive mapping, expressing a longing to get his bearings, to orient himself in what are clearly for him and others disorienting times, to reassert some feeling of a control which seems to have been lost. And indeed there is today all too much evidence of the emergence of disquieting forms of place-bound loyalties. There are the new national-isms springing up in the east of Europe (which are in total contradiction to the argument, being made at the same time, that the national level in these global-local times is becoming increasingly irrelevant – but no one seems to have addressed this conflict). There are also burgeoning exclusive local-isms, the constructions of tightly bounded place-identities. There is talk of 'the new enclosures', and yuppies build walls around their new inner urban enclaves to protect themselves, physically and by simple spatial definition, from the others who also live in inner urban areas. Nor is this appeal to an unproblematized identity of place confined to the right wing of the political spectrum. In the long battle over London's Docklands, some of the notions of place-identity constructed by those defending themselves against the new invaders were equally static, self-enclosing and defensive. A main argument of this article is that notions of a sense of place do not have to be so.

The most commonly argued position, then, is that the vast current reor-ganizations of capital, the formation of a new global space, and in particular its use of new technologies of communication, have undermined an older sense of a 'place-called-home', and left us placeless and disoriented.

But is it really so? Clearly something is going on, but before we get carried away by the simplicity and appeal of this argument, we would be wise to stop and think more clearly about its form. First, there are reservations about how the argument is usually posed. Second, there are debates to be had about how, anyway, we think about space and place.

The reservations move from relatively trivial to really quite serious. Beginning, then, at the beginning, there is the question of language. A spe-cial style of hype and hyperbole has been developed to write of these matters. The same words and phrases recur; the author gets carried away in a reeling vision of hyperspace. For that reason I have deliberately tried to be downbeat

---

8   D. Harvey, *The Condition of Postmodernity*, Basil Blackwell, Oxford 1989.
9   Robins, *op. cit.*, p. 41.

in the opening section of this paper. For amid the Ridley Scott images of world cities, the writing about skyscraper fortresses, the Baudrillard visions of hyperspace ... most people actually still live in places like Harlesden or West Brom. Much of life for many people, even in the heart of the first world, still consists of waiting in a bus-shelter with your shopping for a bus that never comes. Hardly a graphic illustration of time-space compression. There is also the question of how new it all is. The oft-quoted Saatchi remark that there are now more cultural contrasts between the Bronx and midtown Manhattan than between midtown Manhattan and the 7th Arrondissement of Paris is convincing until one remembers, say, the social gulf that separated, even in the nineteenth century, the west end from the east end of London, for example, and how the denizens of the former viewed the inhabitants of the latter as exotic and as potentially threatening as the indigenous populations of the farthest-flung outposts of Empire. So, quite simply, a preliminary word of caution. We must not get too carried away in our own excitement.

Again, it has for long been the exception rather than the rule that place could be simply equated with community, and by that means provide a stable basis for identity. In the United Kingdom, with the exception of a few small mining towns and cotton towns and (maybe) parts, for instance, of the Docklands of London, 'places' have for many centuries been more complex locations where numerous different, and frequently conflicting, communities intersected.[10] Nor do 'communities' necessarily have to be spatially concentrated. The strong distinction which Giddens and Jameson make between presence and absence, and the greater problems of effective understanding encountered as time-space distanciation is increased, raise more questions about their assumptions of the directness of face-to-face communication than about the impact of distance on interpretation. Of course geography makes a difference – it is a point which geographers have been arguing for a decade[11] – but 'presence-availability' does not somehow do away with issues of representation and interpretation. That place called home was never an unmediated experience.

Further, there are potential problems of deep economism in some of these accounts, and also of class reductionism. It is not only capital which moulds and produces changes in our understanding of and access to space and time. The recent changes in space-time have clearly been propelled by shifts in capitalism and developments in technology. But that is not all. To reduce them to the cultural logic of late capitalism (Jameson) or of flexible accumulation (Harvey) is severely to reduce their meaning and their variety. Although such groundings in a material base may come as a relief after years of analysis

---

10 D. Massey, 'A Global Sense of Place'. *Marxism Today,* June 1991, pp. 24–9.

11 See, for instance, Massey, 1984, *op. cit.*

which seemed ready to blow away in a whirl of rhetorical self-referencing, these economic interpretations come far too close to depriving the cultural (or the non-economic more generally) of any autonomy at all. Nor is our experience and interpretation of all these changes dependent only upon our place within, or without, capitalist class relations. Ethnicity and gender, to mention only the two most obvious other axes, are also deeply implicated in the ways in which we inhabit and experience space and place, and the ways in which we are located in the new relations of time-space compression.

Which begins to bring us to more serious reservations about the normal formulation of the argument about the new, disturbing placelessness. There is reference to *the* condition of postmodernity, but in fact there are many such conditions. Different social groups, and different individuals belonging to numbers of social groups, are located in many different ways in the new organization of relations over time-space. From jetsetters, to pensioners holed-up in lonely bed-sits, to Pacific Islanders whose air and sea links have been cut, to international migrants risking life and livelihood for the chance of a better life … all in some way or another are likely to be affected by the shifting relations of time-space, but in each case the effect is different; each is placed in a different way in relation to the shifting scene.[12] Even as you wait, in a bus shelter in Harlesden or West Brom, for a bus that never comes, your shopping bag is likely to contain at least some products of the global raiding party which is constantly conducted to supply the consumer demands of the world's relatively comfortably-off. The point, however, is that much, if not all, of what has been written has seen this new world from the point of view of a (relative) élite. Those who today worry about a sense of disorientation and a loss of control must once have felt they knew exactly where they were, and that they *had* control.

For who is it in these times who feels dislocated/placeless/invaded? To what extent, for instance, is this a predominantly white/first-world take on things? There are a number of ways in which this question can be addressed, but one of them concerns the newness of the changes under discussion. The assumption which runs through much of the literature is that this openness, this penetrability of boundaries is a recent phenomenon. It has already been argued that even in the first world some aspects of the newness have been exaggerated. But the point is even clearer when, as is more fitting, a global perspective is taken. Thus, even Robins, one of the more perceptive writers on the subject, finds himself lured into the rhetoric. He writes, for instance, that 'Globalization, as it dissolves the barriers of distance, makes the encounter of colonial centre and colonized periphery immediate and

---

12 Massey, 1991, *op. cit.*

intense.'[13] While there is clear recognition here that the 'periphery' has been colonized, there is no such recognition that *from the point of view of* that colonized periphery that encounter has for centuries been 'immediate and intense'. Or again,

> Whereas Europe once addressed African and Asian cultures across vast distances, now that "Other" has installed itself within the very heart of the western metropolis. Through a kind of reverse invasion, the periphery has infiltrated the colonial core. The protective filters of time and space have disappeared, and the encounter with the "alien" and "exotic" is now instantaneous and immediate. The western city has become a crucible in which world cultures are brought into direct contact ... Time and distance no longer mediate the encounter with "other" cultures.[14]

Once again there is both recognition and slippage within this formulation. There is recognition of a past colonialism, that the present 'invasion' is a 'reverse' of a previous one. And yet ... did Europe once address its colonies, formal and informal, only across vast distances? To those living in those colonies it cannot have seemed so. To say that 'Time and distance *no longer* mediate the encounter with "other" cultures' is to see only the present form of that encounter, and implicitly to read the history from a first world/colonizing country perspective. For the security of the boundaries of the place one called home must have dissolved long ago, and the coherence of one's local culture must long ago have been under threat, in those parts of the world where the majority of its population lives. In those parts of the world, it is centuries now since time and distance provided much protective insulation from the outside.

That is one way of looking at these changes: that certainly there has been in recent years a quickening of globalization, a new stretching of social relations over space, but that what is also at issue is a change in the nature and direction of those relations. It is often commented that the UK economy is extremely open. But this has been so for centuries. What has changed in the last two decades is the nature of that openness, its directionality, and the power relations which are embedded in it. In the past the openness was represented by the UK being 'the workshop of the world' (i.e. a major exporter of manufactured goods – frequently undermining local production elsewhere), a major participant in the plunder of the world's natural resources, and the chief financier and insurer for much of the world's production and exchange.

---

13 Robins, *op. cit.,* p 25.
14 *Ibid.,* pp 32, 33.

Today, as Nissan, Toyota, Hitachi and others invest within these shores the openness is, and is seen as, very different. As was pointed out in the opening section, one of the main changes in the flow of foreign direct investment in recent years has been that the US, too, is no longer almost exclusively a source of such investment; it is also a recipient.

But there are also questions at what might be called a more 'local' level. bell hooks argues that the very meaning of the term 'home', in terms of a sense of place, has been very different for those who have been colonized, and that it can change with the experiences of decolonization and of radicalization.[15] Toni Morrison's writing, especially in *Beloved*, undermines for ever any notion that everyone once had a place called home which they could look back on, a place not only where they belonged but which belonged to them, and where they could afford to locate their identities. The nature of the impact of the current phase of globalization has so far perhaps – and ironically – been analyzed from a very *un*-global perspective.

Moreover, if one accepts that the identification of a current feeling of disorientation and placelessness has to be restricted primarily to the first world and even then differentially, and in different ways, to different strata of the population, there is still another curious anomaly to be investigated. Much of the current disorientation, as we have seen, is put down to the arrival in one form or another of the 'Other'. Yet some 'Others' of the dominant definers in first-world society have always been there – women. It is interesting to note how frequently the characterization of place as home comes from those who have left, and it would be fascinating to explore how often this characterization is framed around those who – perforce – stayed behind; and how often the former was male, setting out to discover and change the world, and the latter female, most particularly a mother, assigned the role of personifying a place which did not change. Moreover, it is not simple spatial proximity but the relations of power in which that proximity is embedded which are crucial. Thus Wilson argues that in small-scale settlements, where social control can be relatively tight, women have represented little threat to men – although of course there have always been honourable exceptions. The scale and the complexity of life in the big city, however, makes such regulation and control more difficult. 'Almost from the beginning, the presence of women in cities, and particularly in city streets, has been questioned, and the controlling and surveillance aspects of city life have always been directed particularly at women. Urban life potentially challenged patriarchal systems.'[16] The point to draw from this is that it is not proximity in itself which is unsettling but

---

15 bell hooks, *Yearning: Race, Gender, and Cultural Politics*, Turnaround, London 1991.

16 E. Wilson, *The Sphinx in the City: Urban life, the Control of Disorder, and Women*, Virago, London 1991.

also the nature of the social relations, and most particularly in their aspect of power relations, of which proximity is the geography. Just to talk of the collapse of time and distance, or to see it in terms only of movement and flows, is insufficient; what is at issue is the changing geography of (changing) social relations. And to analyze the impact of those changes it is necessary to take account of both sides of the formulation. *Both* the geography (proximity, time-space distanciation, etc.) *and* the content of the social relations themselves (full of the implications of sexism, or of the power relations of colonialism present or past, or of the relations of capital accumulation) must be taken into account. Moreover each aspect – spatial form and social content – will affect the other. It is through this lens, too, that statements about the 'newness' of the encounter with a colonial past must be interpreted. It is not only time and distance (after noting the ethnocentricity of even this formulation) which have changed.

III IDENTITY AND PLACE

There is, then, an issue of whose identity we are referring to when we talk of a place called home and of the supports it may provide of stability, oneness and security. There are very different ways in which reference to place can be used in the constitution of the identity of an individual, but there is also another side to this question of the relation between place and identity. For while the notion of personal identity has been problematized and rendered increasingly complex by recent debates, the notion of *place* has remained relatively unexamined.

The most common formulations of the concept of geographical place in current debate associate it with stasis and nostalgia, and with an enclosed security. Harvey, for example, sees all place-based politics (which he significantly conflates with place*bound* politics) as suffused with aestheticization (which he sees as almost necessarily 'bad') and a longing for stability and coherence. Equating Time with Becoming and Space with Being (and dichotomizing and opposing them in a way that Heidegger never did) he rejects the latter in favour of the former.[17] In political and social life, also, recent years have seen the emergence of many arguments, policies and movements which indeed, in their attempts to establish a relationship between a place and an identity, a place and a sense of belonging, do depend precisely on such notions – of recourse to a past, of a seamless coherence of character, of an apparently comforting bounded enclosure. Such views of place have been

---

17 See Harvey, 1989, *op. cit.*, and the critique in D. Massey, 'The Political Place of Locality Studies', *Environment and Planning A*, no. 23, 1991, pp 267–81.

evident in a whole range of settings – in the emergence of certain kinds of nationalisms, in the marketing of places, whether for investment or for tourism, in the new urban enclosures, and even – on the other side of the social divide – on occasion by those defending their communities against yuppification by recourse to concepts such as 'the real Isle of Dogs'. All of these have been attempts to fix the meaning of places, to enclose and defend them; they construct singular, fixed and static identities for places, and they interpret places as bounded enclosed spaces defined through counterposition against the Other who is outside.

Yet this is not the only way in which the notion of 'place' can be conceived. If *space* is conceptualized in terms of a four-dimensional 'space-time' and, as hinted at above, as taking the form not of some abstract dimension but of the simultaneous coexistence of social interrelations at all geographical scales, from the intimacy of the household to the wide space of transglobal connections, then *place* can be reconceptualized too. This was the point of the stress laid earlier on seeing phenomena such as globalization and time-space compression as changing forms of the spatial organization of social relations. Social relations always have a spatial form and spatial content. They exist, necessarily, both *in* space (i.e. in a locational relation to other social phenomena) and *across* space. And it is the vast complexity of the interlocking and articulating nets of social relations which is social space. Given that conception of space, a 'place' is formed out of the particular set of social relations which interact at a particular location. And the singularity of any individual place is formed in part out of the specificity of the interactions which occur at that location (nowhere else does this precise mixture occur) and in part out of the fact that the meeting of those social relations at that location (their partly happenstance juxtaposition) will in turn produce new social effects.

On this reading, the 'identity of a place' is much more open and provisional than most discussions allow. First, what is specific about a place, its identity, is always formed by the juxtaposition and co-presence there of particular sets of social interrelations, and by the effects which that juxtaposition and co-presence produce. Moreover, and this is the really important point, a proportion of the social interrelations will be wider than and go beyond the area being referred to in any particular context as a place. Second, the identities of places are inevitably unfixed. They are unfixed in part precisely because the social relations out of which they are constructed are themselves by their very nature dynamic and changing. They are also unfixed because of the continual production of further social effects through the very juxtaposition of those social relations. Moreover, that lack of fixity has always been so. The past was no more static than is the present. Places cannot 'really' be characterized by the recourse to some essential, internalized moment. Virtually all the examples cited above – from forms of nationalism,

170

to heritage centres, to ascriptions of 'the real Isle of Dogs' – seek the identity of a place by laying claim to some particular moment/location in time-space when the definition of the area and the social relations dominant within it were to the advantage of that particular claimant-group. When black-robed patriarchs organize ceremonies to celebrate a true national identity they are laying claim to the freezing of that identity at a particular moment and in a particular form – a moment and a form where they had a power which they can thereby justify themselves in retaking. All of which means, of course, that the identity of any place, including that place called home, is in one sense for ever open to contestation. [...]

But, finally and most importantly, on this reading of space and place the identity of place is in part constructed out of positive interrelations with elsewhere. This is in contrast to many readings of place as home, where there is imagined to be the security of a (false, as we have seen) stability and an apparently reassuring boundedness. Such understandings of the identity of places require them to be enclosures, to have boundaries and – therefore and most importantly – to establish their identity through negative counterposition with the Other beyond the boundaries. An understanding of the socio-economic geography of any place, certainly in those parts of the world where the debate is now rife, reveals that such a view is untenable. The identity of a place does not derive from some internalized history. It derives, in large part, precisely from the specificity of its interactions with 'the outside'.

It is here that the debate about place, and particularly about place and belonging, place and home, links up to discussion about identity more generally. While it is frequently accepted that identities are relational, the possibilities are often closed down by the assumption that such relations must be those of bounded, negative counterposition, of inclusion and exclusion. Yet, as has been seen, it has in principle always been difficult, and has over the centuries become more so, to distinguish the inside of a place from the outside; indeed, it is precisely in part the presence of the outside within which helps to construct the specificity of the local place.

The question of the extent to which this is a gender-related issue [...] reverberates, I would argue, through our currently dominant notions of place and of home, and very specifically through notions of place as a source of belonging, identity and security. Moreover, it reverberates – and most importantly – in the fear which is apparently felt by some, including many writers on the subject, when the boundaries dissolve (or are felt to do so), when the geography of social relations forces us to recognize our interconnectedness. On the one hand, then, that kind of boundedness has not for centuries really been characteristic of local places. A large component of the identity of that place called home derived precisely from the fact that it had always in one way or another been open; constructed out of movement, communication, social relations which always stretched beyond it. In one sense or another most places have been 'meeting places'; even their 'original inhabitants' usually came from somewhere else. This does not mean that the past is irrelevant to the identity of place. It simply means that there is no internally produced, essential past. The identity of place, just as Hall argues in relation to cultural identity,[18] is always and continuously being produced. Instead of looking back with nostalgia to some identity of place which it is assumed already exists, the past has to be constructed. bell hooks, in *Yearning*, returns again and again to the phrase 'our struggle is also a struggle of memory against forgetting', but she is talking of 'a politicization of memory that distinguishes nostalgia, that longing for something to be as once it was, a kind of useless act, from that remembering that serves to illuminate and transform the present.'[19]

Yet, on the other hand, is also true that the balance between the internally focused and externally connected social relations which construct a place has shifted dramatically, in recent years and in certain parts of the world, towards the latter. Yet the argument that this necessarily produces fear and disorientation depends on a very particular view of both personal identity and the identity of place, and one which is contestable. Wilson writes of the way in which the big city – a 'place' which is by its very nature open and in flux – has produced in many a feeling of fear; fear of the disorder, the uncontrollable complexity, the chaos. But not all have felt this fear. Women, argues Wilson, have often appeared less daunted by city life than have men. While

> most of the male modernist literary figures of the early twentieth century drew ... a threatening picture of the modern metropolis (an exception being James Joyce) ... modernist women writers such as Virginia Woolf and Dorothy Richardson responded with joy and affirmation. In *Mrs Dalloway*, Virginia Woolf exulted in the vitality of a summer's morning in London, in the 'swing, tramp and tread; in the bellow and uproar ... in the triumph and the jingle and the strange high singing of some aeroplane overhead'. Acknowledging the unstable and uncertain nature of personal identity, she does not find this alarming, as did Kafka and Musil.[20]

bell hooks writes of how at times of estrangement and alienation

---

18 S. Hall, 'Cultural Identity and Diaspora', in J. Rutherford (ed.). *Identity: Community, Culture, Difference*, Lawrence & Wishart, London 1990.

19 hooks, *op. cit.*, p 147.

20 Wilson, *op. cit.*, p 157.

home is no longer just one place. It is locations. Home is that place which enables and promotes varied and everchanging perspectives, a place where one discovers new ways of seeing reality, frontiers of difference. One confronts and accepts dispersal and fragmentation as part of the constructions of a new world order that reveals more fully where we are, who we can become.[21]

In other words, for the new complexities of the geography of social relations to produce fear and anxiety, both personal identity and 'a place called home' have had to be conceptualized in a particular way – as singular and bounded. Of course places can be home, but they do not have to be thought in that way, nor do they have to be places of nostalgia. You may, indeed, have many of them. Michèle le Doeuff has written

> I was born just about everywhere, under the now shattered sky of the Greeks, in a Brittany farmer's clogs, in an Elizabethan theatre, in my grandmother's famines and destitution, and in the secular, compulsory and free schooling that the state was so good to make available to me, but also in the rebellions that were mine alone, in the slaps that followed or preceded them, in Simone de Beauvoir's lucid distress and in Descartes' stove. And there is more to come.[22]

And what is more, each of these home-places is itself an equally complex product of the ever-shifting geography of social relations present and past.

---

21 In 'Choosing the Margin', p 149; in bell hooks, *op. cit.*
22 M. le Doeuff, *Hipparchia's Choice: An Essay Concerning Women, Philosophy, etc.* Blackwell, Oxford 1991, p 172.

CHAPTER 11

MASCULINITY, DUALISMS AND HIGH TECHNOLOGY (1995)

One important element in recent feminist analyses of gender has been the investigation and deconstruction of dualistic thinking. This paper takes up one aspect of this issue of dualisms and the construction of gender. It examines the interplay between two particular dualisms in the context of daily life in and around high-technology industry in the Cambridge area of England. The focus on dualisms as *lived*, as an element of daily practice, is important (see Bourdieu 1977; Moore 1986), for philosophical frameworks do not exist 'only' as theoretical propositions or in the form of the written word. They are both reproduced and, at least potentially, struggled with and rebelled against in the practice of everyday living. The focus here is on how particular dualisms may both support and problematize certain forms of social organization around British high-technology industry.

High-technology industry in various guises is seen across the political spectrum as the hope for the future of national, regional and local economies (Hall 1985) and it is important, therefore, to be aware of the societal relations, including those around gender, which it supports and encourages in its current form of organization. In the United Kingdom, 'high tech' has been sought after by local areas across the country and has been the centrepiece of some of the most spectacular local-economic success stories of recent years. In particular, it is the foundation of what has become known as the 'Cambridge phenomenon' (Segal Quince and Partners 1985). The investigation reported on here is of those highly qualified scientists and engineers, working in the private sector in a range of companies from the tiny to the multinational, who form the core of this new growth. These are people primarily involved in research and in the design of new products. This is the high-status end of high tech. The argument in this paper takes off from two important facts about the scientists who work within this part of the economy: first, that the overwhelming majority of them are male; and, secondly, that they work extremely long hours on a basis which demands from them very high degrees of both temporal and spatial flexibility (see Henry and Massey 1995). It was the conjunction of these two things which led to the train of inquiry reported here.

HIGH TECHNOLOGY AND LONG HOURS OF WORK

There are three bundles of reasons for the long hours worked by employees in these parts of the economy. The first group of reasons arises from the nature of competition between companies in hightechnology activities. This is the kind of competition which has been characterized as classically 'post-Fordist'. Production frequently takes place on a one-off basis, as the result of specifically negotiated and competitive tenders. High among the criteria on which tenders are judged is the time within which the contract will be completed. Moreover, both during and after production there is a strong emphasis on responsiveness to the customer: in answering inquiries, in solving problems which emerge during and after installation/delivery of a product, in being there when needed – even if the telephone call comes through from California in the middle of the night. It is not so much the inherent unpredictability of R&D as the way in which it is compressed into the spatio-temporal dimensions required by this particular social construction of competition which is the issue. 'Time' is important to successful competition. The results should give pause for thought, for these are high-status core workers in what is frequently heralded as a promising flexible future. The demands which this flexibility places even on these workers are considerable.

Moreover, these pressures for long hours are added to by a second bundle of reasons: those which revolve around the nature of competition within the labour market. There are a number of strands to this but the most significant derives from the general character of this market as a knowledge-based labour market. It is a market in individualized labour power, valued for its specific learning, experience and knowledge. In order to compete in this labour market (and others like it) employees must, beyond the necessity of working the already long hours required by their companies, continue to reproduce and enhance the value of their own labour power. They must keep up with the literature, go to conferences and maintain the performance of networking and of talking to the right people. This is additional labour, put in outside the hours required by the company and necessary for its success but equally necessary for the success of the individual employee. Within the workplace, interaction between employees can produce a culture which glorifies long hours of work. Again, this may derive from competition between individuals but it may also result from various peer-group pressures – the

> We don't *need* to work longer – I think people choose to because they enjoy their work, because they own the project ... and there's also ownership of the client.
>
> The clock doesn't matter at all. The only restriction for me is I don't like to get home too late. The landlady's given me a key but I don't like to arrive much after midnight.
>
> I've got so much holiday I don't know what to do with it.
>
> ... because I enjoy it ... I enjoy the work ... I enjoy computers ... I often wonder what I would have done if I'd had to get a job in the days before computing.
>
> One person was sent abroad to a conference because they would not take time off.
>
> But the thing we have discovered over the years is that people who work here, and get into it, become addicted ... we find the problem of getting some people to leave; they do get very engrossed in the thing ... This circuit of people working on the system here, the difficulties are extracting them for some other thing that may be necessary, like they haven't had any sleep for the last 40 years!

Figure 11.1 Enthusiasm for work leading to longer hours

need 'not to let the team down', for instance, can become a form of social compulsion (Halford and Savage 1995).

But the third cluster of reasons for the long hours of work in high-tech sectors is completely different. It is, quite simply, that the scientists love their work. Figure 11.1 illustrates some aspects of this; the first four quotations are from scientists themselves, the last two from company representatives. These scientists and engineers become absorbed by their work, caught up by the interest of it; they don't like to leave an element of a problem unsolved before they break off for the evening. The way in which this involvement is interpreted or presented by different groups varies. Company representatives speak of the kinds of people they seek to employ as committed and flexible, as 'motivated', as 'able to take pressure', as not being the kind to watch the clock, and they frequently acknowledge that such characteristics may derive from pure interest in the work itself. A number of company representatives were quite clear that their search for employees was directed towards finding these characteristics. The scientists themselves often talk of their delight in the nature of the work, of its intrinsic interest. However, where these male scientists have partners (and all the partners we identified were women), their views were more cynical, often pointing up obsessiveness or workaholism. [...]

DUALISMS AND MASCULINITIES

Dualistic formulations

One of the specificities of these high-technology sectors is bound up with the reasons why the employees are so attached to their jobs and how these reasons are interpreted. The dynamics in play here are associated with elements of masculinity and of a very specific form of masculinity. Above all, the attachment to these jobs is related to with their character as scientific, as being dependent upon (and, perhaps equally importantly, confined to) the exercise of rationality and of logic. Within the structure of the economy, these jobs represent an apex of the domination of reason and science. It is this which lends them much of their status and which, in part, accounts for the triumphalist descriptions they are so often accorded in journalistic accounts. What they demand is the ability to think logically. They are in a sector of the economy whose prime characteristics are, for these employees, structured around one of the oldest dualisms in western thought – that between reason and non-reason; it is a sector identified with that pole – reason – which has been socially constructed, and validated, as masculine (see, especially, Lloyd 1984).

Moreover, in this dualistic formulation, science is seen as being on the side of History (capital H) as progression. It makes breakthroughs; it is involved in change, in progress. And it is here that it links up to a second dualism: that between transcendence and immanence. In its aspect of transcendence, science is deeply opposed to that supposed opposite, the static realm of living-in-the-present, of simple reproduction, which has been termed 'immanence'. This opposition between transcendence and immanence is also a dualism with a long history in western thought. And again it is transcendence which has been identified and constructed as masculine (he who goes out and makes history) as against a feminine who 'merely' lives and reproduces. [...]

Dualistic thinking has been criticized both in general, as a mode of conceptualizing the world, and in particular, in its relation to gender and sexual politics. Dualistic thinking leads to the closing-off of options and to the structuring of the world in terms of either/or. In relation to gender and sexuality, it leads, likewise, to the construction of heterosexual opposites and the reduction of genders and sexualities to two counterposed possibilities. Moreover, even when at first sight they may seem to have little to do with gender, a wide range of such dualisms are thoroughly imbued with gender connotations, one side being socially characterized as masculine, the other as feminine, with the former thereby being socially valorized. The power of these connotational structures is immense and it is apparently not much lessened – indeed, it is possibly rendered only more flexible – by the existence among them of inconsistencies and contradictions.

Dualistic practices

It was only gradually, in the course of considering the interview material and the nature of work in the scientific sectors of the economy, that the issue of dualisms emerged as significant in this research. It was the things which people said, the way life was organized and conceptualized, the unspoken assumptions which emerged repeatedly, that pushed the inquiry in this direction.

Thus, for example, it was evident that in Cambridge these scientific employees were specifically attached to those aspects of their work which embody 'reason' and 'transcendence'. What they really enjoy is its logical and scientific nature: they may glory in the scientificity of their work and frequently exhibit delight in the puzzle-solving logical-game nature of it all. Their partners comment upon their obsession with their computers, and both partners and company representatives talk of boys with toys. [...]

The attachment to computers may be seen in this context as reflecting two rather different things, both of which are distinct from the more technologically orientated love of 'fiddling about with machines'. On the one hand, these machines, and what can be done with them, embody the science in which the employees are involved. They are aids and stimuli to logical thought. On the other hand, their relative predictability (and thus controllability) as machines insulates them from the uncertainties, and possibly the emotional demands, of the social sphere (see below).

The aspect of transcendence comes through in the characterizations of the job as 'struggling' with problems, as 'making breakthroughs'; whether these workers think of themselves as far from it or right up against it, there is the notion of a scientific-technical 'frontier'. One scientist, reflecting on the reasons for his long hours of work, talked of being 'driven by success' and of the fact that he was 'always reaching higher'. A scientist in the same company, who was quite critical of the hours worked by others, argued that for some people crisis is part of the job culture: 'it's a sort of badge of courage'. Other words too reflect the effort and the struggle of it all: 'If I stagger out of here

179

at 11 o'clock at night I really don't feel like going home and cooking'. There's the quest: 'As a parent I try to spend as much time as I can with [the child] but in my quest for whatever it is I tend to work very hard'. [...]

[T]he self-conception of many of these employees is built around the work that they do and specifically around this work as scientific activity:

> the machine in front of them is their home.
> It is their science which dominates their lives and interests ...

Moreover, this glorification of their scientific/research and development capabilities on the part of the scientists can go along with a quite contrasting deprecation of their ability to do other things, especially (in the context of our interviews) their incompetence in the face of domestic labour. This is work which it is quite acceptable *not* to be good at. Thus:

> *laundry?* 'I shove it in the machine'; *cleaning?* 'I do it when it gets too much'; *shopping?* 'Tescoes, Friday or Saturday'; *cooking?* 'I put something in the microwave. Nothing special. As long as it's quick and easy that's good enough for me'; *gardening then?* 'when necessary'.

There is here none of the pleasurable elaboration on the nature of the tasks which typifies descriptions of the paid scientific work. The answers are short and dismissive.

Such attitudes are important in indicating what is considered acceptable as part of this scientist's own presentation of himself. Not only is the identification with scientific research very strong and positive but it seems equally important for him to establish what is *not* part of his picture of himself. Domestic labour and caring for his daily needs and living environment is definitely out. It is not just that scientific activity is positively rated which is significant but also that it is sharply cut off from other aspects of life. This is precisely the old dualism showing its head in personal self-identification and daily life. What was going on was a real rejection of the possibility of being good at *both* science *and* domestic labour. A framing of life in terms of 'either/or'.

In this case, and in some others, such downplaying of the rest of life extended to all non-work/scientific activities. But such extreme positions were not common and seem to be more evident among single men than those with partners and, even more markedly, than among those with children. Some men were clearly aware of the issue. For one scientist, a new baby had 'completely changed his life' (what this meant was that he went home early almost every other night) and yet the difficulty of balancing or integrating both sides of his life was evident:

> I feel frustrated ... when ... after this baby that's changed my life ... I go home early every other day (almost) and pick her up at 4.35, take her home, play with her until bedtime, and ... I find that sometimes that's quite frustrating, and keeps me away from work. I mean – it's fulfilling in its own right, but it's ... I'm conscious of the fact that ... I call it a half-day, you know. I find it frustrating.

Finally, some of the comments made about the scientists by (some of) the partners were particularly sharp and revealing, describing them as

> not very socially adequate ... better with things than with people.
> work gets the best of him, work is the centre of his ... life.

One of the very few female company representatives (that is, a member of management, not of the scientific team) reflected:

> Well, when I first joined the company there were twelve people here and they stuck me in an office with the development team and it was a nightmare. I really hated it. They didn't talk, they didn't know how to talk to a woman, they really didn't.

What appears to be going on, in and around these jobs, is the construction/reinforcement of a particular kind of masculinity (that is, of characteristics which are socially coded masculine) around reason and scientificity, abstract thought and transcendence. It is a process which relates to some of the dualisms of western thought and which, as we shall see below, has concrete effects on people's lives.

Such characteristics of the employees, it must be stressed, relate to the more general nature of these jobs. These are jobs which derive their prestige precisely from their abstract and theoretical nature. The very construction and content of these jobs are the result of a long process of separation of conception from execution (and of the further reinforcement of this distinction through social and spatial distancing). They are jobs, in other words, which enable and encourage the flourishing of these kinds of social characteristics. Moreover, the long hours which, for the various reasons discussed above, are worked in them enforce both their centrality within the employees' lives and a transfer of the bulk of the work of reproduction to others. In Cynthia Cockburn's (1981, 181) words:

Family commitments must come second. Such work is clearly predicated on not having responsibility for childcare, indeed on having no one to look after, and ideally someone to look after you.

The implication of all this is not only that these jobs are an embodiment in working life of science and transcendence but also that, in their very construction and the importance in life which they thereby come to attain, they enforce a separation of these things from other possible sides of life (the other sides of reason and transcendence) and thus embody these characteristics as part of a dualism. Moreover, by expelling the other poles of these dualisms into the peripheral margins of life and frequently on to other people (whether unpaid partner or paid services), they establish the dualisms as a social division of labour. The pressure is for someone else to carry the other side of life.

Moreover, if there is indeed a form of masculinity bound up with all this, then the companies in these parts of the economy let it have its head; they trade on it and benefit from it and – most significantly from the point of view of the argument in this paper – they thereby reinforce it. Furthermore, the possession of these characteristics, which are socially coded as masculine and which are related to *forms* of codification which resonate with dichotomous distinctions between two genders, makes people more easily exploitable by the forms of capital in these sectors. There is here a convergence of desires/ interests; between a certain sort of masculinity and a certain sort of capital.

This is not to say that what is at issue here is simple 'sexism'. Our interviews – certainly as analysed so far – did not reveal the explicit sexism found in some other studies, including Cockburn's (1985). We did not encounter much in the way of strong statements about the unsuitability of women for these jobs. There were a few such statements but they were infrequent in the overall context of our interviews. Nor was it clear that the male scientists who displayed the characteristics described always recognized them explicitly as masculine (although further probing may well have unearthed more evidence on this score). The point, however, is that what is at issue here is not so much overt discrimination or sexism as deeply internalized dualisms which structure personal identities and daily lives, which have effects upon the lives of others through structuring the operation of social relations and social dynamics, and which derive their masculine/feminine coding from the deep socio-philosophical underpinnings of western society.

THE WORK/HOME BOUNDARY

The boundary between work and 'home' has often been seen, and in this case can be seen, as an instanciation of the dualism between transcendence and immanence. At work, the frontiers of history are pushed forward; at home (or so the formulation would have us believe), there is a world of feelings, emotions and (simple) reproduction. [...] What is at issue in the ideological power of these dualisms is not only the material facts to which they (often only very imperfectly) relate (many women don't like housework either and many female paid employees negotiate a work/home boundary) but the complex connotational systems to which they refer. Moreover, the negotiation of this boundary has emerged in our research as a crucial element in the construction of these men's attitude to their work and in their construction of themselves.

One of the avenues of inquiry which originally sparked my interest in designing this research derived from statements made in interviews in a previous project (Massey *et al.* 1992). That project was also concerned with investigating high-tech firms, specifically those located on science parks, and one of the recurring themes in a number of the interviews concerned the blurring of boundaries. 'The boundary between work and play disappears' was a response which stuck in my mind from that earlier research. What absorbed me at that point was the characterization of everything outside paid work as 'play' and, especially given the very long hours worked in the companies we were investigating, it prompted me to wonder who it was that performed the domestic labour which was necessary to keep these men fed and watered and able to turn up for work each morning. But what the earlier respondent had in mind was that work itself had many of the characteristics of play: that you get paid for doing things you enjoy, you have flexible working arrangements, you take work home, you are provided with expensive toys. In this formulation, there really is no boundary between paid work and play. In this way of understanding things, 'the home' in the sense of the domestic, of reproduction, of the sphere of emotions, sensuality and feelings, or of immanence, does not enter the picture at all. How, then, do we interpret what actually happens to the boundary between work and home in the case of these scientists in Cambridge? There are two stages to the argument.

First, there is indeed a dislocation of the boundary between work and home. This is particularly true in a temporal and spatial sense. Moreover, it is a dislocation which primarily takes the form of an invasion of the space and time of one sphere (the home) by the priorities and preoccupations of the other (paid work). This can be illustrated in a whole range of ways. The high degree of temporal flexibility in terms of the numbers of hours worked turns out, in practice, to be a flexibility far more in one direction than in the other. While the demands, and attractions, of work are responded to by working during evenings, at weekends, over Bank Holidays and so forth – and it is expected that this will be so, it is the 'commitment' and 'flexibility' required to be an accepted member of this part of the economy – the 'time-in-lieu' thereby in principle accrued is far less often taken and indeed has to be more formally negotiated; the demands of home intrude into work far less than vice versa (see Henry and Massey 1995). Spatial boundaries are also dislocated as work is very frequently taken home. A high proportion of these employees have machines, modems and/or studies in the space of the domestic sphere but there is no equivalent presence of the concerns of home within the central space of paid work (at the most obvious level, for example, not one of the companies we investigated had a crèche). One of the company representatives we interviewed spoke of the employees being 'virtually here' (in the workplace) even when working at home because of the telecommu-nications links installed between the two places. Moreover, this raises a third and very significant aspect of this one-way invasion. A lot of our interviewees spoke of the scientists' difficulty in turning off thoughts about work, of not continuing to think about a problem even when physically doing something quite different. The men wondered if they should charge to the company time spent thinking in the bath. A few men and their partners spoke of episodes when he would get up in the middle of the night to go and fiddle with some puzzle. Men, partners and sometimes children commented on minds being elsewhere when notionally it was time for playing with the children or driv-ing the car on a day out. Here there is a real 'spatial' split between mind and body; a capsule of 'virtual' time-space of work within the material place of the home. While the body performs the rituals of the domestic sphere, the mind is preoccupied with the interests and worries of work:

> I am well aware of the fact that in many areas, that you are bet-ter having the 9–5pm and everything like that, but I have never found it at all compatible with trying to work or trying to pursue a bit of research or a bit of development, to have to give up at the magic hour or whatever ... and I mean you can't say to somebody you will think between 9 and 5pm and you will not think between 5.05pm and 8.55am.

This is eminently understandable and, in many ways, attractive: it is good to have paid employment which is interesting and it is a challenge to resist the compartmentalization of life into mutually sealed-off time-spaces.

But what is important is that once again this works in only one direction. While domestic time is porous, work time is not. Indeed, and this is the significant point, it *cannot* be so. While it is assumed that one may think about work while playing with the children or while out for the day with the partner, the reverse is not the case. Indeed, a reason quite frequently given for working late nights and weekends at the office is that the time-space is less disturbed then – even if other people are doing the same thing, there is less in the way of incoming phone calls and so forth. One of the dominant characteristics of this kind of work is that it demands, and induces, total concentration. [...]

This does not mean that levels of concentration within the workplace do not vary, nor that time-out cannot be taken. Indeed time-in-lieu, trips to the shops, etc. provide occasional windows within the working day. But, within the workplace, everything – even the exercise of the body – is geared to the productivity of the intellect:

> I was amazed when I went there – I'd been working at [a major corporation]. This huge factory in Lancashire had shut and I came down here to the interview with [a smaller company, Cambridge-based] and I walked up the stairway and on every floor there was a series of little offices and ramps around the edge and the middle of each floor was open and there was a ping-pong table or a snooker table and everybody seemed to be playing games and I thought that this is supposed to be a place of work – and then when I saw all the things they were doing – a chap [would] put his bat down and go off and design an IC in a little room in the corner.

What we have here, then, is the workplace constructed as a highly specialized envelope of spacetime, into which the intrusion of other activities and interests is unwanted and limited. For most of these scientists, however, 'the home' is constructed entirely differently. Both temporally and spatially, it is porous and, in particular, it is invaded by the sphere of paid work.

Abstract spaces

One way of beginning to conceptualize the difference between these two kinds of spaces is through the work of Henri Lefebvre. In his account of *The production of space* (1991), he characterizes the space of current western society as 'abstract space' and discusses (and criticizes), as one of its defining features, its fragmentation, its division into subspaces devoted to the performance of specialized activities. His historical analysis explains this process as the result of aspects both of modernity and capitalism on the one hand and of currently dominant forms of masculinity on the other. Although Lefebvre's historical account and the supposed newness of abstract spaces may be questioned, his examples of such specialized and fragmented spaces/space-times resemble very strongly the specialized space-times constructed in high-tech workplaces. They seem to have many of the characteristics of abstract space: they are demarcated against an outside, they are specialized, they are masculine. Yet, in the story we are telling here, they are not coexisting with other similarly specialized and sealed-off time-spaces but with a time-space – that of the domestic sphere – which is porous, which allows entry from other spheres, which is perhaps, in Lefebvre's terms, characteristic of an older and yet, possibly at the same time, a more potentially progressive kind of time-space. Lloyd (1984, 50), it might be recalled, contrasted the wholly rational sphere of reason/transcendence (i.e. evacuated of other things) with 'woman's task' of preserving 'the sphere of the *intermingling* of mind and body' (my emphasis).

Further, Lefebvre (1991, 191) pointedly asks

> Is not social space always, and simultaneously, both a *field of action* (offering its extension to the deployment of projects and practical intentions) and a *basis of action* (a set of places whence energies derive and whither energies are directed).

In other words, social space is both an arena of action and potentially enabling/productive of further effects. Just so the places of work in these high-tech parts of the economy: they are not merely spaces where things may happen but spaces which, in the nature of their construction (as specialized, as closed-off from intrusion, and in the nature of the things in which they are specialized), have effects – in the structuring of the daily lives and the identities of the scientists who work within them. Most particularly, in their boundedness and in their dedication to abstract thought to the exclusion of other things, these workplaces both reflect and provide a material basis for the particular form of masculinity which hegemonizes this form of employment. Not only the nature of the work and the culture of the workplace but also the construction of the space of work itself, therefore, contributes to the moulding and reinforcement of this masculinity. As Lefebvre (1991, 89) writes:

> The dominant tendency fragments space and cuts it up into pieces ... Specializations divide space among them and act upon its truncated parts, setting up mental barriers and practico-social frontiers.

Lefebvre would argue that the currently dominant tendency towards the homogenization/fragmentation and specialization of space is something which should be opposed. This relates to the second stage in the argument here about what is happening to the work/home boundary among the scientists of the Cambridge phenomenon.

186

For what has been discussed so far is an alteration in the boundary between home and work which consists of nothing more than the spatio-temporal transgression by one sphere (one side of the dualism) into the other. As has been noted, this transgression is all one way but the second stage of the argument is that in whatever manner one interprets this 'blurring' of boundaries, it does not overcome the dualism itself. Yet it is the fact of the dichotomies (reason/non-reason; transcendence/immanence) which has been criticized as being part of that same mode of thinking which also polarizes genders and the characteristics so frequently ascribed to them. And it is the parallel fragmentation/specialization which came in for criticism from Lefebvre. What, then, can be learned about the possibility of unification from this study of Cambridge scientists?

RESISTANCE

The characteristics which have been described above are traits of *masculinity*, not of men. As already implied, there is no simple homogeneity among the men we studied. However, these characteristics are strongly embedded within the culture of this part of the economy (with some variation in detail between different types of jobs). Moreover, the strength of this embeddedness means that these characteristics 'pull' all its participants towards them. Individual men have relations to these characteristics which are more or less celebratory or painful. Many of them recognize the need to negotiate the very different personas they inhabit at home and at work – the scientist with the new baby (quoted earlier) was doing just that. And what he was confronting there was precisely the difficulty of preventing his dominant self-conception as a scientist from completely overriding those other potential sides of himself. Other men actively try to resist this potential domination. Their number is small and their reasons varied. Most commonly, resistance is a response to stress or to strongly articulated objections on the part of the partner, or to a genuine sensitivity to the felt need of these men to live a more varied life, not to miss out on the children growing up and so forth.

Moreover, the resistance takes a particular form. It is almost entirely to do with working hours and with the time and space which work occupies rather than with wider characteristics of the job. It also takes place almost entirely at the individual level. These workplaces are not unionized. [...]

Given that the tendency is for work to invade home life, one obvious mechanism for resistance is to protect home life from intrusion. This happens in a number of ways. Some men (a few only but then the resisters in total are not a high proportion of the whole) have decided not to take work home, thereby preserving the space of home and the time spent in it from the intrusion of the demands of paid work. Sometimes this will involve an intrusion in time terms, maybe involving staying longer at the workplace in order to finish a task there rather than take it home. Resistance here is to the violation of the *space* of home. Other men, though again few, have made themselves rules about *time* and insist on keeping to a regular daily routine and on arriving and leaving the workplace at set times. Over the long term, it is possible that this will be detrimental to their careers (see Henry and Massey 1995) but the men are aware of this and indeed in some cases have adopted the strategy because of other problems (personal stress, problems with health or personal relationships) which had been produced by a previous commitment to the high pressure and long hours typical of these companies in general. It must be emphasized that this is not the only way of coping with the pressures of this work. Other scientists, and couples, have found alternative ways of dealing with such demands and compulsions but what is significant about resistance based on time and space is its irony. The 'problem', as we have argued above, has been posed through the working out in everyday life of some of the major dualisms of western ways of thinking. Yet, in the absence of collective resistance, legislative action or wider cultural shifts, individual attempts to deal with some of the conflicts thus provoked may result in a reinforcement of the expression of those very dualisms. The dichotomies are rigidified in order to protect one sphere (the home, the 'rest of life') from invasion by the other (scientific abstraction, transcendence). The problems posed by the dualisms result in their reinforcement.

CONCLUSIONS

The last section concluded on one of a number of ironies analysed in the paper: that those who were attempting to resist the domination of their lives by one side of a dualistic separation most often found themselves reinforcing the divide between the two poles of the dualism. What such a 'Catch-22' indicates is that the way out of the conundra does not lie at that level. The 'solution' must be sought in a deeper challenge to the situation.

Similarly, the empirical material discussed here raises a number of confusions and complexities around the politics of campaigns for a shorter working day/week. They are issues too which relate as much to academe, especially in its present increasingly intensified and individually competitive form, as they do to the high-tech work discussed in the paper. They are issues which touched me personally as an academic and which made me think about my own life as I did the research. It is a privilege to have work which we find interesting. At a recent meeting of feminist academics, where we discussed an early version of this paper, *none* of us wanted our 'work' to be restricted to 35 specified hours in each week. While all of us wanted to resist the current pressures on hours produced by the reinforcement of competitive structures, we did not want to lose either the feeling of autonomous commitment or the possibility of temporal flexibility. But neither did we like the way in which this 'flexibility' currently works in practice – the pressure towards what can only be called a competitive workaholism and the inability to keep things under control. These are things which we as academics, as well as those in the high-technology sectors discussed here, need to confront. For when an important element of the pressure on time results from personal commitment on the one hand and individualized competition on the other, as well as from sectoral and workplace cultures, how can any form of collective resistance be organized?

In the longer term, the aim must be to push the questioning further, to try to find those solutions which may exist at 'deeper' levels. In particular, I suggest, it means questioning the dualisms themselves. Instead of endlessly trying to juggle incompatibilities and to resolve ambiguities which, in reality, point to contradictions, it is important to undermine and disrupt the polarizations which are producing the problem in the first place.

[...]

What I find more problematical as a political issue is the division of the lives of the scientists described in this paper between abstract and completely 'mental' labour on the one hand and the 'rest of life' on the other. In the version of this paper sent to referees, I had unreservedly applauded those few attempts which we had come across in our research to resist the compartmentalization of life into mutually sealed-off time-spaces. At least one referee questioned this, asking simply '*why* is it good to resist compartmentalization?' And I know for myself that one thing I thoroughly enjoy is to sit down in the secluded and excluding space of the Reading Room at the British Museum and devote myself entirely to thinking and writing. And yet – to return to Lefebvre – do we want lives sectioned-off into compartments, into exclusive time-spaces: for the intellect, for leisure, for shopping ...?

This dilemma might relate to, and be partially addressed by, a consideration of the major dualism discussed in this paper – that in which 'science' itself is involved. It is perhaps that the problem lies most fundamentally in the postulated separation of the isolated intellect from the rest of one's being and calling the product of the working of that (supposedly) isolated intellect, 'knowledge'. Among many others, Ho (1993, 168) has argued for an alternative:

> This manner of knowing – with one's entire being, rather than just the isolated intellect – is foreign to the scientific tradition of the west. But ... it is the only authentic way of knowing, if we [are]

to follow to logical conclusion the implications of the development of western scientific ideas since the beginning of the present century. We have come full circle to validating the participatory framework that is universal to all indigenous knowledge systems the world over. I find this very agreeable and quite exciting.

The real irony, then, may be that the longstanding western (though not only western) dualism between abstract thought and materiality/the body may lead through its own logic to its own undermining. And it is on that dualism that much of the separation within the economy between conception and execution – and thus these 'high-tech' jobs themselves – has been founded.

REFERENCES

Bourdieu, P. 1977. *Outline of a theory of practice*. Cambridge Studies in Social Anthropology, Cambridge University Press, Cambridge.

Cockburn, C. 1985. *Machinery of dominance: women, men and technical know-how*. Pluto Press, London.

Halford, S. and Savage, M. 1995. Restructuring organisations, changing people: gender and restructuring in banking and local government, *Work, Employment and Society* 9 1 97–122.

Hall, P. 1985. The geography of the fifth Kondratieff, in Hall, P. and Markusen, A. eds *Silicon landscapes* Allen and Unwin, London, 1–19.

Henry, N. and Massey, D. 1995. Competitive times in high tech, *Geoforum* 26 1 49–64.

Ho, M.-W. 1993. *The rainbow and the worm: the physics of organisms*. World Scientific, London.

Lefebvre, H. 1991. *The production of space*. Blackwell, Oxford.

Lloyd, G. 1984. *The man of reason: 'male' and 'female' in western philosophy*. Methuen, London.

Moore, H. 1986. *Space, text and gender*. Cambridge University Press, Cambridge.

Segal Quince and Partners 1985. *The Cambridge phenomenon*. Segal Quince and Partners, Cambridge.

CHAPTER 12

THE GEOGRAPHY OF POWER (2000)

'Seattle' managed to establish 'globalisation' as an important, and contestable, issue on the political agenda. That debate must be kept going, but has to avoid being fossilised into static oppositions that are difficult to get out of and which finally anyway lead nowhere.

1

The question of globalisation should not be posed as one of local versus global 'Local' may be good or bad, depending on your politics. The peasant farmers in India, being invaded by multinational companies armed with genetically modified products and bits of paper claiming patent rights over plants and seeds, are 'local', fighting to defend 'local rights'. But then so are the proponents of Fortress Europe, or those in California who vote for propositions banning 'illegal' Latin Americans from access to public services. The arguments against 'global' multinational capital's ability to roam the world, playing one group off against another, are certainly appealing. But then so are the arguments for more cultural exchange between countries and peoples. 'Going global' can be attractive or pernicious.

There has been a tendency on the left to treat the 'global' level with a degree of suspicion, partly because there is a feeling that nothing can be done about it. But this acquiesces to the dominant rhetoric – that globalisation is inevitable and we just have to work out the best ways of adapting to it. But globalisation we see at present is not inevitable, it is a project.

One example of the duplicity of this rhetoric of inevitability concerns the nation state. We are constantly being told that individual countries are powerless in the face of multinational capital, and it would be foolish to deny the changes in the relationship between capital and nation states. But many governments (and most particularly those of the USA and the UK) are active participants in the promotion of the current form of globalisation. It was the governments, not the companies, that signed up to the Uruguay round of world trade negotiations. Who gathered inside the splendid halls in Seattle for the World Trade Organisation meeting? Who began the process of nations giving away foreign-exchange control? (Margaret Thatcher, the supposed great defender of our sovereignty, as it happens.) We must not cede the global level of politics to the right.

The left is also suspicious of the global level itself. This is both dangerous and contradictory. First, we need particular kinds of global preconditions to preserve the ability to act locally, to continue the recognition of local specific-ity. Second, we need some kind of global bodies to prevent a further slide into a politics of might is right. The fact that the current bodies (the World Trade Organisation, the International Monetary Fund, the World Bank) do not cur-rently prevent this, and on many fronts are actually agents of the most pow-erful, does not mean that some kinds of global forums are not necessary. One of the biggest dangers, especially since Seattle, is the potential burgeoning of bi-lateral negotiations along the lines of the old Multi-lateral Agreement on Investment (MAI), and from which less powerful voices would be excluded from influence altogether.

Third, surely we want a kind of globalisation? Our political aim should be internationalist: an internationalism that respects local differences and the possibility of certain kinds of local action, yes; but emphatically not a localist future of hermetically sealed countries or cultures.

We are faced here with a problem of language. The word 'globalisation' has been hi-jacked to mean only the particular form of globalisation (neo-liberal and overwhelmingly concerned with the economic) that we suffer at the moment. But 'globalisation' really just means global interconnectedness, and it could take other forms, on different terms and embodying different kinds of power relations. Perhaps, indeed, there are the beginnings of ideas about how this might work in the decidedly international networks already being invented within the radical protest movements themselves. Either way, we need to wrest back the term for ourselves and argue for and imagine not the local rather than the global, but an alternative form of globalisation.

2

Setting up the question as local versus global is to accede to spatial fetishism. That is: imagining that 'space' or 'spatial scale' has a political meaning – to assume, for instance, that the local is always better simply because it is local. This is to side-step the real problem.

What is really at issue is the geography of power. The highly protected local economy of the USA is immensely powerful, the opened and invaded local economy of Mozambique is vulnerable. The global mobility of multinational capital is one thing, the global mobility of the world's poor would be another. There are, then, no formal spatial rules; it all depends on the power relations embedded in the specific situation.

On the political left we deplore the restrictions on international migration, we often point to the blatant inconsistency with the fact that capital (in the form of investment and trade etc) is encouraged to roam freely about the planet, and is admired for its ability to do so. Why should people not have the same rights?

But consider the following (probably apocryphal) tale. Some time during the 19th century a native American chief was asked by members of his society what had been the biggest mistake of the past generations' leaders. After pondering the new society that had grown up all about he answered: 'We failed to control immigration.'

Setting the native American chief against the likes of French rightwinger Jean-Marie Le Pen makes clear that it is not possible to base one's view of international migration on a simple notion of inalienable spatial rights. There are no abstract, generalisable answers to political questions of space and place. What is at issue is not just 'space' but the geography of social, political, and economic power.

3

'Globalisation' is about the restructuring of the world's geography, and the world is immensely varied and grotesquely unequal in terms of power. In such a situation, not only is an appeal to abstract spatial rights inappropriate, but so also may be many kinds of universal rules, which are just another kind of 'abstract and general' approach. They assume the spatial form matters over social content. It is the two together which we must address.

Take the 'rule' of free trade. It may be invoked to allow into a Third World country the likes of agricultural goods that will lay waste to a whole region, where production had undoubtedly been 'inefficient' but where it sustained a livelihood for far more people than now are needed, and formed the basis for far more than 'economics'.

Or resistance to free trade might be mounted by a First World country and its trade unions to protect a declining sector (textiles and clothing, say) against imports from a Third World country for which this is the most promising route for development – if the First World country would open up. On the other hand, these workers in the First World country are already among the lowest paid in that economy. Or again, a newly industrialising country is forbidden (because of 'the rules') to erect protective barriers to enable a nascent high-technology sector to gain a hold. In other words, the application of such a 'rule' may be perverse from whichever position of power or politics it is viewed.

The 'universal rules' currently wielded by bodies such as the WTO [World Trade Organization] are not applied evenly. There are special circumstances, there are politically difficult situations, appeals must be made. And the arguments of the already-powerful (their special circumstances, their politically difficult situations) usually win the day. Free trade is not anyway in truth 'free'. So one claim that we might make, and which many do make, is that the rules be applied with fairness.

And yet we might go further and ask: in such a situation of social and cultural variation and economic inequality, can any abstract set of rules be adequate? Even the powerful find that such rules produce perverse outcomes. It is for this reason that they negotiate around their exceptional circumstances. But would absolute 'fairness' in the application of such rules be any less perverse, from more progressive political points of view? If we vote for total free movement of both trade and people, is it 'fair' that it will be the relatively poor of the First World who will lose their jobs and find their council-housing stock coming under pressure?

'Judging' between the relatively poor of the First World and the ferociously poor of the Third World shows the lack of adequate relation between these rules and the social actors, with their highly differential powers, who are the agents of globalisation. Or our (caricatured) Third World country might want, quite reasonably, to argue for free trade in clothing and textiles but the right to some protection for the new economic sectors it is trying to grow. 'Quite reasonably', because, it argues, only in that way can it lever into action the development potential it believes it has.

But there are general considerations. Trade has environmental costs, for instance. And protection can result in a monopoly for local owners. (One of the dangers of the globalisation debate is thinking of countries as undifferentiated entities. Macro-economic statistics can conceal growing inequalities within countries. The IMF can pronounce 'a success' a country in which there is increasing poverty. The elites in many a Third World country stand to gain from globalisation in its present form.) But it is to argue that the equal application of abstract rules in unequal situations can lead to unfair outcomes. So we need the possibility of a more situated response, the exercise not of a geometrical logic, or the abstract spatial fetishism of a rule such as 'free trade', but of a practical reason.

4

This means asking what we are aiming at. There are many things that can be done: introducing a tax on financial speculation (Tobin tax), countering the decimation of public sector provision, arguing against the anti-developmental requirement of 'structural adjustment policies' for cuts in, for instance, education spending. But the big question must be: what kind of globalisation do we want? We need equalitarian, sustainable ethics of development.

We must first recognise that *almost nothing about 'globalisation' is simply a technical issue, nor simply self-evident.*

An example is 'subsidiarity' – a word about which everyone seems to agree. Of course it is best to have government 'as close as possible to the people'. But then other questions arise. What, for instance, about the wider impact, on other people in other places, of decisions taken 'locally'? Should not such people also be consulted? Or again, keeping all decisions local can make redistribution impossible and lead to a competition between localities in which the richest, the most powerful etc, would win. The point is that there is likely to be political disagreement over how to resolve these issues. Subsidiarity, and the question of which kinds of policy can best be dealt with at which levels, is not a purely technical question.

Rules such as the one that imposes free trade on all parts of the world regardless of their very different circumstances are presented as neutral. Their 'neutrality' is said to derive, indeed, from their universality. And yet the results can be devastatingly unequal.

Perhaps we should come at this another way. Why not begin from the outcomes that are sought and make them the principles by which actions have to be guided? Free trade is a means, not an outcome.

Could there be principles (rather than universally-applicable rules) against which to evaluate particular issues, specific situations? Principles of a globalisation that might put equality and environment above some socially unexamined notion of 'growth' which in fact is no more than a calculus of assets and profits, and which might include more than the most arid definition of economics? Could we, for instance, use quality-of-life and distributional measures?

The agreements on environmental goals involve precisely such principles and aims, but nowhere have they been taken as seriously as the trade rules. What is necessary is for agreed general aims, such as the desirability of cutting back on environmental degradation, to be backed up by targets (appropriately varied between different parts of the world) and sanctions for failing to meet those targets.

Agreeing such aims will not be easy in any international forum. We shall still need global bodies, and they will still need overarching remits. There are few 'purely technical' issues in this globalisation debate, and few things are 'self-evident' either. Even the principle of democracy, which seems self-evident in the West is challenged elsewhere. And we all know that the defence of 'local cultural forms' can be a way of maintaining intra-cultural domination (the suppression of women, for instance). Nonetheless, it can hardly be an advance simply to impose Western principles on other parts of the world – they have to be argued for. What we have to accept is the 'non-foundational' nature of such principles, that taking difference (the local) seriously means we cannot assume any particular principles as self-evident. They are the subject of political contestation.

But for this political contestation to be even dreamable, the globalisation process must be opened up to democratic influence.

Disgracefully, the Uruguay round barely registered in the UK's public political debate. But post-Seattle, debate must be pursued through protest movements, while multinational bodies such as the WTO need opening up and making more democratic. Both within and between countries there needs to be democratic debate. And, once again, a formal appearance of equality (one country one vote) is not enough.

International forums must provide the conditions for a democratic opening. The current disparity in resources for the delegations of different countries makes the idea of equal negotiations laughable. Funds and facilities need to be provided to even this up somewhat (although the USA, for instance, will always have more power).

In the UK we must contest the New Labour line that globalisation is inevitable; we should also contest its form. We should put on the agenda the question: what is globalisation for? What principles might we be aiming at for the international (internationalist) organisation of economy and society? Opening up that kind of a question to political debate will be endlessly difficult (and indeed possibly endless in that it may have to be periodically renewed) – but that is the nature of genuinely political debate. Learning to talk across difference in an interconnected world might be one step towards imagining an alternative form of globalisation.

CHAPTER 13

GLOBALISATION: WHAT DOES IT MEAN FOR GEOGRAPHY? (2002)

Let me begin, briefly, with two observations which provoke geographical reflection: the first concerns governments in the UK and USA (and lots more besides) who tell us that 'globalisation' is inevitable. (They really mean globalisation in its current form – which is to say 'neoliberal'.) They tell us it is the only possible future. And if you point to Nicaragua, Mali and Mozambique, which do not yet seem to be part of this future, they will tell you that such countries are just 'behind' and that eventually they will follow along the path which we have led. Perhaps my favourite example of this came in 1998 when Bill Clinton delivered himself of the reflection that we can no more resist the current forces of globalisation than we can resist the force of gravity. We might note in passing that this comes from a man who spends his life flying about in aeroplanes and thus quite effectively resisting the force of gravity! But, more seriously, of course globalisation is *not* a force of nature. It is a product of society – a political and economic *project* which requires the mighty efforts of the World Trade Organisation, International Monetary Fund, United States of America, multi-national corporations, World Bank, etc., to push it forward. The aim of Clinton's statement is to persuade us that there is no alternative. This is not a description of the world as it is, so much as an image in which the world is being made. Now, many criticisms can be made of this formulation, but I want to focus on one thing – that within Clinton's statement is a kind of sleight of hand in terms of how we think about space and time.

When we ask about Mozambique and the answer is that that country is just 'backward', what is really at issue is a denial of Mozambique's *difference* from us – or at least a reduction of that difference merely to the fact that Mozambique is 'behind' us in development. Co-existing difference is reduced to place in the historical queue. Effectively this is turning geography into history – space into time. The implication is that there is only one history; we are just all at different stages in it. We are not to imagine such other places as having their own trajectories, their own particular histories and – and this is the point – the potential for their own futures. (What if Mozambique does not *want* to follow us?) What this is saying is that they are merely at an earlier stage in the one and only narrative it is possible to tell. For me one of the most significant things about 'space' is that it is the dimension of the coexistence of others. The fact that *right now* other stories are going on: right now green beans are being grown for our table; people are hiding in the Church of the Nativity in Bethlehem. Clinton's is a 'geographical imagination' with no real geography in it at all. *Really* thinking spatially means looking out beyond ourselves; a recognition of others. Clinton's (and others') is a failure of geographical imagination.

The second observation concerns those who argue most strongly for 'free trade' as though there were some self-evident right to global mobility; the term 'free' immediately implying something good, something to be aimed at; as if it is self-evidently good to be able to roam the world. This is a geographical imagination of a world without borders. Yet come a debate on international migration and the same people will often have recourse to another geographical imagination altogether – equally powerful, equally (apparently) incontrovertible – yet in total contradiction. This is the imagination of defensible place, of the rights of local people to their own local places, of a world divided by difference and the smack of firm boundaries. It is a geographical imagination of nationalisms. Two apparently self-evident truths, two completely different geographical imaginations, are called upon in turn. No matter that they contradict each other, because it works. And so in this era of the 'globalisation' of capital, we have people risking their lives in the Channel Tunnel, and boats full of people going down in the Mediterranean. And part of what makes this possible is a duplicitous manipulation of geographical imaginations.

GEOGRAPHY'S INTELLECTUAL CONTRIBUTION

One of the reasons, for me, that 'geography' as a discipline is so inspiring is that it ranges so widely. Through the social, the cultural and the economic; and through human geography and physical geography. The problem this can lead to is that it may be seen as some kind of glorified general knowledge. I have to confess that I have a complicated response to this characterisation. I am really in favour of 'general knowledge', in the sense of a broad awareness of the world. It is an important element in the fulfilment of human potential. On the other hand I do want to assert that geography is *more* than general knowledge. It has its own distinctive intellectual contribution to make to an understanding of the world; as the above two reflections were meant to indicate, and for which the spatial turn in social science research provides abundant evidence. The rest of this brief article explores two other examples. They concern issues on which I am working at the moment, which are set within the wider theme of globalisation, and which illustrate the distinctive contribution which geography can make to the debate about what it might mean to live in, and to be a 'citizen' in, these times.

UNDERSTANDING PLACE

First, we have, as geographers, and in the context of the changed landscape of globalisation, reworked one of our central concepts: *place*. No longer do we think of place – or region, or nation – as simply bounded territories with 'eternal' 'essential' characteristics which somehow grow out of the soil. Rather we (or many of us) now lay stress on understanding the identity of place as the product also of its relations with elsewhere. We know we cannot understand the character of any place without setting it in the context of its relations with the world beyond. This is place as meeting place: different stories coming together and, to one degree or another, becoming entangled. This is the thrown-togetherness of physical proximity, and it is even more marked in an age of globalisation. 'A global sense of place.' This is the specifically geographical version of the more general social scientific argument about 'the relational construction of identity'. Moreover, it implies that places (as meeting places) are internally complicated. They are not simply coherent 'communities'. Rather than focusing on 'local communities', what this view emphasises is that places *need to be negotiated*. And yet, in government policy responses to urban poverty we hear invocations over and over again of 'the local community' in a completely unquestioned way. Either such a community is assumed to be there, or – if it is lacking – it must be made.

A number of geographers are now trying to use our work on place to get some messages across. First, that there is *no* unproblematic place-based local community. Second, what is more, that the *creation* of such a community should not even be the aim. What we want to emphasise is a notion of place as one of the arenas where people (of all ages) learn to negotiate with others – to learn to form this thing called society. It is a practice of daily negotiation which we could understand as the beginnings of democracy. In a way it is incredible that places – most places – 'work' as well as they do. And when they break down we should not try to force upon them an old notion of coherence. Because a healthy democracy requires, not pacification into conformity, but an open recognition of difference, and an ability to negotiate it with mutual respect. [...]

The second area I wish to discuss relates to the Geographical Association's position statement. The statement on the purpose of geographical education identifies as one of its aims the development of 'an ability and willingness to take positive action both locally and globally' (GA, 1999, p. 57). And it is with some thoughts about that, and with a focus on the global, that I want to conclude.

GLOBAL PLACE/LOCAL PLACE

John Berger – writer, artist and political progressive – has written that, in these days, 'it is space rather than time that hides consequences from us'. In other words, how difficult it is in our daily lives to remember the wider relations through which the green beans arrive on our plate. Can we, as geographers, play some part in grappling with this? Let me take up again this question of 'local place'. So often, when we talk about 'local place', we also use terms like real, every day, lived; such words hang in the air, reverberate, evoke 'place' as somehow especially meaningful. And lots of 'intellectuals' would back that up with high-sounding propositions. Thus Edward Casey has written that: 'To live is to live locally, and to know is first of all to know the places one is in' (1996, p. 18). Arif Dirlik likewise argues: 'The struggle for place in the concrete is a struggle against power and the hegemony of abstractions' (1998). And Carter, Donald and Squires, in their book *Space and Place*, write that 'Place is space to which meaning has been attached' (1993, p. xii). Indeed we probably all make such associations at one time or another.

But I think it is quite dangerous. If place really *is* a meeting place then 'the lived reality of our daily lives' is far from being localised – in its connections, its sources and resources, and in its repercussions, that 'daily life' spreads much wider. Where would we draw the line around 'the grounded reality of the everyday'? That is one question 'thinking geographically' might throw up. But there is another. If we imagine place as the meaningful side of space then that implies that 'space', the 'global', the wider world, is in contrast somehow abstract: *not* real and lived; *not* meaningful. Yet a lot of our work – as geographical researchers and as geography teachers – is concerned to demonstrate precisely the opposite: precisely to track the routes by which the green beans arrive on your plate; to trace in great detail (to give just one example) the commodity chains through which our lives are sustained. What we are showing when we research and teach such things is not that local places are *not* grounded, real, etc., but that global spaces *are so too*. If we really imagine 'local places' relationally – as meeting places – then those relations may go around the world. In that sense 'the global' is just as 'real' and 'grounded', even just as 'everyday', as is the so-called local place.

Now I believe that argument to be important both generally in an ethical and political sense and in relation to the GA's statement of geography's purpose. For we have, in general in society at large, a very particular geography of how we think about care and responsibility. It is a kind of nested, Russian-doll, geography. First there is home and family, then perhaps locality, then nation, and so on outwards. There is a kind of accepted understanding that we care first for and have our first responsibilities towards those nearest in. Yet in an age of globalisation, and in the light of the way of imagining space and place that I have been talking about, could we not open up that set of nested boxes? Could we not consider a different geography of care and responsibility? We might think of it as an ethics, a politics, of connectivity rather than of nested territories. Specifically we could open up a bit more *the question of (the possibility of) responsibility and care at a distance.*

IMAGINED GEOGRAPHY

In a world as unequal as this one is, and where the whole planet is, in one way or another, implicated in the daily lives of each of us, this is a question which *has* to be addressed. There are many reasons for that Russian-doll geography which dominates at the moment. There is the still-remaining impact – in this world said to be increasingly virtual – of material, physical, proximity (place). There are all the rhetorics of territory – of nation and of family – through which we are daily urged to construct our maps of loyalty. There is a perhaps obsessive focus – when thinking of care and responsibility – on parent-child relationships. But there are also those notions of the local as more real than the global, of place as more real than space. And this is where 'geography' can make a specific contribution to the debate. In *Globalising Care*, Fiona Robinson (1996) explicitly draws on the work of geographers in order to address these issues. She argues that in order to think about duties and responsibilities we have to imagine the world in terms of social relations. She argues, too, that abstract appeals to a shared humanity will not be an adequate motivation – that what is needed is a practical understanding of the relations which connect us. Or again, Moira Gatens and Genevieve Lloyd, two important contemporary philosophers, have argued (in *Collective Imaginings*, 1999) in relation to our *historical* responsibilities that we have to take responsibility for the past because it is out of that past that we have been produced. The case which they are considering is modern-day Australia's responsibility for the historical treatment of aboriginal people and culture. They write: 'we are responsible for the past not because of what we as individuals have done, but because of what we are' (1999, p. 81) – in other words, because that past has made us (it is that relational construction of identity again). And the geographer's reply (my reply) should be: can we not argue that same case for geography too? That we should take responsibility for the *geographical* as well as the historical relations that make us what we are. After all, we eat those green beans.

That of course would be a far greater challenge. But what seems to be widely agreed is that crucial *both* to the recognition of that challenge *and* to the motivation to take it up is the nature and capacity of our imaginations. So Gatens and Lloyd write that imagination crucially involves an active awareness of others. And I would extend that observation to argue that the geographies of our imaginations are a crucial aspect of that proposition. Indeed Richard Rorty – another eminent philosopher of our day – has written that:

> Intellectual and moral progress is not a matter of getting closer to the True or the Good or the Right … It is an increase in imaginative power … moral progress consists in an increasing responsiveness to the needs of a larger and larger variety of people and things. (1999, pp. 87 and 81)

And – reflecting back on the GA's position statement – the specifically geographical aspect of that 'imaginative power' – in its potential richness and also in its intellectual rigour – is absolutely central to such progress. If, as John Berger argues, it *is* space that currently hides things from us then it is part of our responsibility and our contribution as teachers of geography to expand both our knowledge and our imaginations to make that less the case.

REFERENCES

Dirlik, A. (1998) 'Globalisation and the politics of place', *Development*, 41, 2, pp. 7–13.

Casey, E. (1996) How to get from space to place in a rainy short stretch of time' in Field, S. and Baso, K. (eds) *Senses of Place*. Santa Fé: School of American Research, pp. 14–51.

Carter, E., Donald, J. and Squires, J. (1993) *Space and Place: Theories of identity and location*. London: Lawrence and Wishart.

Geographical Association (1999) Geography in the curriculum: a position statement from the GA, *Teaching Geography*, 24, 2, pp. 57–9.

Gatens, M. and Lloyd, G. (1999) *Collective Imaginings: Spinoza, past and present*. London: Routledge.

Robinson, F. (1999) *Globalizing Care: Ethics, feminist theory, and international relations*. Boulder: Westview Press.

Rorty, R. (1999) *Philosophy and Social Hope*. Harmondsworth: Penguin.

PART III

SPACE

SPATIALIZING POWER: DOREEN MASSEY ON SPACE AS DOMINATION AND POTENTIAL

Marion Werner, Rebecca Lave, Brett Christophers and Jamie Peck

In the 1980s and 1990s, academics increasingly turned to space as an explanatory concept. In cultural studies and political philosophy, space was mobilized primarily as a metaphor to aid in conceptualizing the "posts" of poststructuralism and postmodernism, while the social sciences repurposed space to make globalization tractable. As Henri Lefebvre observed, space was at once conspicuously absent and on every page of much social theory. But for Massey, the crux of the problem was not that the idea of space being circulated was vague. Rather, the problem was that the term was utilized to indicate a sphere of closure, of stasis, and, fundamentally, an absence of politics. Over numerous publications, Massey detailed the stakes involved in perpetuating this theoretical blind spot and offered a positive and dynamic theory of space instead. She argued that space was the product of relations and multiplicity; space was thus the condition for imagining a future not already foretold by the dominant temporal frames of modernism (i.e., progress, development, 'the West'). Central to Massey's theory of space was the problematic of hierarchical dualisms. Space and time were framed in Western thought in ways not only analogical to other central dualisms (man/woman, culture/nature, reason/emotion, etc), but also in combination with them; it was these combinations, of economic inequality with racial oppression, for example, that produced spatial relations of domination and subordination. Massey thus insisted upon an understanding of space that was shot through with the symbolic and material conditions of exclusion and oppression, on the one hand, and the potential of forging "relations otherwise," on the other.

The essays in this section offer the reader a view of the arc of Massey's thought on space as a relationship of power. Her approach to space developed first and foremost in the wake of the radical turn in geography of the 1970s. During that decade, the discipline was upended by a rejection of the quantitative revolution and an embrace of social constructivist approaches to spatial forms. The implications of this epistemic shift were profound: rather than search for spatial causes of observed spatial patterns, radical geographers, influenced by the work of Marx, instead identified generalizable spatial dynamics of capitalist restructuring.

Massey considered this exclusive focus on general principles a mistake, however, and offered a remarkably concise assessment and critique of these developments in her essay titled "New Directions in Space" written in 1985 (Chapter 14). Here, reflecting the influence of critical realism on her thinking at the time, Massey argued that the radical turn in geography – and its strong claims to space as a social construction – had mistakenly thrown the baby out with the bathwater. Ultimately, the place-specific outcomes of a process such as industrial restructuring – while partially attributable to capital's relentless pursuit of value – could not be fully explained by it. To Massey, the political impetus to identify the underlying causes of place-based disinvestment in general terms should not be pursued at the cost of relegating particularity to the margins. "The unique is back on the agenda," Massey famously concluded. If space were truly constitutive of social relations, then the task of the discipline was to identify precisely where and how space – that is, geography – mattered.

To specify exactly how space mattered, Massey developed her relational approach to space over more than a decade of work, beginning with her 1984 monograph *Spatial Divisions of Labour*. As we have discussed in our other editorial contributions in this volume, Massey insisted on approaching the objects of her study – firms, jobs, branch plants, places and regions – as sets of socio-spatial relations, that is, inter-dependent phenomena stretched out over space. Massey illustrated this point at length in her analysis of uneven development in *Spatial Divisions of Labour*. In subsequent publications, she extended her framework to unpaid work and household relations, and to occupations central to the much-trumpeted knowledge economy. In an essay titled "Reflections on gender and geography" (Chapter 16), written for a collection on social change and the middle class, Massey elaborated on her insights into the socio-spatial dynamics of the managerial and professional classes. Foreshadowing later work on London as a world city, Massey insisted that the clustering of managerial "command" and research "conceptualization" occupations in the southeast of England was inseparable from industrial restructuring and gendered productions of class. The social status of new scientist-entrepreneurs was achieved through reinforcing the position of their "service wives," who sacrificed their careers for their male partners, whose positions demanded maximum flexibility, that is, minimal responsibilities for care work (see also Chapter 11). But the reproduction of these masculinized occupations was tied not only to the intimate spaces of the household, but also to place-based practices of race and class segregation. A far cry from later celebrations of the so-called creative class, Massey argued that the increased spatial division between conception and execution under monopoly capitalism created key geographies of exclusion, such as the "quintessential" English countryside of the outer South East tied to the cultural production of a particular sort of English whiteness. For Massey, then, power, was indeed spatialized: it determined the degree, relation and control over spatial flexibility while simultaneously producing rarefied places of social exclusion.

As Massey continued to engage in debates over the mobilization of "space" in social theory in the 1990s, she expanded upon her notion of relational thinking. She did this in large part by mobilizing feminist theory to unpack key masculinist assumptions that underpinned reductive, economistic approaches to Marxism and social theory more broadly. She famously undertook this task in her essay "Flexible sexism" (Chapter 15). Here, Massey offered withering critiques of two major figures in geography – Ed Soja and David Harvey – and their work on postmodernism. Neither author accounted for how his own position shaped his understanding of the modernism/postmodernism debate (see also Chapters 9 and 10). In failing to do so, both Harvey and Soja had missed the significance of feminist critiques of modernism and the political potential of postmodernism, and thus had fundamentally misunderstood the sociospatial relations they attempted to analyze.

Critique for Massey was never merely a scholastic exercise; it was always part of a process of offering alternative approaches. In this section, we are pleased to reprint selections from the concluding chapter of the second edition of *Spatial Divisions of Labour*, titled "Reflections on debates over a decade" (Chapter 18), which offers a unique perspective on that process. The selection includes what we believe to be the most extensive, detailed reflections on Massey's formulation of an anti-essentialist, feminist Marxism through her readings of Marx, Althusser, Poulantzas, Laclau and many feminists – especially Chantal Mouffe, Donna Haraway, and Jane Jenson – in whom she saw her own intellectual journey in part reflected. Massey drew on these thinkers to elaborate her notion of relationality, intimately tied to the concept of articulation as "an approach to the contingencies and uniquenesses, as well as the broad structures, of space-time" (Chapter 18: 302). In her "Reflections", as in her better-known essay, "The politics of space/time" (Chapter 17), Massey recognized the political potential of thinking of identity in terms of relations – especially in the work of Ernesto Laclau – but recognized how that potential was undercut by the mobilization of space as a separate dimension from time, and ultimately, as devoid of politics. Drawing upon her early critiques of the radical turn in geography and gendered hierarchical dualisms, as well as sympathetic readings of theoretical physics, Massey made the case for an alternative, relational view of space-time to a wide audience. Her approach would indeed be picked up far beyond geography, as scholars recognized the significance of her claims to rethink fields as disparate as ethnography, architecture and design, and cultural studies in relational terms.

Massey continued to explore the relationship between identity and space, and its implications for politics, throughout the 1990s. Her efforts, as we discussed in the introduction to Part II, were spurred by resurgent nationalisms as the former Soviet Union and Eastern bloc countries faced emboldened, exclusivist identity claims tied to homogeneous, closed and essentialist constructions of place. In her essay "Philosophy and politics of spatiality" (Chapter 19), delivered as the distinguished Hettner Lecture in Heidelberg in 1998, Massey systematized her relational approach to space and its implications for identity and politics. Many of the themes summarized here would figure prominently in her 2005 book, *For Space*. Fundamentally, Massey argued that for there to be the possibility of difference, there must be space. In other words, if thinkers were to avoid the trappings of reducing space to time, that is, of casting "non-Western" places as merely stages (backward, developing) along a unilinear trajectory of modernity, then space had to be understood as an active category of multiplicity, of becoming. In short, a relational conception of space – that is, space-time – was the pre-condition for the possibility of multiple histories, multiple trajectories, and thus the possibility of coexistence. The lecture deepened the philosophical underpinnings of what was already one of her most well-known ideas: a progressive, or global, sense of place (Chapters 9 and 10). If place were to be conceived as a set of relations – as open, evolving and becoming – then one could both be deeply rooted to place, and defend its specificity, while also having internationalist commitments and responsibilities.

Massey's ideas of space and power traveled across disciplines and borders. Her basic insight that space was not only a production of relations of power, but also that power itself was spatialized was summarized by her concept of power-geometry (Chapter 9). In the mid-2000s, this concept was adopted by the government of Hugo Chavez as one the five "motors" of the Bolivarian revolution in Venezuela. In "Concepts of space and power in theory and in political practice", Massey reflected on the experience of her geographical concept "being put to positive political use" (Chapter 20: 321). She explored the significance of thinking of place as relational and space as potential in the actual ferment of Venezuela's socialist experiment.

As the essays collected here demonstrate, space for Massey was a dimension that opened up the potential of other worlds and becomings, while also manifesting and reproducing social inequality and injustice. These two notions of space subtended both the everyday, seemingly mundane as well as the overtly political. Space can thus be understood as the possibility for contingency and the unexpected as our identities form in-relation, and, therefore, the terrain where political articulations and antagonisms are forged. In short, space is where the shape of the future – never foretold – is played out. In this way, as her eponymous monograph powerfully demonstrated, Massey was "for space". Many have found it difficult to hold these two conceptualizations of space – as the site of emancipatory potential and of entrenched domination – together. Massey, throughout her career, was uncompromising in her insistence that scholars and activists committed to social change had no other choice.

CHAPTER 14

NEW DIRECTIONS IN SPACE (1985)

ELEMENTS OF THE STORY SO FAR

Those in the 'discipline' of geography have for long had a difficult relation to the notion of 'space' and 'the spatial'. There has been much head-scratching, much theorising, much changing of mind. Sometimes the notion has been clasped whole-heartedly as the only claimable distinguishing characteristic within the academic division of labour. Sometimes it has been spurned as necessarily fetishised. There have also, along with these switchbacks, been major shifts in the way in which 'space/the spatial' was itself to be conceived.

The 1960s and 1970s respectively provide instances of two extremes in this lurching relationship, and it is out of that history that emerges the first argument of this essay. The fundamental message is simple; that the radical critique of the 1970s – for very understandable reasons both intellectual and political – went far too far overboard in its rejection of the importance of the spatial organisation of things, of distance and perhaps above all, of geographical differentiation.

Go back a moment to the period before 1960; that bygone age when human geography, or at least a central part of it, was plainly about 'regions'. School and university courses were organised around sections of the world. There were courses on 'Africa', on 'Asia', on 'The Regions of the British Isles'. The focus was on place, on difference, on distinctiveness – on uniqueness. The concern was to understand how localities come to be as they are, how they get their particular character. Certainly, it was not always the most sophisticated theoretical work. There tended to be rather a lot of chapters which simply started with geology and ended up with politics. But what this focus *did* give to this section of the social sciences was an element of distinctiveness. First, it was concerned with putting things together, rather than tearing them apart; with trying to understand links, relationships, synthesis, rather than being concerned only with the dissection of analysis. It was, therefore, necessarily concerned with the unique. Second, this focus gave geography an object of its own, a bit of the world (quite literally) on which it could focus – the place, the region, the locality.

All this was overthrown in the 1960s. Along with other social sciences, geography too was hit by the 'positivist revolution' – in particular in its quantitative guise. The old regional geography was hidden away in embarrassment and the door closed firmly on it. It was explained away as part of our own Dark Ages, whence we had now emerged on to the High Plains of truly scientific endeavour. The story is familiar and we need not dwell on it. Such an enterprise, of course, went well with the wider characteristics of the period [...] With the urban problem beginning to nudge its way on to the political agenda, we built mathematical models of trip distribution, of modal split, and agonised over questions of the length of the journey to work. And, of course, all of that was common to many social sciences. Geography shared with them all the problems of that kind of an approach – the trivial notions of causality, the idea that a scientific 'law' was something that could be spotted simply through empirical regularity (so long as you had enough observations), the mathematics (or problems in the mathematics) leading the direction of enquiry rather than questions which arose from the real world processes themselves. But the new wave posed 'geographers' with a problem in addition to all these. For what exactly was being modelled? What kinds of laws and relationships were being sought? Laws about *what*, precisely? What had happened was that the convergence of method had left geography without an object. The insistence that only the general and the generalisable were scientific left geography shorn of one of its central concerns. The last thing in which one should be interested in this brave new world was the unique, the particular, the specific. Such stuff was to be disposed of by normalisation; it was a hindrance to the cause of science. Things were relatively easy for economics, for sociology, for politics – or so it seemed. However difficult it was to define, they had a section of the substantive world to study – the economy, the social, the political. Geography had no such segment of the world to claim for its own, no particular bit of social relations to section off and study. All it had – or all it appeared to have – was a dimension: space, distance.

So what happened was that geography set itself up as 'the science of the spatial'. There were spatial laws, spatial relationships, spatial processes. There was a notion that there were certain principles of spatial interaction which could be studied devoid of their social content. At a less highflown, but socially more significant, level, there was an obsession with the identification of spatial regularities and an urge to explain them by spatial factors. The explanation of geographical patterns, it was argued, lay within the spatial. There was no need to look further. As we have said, the inner city problem was coming to prominence at that time, and it provides a good case in point. For *there* was a clear spatial regularity. Geographers (and by no means only geographers), assuming that behind every spatial pattern lies a spatial cause, looked to the characteristics of the inner cities (in other words to the characteristics of the location itself) to explain their demise. This was probably the initial geographical version of blaming the victims for their own problems. What had happened in this combination of the rush for positivism and the need for an identity in the institutionalised academic division of labour was that geographers and geography had made some astonishing claims – that there was a world of the purely spatial, spatial laws devoid of substance or content, and spatial processes it was possible to wrench out of their social context.

The bulk of the 1970s and indeed until now, has been taken up with arguing that this is an untenable position, that there are no such things as purely spatial processes; there are only particular social processes operating over space. It was now argued that what was happening in the inner cities – the loss of industrial jobs – had more to do with industry than with the cities, that the cities were at the sharp end of what was to become a much more general process of deindustrialisation. It was also argued that the fact that they *were* at the sharp end had more to do with the character of their industry (that it was less competitive, more labour-intensive, with lower productivity) than with the cities' characteristics as locations. In other words, it was argued – to such an extent that it became a theme tune of the times – that the spatial is a social construct. It is a position which, in very general terms, still holds good.

But, in its turn, it also entailed some serious problems. First – and to talk only in terms of the academic division of labour – it meant that geography was deprived of its spatial role. It discovered, in other words, that the root causes of what it wanted to explain lay outside the discipline. Geographers either had to go off and learn another social science, or take up a position at the end of the transmission belt of the social sciences, dutifully mapping the outcomes of processes which it was the role of others to study. That problem of job demarcation in academe would not in itself have been important, had it not been also for its obverse. For conceptual work in many other social sciences continued to proceed blithely as though the world existed on the head of a pin, as though it were distanceless and spatially undifferentiated. The substance laws of the other social sciences, in other words, continued for the most part to be spatially blind. And what *that* meant, ironically, was that both spatial and substantive disciplines were now underestimating the importance of geography.

This was true in another way too. For along with this down-playing of the role of geography in general went a continued down-playing of the importance of the particularity, the individuality, of places. The focus of the radical critique of the 1970s was far less on the huge variety of outcomes we see in the world around us than in unravelling their common underlying cause. The argument on the whole was not just that spatial patterns are caused by social processes, but that they are caused by *common* social processes. This was an important argument to make, especially at that time. The inner cities were now beginning to vie with the regions as a political problem. And in such circumstances it was not inconvenient to government and policymakers to let the two compete with each other. This story of divide and rule is now well known. And it was therefore of fundamental importance for those of us concerned with this problem to point out not only that you cannot just blame the victim, but that the victims were all going down to a common malady, that far from competing over *regional* policy it would be better to make common cause about *national* policies. So it *was* important and it is still important to stress what was general to those different geographical outcomes. But it was nonetheless done at some cost, and the cost once again was the downplaying of the importance of geography – in this case of geographical variations, of the uniqueness of outcomes.

My summary critique of the critique of the 1970s would be, then, that 'geography' was underestimated; it was underestimated as distance, and it was underestimated in terms of local variation and uniqueness. Space *is* a social construct – yes. But social relations are also constructed over space, and that makes a difference.

INDUSTRIAL CHANGE AND SPATIAL CHANGE

Within studies of industrial location the big advance of the 1970s was to get production itself into the equation. Instead of the exclusive concentration on 'location factors' and on explaining one spatial pattern by another, it was argued that it was necessary to examine what was going on inside the factory or office, that 'location factors' were themselves the result of changes in production, and that in order to understand spatial change it was necessary to go behind 'spatial factors' and spatial pattern [...] Formally it led to a whole series of studies in which the dominant lines of causality were understood to run from causes of changes in production, through those changes themselves (changes in technology, reorganisations of the labour process, etc.) to an evaluation of the impact of those changes on the locational requirements of production, to the explanation of the (changes in) spatial pattern. There were, of course, variants. There was a strong line of argument that in many situations spatial considerations might be totally unimportant in the production of spatial outcomes. This might be true in cases where decisions were being made about closures, for example, or jobs were being lost through intensification of the labour process. In such circumstances spatial patterns of job loss (whether resulting from the operation of the market or from decisions within multi-locational companies) might result entirely from internal characteristics of individual plants rather than from any more obviously spatial factors, such as the wider characteristics of the areas within which plants were located. But in very general terms the explanations tended to follow the stages indicated above. It was essentially a one-way, linear sequence. What was crucial to it (and what was new) was that spatial change was understood as being an outcome of production change.

It was, as I have said, an important point to make at the time, and it needed driving home, but it also now needs to be modified, for it is not the whole of the story – or rather, the story is not quite so simple. The sequence 'production change → spatial change' ignores the crucial impact of spatially-organised locational opportunities (or the lack of them) and of the use of distance and spatial separation themselves. Each of them can have an impact on what happens to production. The use by capital of locational change as part of a wider strategy for weakening workers' resistance is now well-known. It may also (perhaps more interestingly, though certainly more difficult to 'prove') work in the opposite direction – so that the spatial *im*mobilisation of certain elements of capital is part of what conditions the introduction of changes in the organisation of production. The accelerated development of sweated labour and homeworking in the clothing industry in the East End of London in the late 1960s was in part a product of the fact that this section of the industry (small family capital, short production runs, more connection to fashion outlets) was far less spatially mobile than that part of the industry under the control of large capital and concentrating on more mass-produced clothes. Both sections of the industry were under severe cost-pressures, mainly on labour-costs, but they solved their problems in entirely different ways. Big capital left the city, seeking out cheaper labour elsewhere. For the rest, such a strategy was impossible and a solution had to be found on site. For them new, cheaper and more vulnerable sources of labour were sought out by changes in the social organisation of production.

[...]

Very much the same kind of argument can be made of the relation between the spatial organisation of production, on the one hand, and that of occupational and social structure, on the other. One significant development since the 1960s has been the concentration on the increasingly important elements of spatial differentiation of occupational structures within firms. In some cases this has gone along with the separation, within individual firms, of different stages of production (part-process spatial structures); in others it has been organised around 'product-cycle' hierarchies of plants; in yet others it has simply been a case of large numbers of branch plants each producing the same commodity (Massey, 1984). In all these cases, however, lengthening managerial hierarchies were stretched out over space.

The fact that this was happening was recognised quite early. The work of Hymer (1972) and of Westaway (1974) was pre-eminent in pointing out the performance of different levels and kinds of managerial functions at different locations. There was a hierarchy, social and spatial, from the strategic to the routine. There are two points to be made about this. First, what are really 'stretched out over space' are the relations of economic ownership and possession (Massey, 1984). It is a hierarchy of particular places in these relations, related to the performance of particular functions. And those members of the managerial structure occupying different places within that hierarchy thereby have different places also in relation to the overall antagonism, within the relations of production, between capital and labour. Such differences are one element only in the determination of place in social structure. Roughly, the nearer to headquarters you are functionally, the higher your social status, and since the hierarchies have a spatial form, social and spatial differentiation are clearly related.

But second, it is the nature of this relationship (between social form – or in this case more accurately, *place* in the relations of economic ownership and possession within capitalist production – and spatial form) which is interesting. It is usually characterised, at least implicitly, as though a pre-existing managerial hierarchy is, in explanatory terms, subsequently allocated across space, as though the process is akin to dealing out between locations a pre-existing pack of cards. There is an implicit, perhaps unnoticed, assumption that the extended hierarchies of management and control were developed with the *aspatial* concentration of capital and *then* were distributed between plants as the large firms developed multi-locational patterns.

It did not, of course, happen like that. Becoming multi-locational was part and parcel of the growth of large firms; it was also part of the extension of the hierarchies of management and control. What is important to the argument here is that that very fact was one of the things which influenced the social divisions which developed within managerial hierarchies. The fact of multi-locationality itself will push towards the adoption of particular kinds of divisions in terms of the formal disaggregation of functions within the overall social relations of production. The hierarchy of managerial functions, and of managerial personnel, which stretches, say, from the headquarters in the metropolitan region, to a regional headquarters in a smaller city, to an outlying branch plant, is in part moulded in its form by the fact of spatial separation. So, too, is the hierarchy of social status and the detail of social structure. These are not just social divisions of labour distributed over space; the form of the social division is itself influenced by the *fact* that it is distributed over space.

216

It is also more than that. Spatial distribution and contrasting geographical contexts – spatial structure in a wider sense – will also mould the social divisions which exist. Certainly there is evidence for this in Britain today. At the lower end of management hierarchies, at the level of a lowly local branch-plant, management can be reduced to fairly routine administration and management can feel almost as much on the receiving end of, and in the dark about, decisions handed down from above as is the production workforce. That sense of differentiation, and potential antagonism, can be reinforced both by relative geographical isolation from other elements of 'their managerial class' and, when branch plants are in far-flung, production only regions, by their very different social context [...]

Thus the fact that social processes take place over space and in a geographically-differentiated world affects their operation. Many of the most significant changes in social structure which have taken place in recent years in the UK could not really even be sensibly conceptualised outside a spatial geographically variegated form. From a point in the early 1960s where shortage of labour seemed for a moment to be a block on the hoped-for expansion of production, what has actually emerged is that the restructuring of British capital has taken place in a context of decelerating job-growth and subsequent decline. At the beginning of the period what was necessary was an expanded supply of labour. Later the requirement became much more simply cheaper labour. In both cases spatial expansion, geographical movement, was essential to capital's way out of its problems. In the first place the peripheral regions were needed as extensions to the supply of labour. Later their labour was used to undercut the strength of labour elsewhere [...]

Understanding the spatial organisation of society, then, is crucial. It is central to our understanding of the way in which social processes work out, possibly to our conceptualisation of some of those processes in the first place, and certainly to our ability to act on them politically.

THE QUESTIONS AHEAD

While this is easy to say – or seems so now as we forget the enthusiasm with which we denied spatiality in the 1970s! – it is not always so easy to see how to incorporate that understanding into analysis. Some things, perhaps, are clear enough. A re-recognition of the importance of spatial structure does not, for instance, imply that spatial structure in itself has determinate effects. Take for instance that well-known spatial form – small local labour markets with single dominant employers. It is a form frequently invoked in explanations of the state of labour relations within particular industries. But it is invoked, with equal equanimity, to 'explain' two very different results. For every time that it is invoked to explain 'paternalism' and labour quiescence (for instance in the textile-related industry of north-east Lancashire) it is also invoked as a part of the backcloth to militancy and solidarity (for instance in the colliery towns of the Welsh valleys). It is not, in other words, the spatial form in itself which has determinate effects. The social structures of which this *was* the spatial form were utterly different in the two locations – the kind of capital and the kind of labour were in complete contrast. It was these different social structures *in* these particular spatial forms which had such well-recognised outcomes.

I would argue then that one cannot formulate a world of spatial forms and spatial effects, in a manner reminiscent of the 1960s. But what of the obverse of that problem? Can we have social theories without spatial content or delimitation? Can we validly conjure with processes, structures, generative mechanisms or what have you, as though they occur on the head of a pin? In what sense is spatial form constitutive of social relations? If the spatial is not autonomous from the social, can the social be theorised autonomously from its spatial form, requirements and implications? What, in other words, is the effective import for research of this widening recognition of the significance of the spatial and the geographical?

[...] If we really mean that it is impossible to conceptualise social processes and structures outside their spatial form and spatial implications, then the latter must also be incorporated into our initial formulations and definitions, into our basic concepts – of capital, for instance, to point to the most obvious. That is no easy task. There are some clear possibilities – in the spatial implications of the self-expansion of capital, for instance. Yet so often the results seem either incredibly limited and banal (reinforcing the difficulties already being experienced in elaborating a wide and full range of generative mechanisms and causal properties) or we get involved in rather arbitrary series of multiple possibilities for how social processes will operate in a range of different and individually and formally-specified 'spatial contexts'. Neither seems on the face of it a very attractive possibility.

Yet necessary relations are not aspatial. How can 'necessary' relations be necessary if they depend, for example, on contiguity – unless that contiguity is specified? Inherent causal properties may depend on spatial form. What then happens to the argument that 'the spatial' is necessarily contingent? As a number of commentators have remarked, the whole realm of politics and culture, like the spatial, often also seems to be relegated to the arena of the contingent. The two seem to be closely related. But to accept that position would leave the range of possible necessary relations extremely limited, and limited primarily to the economic. Part of what is fundamentally at issue here is the reassessment of our definition of necessary relations within the social sciences.

It may indeed be argued that 'geography' only comes on to the scene at a later stage of analysis – that it is inherently contingent. The question then is what becomes of the injunction that social processes are constituted spatially? Williams (1981) has made a trenchant argument on the parallel relations between the social and the natural; that they are impossible to conceptualise separately and then 'put together'. And what of Urry's (1981) important point that the operation of social laws over space may change the nature of those laws themselves? Equating the geographical with the concrete seems to be a very minimalist position.

[...] The unique is back on the agenda. The recognition and understanding of particularity is theoretically the mirror image of, and politically the equally-necessary obverse of, pointing to the generality and necessity of underlying mechanisms. And much of this particularity is spatially structured. In that sense the widening recognition of the importance of the geography of social structures, and of the fact that social structures are in the concrete world constituted geographically, is in tune with a widening and more general appreciation of specificity and of internal form. It is certainly important, both politically and theoretically, to developments within the social sciences. Even while some of the more fundamental theoretical questions remain unresolved (or, as they may remain, forever in dispute), it is vital that we accept, and continue to insist upon, the importance of space and spatial variations in *concrete* analysis.

REFERENCES

Hymer, S. (1972) 'The Multinational corporation and the Law of Uneven Development' in Bhagwati, J. N. (ed.) *Economics and World Order.* Macmillan, London, 133–40.

Massey, D. (1984) *Spatial Divisions of Labour: Social Structures and the Geography of Production,* Macmillan, London.

Urry, J. (1981) *The Anatomy of Capitalist Societies: The Economy, Civil Society and the State.* Macmillan, London.

Westaway, J. (1974) 'The Spatial Hierarchy of British Business Organisations and its Implications for the British Urban System', *Regional Studies,* vol. 8, pp. 145–55.

Williams, S. (1981) 'Realism, Marxism and Human Geography', *Antipode* 13(2) pp. 31–8.

CHAPTER 15

FLEXIBLE SEXISM (1991)

INTRODUCTION

In the current debate around modernism and postmodernism, which is having its reflection in our field, both sides claim feminism for their own. Moreover, to feminists each offers possibilities. Postmodernism holds out the potential democracy of a plurality of voices and points of view, the end to a notion of science and society which has in fact (to be distinguished from 'by necessity') been unremittingly and tediously male, a patriarchal hierarchy with a claim to truth. Modernism, on the other hand, points to the possibility of progress and change. Things may be patriarchal now (including, OK let's admit it, modernism itself) but they need not always be so; more than that, it is possible to judge between alternatives, and history is on our side.

However, that it may be difficult to choose between the attractions they each at least in their rhetorics appear to offer, has as its other side that both postmodernism and modernism remain so frequently, so unimaginatively, patriarchal. This has been said before about the wider debate (for instance, see Fraser and Nicholson, 1988). If there is one thing which has most certainly demonstrated its flexibility in an age which as a whole is frequently accorded that epithet, it is sexism.

This feature is also disappointingly characteristic of the way in which at least some of the modernism-postmodernism debate has been conducted in our field, and it is the purpose of this paper to examine some of the ways in which this happens and to explore some of its implications. To this end I am focusing on two books which have been published recently: Soja's *Postmodern Geographies* (1989) and Harvey's *The Condition of Postmodernity* (1989). These books have been chosen not because they are in any sense representative of the debate between postmodernism and modernism (indeed there is argument about even how they might be classified) but because they are, or may become, central to the discussion within geography [...] For it seems to me that the absence from, indeed denial by, both these books of feminism and the contributions it has recently made, raise issues which are important for all of us, and which range from our style as academics to the way in which some of the central concepts of the debate are formulated. Indeed, the implications are perhaps in the end even wider than that. For both these books are centrally concerned with the relation between the poles of that impossible dichotomy: space and society. And, as the debate about this relation is crucial in the whole modernism-postmodernism exchange, it seems important to address its shortcomings. As we shall see, introducing feminism into this exchange challenges the views, not just of society but also of space, which these books develop.

I should also like to report that I had some hesitation about writing this paper. I do not like public mudslinging and have tried not to indulge in it here, but the paper is at times very critical. Nor do I relish gladiatorial combats and I hope that the result of this paper will be more to open (or continue) a wider debate. For it is certainly not just with these two particular authors that I want to take issue. Similar critiques could be made of much of our work, probably including some of my own and other feminists'. These particular books, however, claim a generality and a breadth of scope which others do not, and it is for this reason that they are particularly important to examine. The questions, though, are ones which we should all address [...]

POSTMODERN PROBLEMS FOR FEMINISTS

Democracy and academic style

One of the main attractions of the postmodern perspective is that it would seem on initial viewing to offer the prospect of a greater democracy through its recognition of the reality of a variety of viewpoints, a plurality of cultures. This has its underside: those viewpoints and cultures may, for example, run counter to what we have been accustomed, from a modernist perspective, to think of as progressive, and postmodernism forbids us from evaluating. Moreover, as Harvey argues very well, mere recognition of the existence of something does not empower it.

Nonetheless, one of the promises of postmodernism is that it will allow fuller appreciation of those who have for so long been banished to the margins, whether these be non-Western societies, women/feminists, or subordinated class strata.

In such a context one of the emancipatory roles of the writer and intellectual could be precisely to help give voice to the previously excluded. This is not itself an unproblematical possibility, as the intricate debates in other disciplines, most particularly anthropology, bear witness [...] It is a debate which could profitably be further developed within geography. Nonetheless, postmodernism can to some extent be seen as holding out some such progressive possibilities. And to some extent they have been taken up.

There is, however, another view of the role of intellectuals (particularly the paid professional intellectuals of academe) within the postmodernist project/era. And it is this one which I wish to take up here, for it raises important issues about who and how we are as 'academics'. Thus, Bauman (1988) has interpreted the concept of postmodernism as a response by intellectuals to their own discomfiture, their sense of dislodgement from previous authority. (The deliberate ambiguity of 'project/era' was thus apt in the context of this discussion.) Bauman's argument is that the concept of postmodernity has value precisely because it captures and articulates the changing experience of contemporary intellectuals [...] Owens (1985) emphasizes not just the often-referred-to demise of the dominance of Western culture but also the challenge to modernity from within the geographical bases of that culture: "the causes of modernity's demise ... lie as much within as without" (page 58). And among the many different challenges to modernity from within has been the challenge from feminism. Bondi (1990) argues that postmodernism "may he understood as a crisis in the experience of modernity among white, western men, and as a response centred on that experience" (page 5). Moreover, it is argued, the nature of the response to the crisis is such as to find, somehow, a way of hanging on to intellectual hegemony, or at least of not letting anyone else have it. Thus Hartsock (1987, page 196) argues:

> "Somehow it seems highly suspicious that it is at this moment in history, when so many groups are engaged in 'nationalisms' which involve redefinitions of the marginalised Others, that doubt arises in the academy about the nature of the 'subject', about the possibilities for a general theory which can describe the world, about historical 'progress'. Why is it, exactly at the moment when so many of us who have been silenced begin to demand the right to name ourselves, to act as subjects rather than objects of history, that just then the concept of subjecthood becomes 'problematic'? Just when we are forming our own theories about the world, uncertainty emerges about whether the world can be adequately theorized? Just when we are talking about the changes we want, ideas of progress and the possibility of 'meaningfully' organizing human society become suspect?"

[...] There are a number of issues here. First, if there is anything at all in these interpretations (and I think there is, though it is by no means a whole explanation), then it is inadequate to try to explain the condition of postmodernity and the associated debates about representation simply as the result of 'time-space compression', as Harvey does. The arguments just cited give more autonomy than does Harvey, not only to the sphere of culture and intellectual debate, but also – and more significantly from the point of view of the discussion here – to the sphere of political action. What is more, as Hartsock argues, political action and intellectual activity have been much more closely linked together in fields such as feminist studies, ethnic studies, and Third World studies, than they have been in more mainstream white male modernism (including much Marxism) for all its claims to political relevance.[1]

But second, if this is a crisis in part within the groves of academe itself then, it has been argued, it is frequently conducted more with an eye to positions of power and influence within the academy than with any liberating project of the full recognition of others. This point has been made most sharply by Sangren (1988). Writing of ethnography, he says

> "whatever 'authority' is created in a text has its most direct social effect not in the world of political and economic domination of the Third World by colonial and neocolonial powers, but rather in the academic institutions in which such authors participate" (page 411).

And Mascia-Lees et al (1989, page 16) add

> "While postmodernist anthropologists such as Clifford, Marcus, and Fisher may choose to think that they are transforming global power relations as well as the discipline of anthropology itself, they may also be establishing first claim in the new academic territory on which this decade's battles for intellectual supremacy and jobs will be waged."

Third, it is necessary in other words to recognize the power relations within academe and within intellectual debate. [...]

These arguments raise serious issues for all intellectuals/academics about their behaviour within their own social group, about the nature of their writing, about the power-structures of academe, and so on. And these issues

---

1 But if modernist accounts such as Harvey's miss out resistance and political struggle, this is absolutely not to argue that the majority of postmodernists do the opposite. All those lists of dualist differences between modernism and postmodernism (or Fordism and post-Fordism) obscure the fact that an awful lot remains tediously the same. One of the problems of some postmodernism is its treatment of 'others' as titillating exotica and as primarily constituted, in effect, to affirm the identity of the central character.) [...]

arise most acutely for those who are already established and, within these, for those who are members of the already dominant group of white males. For them, if ventures into postmodernism are not to represent simply an attempt at the restoration of their shaky authority as purveyors of truth (even if it is that the whole concept is a lot more complicated than it was previously thought to be), and if it is to be more than another play for status within academe on the part of those who already hold, as a group, most of the positions of power, then there has to be a fundamental questioning of the way they go about their craft.

One aspect of this which is highly symptomatic revolves around the question of 'style', and in particular writing-style. Much writing in and about postmodernism verges on the pretentious, and on occasions the virtually incomprehensible to those not in a (fairly small) group. Moreover 'the left' is not immune from this (and not only among the postmodernists) – and indeed has provided over the years some of the worst examples of undemocratic writing. It is an issue which I should like to see debated, and that is why I raise it now.

For it occurred to me again while reading Soja's book. *Postmodern Geographies* has a strong, central argument, one which is extremely important to communicate, and one which might in general terms be accepted at least in part by many social scientists, whether or not they agreed in detail either with the manner of getting there or with whether it was demonstrated in practice by Soja's own examples. The book is full of rich insights and thought-provoking connections and ideas. I learned a lot from reading it. But the presentation of the argument is bemusing.

First, there is the question of structure. The book begins with a section called "Preface and Postscript" and its opening sentences are:

"Combining a Preface with a Postscript seems a particularly apposite way to introduce (and conclude) a collection of essays on postmodern geographies. It signals right from the start an intention to tamper with the familiar modalities of time, to shake up the normal flow of the linear text to allow other, more 'lateral' connections to be made" (page 1).

In fact, what follows is a very conventionally structured argument (for which we should perhaps be grateful). [...] Most conventionally, the considerable amount of history which the book presents (for instance, about the development of the social/spatial line of thought amongst geographers) is both structured in an extraordinarily linear manner and leads with an ineluctable inexorability to the author and his current argument [...] This is not, of course, unusual. There have been a few such 'histories' written recently, with

225

the apparent authority of the overseer, where many of us involved recognise neither our individual roles nor the play as a whole. What makes it particularly jarring in this book, though, is the fact that it contradicts so completely both those opening sentences and the expressed commitment to multiple voices and plurality. One effect of this is that it leads to problems with the construction of Soja's own argument. By focusing so unremittingly on one characteristic (historicism), and homing in on all examples which exemplify his point, he misses other themes, other examples, and indeed counterexamples. [...]

But another effect of the linear way in which Soja constructs his history is that it omits, not just other themes, but other voices. It has a hermetic coherence which excludes deviant contributions. Non-Marxist geographers, for instance, are not heard from very much. Again, in complete contrast with the promise of the first paragraph of the book, there is little simultaneity here, just a procession of those *who are seen to have been* dominant or important. It is a disappointment because it belies the evident democratic intent. It is very un-postmodern in the best sense of postmodern.

In contrast, however, to the conventionality of the overall structure, the language in which the argument is couched is arcane and tortured. Presentations which play with form, which take a delight in their own artistry, are surely to be applauded, but the taste this book left with me was one of pomposity rather than of an attempt to communicate. There has been much debate recently about the construction of texts, and the effects and implications of different modes of construction. The case of the linear history was an example of this, and here we see a similar effect in relation to linguistic style. *Postmodern Geographies* left at least this reader (and I know I am not the only one; it has been the subject of some discussion) wondering what the author was trying to achieve. The concern most often expressed is that this kind of writing is less about communication than about self-presentation. This is a difficult issue, and I realise that to some extent at least it is subjective. Moreover, in this case I have some sympathy in the sense that Soja is trying to get geographical issues on to the agenda of the intellectual left. Writing to one's audience is an important skill, and I can well understand if he felt that the only way to gatecrash those august portals was to write like too many of them do. I suppose all I am arguing is that we should try to resist the temptation. For, if those of us who would in some way or measure sign up under the banner of postmodernism are to avoid the accusation of using the claimed potential democracy of the message simply to show off to each other, then we have to be very careful how, and for whom, we write. This of course applies to all of us, not just those who align with postmodernism. It is just that postmodernists' proclamations against authority, and their explicitly stated concern with the nature of the text, make such writing in their case particularly ironic. Nor am I trying to make the case that everything we write should be 'for the proletariat' otherwise known in the United Kingdom as the man (sic) on the Clapham omnibus. Styles will, and should, vary with the audience addressed (which is not the same as falling into their bad habits). It is not a question of being anti-intellectual, either; indeed it is in part bound up with precisely the distinction between being an *intellectual* and being an *academic.*

Moreover, the issue is reinforced in Soja's book because we are given clues as to what he was trying to establish himself *as.* We are told, for instance, that the author once went for a trip around Los Angeles with Fredric Jameson and Henri Lefebvre. What are we to make of this information? Perhaps what is being communicated is the sense of an in-crowd, and the fact that the author may be part of it [...]

The combination of all these characteristics of style and presentation is, however, alienating. It seems designed to create a sense of a centre and a periphery. If the arguments cited earlier are correct and academics (and especially white male academics) today are feeling that there *is* a loss of status, a feeling that we (they) are not being regarded with the customary awe (at least, among those from whom most academics are accustomed to receive it – those on the currently fashionable 'margins' never cared much for most of us anyway), then this is not the way to regain any kind of respect. This kind of response to a crisis chimes only too well with that negative aspect of postmodernist analysis, which can only confirm the mutual incomprehensibility of self-defining groups, and greet it with a shrug of indifferent shoulders. On the other hand, it is a style which is in total contradiction to that more emancipatory aspect of postmodernism, the pulling down of hierarchies, the entry of the previously marginalised into the central forum of debate.

On page 74 of his book, in the middle of all this, Soja writes:

> "This reconstituted critical human geography must be attuned to the emancipatory struggles of all those who are peripheralized and oppressed by the specific geography of capitalism (and existing socialism as well) – exploited workers, tyrannized peoples, dominated women."

The comment in the margin of my copy is unprintable.

Difference and distance

But that quotation reveals something else as well. For it is not just in terms of style and textual strategy that *Postmodern Geographies* is ambivalent in its relation to postmodernism. So it is in the content of its theoretical stance

227

and its arguments.

That quotation reveals on the one hand the recognition that a simple dualism of capital versus labour is not enough. Notions of peripherality, and of tyrannised peoples and dominated women get a mention. Yet, on the other hand, the thing by which they are peripheralised, tyrannised, or dominated is assumed to be – uniquely – the geography of *the mode of production* (capitalism or 'existing socialism'). It recognises that there are more things in life than can be captured in the classic formulation, but it does not really take them on board.

This is not an ambivalence particular to that quotation. It is present throughout the book. The existence of racism and sexism, and the need to refer to them, is recognised, but it is assumed throughout, either explicitly or implicitly, that the only axis of power which matters in relation to these distinct forms of domination is that which stems fairly directly from the relations of production. No other relations of power and dominance are seriously addressed. The fact that patriarchy, for instance, is not reducible to the terms of a debate on modes of production, is not considered. Indeed, to take the point further, modernity itself is defined entirely in relation to capitalism, at times seeming almost equivalent to it. Thus, in the key section on the deconstruction and reconstruction of modernity, an initially rich and broad-ranging definition is step-by-step narrowed down. We move from a recognition that "the experience of modernity captures a broad mesh of sensibilities" (page 25) and an argument (still very broad in what it potentially encompasses) that "spatiality, temporality, and social being can be seen as the abstract dimensions which together comprise all facets of human existence" (page 25). The breadth of this statement is confirmed by the definition of social being as "revolving around the constitution of society, the production and reproduction of social relations, institutions, and practices" (page 25). Yet within a few pages, this focus has been reduced and modernisation, each accelerated period of which is seen as giving birth to new forms of modernism, and which becomes conflated with modernity, is reduced to capitalism … "Modernization can be directly linked to the many different 'objective' processes of structural change that have been associated with the ability of capitalism to develop and survive. … This defining association between modernization and the survival of capitalism. … Modernization … is a continuous process of societal restructuring … that arises primarily from the historical and geographical dynamics of modes of production" (pages 26–27).

Yet between the last two of these statements there is a fleeting moment of doubt, of acknowledgement that it is not as simple as this. "Modernization", it is conceded, "is not entirely the product of some determinative inner logic of capitalism, but neither is it a rootless and ineluctable idealization of history" (page 27). Of course, it partly depends on how you want to define modernisation, but there is clearly here a drawing-back from the earlier simple equation of it with capitalism. Yet the revised formulation is also unsatisfactory. The alternatives are not, in fact, limited to a single determinative inner logic on the one hand and total rootlessness on the other. For one thing, and quite apart from the ramifications of wider debates, there are other axes of social power relations by which our current societies are characterised, as well as those of class and capitalism. In Soja's formulation structures such as patriarchy are reduced to noises-off which account for the fact that there is no simple deterministic relation between capitalism and modernisation. But why cannot such other axes of power and of social structuring be considered in their own right?[2] Patriarchy is not in the index. Feminism gets one mention, and it is in the passage following the quotation cited at the end of the last section [...]

The characterization of modernism mainly in relation to modes of production is paralleled by an unusual definition of postmodernism. Soja produces a carefully modulated argument here, and is careful too, as we shall see later, in stating his own relation to the wider projects of postmodernism, but in the end the most significant axis of his definition seems to be based around the importance of space. This leads to what seem to me to be some unexpected results. Both Harvey and Mandel turn out to be postmodernists, for instance. And, although the arguments in the chapters on Los Angeles do not establish how or why space is more important now, the arguments about the ontological significance of space (which are very interesting) are general ones: they are not specific to the recent period. But apart from these apparent confusions there is a deeper issue, for the postmodern questioning of modernism has involved far more than that. Among other things it has challenged the existence of a single coherent narrative of a causal structure to which everything can be related, it has challenged the authority of the single author or viewer, and it has challenged the notion of a single universal subject, constructed – usually with blithe unintentionality – in the shape of a white Western male heterosexual. In particular, it has been related to, though it is not equivalent to, the feminist critiques of modernism (see, among many writings in this area, Nicholson, 1990). None of this receives any attention.

Now, a number of people have already pointed out that *Postmodern Geographies* is, after all, a thoroughly *modern* text (for instance, see Dear, 1990; Gregory, 1990). Moreover, to be fair to Soja it should also be pointed out that he himself explicitly *dis*claims any intention to be thoroughly *post*-modern (page 5). Nonetheless, he also says that he does now feel comfortable

---

2   To argue this is, in my view, absolutely not to be anti-Marxist, still less is it to be anti-materialist. The point is more that what we are offered in this analysis is a very reconstructed Marxism.

with postmodernism's "intentional announcement of a possibly epochal transition *in* both *critical 'thought* and material' life" (page 5, my emphasis). Moreover, some of his reticence about postmodernism seems, in my view quite legitimately, to come from its frequent abandonment of any progressive project other than multiplicity. But, given this, it is possible to make use of some of the changes in critical thought (including some of the uncomfortably searching questions posed by postmodernism) both to address the ways in which modernism was also profoundly flawed and to retain a position of political commitment. Yet there is here no recognition that modernism was or is profoundly patriarchal (for instance) nor that there are possible alternatives which can go some way to addressing the central dilemmas of modernism without leaving us floating in an apolitical void. Perhaps the strongest case for an alternative of this sort has been made by feminists (for instance, see Mascia-Lees et al, 1989).

That arguments such as these have not been taken on board is evidenced in Soja's treatment of his central concepts of space and place. The chapters on Los Angeles are crucial here. They are innovative and fun, and they reveal some worthwhile insights (although they do not seem to do any more in the end than move from the socioeconomic to the spatial. It is unclear how, in the real content of the relation they posit between the social and the spatial they are distinct from much previous writing, or are an exemplification of the theoretical propositions laid out in the early part of the book). But they are designed in a particular way. They are very much long-distance views, overviews (literally, from a height, whether it be from the air or from City Hall).

This raises two issues. First, this is very much a visual approach, and in modernism, vision was systematically and symptomatically prioritised over other senses. It has been argued to be the sense which allows most mastery; in part deriving from the very detachment which it allows and requires. And second this detachment, and the authority of the viewer which it helps to construct, is underscored in *Postmodern Geographies* by the very vantage points which Soja chooses to look from. The question of how one presents spaces, places and local cultures is a complex and unresolved one, or certainly that is true of how to do it democratically. The stance which Soja adopts is similar to that from which he writes his history. But such a stance ignores the major debates about the difficulties of such an approach. The work of Clifford and others has already been referred to. The collection by Clifford and Marcus (1986) is precisely concerned with how one constructs a text adequately to take account of the problems both of what he (Clifford) calls "visualism" and of the recognition and reporting of distinct views and interpretations which are not simply absorbed into and re-presented by the "author". These writers, and others in the same vein, have in turn been criticised by feminists on a number of grounds: for the degree to which the complexity of the text can lead to such obscurity that few can understand; for the lack of recognition that they still remain unquestionably 'the authors'; for the introspective self-regard which some postmodern strategies can produce among anthropologists themselves; perhaps most of all, and which is related to commitment, for a lack of regard to the question of whom they are speaking *for*.

EXCLUSIVELY MASCULINE MODERNISM

[...]

Harvey's *The Condition of Postmodernity* is also, like *Postmodern Geographies*, and especially given the intrinsic difficulty of the argument it is developing, a major achievement.

But here again, reading it as a feminist, I was troubled. In some ways it is difficult to know where to get into this argument, partly because the book is such a seamless whole and partly because the main problem is precisely one of absence.

The absence is that of other points of view. Whereas Soja's ventures into postmodernism at least provoke him into wrestling with the necessity of recognising the existence of a multiplicity of '*auteurs*', Harvey's modernism is constructed (or perhaps I should say unreconstructed) around an assumed universal whose particular characteristics are not even recognised. Women, for instance, do not figure in the development of the argument, and neither does the possibility of feminist readings of the issues under consideration. The same could be said of other voices currently subordinated in this society and its dominant lines of intellectual debate. The issue is not confined to feminism. Nor is it that there should be a few paragraphs here and there on "women, ethnic minorities, etc". It is that the dominant view is assumed to be the universal, and that view is white, male, heterosexual, Western.

The analyses of film are symptomatic [...] Let us take the case of *Blade Runner* [discussed in Chapter 18 of Harvey]. One of the key threads in this movie is the struggle by the female replicant Rachel to prove that she is not a replicant. However, in order to do this, and thereby to survive, replicants have to prove a history, and their relationship to it; they must, most crucially, enter and establish a place in the symbolic order. And the symbolic order used in *Blade Runner* is that of Freud. So Harvey, drawing on this analysis of the film, which as he says is that of Giuliana Bruno (1987), describes Rachel's (ultimately successful) attempt at survival through the establishment of a (human) identity. As he writes,

"But she can re-enter the symbolic realm of a truly human society

231

only by acknowledging the overwhelming power of the Oedipal figure, the father. ... In submitting to Deckard (trusting him, deferring to him, and ultimately submitting to him physically), she learns the meaning of human love and the essence of ordinary sociality. In killing the replicant Leon as he is about to kill Deckard, she provides the ultimate evidence of the capacity to act as Deckard's woman" (page 312).

There are a number of points to be made here. First of all, Harvey does not comment on the particularity of this process of a replicant finding an identity as a woman. She learns the meaning of love through submission (Harvey's word) to a man; she establishes an identity – as "Deckard's woman". It is not an appetising prospect, and one wonders whether, if survival had not been dependent on it, she would have bothered. This point is a more significant one than it perhaps sounds in that one of the things which Harvey misses is that Rachel is not just establishing *an* identity, she is establishing a sexual and specifically a *female* identity. In Bruno's terms "To survive for a time, the android has to accept the fact of sexual difference, the sexual identity which the entry into language requires" (page 71).

It is interesting, and surely significant, moreover, that it is precisely and only at this point that Harvey disagrees with Bruno (nor, possibly, is it insignificant that he talks of Bruno as 'he' and calls her Giuliano!). Bruno writes

"Of all the replicants, only one, Rachel, succeeds in making the journey. She assumes a sexual identity, becomes a woman, and loves a man. ... Rachel accepts the paternal figure and follows the path to a 'normal', adult, female, sexuality: she identifies her sex by first acknowledging the power of the other, the father, a man. But the leader of the replicants, Roy Batty, refuses the symbolic castration which is necessary to enter the symbolic order" (page 71).

It is precisely this contrast with which Harvey disagrees. He put Roy's refusal simply down to the fact that survival in his case is unlikely anyway. I do not know which interpretation is more valid in relation to the film, but it is interesting that this disagreement precisely underlines Harvey's unwillingness to engage on the terrain of sexual identity. For that, of course, might further undermine the supposed universality of one fraction of humanity, the heterosexual male.

This disagreement with Bruno, moreover, is linked back to the earlier lack of comment on the manner of Rachel's acquisition of an identity. Bruno makes it clear that what is involved is submission, and that some may go along with it, and others may refuse. Although he recognises submission, it is not seen as so problematical a process by Harvey, and later he clearly believes that Rachel really does fall in love with Deckard. Thus, for instance, the possibility that she might be feigning, in order to survive, does not seem to occur to him. Yet women have often had to resort to feigning, in various ways, and often with far less at stake than survival (as another recent movie *When Harry met Sally* recently pointed out!) Moreover, not only does Harvey believe that Rachel really falls for Deckard, but he is disappointed because

> "The strongest social bond between Deckard and the replicants in revolt – the fact that they are both controlled and enslaved by a dominant corporate power – never generates the slightest hint that a coalition of the oppressed might be forged between them" (page 313).

Now that quite took my breath away. On page 312 we are reading all this about Rachel having to submit to Deckard, and on page 313 we are wondering why she does not enter into an alliance with him. The wider political implications of this kind of male-based analysis have recently been analysed by Hart (1989). [...] But wishing for coalitions of the oppressed without first analysing the contradictions and power-relations within those potential coalitions is to court political failure.
[...]

'Other' spaces of modernism

The spaces of modernism which are mostly celebrated are the public spaces of the city. It was in the rapidly growing Western cities, especially Paris, that modernism was born. And the standard literature from Baudelaire onwards is replete with descriptions of boulevards and cafés, of fleeting, passing glances and of the cherished anonymity of the crowd. The spatial and social reorganization, and flourishing, of urban life was an essential condition for the birth of the new era. But that city was also gendered. Moreover, it was gendered in ways which relate directly to spatial organisation.

First, it was gendered in the very general sense of the distinction between the public and the private (Wolff, 1985). This period of the mid-nineteenth century was a crucial one in the development of the notion of 'the separation of spheres' and the confinement of women, ideologically if not for all women in practice, to the 'private' sphere of the suburbs and the home (Davidoff and Hall, 1983; Hall 1981). The public city which is celebrated in the enthusiastic descriptions of the dawn of modernism was a city for men. The boulevards and cafés, and still more the bars and brothels, were for men - the women who did go there were for male consumption. Nineteenth-century

233

Paris presented very different impressions and possibilities for men and for women. Thus Pollock (1988), in thinking through the relation between "space and social processes" (her terms) in relation to art history argues that one possible approach might lie "in considering not only the spaces represented, or the spaces *of* the representation, but the social spaces from which the representation is made and its reciprocal positionalities" (page 66).

But the social spaces from which the generally cited central cultural products of modernism were made were the public spaces of the city – the spaces of men. [...]

What all this together implies is that the experience of modernism/modernity as it is customarily recorded, the production of what are customarily assumed to be its major cultural artefacts, and even its customary definition, are all constructed on and are constructive of particular forms of gender relations and definitions of masculinity and of what it means to be a woman. This is not ('just') to say that modernism was or is patriarchal (this would hardly be news, nor differentiate it from many other periods in history); it is to say that it is not possible fully to understand modernism without taking account of this. To return more directly to Harvey, modernism is about more than a particular articulation of the power relations of time, space, and money. Harvey has produced a fascinating, if arguably economistic, exploration of the relation between the definition, production, and experience of space, on the one hand, and modes of production and class formation on the other. But it completely misses other ways, other power-relations, in which space is also structured and experienced. Harvey mentions none of the arguments which have been addressed in this section. [...]

It has been argued by a number of women that the usual view of modernism, and perhaps most specifically of its art, is frequently only a partial conception of modernity (for instance, see Wolff, 1985). If that is true of many of the male 'authorities' on the subject, it is a fortiori the case with Harvey who, through his whole argument (and this is a more general concern about the discussion) draws only on mainstream (or what was to become mainstream) culture, whether this be gallery art, famous architects, or big-budget movies. This leads to an unnecessarily monolithic view of the modernist period; it shifts the definition of what it was and, by missing out the voices on the margins and in the interstices of what was accepted, it also misses the full force of the critique which those voices, among them feminists, were making of the modernism he does discuss.

All this becomes fully apparent in another way when Harvey considers the work of Cindy Sherman. She is postmodern and female. Harvey clearly does not like what she does and is more than a little disturbed by it. He describes visiting an exhibition of her photographs:

234

"The photographs depict seemingly different women drawn from many walks of life. It takes a little while to realize, with a certain shock, that these are portraits of the same woman in different guises. Only the catalogue tells you that it is the artist herself who is that woman. The parallel with Raban's insistence upon the plasticity of human personality through the malleability of appearances and surfaces is striking, as is the self-referential positioning of the authors to themselves as subjects. Cindy Sherman is considered a major figure in the postmodern movement" (page 7).

There is a whole host of problems here. Later, Harvey refers to Sherman and a range of other postmodernists in a discussion of the current crisis of representation. That there *is* such a crisis is not in doubt. But Harvey here (page 322) and throughout the book identifies the cause of this crisis as "the experience of time-space compression in recent years, under the pressures of the turn to more flexible modes of accumulation" (page 322). After all the feminist debate about representation, to which I have just referred, and the directly political critique of modernist representation, it is surely inadequate to put the whole crisis down to time-space compression and flexible accumulation. There was *political* and a specifically feminist criticism of the mode of representation which was dominant prior to the crisis. Much of this postmodern work is thus not just part of a crisis, it is also a social comment. Thus when Harvey writes "The interest in Cindy Sherman's photographs (or any postmodern novel for that matter) is that they focus on masks without commenting directly on social meanings other than on the activity of masking itself" (page 101), he is missing much of the point [...]

Moreover, it is not just a general sociopolitical point which can be drawn from Sherman's photographs, but a specifically feminist one. Harvey says he was shocked to find that all these different images were of "the same woman". It is an unintended admission, for that is precisely the effect they are supposed to have on the patriarchal viewer. Thus Owens comments that they "reflect back at the viewer his own desire (and the spectator posited by this work is invariably male) – specifically the masculine desire to fix the woman in a stable and stabilizing identity. But this is precisely what Sherman's work denies: for while her photographs are always self-portraits, in them the artist never appears to be the same ... while Sherman may pose as a pin-up, she still cannot be pinned down" (page 75). It is, precisely, a way of disrupting the normally dominant pleasures of the patriarchal visual field.

Moreover, maybe she *is* all of these things, *and* they are masks. Sherman's work reveals how socially constructed and how unstable 'gender' is and how, indeed, the last few centuries of Western culture has produced a 'femininity' which does indeed have a lot to do with self-presentation, in masks for others, in masquerade (Chadwick, 1990, pages 358–359; Owens, 1985, page 75).

Finally, Harvey seems to object particularly to the fact that Sherman took these pictures of herself ("the self-referential positioning of the authors to themselves as subjects"). Would it have been less disturbing had a man taken an authoritative picture of this woman? – like Manet painting Olympia, perhaps?

Gender, then, is a determining factor in cultural production. It must be so also in relation to its interpretation. We have seen this, in this section, in specific relation to modernism. At the end of *The Condition of Postmodernity*, Harvey argues for a recuperation of one form of modernism – Marxism. He recognises, too, that it must be reworked in order to treat more satisfactorily of difference and 'otherness', and that it is not enough simply to add categories on: they should be present in the analysis from the beginning. Yet in his own analysis of modernism and postmodernism one of the most significant of those 'differences' – that which revolves around gender – is absent.

POLITICS – AND ACADEME

I have great sympathy with the overall projects of both these books. Soja is struggling to be postmodern, but really remaining in many ways modern; Harvey is quite clearly for modernism but wanting, he says, to change it in ways which will respond to certain inadequacies. I, too, would like to retain strong aspects of what characterises the modernist project, most particularly its commitment to change, hopefully progressive; I also agree strongly with Harvey's defence of much of what has been achieved in its name. But it is necessary also to recognise the inadequacies of the modernist project in its dominant form. One problem of both these books is that they neither fully recognise the issues nor adequately respond to them. The answers which most postmodernism has so far provided may well be mistaken, but the challenges it poses must surely be addressed.

Moreover, one stream of thought which has been raising many of the same issues for far longer, which has been debating a set of answers which do not fall into the traps of postmodernism, which do not disintegrate into localism (in Lyotard's sense, which has nothing to do with the specifically geographical – see Massey, 1991), which do not abandon theories which have sufficient scope to deal with issues such as gender and class, which are historical and sensitive to differentiation ... is feminism. The list of characteristics just mentioned is taken from Fraser and Nicholson (1988), but many others have been debating similar issues. Other than contributions already mentioned there are, for instance, Flax (1986), Harding (1986, 1987, and many others), Haraway (1983), Jardine (1985), and Morris (1988).

This literature is not mentioned by Soja or Harvey. Not one of the above authors is mentioned by either of them.[3] At a number of points in this paper it has been noted that the potential contributions of feminism have simply been ignored. This is perhaps particularly glaring because so many feminists have written on the issues of space and society which are central to the debate in hand. Why, then, are they not considered? Is it that many men feel they do not have to read the feminist literature? Is it seen as a 'specialism'? Harvey has said (1985) that he likes to think of himself as "a restless analyst". It is an attractive and appealing image. But maybe he has not been restless enough. It should not be acceptable that a large part of the central literature is simply missing from what sets out to be a comprehensive overview, and that whole lines of debate are simply ignored.

Fraser and Nicholson mention a number of other features which are potentially characteristic of a new mode of theorising which is neither modern in the old sense nor postmodern in its usual style. The attention to cultural specificity and to differentiation within society and over time is developed into the statement that such theory "would be non-universalist. When its focus became cross-cultural or trans-epochal, its mode of attention would be comparativist rather than universalising, attuned to changes and contrasts instead of to 'covering laws'" (1988, pages 390–391). I have to say that I am uncertain about this in some ways. (These are confusing times and I think we should be open enough to admit that on some things we may remain undecided.) But this characterisation of theory does contrast strongly with Harvey's. Harvey constantly runs together universalism and internationalism. But, often, they are absolutely not the same thing. Indeed in some ways they are potentially antagonistic to each other. A true internationalism is surely a nonstarter without the prior recognition of diversity. And the 'universals' on which so much analysis is based are so often in fact quite particular; not universals at all, but white, male, Western, heterosexual, what have you. The long attempt to force such universals down unwilling throats is now demonstrating its failure in part precisely by provoking the most reactionary forms of cultural specificity.

---

3   Harvey has one reference to Hartsock (1987) which he uses simply to take an unsubstantiated swipe at postmodernism. Noting that some authors emphasise "the opening given in postmodernism to understanding differences and otherness, as well as the liberatory potential it offers for a whole host of new social movements (women, gays, blacks, ecologists, regional autonomists, etc.)" [!] he goes on to assert "Curiously, most movements of this sort, though they have definitely helped change 'the structure of feeling', pay scant attention to postmodernist arguments, and some feminists (e.g. Hartsock, 1987) are hostile ..." (page 48). This is grossly to misrepresent a complex debate. Moreover dissatisfaction with the answers of postmodernism, as I indicated above, does not mean that we are happy to tag along behind an exclusively masculine modernism such as Harvey's.

> "Finally", write Fraser and Nicholson "postmodern-feminist the-
> ory would dispense with the idea of a subject of history. It would
> replace unitary notions of 'women' and 'feminine gender iden-
> tity' with plural and complexly constructed conceptions of social
> identity, treating gender as one relevant strand among others,
> attending also to class, race, ethnicity, age and sexual orientation"
> (1988, page 391).

Again, this is easier said than done. But in all kinds of ways, the approaches
in the two books which have been discussed here show how poverty-stricken
is the analysis, and how open to progressive political criticism is a failure
even to wrestle with these problems, and their attendant possibilities. The
question of 'authorship' seems to be central. White Western men write academic texts and interpret the world for each other; and the universal author
of history is understood to be a male, heterosexual, and modernising in the
Western image. So Harvey fails to understand what Sherman is saying precisely because it is about these things – author(ity), and feminism. Although
he discusses perspectivism, for example, and its relation to individualism (for
example, page 245) and the modernist 'aura' of the artist as producer (pages
55, 245), the full implications are not drawn out and explored. Yet those
implications are political, in the widest sense of the word. [...]

There are implications also, therefore, for the way we are, and could be,
as academics. There are huge questions being raised, in parts of geography,
in anthropology and elsewhere, about our role as interpreters of the world.
Yet neither of these books addresses these questions. There are issues about
the hierarchies within our own fields, and whether we really need to take
ourselves *quite* so seriously [...]

All this finds its reflection in the wider politics which these books advocate. Here too the difficulties of difference – perhaps, at its simplest, the fact
of complexity – are simply erased by the steamroller of an analysis which
insists that capital and labour (and in fact mainly capital, for neither book
allows much space for resistance, even from labour) are all there is to it. Soja
is the more reticent about setting out a political position, though it is implicit
throughout and the quotation cited earlier demonstrated his conviction that
what we should be fighting in the West is capitalism, and only capitalism [sic],
for via that the problems of sexism and racism would also be confronted. At
one point he argues that: "The political challenge for the postmodern left, as
I see it, demands first a recognition and cogent interpretation of the dramatic
and often confusing fourth modernization of capitalism" (page 5). This is
necessary, surely, but it is not enough (and though this is labelled "first" we
are not given any more). If there is one thing to be taken on board by the
political and social shifts of recent decades it is that, unfortunately maybe,
things are just not that simple.

Harvey is much more explicit about his politics. It is absolutely stated that everything must be subordinated to – just as, theoretically, it is reduced to – a question of class. Thus on page 46 he is discussing ideas, such as Foucault's, which "appeal to the various social movements that sprang into existence during the 1960s (feminists, gays, ethnic and religious groupings, regional autonomists, etc.)" [!]. But, he argues, such movements leave open "the question of the path whereby such localized struggles might add up to a progressive, rather than regressive, attack upon the central forms of capitalist exploitation and repression. Localized struggles ... have not generally had the effect of challenging capitalism...." There are two major points here. First, in what sense, precisely, is feminism (to take the case under discussion in this paper) a 'local' struggle while class struggle, it is to be presumed, is 'general'? One can only argue such a position if it is held that there are no patriarchal structures not reducible to class. Second, and consequently, why is there an assumption that what these 'local' struggles are fighting is capitalism? Surely what feminists are fighting is patriarchy. People, such as myself, may be both feminists and socialists and see themselves trying to struggle on both fronts (though sometimes with despair, as when reading passages such as these). One's identity, and the struggles we are engaged in, are far more multifaceted than Harvey's position is capable of conceiving.

At the end of his book, Harvey pulls together his theoretical and his political positions, arguing for a further development of Marxist formulations. This, surely, is a positive step, and one which I would wholeheartedly support. But as it is spelled out it becomes clear that what this would mean in Harvey's formulation is continued subordination for all those people in parentheses, those who do not in their complex identities match the postulated, uncomplicated-because-unanalysed, universal. Thus, consider the following:

> "The importance of recuperating such aspects of social organiza-
> tion as race, gender, religion, within the overall frame of historical
> materialist enquiry (with its emphasis upon the power of money
> and capital circulation) and class politics (with its emphasis upon
> the unity of the emancipatory struggle) cannot be overestimated"
> (page 355).

How to have your cake and eat it too! There are four comments. First, I am absolutely in favour of thinking through issues of gender "within the overall frame of historical materialist enquiry". Second, however, we have to be sure what that means. Materialism is far wider than an "emphasis upon the power of money and capital circulation". This is less materialism than economism; and it simply could not deal even with many of the gender issues raised earlier in this paper. Third, again yes – we need to think through ways of constructing "the unity of the emancipatory struggle"; but, fourth, this emphatically cannot be achieved by forcing all struggles under "the overall frame of ... class politics". What Harvey's position means is a unity enforced through the tutelage of one group over others. As Hadjimichalis and Vaiou have recently written, in the context precisely of debates within our field,

> "In a contradictory way, by advocating 'unity' and ignoring divisions (theoretically, practically and prospectively) the left itself has contributed to deepening divisions .... 'Unity' must be gradually built up upon the articulation of differences and individual experiences" (1990, page 21).

Yet even while he recognises the need to construct alliances in the search for unity, Harvey forces everyone into one mould: "The very possibility of a genuine rainbow coalition defines a unified politics which inevitably speaks the tacit language of class, because this is precisely what defines the common experience within the differences" (page 358). Any on-the-ground experience of trying to build alliances would demonstrate the inadequacy of this view. There is here no understanding of the need to recognise conflicts (remember *Blade Runner?*) and complexity and to deal with them in their own right, as unities which are articulations of genuine and often contradictory differences.

REFERENCES

Baudrillard J, 1988 *America* (Verso, London).

Bauman Z, 1988, "Is there a postmodern sociology?" *Theory, Culture and Society* 5 217–237.

Bondi L, 1990, "On gender tourism in the space age: a feminist response to *Postmodern Geographies*", paper presented to the panel: Author meets critic: Ed Soja's *Postmodern Geographies*, AAG, Toronto, April; copy available from the author, Department of Geography, University of Edinburgh, Edinburgh.

Bruno G, 1987, "Ramble city: postmodernism and *Blade Runner*" October **41** 61–74.

Chadwick W, 1990 *Women, Art, and Society* (Thames and Hudson, London) .

Clifford J, Marcus GE, (Eds), 1986 *Writing Culture: The Poetics and Politics of Ethnography* (University of California Press, Berkeley, CA).

Davidoff. L, Hall C, 1983, "The architecture of public and private life: English middle-class society in a provincial town 1780–1850", in *The Pursuit of Urban History* Eds D Fraser, A Sutcliffe (Edward Arnold, Sevenoaks, Kent).

Dear M, 1990, "*Postmodern Geographies*: review" *Annals of the Association of American Geographers* **80** 649–654.

Flax J, 1986, "Gender as a social problem: in and for feminist theory" *American Studies/ Amerika Studien* June.

Fraser N, Nicholson L, 1988, "Social criticism without philosophy: an encounter between feminism and postmodernism" *Theory, Culture and Society* 5 373–394.

Gregory D, 1990, "Chinatown, part three? Soja and the missing spaces of social theory" *Strategies* **3** 40–104.

Hadjimichalis C, Vaiou D, 1990, "Flexible labour markets and regional development in northern Greece" *International Journal of Urban and Regional Research* **14** 1–24.

Hall C, 1981, "Gender divisions and class formation in the Birmingham middle class, 1780–1850" in *People's History and Socialist Theory* Ed. R Samuel (Routledge and Kegan Paul, Andover, Hants).

Haraway D, 1983, "A manifesto for Cyborgs: science, technology and socialist feminism in the 1980s" *Socialist Review* **80** 65–107.

Harding S, 1986 *The Science Question in Feminism* (Cornell University Press, Ithaca, NY).

Harding S (Ed.), 1987 *Feminism and Methodology* (Indiana University Press, Bloomington, IN).

Hart N, 1989, "Gender and the rise and fall of class politics" *New Left Review,* number 175, pp 19–47.

Hartsock N, 1987, "Rethinking modernism: minority vs majority theories" *Cultural Critique* **7** 187–206.

Harvey D, 1985 *Consciousness and the Urban Experience: Studies in the History and Theory of Capitalist Urbanisation* (Basil Blackwell, Oxford).

Harvey D, 1989 *The Condition of Postmodernity* (Basil Blackwell, Oxford).

Jardine A, 1985 *Gynesis: Configurations of Women and Modernity* (Cornell University Press, Ithaca, NY).

Mascia-Lees F E, Sharpe P, Cohen C B, 1989, "The postmodernist turn in anthropology cautions from a feminist perspective" *Signs* **15**(1) 7–33.

Massey D, 1991, "The political place of locality studies" *Environment and Planning A* **23** 267–281.

Morris M, 1988 *The Pirate's Fiancée* (Verso, London).

Nicholson L J (Ed.), *Feminism/Postmodernism* (Routledge, Chapman and Hall, Andover, Hants).

Owens C, 1985, "The discourse of others: feminists and postmodernism", in *Postmodern Culture* Ed. H Foster (Pluto Press, London) pp 57–82.

Pollock G, 1988 *Vision and Difference: Femininity, Feminism and Histories of Art* (Routledge, Chapman and Hall, Andover, Hants).

Sangren S, 1988, "Rhetoric and the authority of ethnography" *Current Anthropology* **29** 405–424.

Soja E, 1989 *Postmodern Geographies: The Reassertion of Space in Critical Social Theory* (Verso, London).

Wolff J, 1985, "The invisible flâneuse: women and the literature of modernity" *Theory, Culture and Society* **2**(3) 37–46.

CHAPTER 16

REFLECTIONS ON GENDER AND GEOGRAPHY (1995)

CLASS AND OTHER AXES OF DIVISION

One strand of change within class analysis over the years, and one that is widely if not universally reckoned to have represented "progress", has been the increasing attention paid to the intersection of class with, or its incorporation of, other axes of social differentiation and inequality. [...]

It also seems clear [...] that the debate over what one might call the "depth" of the relationship between class and other axes, has shifted. On the whole, it seems, the claims now being made are for a deeper level of interaction. At a number of points it is argued, for instance, that not only are social classes in their social outcomes empirically gendered or racialized but so too are the processes of class formation themselves. Thus Anne Witz, focusing on gender, provides a detailed explication of this in her examination of occupational structures, arguing that "gender matters in a *further*, more embedded, sense that has much more to do with the processes and mechanisms ... underlying the historical specificities of forms of the social division of labour, of which occupational structure is one aspect" (p. 43).[1] In other words, the construction of occupational positions must be taken to be part of class theory, and not assumed to be pre-given to it, and moreover that process of construction is itself gendered. For these reasons, she argues, "we need a new concept of class formation in order to describe the processes and mechanisms whereby occupational structures of 'places' emerge and gendered 'persons' come to be associated with them over time and, indeed, how these two processes are not necessarily sequential" (p. 43). Now, there are a number of ways in which such processes and mechanisms may operate, and both Witz and other authors in

---

1 Editorial note: here and elsewhere in this essay, Massey references chapters from the volume edited by Butler and Savage (1995), where this text was first published.

the collection engage with a range of them. There is, for instance, the way in which the bureaucratic career has been constructed as a male career. There is the dependence of career jobs on the existence of routine and non-career jobs, the former held more by men, the latter more by women. There is the legitimation of certain jobs as being of high status simply because of the maleness of those who hold them. There are gendered processes of exclusion, demarcation and segregation enacting social closure around, for instance, positions based upon the possession of specialist knowledge.

I want here to take this argument a little further. Most of the mechanisms referred to above are examples of the joint operation of class and gender in the production of gender-exclusive, or dominated, occupational positions. It may be, however, that the intermeshing of class and gender operates at an even deeper level, and that the process is one not only of class (or occupational structure) formation, but also of gender formation.

The co-constitution of class and gender

Take, as an example, the relatively recently established, and growing, occupation of research-scientist in high-technology industry. It is an occupation that has emerged as a separate element in the social division of labour with the increasing separation of knowledge-based jobs (such as research engineering) from the process of direct physical production (see Massey et al. 1992). The jobs that now fall into this occupational grouping involve intellectual research, quite high levels of abstract thought, and the concentrated application of scientific logic. They are reasonably paid and, more important than that, are surrounded by a high level of hype, both journalistic and academic. They are jobs with a high degree of cachet, and are seen as being "on the frontiers"; their holders are sought after and applauded, in different ways, by politicians on both left and right of the political spectrum. Approximately 95% of the holders of these jobs in the UK today are men.[2]

How are these facts to be interpreted? Certainly there are issues here of social closure around these jobs based on specialist knowledge. Much has, for instance, been written about the culture of high-technology workplaces and the difficulties that it frequently presents to women. The time-space organization of the jobs is also highly demanding, and thus restricts the range of people who would be prepared to take them up. The hours are frequently very long and – equally important – unpredictable. Work continues into the night, over weekends, into Bank Holidays. And although in some ways these knowledge-based jobs might be done anywhere (so long as you have

---

2   See, for a general analysis, Massey et al. (1992). [...]

a computer on hand), in fact considerable geographical demands are placed on these employees. They may have to be "on call" to go out and fix problems, they may have to fly off to California at a moment's notice, their very progress in their careers may require a period of worldwide geographical mobility. These are jobs that demand a particular form of what is now usually referred to as flexibility – in this case time-space flexibility. They are also, and for that reason, jobs that prefer that you don't have too many commitments outside of work, and certainly not commitments – such as those of caring for others – which themselves require a degree of time-space flexibility. In our interviews we found no-one to disagree with the statement that "a single parent could not do this job". In these and a multitude of other ways, then, already-gendered persons have highly differential abilities (whether through availability or through inclination) to enter this profession.

Certainly, too, it is the case that the way in which these jobs are socially constructed generates a demand for help with personal servicing. In our interviews the younger single men sometimes got by on junk food and night-time visits to the launderette, there was a medium degree of reliance on other family, on cleaners and on childminders, but the bulk of the burden fell, in the 66% of cases where the scientists were cohabiting, on the female partners. It is, then, a classic segment of the service class whose possibility of existence in this form depends on the existence also of "service wives" [...] And this in turn of course made it even more difficult for these (mainly professionally qualified) women to enter fully into their own professional careers. And thus the masculinity of the occupational middle class is further reinforced.

It is also surely the case that the fact that these occupations are peopled by self-confident (and mainly young) men further reinforces the high status in which they are so frequently held. The mythologizing of the lives of young male scientist-entrepreneurs was, particularly in the 1980s, a regular feature of newspaper business pages (see Massey et al. 1992).

In all these ways, then, gender makes these occupations what they are: in terms of who fills these spaces in the social division of labour, in terms of the design of the spaces and of their dependence on other gendered work, and in terms of the status that they are thereby accorded.

It may be, however, that the nature of this patch within the overall social division of labour is even more fundamentally gendered than this. These jobs are the apex of abstract thought within the overall process of production. They are the result of a long process (which even now may be being re-evaluated) of separation, within industry, of conceptualization from execution. These jobs are at the "conceptualization" end of that dualism. They are occupations/roles in society whose status derives from the (perceived-as) elevated abstraction of their work-content. [...]

Certainly, the separation of conceptualization from execution is part of a process of the division of tasks propelled by the requirements of competitive production, by the requirements of capitalist calculation (see, for instance, Braverman 1974). It is a necessary part of the capitalist division of labour. However, the fact that the division of tasks historically took the *form* of the separation of conception from execution can also be read in the light of a longer historical distinction – the philosophical separation of Mind from Body that has been so prominent in Western philosophy since Descartes and that was itself a more precise, and in many ways more extreme, version of an even longer-lasting distinction between Reason and non-Reason. The separation-out of conceptualization as a social function is not particular to capitalism, although of course its forms in this case are distinct. Nor is it only a distinction around which *class* divisions may be articulated. Genevieve Lloyd (1984) among many others has pointed to, and analyzed in detail, the imbrication of the establishment of these dualisms with the establishment of the dichotomous gender system and its particular ascribed characteristics. It was with masculinity that were associated the "Reason" and the "Mind" sides of these dualisms. And it was with the establishment of masculinity as dominant that the very nature of these dualisms (the fact of their mutually-exclusive dichotomous nature, the lines of divide that they describe) was associated. More generally, indeed, it might also be remembered that such dualisms are by their very nature "relational" [...], but that the *form* of this relational connection is precisely what has been argued to be characteristic of, and related to, our societies' dualistic approach to gender definition (Lloyd 1984, Massey 1992).

On the one hand, then, it is perhaps no more than the continuance of a long tradition that men should be the ones to get the high-status jobs at the conceptual end of the current spectrum in the social division of labour. But on the other hand, and in the end much more importantly, the very fact and nature of the divide itself is utterly tied up not with already defined genders, but with processes of gender-dividing and the ascription of gender characteristics – the formation of gendered identities. David Noble (1992) has written of the gendered history of this set of dualisms and of some of its practical effects in modes of social organization. The subtitle of his book is "The Christian clerical culture of Western science". Maybe the high-tech research laboratory of the late twentieth century has much in common – in status, in symbolism, in the construction of a particular form of masculinity – with the medieval monastery. The long Western (and not only Western) construction of a division of labour that separates Reason from non-Reason, abstract thought from concrete production, conceptualization from execution, has been at the same time a process at the heart of the construction of gender.

Moreover, the process continues today. In the scientific workplace of today this clerical-scientific culture is one that both reflects and helps further to define and reinforce particular aspects of a particular kind of masculinity – that bound up with science, logic and rationality. What is at issue is not individual empirical men – individual men cope with the culture in a variety of ways and with varying degrees of difficulty and ease – but a form of *masculinity*, socially defined.[3]

So, it is being argued here, the terms on which the social division of labour is constructed (the criteria of its lines of divide) are imbued with gender, and the construction of this social division of labour is itself active in the constitution of gender, both the nature of its divisions and the characteristics that they are socially ascribed.

Moreover, the fact of the continued salience of this process of gender-constitution then curls back into another argument [addressed by Nicky Gregson and Michelle Lowe] [...] that there is a strong unwillingness on the part of middle-class men "to do more than the bare minimum in the way of domestic labour" (p. 158). They go on to explore "the place of domestic labour in the identities of middle-class men and women" (p. 158), using a performative account of class in an analysis of domestic labour to distinguish between those elements that such people will do (which they see as being compatible with or confirming of their identities) and those elements that they are happy to delegate to others, given their time-constraints and their financial abilities. The authors urge the need to address "the gender politics of domestic labour" (p. 163). Perhaps, again, the argument can be taken a step further. First, as Gregson and Lowe would concur, there is variation on this issue between masculine and feminine identities. But secondly, and to bring the argument in a sense full-circle, the construction of certain types of middle-class masculinity as not including domestic labour is also, in part, a product of the social division of labour in paid employment. For some of the scientists in our research it was important to their self-conception as scientists to play down their interest in and ability at domestic labour (see Massey, 1995b). Thus, the construction of masculine incompetence about the house, and therefore the construction of a gender politics of domestic labour, happens in part through the joint constitution of gender and occupation within the wider field of the social division of labour.

---

3   The relations between these occupations and the dualisms Reason–non-Reason and Transcendence–Immanence are spelled out in Massey (1995b).

The relation of the categories

The basic argument here, then, is that the interrelation between class and other axes of social differentiation, such as gender, operates at a very profound level and that what will frequently be involved will in fact be the *joint*, or simultaneous, constitution of the dimensions and the character of both class and these other axes. The status of the particular kind of specialist knowledge possessed by the men in these examples reflects and confirms, and constitutes, both their middle-class status and their masculinity.

It is still, none the less, the nature of *class* that is the focus of attention in this volume, and to argue that things are interrelated is by no means to argue that they should be collapsed into each other. Indeed, to retain any notion of interrelation one must previously have established a distinction. The categories race, class, gender are not *the same*. [...]

A similar point might be made in relation to Phillips and Sarre's argument in [their chapter] about the relation between "race" and class. They criticize Savage et al. (1992) for maintaining race and gender as "contingent" to the process of class formation. The alternative is, in the terms of realist explanatory categories, that they are "necessary". It seems to me that there is an implicit reading here of "contingent" and "necessary" as less and more significant respectively. Certainly in this context quite the opposite is the case. For race and class to be *contingent* causal axes to the process of class formation means that they have an analytically autonomous causal structure. It means, precisely, that they are not subsumed within the logic of class, as would be implied by the term "necessary". To say that, empirically, class and race and gender are often (always? how would we know?) mixed up together is *not* to establish that they are part of the same necessary logic. [...]

What is at issue is not accounting for proportions of variation in outcomes, but recognizing the active mutual engagement of dimensions of social differentiation so that they produce an outcome in which specific forms of gender and class relation are in effect fused. But here there is a problem that some recent formulations of class, notably Goldthorpe's own (1983, Erikson & Goldthorpe 1992), are couched in such a way as to make it difficult to examine this interface. Goldthorpe's recent formulations emphasize that class is based around employment relations rather than the experience of work itself. An important thread in this argument, however, is that the experience of class on the second view happens primarily within the workplace, whereas on the first view the experience extends to the members of the worker's family. This poses two problems. First, [...] the experience of class within the workplace helps construct individuals with particular identities, which they continue to inhabit outside the workplace as well. The construction of one's identity around status and career, for instance, is not something one leaves behind in the office. You take it, for instance, back home to the domestic sphere. Nor are such characteristics exclusively ones of class. In the case of the scientists-professionals in my own recent research, they were also characteristics of (a particular form of) masculinity. And [...] the construction of such work identities has considerable effects on people outside the workplace, not least the other members of "the conjugal family".

Secondly, there is a problem for those – such as Goldthorpe – who insist that the family is the unit of class analysis. As the research cited above shows, the effects of work relationships are frequently brought back into the home in ways that are divisive. This is particularly true of non-economic effects. Thus scientific masculinity on occasions discouraged the performance of domestic work, and, as Gregson and Lowe point out, the impact of careerism (and the possession of a career is a central criterion in Goldthorpe's definition of the middle class) can have similar, contradictory impacts. Moreover – and this is the point – these can set up members of a conjugal family with conflicting interests. And, although Erikson & Goldthorpe state that they are aware of possible gender divisions within the family (Erikson & Goldthorpe 1992: 233), it seems important not just to admit these as a possibility, but to point to clear links between the construction of specific forms of class identity and domestic relationships. There is widespread evidence both that the man's career is pursued as much for himself as for his family (in our group, for his status as a scientist rather than for monetary reward) and that (certainly in many of our cases) the women could have had equally well-remunerated careers – it was just that their priorities were different (they put family and children higher up the list).

THE GEOGRAPHIES OF CLASS

At a number of points in the course of this book reference has been made to the importance of "place" in any consideration of the nature of class and of the middle class in particular. There is something intuitively appealing about this – the sharpness of the spatial differentiation between social groups in Western society is such that it is easy to think of emblematic class-related places. The more difficult questions are those that try to push beyond this (not unimportant) level of analysis [...]. There are two particular lines of thought that I wish to pursue here. The first is to argue that what is at issue is somewhat wider than simply "place". Rather, I think, what we may be able to begin to think about is different relations between particular social groups and *geography*. [...] What *will* be argued, however, is that, as well as distinctive relations to *place*, different social groups may also have particular identifiable and characterizable relations to space – what I shall term here *social spatialities.* The second aim is to explore the nature of the relationships that may exist between these aspects of geography and distinct social groups and – even more difficult to pin down – the nature of the connection (if any) to class. The two themes are intertwined in what follows. [...]

Place

The relationship of social groups to place is more generally recognized to be significant than is that to spatiality, even though the nature and coherence of the relationship are disputed. The connection of the middle class to the countryside, which is the focus of a number of discussions in this book, raises a range of issues.

To begin with, it underlines that what is at issue here is not just the happenstance congregation of different social groups into distinct geographical locations but the active *making of places.* Moreover, this making of places is itself part and parcel of constructing and confirming the identity of the social group. A social group does not merely make a place after its own (thus pre-given) image; rather the process of construction of the place is integral to the imagination and affirmation of the social identity itself. That this is so is evident from many of the discussions of the relationship between elements of the middle class and the countryside, both in the articles in this collection and elsewhere. (This is emphatically *not* to argue, as none of the papers here would argue, that there is some one single coherent relation between the middle class and the countryside. It is simply to argue that, insofar as there are such relationships, fractured and complicated as they may be, they take this form of constitution rather than merely correlation.)

To the extent, then, that there are constitutive relationships between place and group, they involve not only (re)making the place, for instance the countryside, but also (re)making the group. [One element highlighted in other chapters is that] the countryside (and the discussion is mainly, though not exclusively, of the English countryside) is white. If the notion of the middle-class in Britain brings with it images of whiteness, then that is reinforced when the middle class is linked to rurality. All the classic images of villages and "quintessential" (it seems obligatory to use that word!) English countryside hark back to an imagined past before immigration and stand in rebuke and rejection of the ethnic chaos of the inner city. Cloke, Phillips and Thrift cite evidence of geographical avoidance of ethnic minorities as part of the reason for some white people's desire to live in the countryside. What is going on here is certainly exclusion (Phillips and Sarre talk of "reluctant admission" to the middle class) from both place and the culture of the social group. And it is also the active *making* of both place and culture in a process of mutual reinforcement. In a programme of work on the (re)making of the South East of England during the 1980s we uncovered just such processes underway. What began to emerge was a picture of the Outer South East of England, at least in its more rural parts, as a region – or a set of localities – being produced as part of a project to construct a particular kind of (middle-class) white ethnicity. The place, the particular nature of the articulation of the ethnicity, and the identity of the social groups involved were being constructed together and as largely mutually reinforcing. This is a particular kind of English whiteness, and a particular way of being middle class, articulated into and through a particular kind of place. As Phillips and Sarre so aptly put it in this volume, "The whiteness of the British middle classes turns out to be not just an assumption or an oversight, but an implicit goal of British culture" (p. 91). And, to mirror the argument in the first section, this is not just a matter of exclusion and of discrimination (although it is also both of these); it is also a matter of co-constitution, in which the co-constitution of place may also be a significant element.

It was probably without a flicker of surprise that you read, in Tony Fielding's [chapter], that the process of class formation for managerial and professional strata involves not only interregional migration but migration specifically to the South East of England (and were it possible to draw the boundaries of that region rather more generously I am certain that this observation would be even more emphatic). Yet why should we accept, as though it were apparently "natural", that these social groups should cluster so strongly (although not exclusively) within one corner of the country? Here is a clear correlation between social class (in the most general of terms – I shall return to this) and geography, and one that appears to have been reinforced over recent decades. One way to interpret this geography is as the spatial expression of the (changing) social relations of production (Massey 1995a). Managers may be defined in terms of their control over the relations of economic ownership and possession; and professionals through their autonomy and their possession of specialist knowledge (to remain with the case of scientists and technologists, through their control over conceptualization within the overall process of production). As the social relations involved in both of these dimensions have become more elaborate, as long hierarchies of management have developed (with the concentration of ownership, and so forth) and as conceptualization has become increasingly divorced from execution, so their geographies have changed. It has become less necessary for the upper echelons of these hierarchies to be located alongside the direct process of manual production. Increasingly, in fact, they have pulled away from it. Over the past 100 years the geography of the control over production has become increasingly distinct from the geography of "production itself". And the geography of Research and Development has become more and more removed from

251

the geography of factories. In the process these newly emerging groups have made places that both reflect and actively reinforce their (social) distinctiveness. *They have created a geography of difference.*

The complexities of causality involved in all this are fascinating. At first sight what is going on is that changes in the division of labour (the proliferation of occupational places) along the managerial and conceptual aspects of the social relations of production have enabled a parallel proliferation, and mutual distancing, of spatial locations. (Just note, at this point, that they have only *enabled* these spatial changes; they have not necessitated them.) As the hierarchies of management and conceptualization have been stretched out over space they have responded to other locational demands (other than proximity to production), they have been attracted to other geographical environments, they have established a distance between themselves and manual production and the working class. Yet in fact the changes in the division of labour and the establishment of new occupational categories have not been the simply autonomous "independent variable" from which the definition of new social groups and new social geographies has been a dependent derivation. It has been argued in the first section of this chapter [...] that the emergence of occupations does not happen as some kind of ineluctable technological necessity. The relation between gender and the splitting of conceptualization and execution was discussed above. And the same point can be made in a more general way here: the pushing forward of the division of labour itself has been both stimulated and influenced in its character by forces pushing towards social differentiation and by the possibilities offered by geographically uneven development (see Massey 1995a). Moreover, once again, the different aspects have in many ways reinforced each other. Most importantly, the possibility of spatial distancing from the manual working class and of establishing a social exclusivity of place has been both a stimulus to the development of the division of labour and a reinforcement of the social differentiation that it enabled. In the UK (and there are differences between cultures here) functional distance from production has gone along with, and in its social effects has been reinforced by, geographical distance. The spatial symbolism of science parks may be seen as emblematic of this process (Massey et al. 1992). Their whole construction as places is designed to this effect. Occupational, social and spatial identities are constructed together.

This, of course, has been to concentrate on the relation of "place" to employment and to residence. There are many other ways, as Urry [in his chapter] again reminds us, in which the symbolism of place can be a significant component in the struggle to construct and demonstrate a particular social identity. If the working class goes to Benidorm and Bowness, there are middle-class "honeypots" too. There is (apparently) significance attached to the choice of ski resort; there are highly developed relationships, bearing well-established meanings, with particular parts of continental Europe – the Dordogne, or Tuscany; there is a knowing cultural geography of the sources of consumption – olives from the right grove, olive oil from the right region (even if you have gone out on a limb and found a little place no-one else has ever heard of, the *fact* of geography, and of having an awareness of this kind of "cultural geography", is important). But to wander thus is to raise again a central question. There certainly seem to be important connections between the establishment of social identity and place/spatiality, but what is their nature and how, if at all, are they related to class?

The character of the connections

First, then, it is important to remember that the constitution of social groups necessarily occurs "spatially"; that is, in places and through spatial mobility and interaction. It is, moreover, all these elements rather than just the "in place" aspect of things, which are important. Indeed, it may be the combination of these things, rather than any one of them individually, that produces the greatest degree of distinctiveness between social groups. Thus the commitment to some idea of "village life" by certain middle-class elements is referred to a number of times in these papers. So too is the fact that this space of the village may be shared by other groups that are in no way middle-class. The social difference between these groups is sometimes characterized in terms of the distinct images and symbolisms of the village that each mobilizes. But there is also a clear differentiation between such groups (and also between genders) in terms of the wider spatiality within which this village location and imagery are set and indeed with which it interplays.[4] The "idyllic village in the mind" is in fact most likely to be found precisely in the minds of those who are more spatially mobile, those who travel abroad for holidays, who go frequently to London for business and for culture, who travel frequently and internationally as part of their working lives. The one aspect, indeed, could well be the stimulant to the existence of the other: the rapid and perhaps disorienting spatial flexibility on the one hand generating a desire for stability in place on the other. The (tentative) argument being developed here, then, is that maybe it is possible to think in terms of different social groups being characterized by distinct spatialities, where that term is used in the widest possible way – as degree of and relation to spatial flexibility, as commitment to place, as level of control over both. And, if that is so, then maybe at least some significant elements in the middle class in the UK today (I am thinking particularly of the upper echelons of professional, managerial

---

4   Again this argument draws on the [Open University's] South East research programme.

and new petit bourgeois groups) embody in their own lives, and more than any other group in society, that tension between the global and the local (between spatial mobility on the one hand and a commitment to place on the other) about which so much is currently being written. It is, perhaps, a measure of their cultural hegemony that it is *their* experience that is taken as the sign of the times. And it is, of course, primarily they who write about it.

A second reflection on the nature of these connections between spatiality and the social is simply that geography plays an "active" role in the constitution of the social. Distinctions of spatiality and place reflect, are actively drawn upon by, and mould and reinforce other social distinctions.

Moreover, thirdly, and leading directly on from this, if the constitution of class-related social groups is, or should be interpreted as, relational (and I would argue so) then distinctions of geography most certainly fulfil this criterion. It is not only that different social groups have different social spatialities and relationships to place but that these distinct spatialities are in many ways mutually-constitutive. At the simplest level, the middle class has in general more *spatial power* than working-class groups. Such power may operate in a variety of ways: through market-power, for instance in the housing market, through greater degrees of mobility through access to transport and the availability of opportunities, and through its power over location in the employment relation (see Massey 1995a), and so forth. And in many ways this power works, and is worked, to reinforce already existing differences. The importance of *distancing,* from direct production, from economic decline and dereliction, *from the working class*; the importance of *exclusion*, from the residential area, from the employment location (the very term "exclusive" being often used in advertising); the importance of "seclusion"; the power of *relative* (rather than absolute) mobility in reinforcing social advantage – all of these are social relationships of geography that are established relationally with other social groups. These things are important at a range of spatial scales: within towns and cities, between urban and rural, and between the South East of the country and "the rest". Indeed, it is the combination of the social and spatial power of middle-class groups that is the most intractable problem standing in the way of addressing the gross inequalities of geographically uneven development in the UK today. Whether it be the commitment to certain kinds of exclusivities of place or the simple refusal of "high-level" managers and civil servants to move outside of the home counties, the mutually reinforcing social and spatial power of these groups is consistently wielded against attempts to tackle problems of spatial inequality. Between them, the upper echelons of managers and professional more or less control the geography of employment in the UK (Massey 1995a). Earlier in this chapter it was asked on what terms the social spatialities of different groups might intersect. The answer must be, at least in part, that they intersect relationally: they constitute, and reinforce the characteristics of, each other.

Yet how, if at all, is all this related to *class*? Much of the foregoing discussion in this chapter has been cautiously (prudently) in terms of "social groups". And even when, as in Fielding's chapter [...], the analysis is in terms of clearly defined classes, what is demonstrated is the empirical fact of notable degrees of variation. At the empirical level this leaves open the question whether an even greater degree of inter-group variation in interregional mobility would have been identified between groups defined along different lines. [...] It seems to me, therefore, that it is not possible to argue for a single geography of the middle class if this is to be defined in terms of place-outcomes (that is, the actual places chosen, whether for residence or whatever). However, such choices may be interpreted as the operationalization or non-operationalization of spatial powers, and it may be that it is the possession of these spatial powers, rather than the particular way in which they are operationalized, that middle-class groups have in common. In other words, it may be the wider *spatialities*, in the broad definition outlined above, that the middle class coherently exhibits, rather than any particular specific set of locations.

However, if such a spatiality can be demonstrated to be a common property of the middle class in what way is that relationship established? Fielding's evidence of a clear empirical correlation, for instance, is just that. We have yet to theorize any *necessary* (constitutive) relation between the middle class and particular spatialities. Indeed it seems to me that this is very difficult to do. It may possibly be the case that spatial powers can be derived from an asset-based analysis, for instance from a combination of property and culture assets, but the connections do not seem to be very direct. On the other hand, an approach to class based in the relations of production does offer some pointers. It is evident, for instance, that the spatial flexibility of managerial and professional groups in terms of employment and residential location derives quite directly from long-term shifts in the organization of capitalist production and that the hierarchies of occupations are quite directly reflected in their geographies. The relational definitions of class in these terms, and their relational geographies, are connected and mutually reinforcing.[5] And what this represents is the operationalization of a potential, located in the social division of labour, where the division of labour is itself

---

5   Savage et al. (1992) argue that a critical realist view of class relations leads to the adoption of an asset-based approach to class. I certainly agree that Savage et al's asset approach is compatible with a critical realist position. However, I would also contend, and it is implicit in the argument at this point, that other approaches may also be compatible – in particular here the approach based on social relations of production.

in part a response to the possibility of such operationalization (see above). In this sense, it would be possible to see the geographical hierarchies of professional and managerial groups as deriving from their socio-spatial causal powers and as feeding back into the process of consolidation of their social distinctiveness. It is also possible to pursue this line of analysis at a finer level of disaggregation and in particular to explore the distinction between managerial and professional groups. Thus, it can be argued that the different places of these two groups within the class schema based on relations of production (drawing on Wright 1976) produce distinct spatial potentials in relation to the geography of employment and residence (Massey 1995a). In direct reflection of their contrasting functions within the overall relations of production, and the distinct locational pressures which relate to them, whereas in the UK managers tend to be more concentrated within conurbations (and especially London), scientific professionals have the greater tendency to be in the more rural parts of the outer South East. This is a difference in geography that is noted in passing in a number of chapters here, especially in the contrasts between London and Berkshire. What I am arguing here is that it can be clearly related to differences in location within the relations of production. Such tentative suggestions, it seems to me, may offer a way forward. What they do not do, of course, is to link up with those aspects of social spatiality that go beyond the sphere of work and home location – the wider social characteristics connected with leisure, tourism and the more elaborated spatialities of social life.

The causal logic of the connection between social class and spatiality may, then, not have been fully established, and may not be there to establish. But what does seem clear is that spatiality in its widest sense is an important differentiator, and moment in the formation, of social identities more generally.

REFERENCES

Braverman, H. 1974. *Labor and monopoly capital: the degradation of work in the twentieth century.* New York: Monthly Review Press.

Butler, T. & M. Savage 1995. *Social change and the middle classes.* London: UCL Press.

Erikson, R. & J. Goldthorpe 1992. *The constant flux: a study of class mobility in industrial societies.* Oxford: Clarendon Press.

Goldthorpe, J. 1983. Women and class analysis: a defence of the conventional view. *Sociology* 17, 465–78.

Lloyd, G. 1984. *The man of reason: "male" and "female" in western philosophy.* London: Methuen.

Massey, D. 1992. Political and space-time. *New Left Review* 196, 65–84.

Massey, D. 1995a. *Spatial divisions of labour: social structures and the geography of production,* 2nd edn. Basingstoke: Macmillan.

Massey, D. 1995b. Masculinity, dualism and high-technology. *Transactions of the Institute of British Geographers* NS 20, 487–99.

Massey, D., P. Quintas, D. Wield 1992. *High-tech fantasies: science parks in society, sciences and space.* London: Routledge.

Noble, D. 1992. *A world without women: the Christian clerical culture of western science.* Oxford: Oxford University Press.

Savage, M., J. Barlow, P. Dickens, T. Fielding 1992. *Property, bureaucracy and culture: middle class formation in contemporary Britain.* London: Routledge.

Wright, E. O. 1976. Class boundaries in advanced capitalist societies. *New Left Review* 98, 3–41.

CHAPTER 17

POLITICS AND SPACE/TIME (1992)

'Space' is very much on the agenda these days. On the one hand, from a wide variety of sources come proclamations of the significance of the spatial in these times: 'It is space not time that hides consequences from us' (Berger); 'The difference that space makes' (Sayer); 'That new spatiality implicit in the postmodern' (Jameson); 'It is space rather than time which is the distinctively significant dimension of contemporary capitalism' (Urry); and 'All the social sciences must make room for an increasingly geographical conception of mankind' (Braudel). Even Foucault is now increasingly cited for his occasional reflections on the importance of the spatial. His 1967 Berlin lectures contain the unequivocal: 'The anxiety of our era has to do fundamentally with space, no doubt a great deal more than with time.' In other contexts the importance of the spatial, and of associated concepts, is more metaphorical. In debates around identity the terminology of space, location, positionality and place figures prominently. Homi Bhabha, in discussions of cultural identity, argues for a notion of a 'third space'. Jameson, faced with what he sees as the global confusions of postmodern times, 'the disorientation of saturated space', calls for an exercise in 'cognitive mapping'. And Laclau, in his own very different reflections on the 'new revolution of our time', uses the terms 'temporal' and 'spatial' as the major differentiators between ways of conceptualizing systems of social relations.

In some ways, all this can only be a delight to someone who has long worked as a 'geographer'. Suddenly the concerns, the concepts (or, at least, the *terms*) which have long been at the heart of our discussion are at the centre also of wider social and political debate. And yet, in the midst of this gratification I have found myself uneasy about the way in which, by some, these terms are used. Here I want to examine just one aspect of these anxieties about some of the current uses of spatial terminology: the conceptualization (often implicit) of the term 'space' itself.

In part this concern about what the term 'space' is intended to mean arises simply from the multiplicity of definitions adopted. Many authors rely heavily on the terms 'space'/'spatial', and each assumes that their meaning is clear and uncontested. Yet in fact the meaning that different authors assume (and therefore – in the case of metaphorical usage – the import of the metaphor) varies greatly. Buried in these unacknowledged disagreements is a debate that never surfaces; and it never surfaces because everyone assumes we already know what these terms mean. Henri Lefebvre, in the opening pages of his book *The Production of Space*, commented on just this phenomenon: the fact that authors who in so many ways excel in logical rigour will fail to define a term which functions crucially in their argument: 'Conspicuous by its absence from supposedly epistemological studies is ... the idea ... of space – the fact that "space" is mentioned on every page notwithstanding.'[1] At least there ought to be a debate about the meaning of this much-used term.

Nonetheless, had this been all that was at issue I would probably not have been exercised to write an article about it. But the problem runs more deeply than this. For among the many and conflicting definitions of space that are current in the literature there are some – and very powerful ones – which deprive it of politics and of the possibility of politics: they effectively depoliticize the realm of the spatial. By no means all authors relegate space in this way. Many, drawing on terms such as 'centre'/'periphery'/'margin', and so forth, and examining the 'politics of location' for instance, think of spatiality in a highly active and politically enabling manner. But for others space is the sphere of the lack of politics.

Precisely because the use of spatial terminology is so frequently unexamined, this latter use of the term is not always immediately evident. This dawned fully on me when I read a statement by Ernesto Laclau in his *New Reflections on the Revolution of Our Time*. 'Politics and space', he writes on page 68, 'are antinomic terms. Politics only exist insofar as the spatial eludes us.'[2] For someone who, as a geographer, has for years been arguing, along with many others, for a dynamic and politically progressive way of conceptualizing the spatial, this was clearly provocative!

Because my own inquiries were initially stimulated by Laclau's book, and because unearthing the implicit definitions at work implies a detailed reading (which restricts the number of authors who can be considered) this discussion takes *New Reflections* as a starting point, and considers it in most detail. But, as will become clear, the implicit definition used by Laclau, and which depoliticizes space, is shared by many other authors. In its simpler forms it

---

1 H. Lefebvre, *The Production of Space*, Oxford, 1991, p. 3.
2 E. Laclau, *New Reflections on the Revolution of Our Time*, London, 1990. Thanks to Ernesto Laclau for many long discussions during the writing of this article.

operates, for instance, in the debate over the nature of structuralism, and is an implicit reference point in many texts. It is, moreover, in certain of its fundamental aspects shared by authors, such as Fredric Jameson, who in other ways are making arguments very different from those of Laclau.

To summarize it rather crudely, Laclau's view of space is that it is the realm of stasis. There is, in the realm of the spatial, no true temporality and thus no possibility of politics. It is on this view, and on a critique of it, that much of my initial discussion concentrates. But in other parts of the debate about the nature of the current era, and in particular in relation to 'postmodernity', the realm of the spatial is given entirely different associations from those ascribed to it by Laclau. Thus Jameson, who sees postmodern times as being particularly characterized by the importance of spatiality, interprets it in terms of an unnerving multiplicity: space is chaotic depthlessness.[3] This is the opposite of Laclau's characterization, yet for Jameson it is – once again – a formulation which deprives the spatial of any meaningful politics.

A caveat must be entered from the start. This discussion will be addressing only one aspect of the complex realm that goes by the name of the spatial. Lefebvre, among others, insisted on the importance of considering not only what might be called 'the geometry' of space but also its lived practices and the symbolic meaning and significance of particular spaces and spatializations. Without disagreeing with that, the concentration here will nonetheless be on the view of space as what I shall provisionally call 'a dimension'. The argument is that different ways of conceptualizing this aspect of 'the spatial' themselves provide very different bases (or in some cases no basis at all) for the politicization of space. Clearly, anyway, the issue of the conceptualization of space is of more than technical interest; it is one of the axes along which we experience and conceptualize the world.

SPACE AND TIME

An examination of the literature reveals, as might be expected, a variety of uses and meanings of the term 'space', but there is one characteristic of these meanings that is particularly strong and wide-spread. This is the view of space which, in one way or another, defines it as stasis, and as utterly opposed to time. Laclau, for whom the contrast between what he labels temporal and what he calls spatial is key to his whole argument, uses a highly complex version of this definition. For him, notions of time and space are related to contrasting methods of understanding social systems [...] Laclau posits that 'any repetition that is governed by a structural law of successions is space'

---

3   E. Jameson, *Postmodernism, or, the Cultural Logic of Late Capitalism*, London, 1991.

(p. 41) and 'spatiality means coexistence within a structure that establishes the positive nature of all its terms' (p. 69). Here, then, any postulated causal structure which is complete and self-determining is labelled 'spatial'. This does not mean that such a 'spatial' structure cannot change – it may do – but the essential characteristic is that all the causes of any change which may take place are internal to the structure itself. On this view, in the realm of the spatial there can be no surprises (provided we are analytically well-equipped). In contrast to the closed and self-determining systems of the spatial, Time (or temporality) for Laclau takes the form of dislocation, a dynamic which disrupts the predefined terms of any system of causality. The spatial, because it lacks dislocation, is devoid of the possibility of politics.

This is an importantly different distinction between time and space from that which simply contrasts change with an utter lack of movement. In Laclau's version, there can be movement and change within a so-called spatial system; what there cannot be is real dynamism in the sense of a change in the terms of 'the system' itself (which can therefore never be a simply coherent closed system). A distinction is postulated, in other words, between different types of what would normally be called time. On the one hand, there is the time internal to a closed system, where things may change yet without really changing. On the other hand, there is genuine dynamism, Grand Historical Time. In the former is included cyclical time, the times of reproduction, the way in which a peasantry represents to itself (says Laclau, p. 42) the unfolding of the cycle of the seasons, the turning of the earth. To some extent, too, there is 'embedded time', the time in which our daily lives are set.[4] These times, says Laclau, this kind of 'time' is space.

Laclau's argument here is that what we are inevitably faced with in the world are 'temporal' (by which he means dislocated) structures: dislocation is intrinsic and it is this – this essential openness – which creates the possibility of politics. Any attempt to represent the world 'spatially', including even the world of physical space, is an attempt to ignore that dislocation. Space therefore, in his terminology, is representation, is any (ideological) attempt at closure: 'Society, then, is unrepresentable: any representation – *and thus any space* – is an attempt to constitute society, not to state what it is' (p. 82, my emphasis). Pure spatiality, in these terms, cannot exist: 'The ultimate failure of all hegemonisation [in Laclau's term, spatialization], then, means that the real – including physical space – is in the ultimate instance temporal' (p. 42); or again: 'the mythical nature of any space' (p. 68). This does not mean that the spatial is unimportant. This is not the point at issue, nor is it Laclau's intent. For the 'spatial' as the ideological/mythical is seen by him as itself part

---

4   See, for instance, the discussion in M. Rustin, 'Place and Time in Socialist Theory', *Radical Philosophy*, no. 47, 1987, pp. 30–36.

of the social and as constitutive of it: 'And insofar as the social is impossible without some fixation of meaning, without the discourse of closure, the ideological must be seen as constitutive of the social' (p. 92). The issue here is not the relative priority of the temporal and the spatial, but their definition. For it is through this logic, and its association of ideas with temporality and spatiality, that Laclau arrives at the depoliticization of space. 'Let us begin,' writes Laclau, 'by identifying three dimensions of the relationship of dislocation that are crucial to our analysis. The *first* is that dislocation is the very form of temporality. And temporality must be conceived as the exact opposite of space. The "spatialization" of an event consists of eliminating its temporality' (p. 41; my emphasis).

The second and third dimensions of the relationship of dislocation (see above) take the logic further: 'The *second* dimension is that dislocation [Massey: which, remember, is the antithesis of the spatial] is the very form of possibility,' and 'The *third* dimension is that dislocation is the very form of freedom. Freedom is the absence of determination' (pp. 42, 43; my emphases). This leaves the realm of the spatial looking like unpromising territory for politics. It is lacking in dislocation, the very form of possibility (the form of temporality), which is also 'the very form of freedom.' Within the spatial there is only determination, and hence no possibility of freedom or of politics.

Laclau's characterization of the spatial is, however, a relatively sophisticated version of a much more general conception of space and time (or spatiality and temporality). It is a conceptualization in which the two are opposed to each other, and in which time is the one that matters and of which History (capital H) is made. Time Marches On but space is a kind of stasis, where nothing really happens. There are a number of ways in which, it seems to me, this manner of characterizing space and the realm of the spatial is questionable. Three of them, chosen precisely because of their contrasts, because of the distinct light they each throw on the problems of this view of space, will be examined here. The first draws on the debates that have taken place in 'radical geography' over the last two decades and more; the second examines the issue from the point of view of a concern with gender; and the third examines the view from physics.

RADICAL GEOGRAPHY

In the 1970s the discipline of geography experienced the kinds of developments described by Anderson in 'A Culture in Contraflow'[5] for other social

---

5   P. Anderson, 'A Culture in Contraflow', [*New Left Review*] 180, March-April 1990, pp. 41–78 and [*New Left Review*] 182, July-August 1990, pp. 85–137.

sciences. The previously hegemonic positivist 'spatial science' was increasingly challenged by a new generation of Marxist geographers. The argument turned intellectually on how 'the relation between space and society' should be conceptualized. To caricature the debate, the spatial scientists had posited an autonomous sphere of the spatial in which 'spatial relations' and 'spatial processes' produced spatial distributions. The geography of industry, for instance, would be interpreted as simply the result of 'geographical location factors'. Countering this, the Marxist critique was that all these so-called spatial relations and spatial processes were actually social relations taking a particular geographical form. The geography of industry, we argued, could therefore not be explained without a prior understanding of the economy and of wider social and political processes. The aphorism of the seventies was 'space is a social construct'. That is to say – though the point was perhaps not made clearly enough at the time – space is constituted through social relations and material social practices.

But this, too, was soon to seem an inadequate characterization of the social/spatial relation. For, while it is surely correct to argue that space is socially constructed, the one-sidedness of that formulation implied that geographical forms and distributions were simply outcomes, the end point of social explanation. Geographers would thus be the cartographers of the social sciences, mapping the outcomes of processes which could only be explained in other disciplines – sociology, economics, and so forth. What geographers mapped – the spatial form of the social – was interesting enough, but it was simply an end product: it had no material effect. Quite apart from any demeaning disciplinary implications, this was plainly not the case. The events taking place all around us in the 1980s – the massive spatial restructuring both intranationally and internationally as an integral part of social and economic changes – made it plain that, in one way or another, 'geography matters'. And so, to the aphorism of the 1970s – that space is socially constructed – was added in the 1980s the other side of the coin: that the social is spatially constructed too, and that makes a difference. In other words, and in its broadest formulation, society is necessarily constructed spatially, and that fact – the spatial organization of society – makes a difference to how it works.

But if spatial organization makes a difference to how society works and how it changes, then far from being the realm of stasis, space and the spatial are also implicated (*contra* Laclau) in the production of history – and thus, potentially, in politics. This was not an entirely new thought. Henri Lefebvre, writing in 1974, was beginning to argue a very similar position: 'The space of capitalist accumulation thus gradually came to life, and began to be fitted out. This process of animation is admiringly referred to as history, and its motor sought in all kinds of factors … This is the road to a ceaseless analysing of, and searching for, dates and chains of events. Inasmuch as space is the locus of all such chronologies, might it not constitute a principle of explanation at least as acceptable as any other?'[6]

This broad position – that the social and the spatial are inseparable and that the spatial form of the social has causal effectivity – is now accepted increasingly widely, especially in geography and sociology,[7] though there are still those who would disagree, and beyond certain groups even the fact of a debate over the issue seems to have remained unrecognized [...][8] For those familiar with the debate, and who saw in it an essential step towards the politicization of the spatial, formulations of space as a static resultant without any effect – whether the simplistic versions or the more complex definitions such as Laclau's – seem to be very much a retrograde step. However, in retrospect, even the debates within radical geography have still fully to take on board the implications of our own arguments for the way in which space might be conceptualized.

ISSUES OF GENDER

For there are also other reservations, from completely different sources, that can be levelled against this view of space and that go beyond the debate which has so far taken place within radical geography. Some of these reservations revolve around issues of gender.

First of all, this manner of conceptualizing space and time takes the form of a dichotomous dualism. It is neither a simple statement of difference (A, B, ...) nor a dualism constructed through an analysis of the interrelations between the objects being defined (capital:labour). It is a dichotomy specified in terms of a presence and an absence; a dualism which takes the classic form of A/not-A... Now, apart from any reservations which may be raised in the particular case of space and time (and which we shall come to later), the mode of thinking that relies on irreconcilable dichotomies of this sort has in general recently come in for widespread criticism. All the strings of these kinds of opposition with which we are so accustomed to work (mind–body;

---

6   Lefebvre, p. 275.
7   See, for instance, D. Massey, *Spatial Divisions of Labour: Social Structures and the Geography of Production*, Basingstoke 1984; D. Gregory, and J. Urry, eds., *Social Relations and Spatial Structures*, Basingstoke 1985; and E. Soja, *Postmodern Geographies: The Reassertion of Space in Critical Social Theory*, London, 1989.
8   It should be noted that the argument that 'the spatial' is particularly important in the current era is a different one from that being made here. The argument about the nature of postmodernity is an empirical one about the characteristics of these times. The argument developed within geography was an in-principle position concerning the nature of explanation, and the role of the spatial within this.

nature–culture; Reason–emotion; and so forth) have been argued to be at heart problematical and a hindrance to either understanding or changing the world. Much of this critique has come from feminists.[9]

The argument is two-fold. First, and less importantly here, it is argued that this way of approaching conceptualization is, in Western societies and more generally in societies where child-rearing is performed overwhelmingly by members of one sex (women), more typical of males than of females. This is an argument which generally draws on object-relations-theory approaches to identity-formation. Second, however, and of more immediate significance for the argument being constructed here, it has been contended that this kind of dichotomous thinking, together with a whole range of the sets of dualisms that take this form (we shall look at some of these in more detail below) are related to the construction of the radical distinction between genders in our society, to the characteristics assigned to each of them, and to the power relations maintained between them. Thus, Nancy Jay, in an article entitled 'Gender and Dichotomy', examines the social conditions and consequences of the use of logical dichotomy.[10] She argues not only that logical dichotomy and radical gender distinctions are associated but also, more widely, that such a mode of constructing difference works to the advantage of certain (dominant) social groups, 'that almost any ideology based on A/Not-A dichotomy is effective in resisting change. Those whose understanding of society is ruled by such ideology find it very hard to conceive of the possibility of alternative forms of social order (third possibilities). Within such thinking, the only alternative to the *one* order is disorder' (p. 54). Genevieve Lloyd, too, in a sweeping history of 'male' and 'female' in Western philosophy, entitled *The Man of Reason*, argues that such dichotomous conceptualization, and – what we shall come to later – the prioritization of one term in the dualism over the other, is not only central to much of the formulation of concepts with which Western philosophy has worked but that it is dependent upon, and is instrumental in the conceptualization of, among other things, a particular form of radical distinction between female and male genders.[11] [...] The argument here is that the definition of 'space' and 'time' under scrutiny [...] is precisely of this form, and on that basis alone warrants further critical investigation.

But there is also a further point. For within this kind of conceptualization, only one of the terms (A) is defined positively. The other term (not-A) is conceived only in relation to A, and as lacking in A. A fairly thorough reading of

---

9   See, for instance, [...] S. Harding and M.B. Hintikka, eds., *Discovering Reality: Feminist Perspectives on Epistemology, Metaphysics, Methodology, and Philosophy of Science*, Dordrecht 1983[...]

10 N. Jay, 'Gender and Dichotomoy', *Feminist Studies*, vol. 7, no. 1, Spring 1981, pp. 38–56.

11 G. Lloyd, *The Man of Reason: 'Male' and 'Female' in Western Philosophy*, London 1984.

some of the recent literature that uses the terminology of space and time, and that employs this form of conceptualization, leaves no doubt that it is Time which is conceived of as in the position of 'A', and space which is 'not-A'. Over and over again, time is defined by such things as change, movement, history, dynamism; while space, rather lamely by comparison, is simply the absence of these things. This has two aspects. First, this kind of definition means that it is time, and the characteristics associated with time, that are the primary constituents of both space and time; time is the nodal point, the privileged signifier. And second, this kind of definition means that space is defined by absence, by lack. This is clear in the simple (and often implicit) definitions (time equals change/movement, space equals the lack of these things), but it can also be argued to be the case with more complex definitions such as those put forward by Laclau. For although in a formal sense it is the spatial which in Laclau's formulation is complete and the temporal which marks the lack (the absence of representation, the impossibility of closure), in the whole tone of the argument it is in fact space that is associated with negativity and absence. Thus: 'Temporality must be conceived as the exact opposite of space. The "spatialization" of an event consists of eliminating its temporality' (p. 41).

Now, of course, in current Western culture, or in certain of its dominant theories, woman too is defined in terms of lack. Nor [...] is it entirely a matter of coincidence that space and the feminine are frequently defined in terms of dichotomies in which each of them is most commonly defined as not-A. There is a whole set of dualisms whose terms are commonly aligned with time and space. With Time are aligned History, Progress, Civilization, Science, Politics and Reason, portentous things with gravitas and capital letters. With space on the other hand are aligned the other poles of these concepts: stasis, ('simple') reproduction, nostalgia, emotion, aesthetics, the body. All these dualisms, in the way that they are used, suffer from the criticisms made above of dichotomies of this form: the problem of mutual exclusivity and of the consequent impoverishment of both of their terms. Other dualisms could be added which also map on to that between time and space. Jameson, for instance, as do a whole line of authors before him, clearly relates the pairing to that between transcendence and immanence, with the former connotationally associated with the temporal and immanence with the spatial. Indeed, in this and in spite of their other differences, Jameson and Laclau are very similar. Laclau's distinction between the closed, cyclical time of simple reproduction (spatial) and dislocated, changing history (temporal), even if the latter has no inevitability in its progressive movement, is precisely that. Jameson who bemoans what he characterizes as the tendency towards immanence and the flight from transcendence of the contemporary period, writes of 'a world peculiarly without transcendence and without perspective ... and indeed without plot in any traditional sense, since all choices would be equidistant and on the same level' (*Postmodernism*, p. 269), and this is a world where, he believes, a sense of the temporal is being lost and the realm of the spatial is taking over.

Now, as has been pointed out many times, these dualisms which so easily map on to each other also map on to the constructed dichotomy between female and male. From Rousseau's seeing woman as a potential source of disorder, as needing to be tamed by Reason, to Freud's famous pronouncement that woman is the enemy of civilization, to the many subsequent critics and analysts of such statements of the 'obviousness' of dualisms, of their interrelation one with another, and of their connotations of male and female, such literature is now considerable.[12] And space, in this system of interconnected dualisms, is coded female. '"Transcendence", in its origins, is a transcendence *of* the feminine', writes Lloyd (*The Man of Reason*, p. 101), for instance. Moreover, even where the transcodings between dualisms have an element of inconsistency, this rule still applies. Thus where time is dynamism, dislocation and History, and space is stasis, space is coded female and denigrated. But where space is chaos (which you would think was quite different from stasis; more indeed like dislocation), then time is Order [...] and space is *still* coded female, only in this context interpreted as threatening.

Elizabeth Wilson, in her book *The Sphinx in the City*, analyses this latter set of connotations.[13] The whole notion of city culture, she argues, has been developed as one pertaining to men. Yet within this context women present a threat, and in two ways. First, there is the fact that in the metropolis we are freer, in spite of all the also-attendant dangers, to escape the rigidity of patriarchal social controls which can be so powerful in a smaller community. Second and following from this, 'women have fared especially badly in Western visions of the metropolis because they have seemed to represent disorder. There is fear of the city as a realm of uncontrolled and chaotic sexual licence, and the rigid control of women in cities has been felt necessary to avert this danger' (p. 157). 'Woman represented feeling, sexuality and even chaos, man was rationality and control' (p. 87). Among male modernist writers of the early twentieth century, she argues – and with the exception of Joyce – the dominant response to the burgeoning city was to see it as threatening, while modernist women writers (Woolf, Richardson) were more likely to exult in its energy and vitality. The male response was perhaps more ambiguous than this, but it was certainly a mixture of fascination and

---

12 See, for instance, D. Dinnerstein, *The Rocking of the Cradle and the Ruling of the World*, London 1987; M. le Doeuff, *Hipparchia's Choice: An Essay Concerning Women, Philosophy, Etc.*, Oxford 1991; and Lloyd.

13 E. Wilson, *The Sphinx in the City: Urban Life, the Control of Disorder, and Women*, London 1991.

fear. There is an interesting parallel to be drawn here with the sense of panic in the midst of exhilaration which seems to have overtaken some writers at what they see as the ungraspable (and therefore unbearable) complexity of the postmodern age. And it is an ungraspability seen persistently in spatial terms, whether through the argument that it is the new (seen-to-be-new) time-space compression, the new global-localism, the breaking down of borders, that is the cause of it all, or through the interpretation of the current period as somehow in its very character intrinsically more spatial than previous eras. In Jameson these two positions are brought together, and he displays the same ambivalence. He writes of 'the horror of multiplicity' (p. 363), of 'all the web threads flung out beyond my "situation" into the unimaginable synchronicity of other people' (p. 362). It is hard to resist the idea that Jameson's (and others') apparently vertiginous terror (a phrase they often use themselves) in the face of the complexity of today's world (conceived of as social but also importantly as spatial) has a lot in common with the nervousness of the male modernist, nearly a century ago, when faced with the big city.

It is important to be clear about what is being said of this relationship between space/time and gender. It is not being argued that this way of characterizing space is somehow essentially male; there is no essentialism of feminine/masculine here. Rather, the argument is that the dichotomous characterization of space and time, along with a whole range of other dualisms that have been briefly referred to, and with their connotative interrelations, may both reflect and be part of the constitution of, among other things, the masculinity and femininity of the sexist society in which we live. Nor is it being argued that space should simply be reprioritized to share an equal status with, or stand instead of, time. The latter point is important because there have been a number of contributions to the debate recently which have argued that, especially in modernist (including Marxist) accounts, it is time which has been considered the more important. Ed Soja, particularly in his book *Postmodern Geographies*, has made an extended and persuasive case to this effect (although see the critique by Gregory).[14] The story told earlier of Marxism within geography – supposedly the spatial discipline – is indicative of the same tendency. In a completely different context, Terry Eagleton has written in his introduction to Kristin Ross's *The Construction of Social Space* that 'Ross is surely right to claim that this idea [the concept of space] has proved of far less glamorous appeal to radical theorists than the apparently more dynamic, exhilarating notions of narrative and history.'[15] It is interesting

---

14 Soja; and D. Gregory, 'Chinatown, Part Three? Soja and the Missing Spaces of Social Theory', *Strategies*, no. 3, 1990.

15 K. Ross, *The Emergence of Social Space: Rimbaud and the Paris Commune*, Basingstoke 1988; Eagleton's *Foreword*, p. xii.

to speculate on the degree to which this de-prioritization might itself have been part and parcel of the system of gender connotations. Ross herself writes: 'The difficulty is also one of vocabulary, for while words like "historical" and "political" convey a dynamic of intentionality, vitality, and human motivation, "spatial", on the other hand, connotes stasis, neutrality, and passivity' (p. 8), and in her analysis of Rimbaud's poetry and of the nature of its relation to the Paris Commune she does her best to counter that essentially negative view of spatiality. (Jameson, of course, is arguing pretty much the same point about the past prioritization of time, but his mission is precisely the opposite of Ross's and Soja's; it is to hang on to that prioritization.)

The point here, however, is not to argue for an upgrading of the status of space within the terms of the old dualism (a project which is arguably inherently difficult anyway, given the terms of that dualism), but to argue that what must be overcome is the very formulation of space/time in terms of this kind of dichotomy. The same point has frequently been made by feminists in relation to other dualisms, most particularly perhaps – because of the debate over the writings of Simone de Beauvoir – the dualism of transcendence and immanence. When de Beauvoir wrote 'Man's design is not to repeat himself in time: it is to take control of the instant and mould the future. It is male activity that in creating values has made of existence itself a value; this activity has prevailed over the confused forces of life; it has subdued Nature and Woman',[16] she was making precisely that discrimination between cyclicity and 'real change' which is not only central to the classic distinction between immanence and transcendence but is also part of the way in which Laclau distinguishes between what he calls the spatial and the temporal. De Beauvoir's argument was that women should grasp the transcendent. A later generation of feminists has argued that the problem is the nature of the distinction itself. The position here is both that the two dualisms (immanence/transcendence and space/time) are related and that the argument about the former dualism could and should be extended to the latter. The next line of critique, the view from physics, provides some further hints about the directions which that reformulation might take.

THE VIEW FROM PHYSICS

The conceptualization of space and time under examination here also runs counter to notions of space and time within the natural sciences, and most particularly in physics. Now, in principle this may not be at all important; it is not clear that strict parallels can or should be drawn between the physical

---

16 S. de Beauvoir, *The Second Sex* (1949), trans. H. M. Parshley, Harmondsworth 1972, p. 97.

and the social sciences. And indeed there continue to be debates on this subject in the physical sciences. The point is, however, that the view of space and time already outlined above does have, as one of its roots at least, an interpretation drawn – if only implicitly – from the physical sciences. The problem is that it is an outmoded one.

The viewpoint, as adopted for instance by Laclau, accords with the viewpoint of classical, Newtonian, physics. In classical physics, both space and time exist in their own right, as do objects. Space is a passive arena, the setting for objects and their interaction. Objects, in turn, exist prior to their interactions and affect each other through force-fields. The observer, similarly, is detached from the observed world. In modern physics, on the other hand, the identity of things is *constituted through* interactions. In modern physics, while velocity, acceleration and so forth are defined, the basic ontological categories, such as space and time, are not. Even more significantly from the point of view of the argument here, in modern physics, physical reality is conceived of as a 'four-dimensional existence instead of ... the evolution of a three-dimensional existence'.[17] Thus 'According to Einstein's theory ... space and time are not to be thought of as separate entities existing in their own right – a three-dimensional space, and a one-dimensional time. Rather, the underlying reality consists of a four-dimensional space-time' (p. 35). Moreover, the observer, too, is part of the observed world.

It is worth pausing for a moment to clarify a couple of points. The first is that the argument here is not in favour of a total collapse of the differences between something called the spatial and the temporal dimensions. Nor, indeed, would that seem to be what modern physics is arguing either. Rather, the point is that space and time are inextricably interwoven. It is not that we cannot make any distinction at all between them but that the distinction we do make needs to hold the two in tension, and to do so within an overall, and strong, concept of four-dimensionality. The second point is that the definitions of both space and time in themselves must be constructed as the result of interrelations. This means that there is no question of defining space simply as not-time. It must have a positive definition, in its own terms, just as does time. Space must not be consigned to the position of being conceptualized in terms of absence or lack. It also means, if the positive definitions of both space and time must be inter-relational, that there is no absolute dimension: space. The existence of the spatial depends on the interrelations of objects: 'In order for "space" to make an appearance there needs to be at least two fundamental particles' (p. 33). This is, in fact, saying no more than what is commonly argued, even in the social sciences – that space is not

---

17 R. Stannard, *Grounds for Reasonable Belief,* Edinburgh 1989. Page references are given in parenthesis in the text.

absolute, it is relational. Perhaps the problem at this point is that the implications of this position seem not to have been taken on board.

Now, in some ways all this seems to have some similarities with Laclau's use of the notion of the spatial, for his definition does refer to forms of social interaction. As we have seen, however, he designates them (or the concepts of them) as spatial only when they form a closed system, where there is a lack of dislocation that can produce a way out of the postulated (but impossible) closure. However, such use of the term is anyway surely metaphorical. What it represents is evidence of the connotations which are being attached to the terms 'space' and 'spatial'. It is not talking directly of 'the spatial' itself. Thus, to take up Laclau's usage in more detail: at a number of points, as we have seen, he presents definitions of space in terms of possible (in fact, he would argue, impossible) causal structures: 'Any repetition that is governed by a structural law of successions is space' (*New Reflections*, p. 41); or 'Spatiality means coexistence within a structure that establishes the positive nature of all its terms' (p. 69). My question of these definitions and of other related ones, both elsewhere in this book and more widely – for instance in the debate over the supposed 'spatiality' of structuralism – is 'says who?' Is not this appellation in fact pure assertion? Laclau agrees in rejecting the possibility of the actual existence of pure spatiality in the sense of undislocated stasis. A further question must therefore be: why postulate it? Or, more precisely, why postulate it as 'space'? As we have just seen, an answer that proposes an absolute spatial dimension will not do. An alternative answer might be that this ideal pure spatiality, which only exists as discourse/myth/ideology, is in fact a (misjudged) metaphor. In this case it is indeed defined by interrelations – this is certainly not 'absolute space', the independently existing dimension – and the interrelations are those of a closed system of social relations, a system outside of which there is nothing and in which nothing will dislocate (temporalize) its internally regulated functioning. But then my question is: why call it 'space'? [...] Insofar as such systems do exist – and even insofar as they are merely postulated as an ideal – they can in no sense *be* simply spatial nor exist only in space. In themselves they *constitute a* particular form of space-time.

Moreover, as metaphors the sense of Laclau's formulations goes against what I understand by – and shall argue below would be more helpful to understand by – space/the spatial. 'Any repetition that is governed by a structural law of successions'? – but *is* space so governed? As was argued above, radical geographers reacted strongly in the 1970s precisely against a view of 'a spatial realm', a realm, posited implicitly or explicitly by a wide range of then-dominant practitioners, from mathematicized 'regional scientists' to data-bashers armed with ferociously high regression coefficients, in which there were spatial processes, spatial laws and purely spatial explanations. In terms of causality, what was being argued by those of us who attacked this view was that the spatial is externally determined. A formulation like the one above, because of the connotations it attaches to the words 'space'/'spatial' in terms of the nature of causality, thus takes us back a good two decades. Or again, what of the second of Laclau's definitions given above? – that the spatial is the 'coexistence within a structure that establishes the positive nature of all its terms'? What then of the paradox of simultaneity and the causal chaos of happenstance juxtaposition which are, as we shall argue below (and as Jameson sees), integral characteristics of relational space?

In this procedure, any sort of stasis (for instance a self-regulating structural coherence which cannot lead to any transformation outside of its own terms) gets called 'space'/'spatial'. But there is no reason for this save the prior definition of space as lacking in (this kind of) transformative dynamic *and*, equally importantly, an assumption that anything lacking in (this kind of) dynamism is spatial. Instead, therefore, of using the terms 'space' (and 'time') in this metaphorical way to refer to such structures, why do we not remain with definitions (such as 'dislocated'/'undislocated') that refer to the nature of the causal structures themselves? Apart from its greater clarity, this would have the considerable advantage of leaving us free to retain (or maybe, rather, to develop) a more positive concept of space.

Indeed, conceptualizing space and time more in the manner of modern physics would seem to be consistent with Laclau's general argument. His whole point about radical historicity is this: 'Any effort to spatialize time ultimately fails and space itself becomes an event' (p. 84). Spatiality in this sense is agreed to be impossible. '"Articulation" ... is the primary ontological level of the constitution of the real', writes Laclau (p. 184). This is a fundamentally important statement, and one with which I agree. The argument here is thus not opposed to Laclau; rather it is that exactly the same reasoning, and manner of conceptualization, that he applies to the rest of the world, should be applied to space and time as well. It is not that the inter-relations between objects occur *in* space and time; it is these relationships themselves which *create/define* space and time.[18]

It is not of course necessary for the social sciences simply to follow the natural sciences in such matters of conceptualization [...] What is being argued here is that the social issues that we currently need to understand, whether they be the high-tech postmodern world or questions of cultural identity, require something that would look more like the 'modern physics' view of space. It would, moreover, precisely by introducing into the concept of space that element of dislocation/freedom/possibility, enable the politicization of space/space-time.

---

18 Stannard, p. 33.

AN ALTERNATIVE VIEW OF SPACE

A first requirement of developing an alternative view of space is that we should try to get away from a notion of society as a kind of 3-D (and indeed more usually 2-D) slice which moves through time. Such a view is often, even usually, implicit rather than explicit, but it is remarkably pervasive. It shows up in the way people phrase things, in the analogies they use. Thus, just briefly to cite two of the authors who have been referred to earlier, Foucault writes 'We are at a moment, I believe, when our experience of the world is less that of a long life developing through time than that of a network that connects points and intersects with its own skein,'[19] and Jameson contrasts 'historiographic deep space or perspectival temporality' with a (spatial) set of connections which 'lights up like a nodal circuit in a slot machine.'[20] The aim here is not to disagree in total with these formulations, but to indicate what they imply. What they both point to is a contrast between temporal movement on the one hand, and on the other a notion of space as instantaneous connections between things at one moment. [...] But while the contrast – the shift in balance – to which both authors are drawing attention is a valid one, in the end the notion of space as *only* systems of simultaneous relations, the flashing of a pinball machine, is inadequate. For, of course, the temporal movement is also spatial; the moving elements have spatial relations to each other. And the 'spatial' interconnections which flash across can only be constituted temporally as well. Instead of linear process counterposed to flat surface (which anyway reduces space from three to two dimensions), it is necessary to insist on the irrefutable four-dimensionality (indeed, n-dimensionality) of things. Space is not static, nor time spaceless. Of course spatiality and temporality are different from each other, but neither can be conceptualized as the absence of the other. The full implications of this will be elaborated below, but for the moment the point is to try to think in terms of all the dimensions of space-time. It is a lot more difficult than at first it might seem.

Second, we need to conceptualize space as constructed out of interrelations, as the simultaneous coexistence of social interrelations and interactions at all spatial scales, from the most local level to the most global [...] On the one hand, all social (and indeed physical) phenomena/activities/relations have a spatial form and a relative spatial location. The relations which bind communities, whether they be 'local' societies or worldwide organizations; the relations within an industrial corporation; the debt relations between the South and the North; the relations which result in the current popularity

---

19 M. Foucault, 'Of Other Spaces,' *Diacritics*, Spring 1986, p. 22.
20 Jameson, p. 374.

in European cities of music from Mali. The spatial spread of social relations can be intimately local or expansively global, or anything in between. Their spatial extent and form also changes over time (and there is considerable debate about what is happening to the spatial form of social relations at the moment). But, whichever way it is, there is no getting away from the fact that the social is inexorably also spatial.

The proposition here is that this fact be used to define the spatial. Thus, the spatial is socially constituted. 'Space' is created out of the vast intricacies, the incredible complexities, of the interlocking and the non-interlocking, and the networks of relations at every scale from local to global. What makes a particular view of these social relations specifically spatial is their simultaneity. It is a simultaneity, also, which has extension and configuration. But simultaneity is absolutely not stasis. Seeing space as a moment in the intersection of configured social relations (rather than as an absolute dimension) means that it cannot be seen as static. There is no choice between flow (time) and a flat surface of instantaneous relations (space). Space is not a 'flat' surface in that sense because the social relations which create it are themselves dynamic by their very nature. It is a question of a manner of thinking. It is not the 'slice through time' which should be the dominant thought but the simultaneous coexistence of social relations that cannot be conceptualized as other than dynamic. Moreover, and again as a result of the fact that it is conceptualized as created out of social relations, space is by its very nature full of power and symbolism, a complex web of relations of domination and subordination, of solidarity and cooperation. This aspect of space has been referred to elsewhere as a kind of 'power-geometry'.[21]

Third, this in turn means that the spatial has *both* an element of order *and* an element of chaos (or maybe it is the case that we should question that dichotomy also). It cannot be defined on one side or the other of the mutually exclusive dichotomies discussed earlier. Space has order in two senses. First, it has order because all spatial locations of phenomena are caused; they can in principle be explained. Second, it has order because there are indeed spatial systems, in the sense of sets of social phenomena in which spatial arrangement (that is, mutual relative positioning rather than 'absolute' location) itself is part of the constitution of the system. The spatial organization of a communications network, or of a supermarket chain with its warehousing and distribution points and retail outlets, would both be examples of this, as would the activity space of a multinational company. There is an integral spatial coherence here, which constitutes the geographical distributions and the geographical form of the social relations. The spatial form was socially

---

21 D. Massey, 'Power-Geometry and a Progressive Sense of Place', in Bird et al., eds., *Mapping the Futures*, London forthcoming.

'planned', in itself directly socially caused, that way. But there is also an element of 'chaos' which is intrinsic to the spatial. For although the location of each (or a set) of a number of phenomena may be directly caused (we know why x is here and Y is there), the spatial positioning of one in relation to the other (x's location in relation to Y) may not be directly caused. Such relative locations are produced out of the independent operation of separate determinations. They are in that sense 'unintended consequences'. Thus, the chaos of the spatial results from [...] happenstance juxtapositions, the accidental separations, the often paradoxical nature of the spatial arrangements that result from the operation of all these causalities. Both Mike Davis and Ed Soja, for instance, point to the paradoxical mixtures, the unexpected land-uses side by side, within Los Angeles. Thus, the relation between social relations and spatiality may vary between that of a fairly coherent system (where social and spatial form are mutually determinant) and that where the particular spatial form is not directly socially caused at all.

This has a number of significant implications. To begin with, it takes further the debate with Ernesto Laclau. For in this conceptualization space is essentially disrupted. It is, indeed, 'dislocated' and necessarily so. The simultaneity of space as defined here in no way implies the internally coherent closed system of causality which is dubbed 'spatial' in his *New Reflections*. There is no way that 'spatiality' in this sense 'means coexistence within a structure that establishes the positive nature of all its terms' (p. 69). The spatial, in fact, precisely *cannot* be so. And this means, in turn, that the spatial too is open to politics.

But, further, neither does this view of space accord with that of Fredric Jameson, which, at first sight, might seem to be the opposite of Laclau's. In Jameson's view the spatial does indeed, as we have seen, have a lot to do with the chaotic. While for Laclau spatial discourses are the attempt to represent (to pin down the essentially unmappable), for Jameson the spatial is precisely unrepresentable – which is why he calls for an exercise in 'mapping' (though he acknowledges the procedure will be far more complex than cartography as we have known it so far). In this sense, Laclau and Jameson, both of whom use the terms 'space'/'spatiality', and so on, with great frequency, and for both of whom the concepts perform an important function in their overall schemas, have diametrically opposed interpretations of what the terms actually mean. Yet for both of them their concepts of spatiality work against politics. While for Laclau it is the essential orderliness of the spatial (as he defines it) that means the death of history and politics, for Jameson it is the chaos (precisely, the dislocation) of (his definition of) the spatial that apparently causes him to panic, and to call for a map.

So this difference between the two authors does not imply that, since the view of the spatial proposed here is in disagreement with that of Laclau, it

concords with that of Jameson. Jameson's view is in fact equally problematical for politics, although in a different way. Jameson labels as 'space' what he
sees as unrepresentable (thus the 'crisis of representation' and the 'increasing
spatialization' are to him inextricably associated elements of postmodern
society). In this, he perhaps unknowingly recalls an old debate within geography that goes by the name of 'the problem of geographical description'.[22]
Thus, thirty years ago H. C. Darby, an eminent figure in the geography of his
day, ruminated that 'A series of geographical facts is much more difficult to
present than a sequence of historical facts. Events follow one another in time
in an inherently dramatic fashion that makes juxtaposition in time easier to
convey through the written word than juxtaposition in space. Geographical
description is inevitably more difficult to achieve successfully than is historical narrative.'[23] Such a view, however, depends on the notion that the difficulty of geographical description (as opposed to temporal storytelling) arises
in part because in space you can go off in any direction and in part because
in space things which are next to each other are not necessarily connected.
However, not only does this reduce space to unrepresentable chaos, it is also
extremely problematical in what it implies for the notion of *time*. And this
would seem on occasions to be the case for Jameson too. For, while space is
posed as the unrepresentable, time is thereby, at least implicitly and at those
moments, *counterposed* as the comforting security of a story it is possible to
tell. This of course clearly reflects a notion of the difference between time
and space in which time has a coherence and logic to its telling, while space
does not. It is the view of time which Jameson might, according to some
of his writings, like to see restored: time/History in the form of the Grand
Narrative.

However, this is also a view of temporality, as sequential coherence, that
has come in for much questioning. The historical in fact can pose similar
problems of representation to the geographical. *Moreover*, and ironically, it
is precisely this view of history that Laclau would term spatial: '... with inex-
orable logic it then follows that there can be no dislocation possible in this
process. If everything that happens can be explained *internally* to this world,
nothing can be a mere event (which entails a radical temporality, as we have
seen) and everything acquires an absolute intelligibility within the grandi-
ose scheme of a pure spatiality. This is the Hegelian-Marxist moment' (*New
Reflections*, p. 75). *Further still*, what is crucially wrong with both these views
is that they are simply opposing space and time [...] It is a counterposition
which makes it difficult to think the social in terms of the real multiplicities of

---

22 H. C. Darby, 'The Problem of Geographical Description', *Transactions of the Institute of
British Geographers*, vol. 30, 1962, pp. 1–14.

23 Ibid., p. 2.

space-time. This is an argument that is being made forcefully in debates over cultural identity. '[E]thnic identity and difference are socially produced in the here and now, not archeologically salvaged from the disappearing past';[24] and Homi Bhabha enquires 'Can I just clarify that what to me is problematic about the understanding of the "fundamentalist" position in the Rushdie case is that it is *represented* as archaic, almost medieval. It may sound very strange to us, it may sound absolutely absurd to some people, but the point is that the demands over *The Satanic Verses* are being made *now*, out of a particular political state that is functioning very much in our time.'[25] Those who focus on what they see as the terrifying simultaneity of today would presumably find such a view of the world problematical, and would long for such 'ethnic identities' and 'fundamentalisms' to be (re)placed in the past so that one story of progression between differences, rather than an account of the production of a number of different differences at one moment in time, could be told. That this cannot be done is the real meaning of the contrast between thinking in terms of three dimensions plus one, and recognizing fully the inextricability of the four dimensions together. What used to be thought of as 'the problem of geographical description' is actually the more general difficulty of dealing with a world which is 4-D.

But all this leads to a fourth characteristic of an alternative view of space, as part of space-time. For precisely that element of the chaotic, or dislocated, which is intrinsic to the spatial has effects on the social phenomena that constitute it. Spatial form as 'outcome' (the happenstance juxtapositions and so forth) has emergent powers which can have effects on subsequent events. Spatial form can alter the future course of the very histories that have produced it. In relation to Laclau, what this means, ironically, is that one of the sources of the dislocation, on the existence of which he (in my view correctly) insists, is precisely the spatial. The spatial (in my terms) is precisely one of the sources of the temporal (in his terms). In relation to Jameson, the (at least partial) chaos of the spatial (which he recognizes) is precisely one of the reasons why the temporal is not, and cannot be, so tidy and monolithic a tale as he might wish. One way of thinking about all this is to say that the spatial is integral to the production of history, and thus to the possibility of politics, just as the temporal is to geography. Another way is to insist on the inseparability of time and space, on their joint constitution through the interrelations between phenomena; on the necessity of thinking in terms of space-time.

---

24 M. P. Smith, 'Postmodernism, Urban Ethnography, and the New Social Space of Ethnic Identity', forthcoming in *Theory and Society*.

25 In 'Interview with Homi Bhabha' in J. Rutherford, ed., *Identity: Community, Culture, Difference*, London 1990, p. 215. At this point, as at a number of others, the argument links up with the discussion by Peter Osborne in his 'Modernity is a Qualitative, Not a Chronological, Category', [*New Left Review*] 192, March-April 1992, pp. 65–84.

CHAPTER 18

REFLECTIONS ON DEBATES OVER A DECADE (1995)

[...]

MARXISM AND THE ANALYSIS OF CAPITALISM

[...]

Flows of value and the analysis of class relations

The phenomena and the causal processes which figure in [*Spatial Divisions of Labour*] are conceptualised in terms of class, and in more general terms social, relations and not in terms of value. This, I have come increasingly to believe, is an important distinction. Value analysis and class analysis are of course not mutually exclusive approaches; they are indeed clearly related. And value itself, as is oft repeated, is a social relation. However, they do often exist uneasily side by side in empirical analysis. Moreover it seems to me to make an important difference to the whole tenor of an analysis, which of the two is adopted as the main entry-point. This is quite apart from the byzantine entanglements into which the 'law of value' has fallen and which make it, in my view, unusable in any empirical economic calculus. This is not to say that the concept of value is not useful for thinking through the broad structures of the economy and for forming the absolutely necessary basis for some central concepts – exploitation, for instance. But that is quite different from the, in my view vain, attempts to use it as a basis for empirical economic calculation – the frequent references in some literature to things such as 'the organic composition of capital', for instance, often being in fact references to capital intensity measured in terms of price. However besides all these technical objections it seems to me that there are also important implications for the nature of analysis which arise from taking class rather than flows of value or even of capital as the initial frame.

Perhaps most obviously, class interests as perceived by the members of any class are not necessarily the same as economic interests and particularly not necessarily the same as short or medium-term economic interests. Moreover class interests may override immediate economic interests, or may hold the key to understanding why long-term rather than short-term economic advantage proved to be decisive as a basis for action. There are many examples of this in foregoing chapters. At a broad level there is Gamble's analysis of that strong strain in British Conservatism 'for which the maintenance of social power and relatively stable class relations has been of far greater importance than any particular "bourgeois" economic ideology, such as that of the free play of market forces' (p. 44).[1] There are frequent analyses of types of capital – maybe old-fashioned, small or middling-sized – where 'accumulate, accumulate' is certainly not the name of the game, where even the smallest positive rate of profit is an enabling condition for being what one primarily is, a maker of shirts for instance. The example of the woolen-textile industry (see Chapter 6, pp. 268 *passim*), is a case in point where there was neither the will to maximize profits nor the willingness to withdraw from production just because profits failed. Or again, there were the anxious introspections of the Confederation of British Industry in the tempestuous early years of Mrs. Thatcher's rule: After 'numerous boardroom battles ... most companies retained their longer-term political and class loyalties above more immediate economic interests' (p. 258). An analysis which thought in terms of categories defined only by the economic, or which expected actions to be simply determined by the economic or, even more, by value, could not account for such apparently anomalous forms of behaviour.

One implication of this is that more thought needs to be given to the way in which we characterise capital. Although 'industry' is the focus of so much analysis – the central object of attention in industrial geography – it still seems to me that remarkably little work has been done on this issue. It is for this reason that an attempt to get to grips with the question is presented right at the beginning of this book (Section 2.2, Characterising capital). For what is clear throughout all the subsequent analyses is that capital is divided in ways far more complex (and including non-economic) than the simple criteria which are usually deployed in industrial studies (sector, size, place in the economy). In any given actual society capital is differentiated also by such

---

1 Editorial note: Here and elsewhere, Massey references numerous sections and specific citations from the second edition of *Spatial Divisions of Labour*, where this text was first published.

things as social character, temperament, regional history. Moreover, as the analyses throughout the book, and perhaps particularly those in Chapter 6, try to show, these differences are of real importance both to any understanding of the behaviour of particular parts of the economy (how they respond to given economic pressures, for instance) and to analysis of the economy as a whole and of its geography. The usual categories of economic geography are simply not good enough; what is needed is an analysis of the class structure of capital.

Behind these points, of course, lies a broader argument: that it is impossible simply to separate-off 'the economic' from the political, cultural and ideological aspects of society. [...] Not only are 'politics and ideology ... not to be interpreted as simple reflections of the economic' but 'politics and ideology are themselves important in the construction of the economic' (p. 43).

One way in which this is clearly true is that economic phenomena have to be *interpreted*. They are not simply objective data to which there will be a knee-jerk response. There is an emphasis on this need for, and importance of, interpretation throughout the book. It is there in the analysis of the response of different kinds of capital to particular economic pressures; it is there in the attempt to characterise capital; it is there in the analysis of the national economy. Thus, on the last, the shift in the later seventies towards monetarism was in part a political shift in the *analysis* of the economy; it concerned '*the political formulation* of the economic situation as being primarily a problem of inflation' (pp. 255–6), for instance; it involved re-working the distinction between 'productive' and 'non-productive' parts of the economy (pp. 256–7) – a reinterpretation which had dramatic effects at both macro-economic and regional levels. 'So it has not just been changing economic circumstances which have been important but also changes in the way in which economic pressures were filtered, moulded and translated through the prevailing political and ideological climate' (p. 227). The motif of all these arguments, and one which is repeated in various forms throughout the book, is that 'the requirements of accumulation do not arrive raw at the factory gate'.

Such a view leaves the analysis open, not just to 'politics, ideology...' etc. in their broad senses but also to all those other social relations and axes of social differentiation which in some sense in their origins (though not in their formation and reproduction) are autonomous from 'the economic' as it is usually defined and yet which are thoroughly implicated in its form. The axis which gets most attention in the analyses here (though far less than it should have got) is gender relations. The *Elaborations* (p. 39) to the class framework, for instance, argue that 'ideologies of race and gender criss-cross the labour market' and talk in terms of 'ideologically determined labour markets'. The 'industrial location decision', in other words, 'is just one moment in a much wider economic, ideological and political field' (p. 42).

And finally, all of these things leave open in the analysis a necessary space for agency, and for politics. The opening discussion in Chapter 2 tries both to insist on this and to differentiate this concept of agency from the voluntaristic, free-floating-individual variety which is often set up in contradistinction to supposed 'determinism' (see pp. 14–15). [...] Thus [...] there is an insistence on the fact that new spatial structures come about, not through some ineluctable shifts, but through active social engagement. [...] 'The process by which one use of space lays the preconditions for another is a complex one and depends on the political and organisational response of the classes and social groups involved' (p. 290); 'The evolution of different kinds of spatial structure, their establishment, maintenance and eventual collapse and change, are not simply determined by the characteristics of the labour process, the requirements of accumulation, the stages of the mode of production, or even the demands of capital. None of these things in themselves "result in" specific spatial forms. Spatial structures are established, reinforced, combated and changed through political and economic strategies and battles on the part of managers, workers and political representatives' ... they are 'the object of political struggle' (p. 82). And in turn, it might be added, managers, workers, political representatives and so forth are moulded in such struggles. 'Classes are a product of history and of social conflict as well as being constituent of them' (p. 35). Exactly the same form of argument, with its insistence on a lack of necessity, is deployed in relation to the level of organisation of trade unions. [...] Chapter 6 concludes with such an example: geography may matter 'but it does not in itself determine any particular social outcome... The changes going on at the moment can be conceptualised in terms of a shift between dominant spatial divisions of labour. But that is to talk of a social process, involving disruption, change, and conflict: as such the outcome is always uncertain' (p. 286)

[...]

EXPLANATION

[...]

Articulation/thinking in terms of relations

We are, then, firmly into the realm of 'multicausality' and again there are numerous examples through the book where it is necessary to draw upon whole constellations of processes, specified in relation to class, to technological level, to gender relations, and with the significance of the spatial organisation of each of these processes underlined. A small but typical example occurs in the analysis of certain strategies within the footwear industry (see pp. 162–3), where a satisfactory explanation could not be arrived at without drawing upon analysis from all these different directions. Each process is in itself theoretically analysable ('necessary' maybe, in the terms of realism) and each in principle could be theorised in terms of its causal powers at a very general level (and remembering that such powers/tendencies are themselves only 'enabling' rather than determinate of any particular outcome), but their intersection, the terms of their intersection, and its results, are contingent. Again this does not mean that the outcomes are totally indeterminate, in the sense that nothing can be anticipated – even in the case of human agency the potential courses of action are frequently restricted (people are boxed-in, there is only bounded indeterminacy). It simply implies that in principle the outcome needs specific investigation.

This, however, is to go beyond the usual meanings of multicausality, which is a very flaccid term. What are at issue here are causal structures in which processes intersect to impact upon each other, to influence/encourage/restrain/mould the operation of each other. It is this which I think of, in a general form, as articulation. In this kind of approach to causality, causes cannot simply be added together, as in certain forms of multiple regression analysis, to approach with mounting excitement a 'significant' level of explanation. A case of this kind of causal thinking is presented in relation to the central question, for the book, of the impact of regional policy. Chapter 6, in the section on 'Modernisation' takes up the issue [...] arguing that 'not only did the economic role of regional policy change over time, its impact also varied between sectors. Most obviously, it was simply more important in some sectors than others as a factor in locational change. But more than this, regional policy combined in different ways in different industries with other developments taking place at the time. The way it actually operated was also different' (pp. 240–1; and see also p. 166).

Further, within such causal structures there may be some processes which in a given instance are more important than others (for instance by having more impact on the operation of other processes than vice versa, or by determining the conditions of operation of other processes). However, the fact, degree and nature of such dominance can only be established by empirical enquiry, and it can change from case to case. It is not valid – in this view of causality – to *assume* that, to take the favourite example, in the end it will always be class which is dominant/determinant.

That last example (characterising capital) makes clear that this notion of articulation applies not only to structures of explanation but also to the very conceptualisation of empirical phenomena. This is one aspect of a more general approach which I have tried to advocate and to pursue in this book and which may be called 'thinking in terms of relations'. Thus, 'jobs' (particular forms of employment) are conceptualised as particular moments within the overall relations of production, as functions set within and defined in articulation with the wider set of social relations. It is this approach which converts an understanding of a particular geographical distribution of employment from being simply a pattern of jobs to being a resultant which indicates the form of spatial organisation of the relations of production which holds those jobs together and of which they are phenomena. This approach, of reinterpreting 'objects in space' as products of the spatial organisation of relations is at the heart of the approach of the book [...]

A final note on variety and specificity

There is no necessary relation, then, between a thoroughgoing recognition of variation and specificity on the one hand and a retreat into 'description' or empiricism on the other. There is more that one can do with the unique than simply contemplate it (p. 116). Apart from the fact that 'description' must always anyway be theory-dependent, what is at issue, perhaps, is more the nature and role of theoretical work. 'General laws' are about causation, connection, interdependence – and therefore conceptualisation – not empirical correlation (p. 116). Indeed, from the point of view of the approach adopted in this work, it would be better to abandon completely the terms 'description' and 'laws' in this kind of discussion. The role of theoretical work is in the conceptualisation of objects of study, in the theorisation of causal powers and relations, in the establishment of frameworks, themselves not as a set of immutable tendencies but more as a way of looking at the world (Sayer, 1984). Indeed the recognition of both variety and specificity is linked up to particular theoretical approaches, or forms of explanation [...]

But still the question has to be asked, and answered, why bother? Does not all this focus on specificity/difference/variety lead only to endless micro studies from which in the end no larger lessons can be learned?

One reply could be that in fact the world is like that: it is indeed endlessly contingent, unique. This is an answer which might emerge from many a strand of postmodernist thought. But it is an unsatisfactory answer in the sense that what is at issue is the role of intellectual work in getting to grips with that world. Simple reproduction of it, or better – representation of it – is not good enough.

But there are other replies. First, it is important to stress that there is no advocacy here for the focus being *only* on difference and variation. This is true both in the sense of what is important to examine and in the sense that the very construction of difference relies on an understanding of broader structures. But second, and given that, internal variation and specificity affect the way the world works. 'Spatial differentiation ... is integral to the reproduction of society and its dominant social relations' (p. 289). This is one of the main messages of this book, and a significant element in the argument that 'geography matters' (see also Massey, 1991). Moreover, a genuine *revaluation* of difference involves more than a parenthetical reference or a gestural aside; it involves recognising *from the start* the existence and importance of variety, and building that into the manner of initial conceptualisation (p. 67). Third, the recognition of difference, spatially as in other ways, must be one of the responsibilities which comes with the privilege which intellectuals have in representing and making sense of the world. I have always been very struck by, and thoroughly agree with, Derek Gregory's argument that the comprehension of difference (in this case, the 'otherness' of other cultures) is one of the raisons d'être of the human sciences and that 'There are few tasks more urgent in a multicultural society and an interdependent world, and yet one of modern geography's greatest betrayals was its devaluation of the specificities of place and of people' (Gregory, 1989, p. 358). Fourth, if one is to go beyond a broad understanding of the world, to intervene in it, then appreciating its specificity is essential [...] This demands an approach precisely for 'conceptualising and examining the apparently endless adaptability and flexibility [in that other, older sense] of capital' (p. 67) [...]. In one sense this is true because 'politics' in one way or another is almost always 'local' even if not in the specifically spatial sense. And if the injunction to 'act locally, think globally' served us well for a while it has now become too glib. This is true both in the sense that many political struggles are far more complex than that in their relation to the local/global nexus (Smith, 1993) and in the sense that this formulation does not pose the major questions. Which are: how then are we to conceptualise the local? if thinking (globally) and acting (locally) are not to be divorced how are we to theorise the relation of the local to the wider context, and to understand the terms and the implications of its specificity?; yet the problem of knowing 'what's best' globally and in relation to distant (in any sense of the word) others should not be underestimated. Yet recognising specificity does not in any way anyway imply a concentration on local politics in the sense usually understood; a focus, that is, on very small-scale actions [...] Taking on any national state, any national class structure, or any set of international relations at any particular moment, requires not just that we see them as capitalist, say, but also that their particular, conjunctural, nature and articulation is also understood.

THE CONCEPTUALISATION OF SPACE

The geography of the relations of production

When I wrote the first edition of *Spatial Divisions of Labour* what I thought I was mainly doing that was new was reconceptualising the central objects of study of industrial geography – firms, jobs, types of jobs, branch plants, and so on – in terms of the social relations which constitute them and thereby – the second crucial move – rethinking the nature of these classic geographical distributions and of economic space itself. Rather than as scatterings of isolated phenomena, these distributions were to be conceptualised as the interconnected phenomena of social relations stretched out to form a space. The aim was that this should enable us to think the politics of place and uneven development in a different way.

There is a sequence of steps in this reconceptualisation of economic space. The first, and the one which is usually omitted thereby leading to an inability to perform the others, is to take seriously the conceptualisation of the object of study (say, jobs and types of jobs). As with capital as a class (see above) these phenomena with which industrial geography conventionally deals are rarely seriously considered in their nature as objects of study. Yet one of the crucial lessons of Marxism, for instance, for work in this area is to recognise things as constituted by relations: capital is a relation, the various classes in a society are constituted relationally with each other, and so forth. Likewise jobs and types of jobs: they are phenomena of different positions within the overall complexity of the social relations of production; the existence and specificity of one type of job (say, specialist manager) depends on the existence and specificity of jobs designed to do other parts of the overall division of labour. One of the attractions of Wright's [1978] framework was the detail with which he had begun to think this through. Moreover his framework not only analyses occupational functions but links them to class position, in particular to intra-class variations (though I disagreed then, and continue to do so, with many of the conclusions he drew from his approach). Thus what was immediately possible was a linking of the conceptualisation of jobs in terms of relations with an analysis of elements of class, between that is industrial geography and the geography of social structure.

If, then, a particular managerial job, say, can be conceptualised as a set of functions both specified by and existing in relation to other jobs within the economy, then the next step is to think of this spatially. Instead of, say, different types of jobs each with their own (same or different) geographical distribution, there are different sets of interdependent functions held together in tension by sets of social relations stretched out between them. Uneven development is then an issue of the geography of that division of labour and of the social relations of production, and not merely of more or different jobs/ investment here than there; a 'core' region is not just, or even necessarily, the one with all the best jobs, or even the most jobs in a particular sector, say, but the one from which run the dominant lines of control, of strategic direction, of crucial connections; a spatial structure of production (as in this book) is not a distribution of jobs but a geography of social relations. Thinking in terms of relations starts from the interdependence of phenomena and thus of the spaces they construct: this applies to jobs within a division of labour (see, for instance, p. 206) and to regions within an economy. What is at issue is the spatial form of certain aspects of social power. Moreover, this matters: 'It matters in what kind of spatial structure a plant is embedded. It matters in terms of the kind of relations of dominance and subordination which exist between plants in different localities, it matters for the people who work in the plants, and it matters politically' (p. 104). Thinking in terms of relations gives access to causality. It enables a more robust approach to the constitution *and reproduction* of the space of a certain set of social relations.

One of the most crucial developments which has taken place, in the UK and most other first world countries, in the decades since the sixties has been the expansion and consolidation of white-collar middle-income professional and managerial strata. The size and power of this group has become a stubborn fact of social structure, a vital stake in the play of politics, and – I would argue, as do the preceding chapters – one of the most important (and probably implacable) problems facing any attempt to work towards less uneven forms of spatial development.

As groups they have emerged from the more detailed structuring and separating-out of functions within the division of labour, and the relations in which they exist with other groups are often ones which give them considerable power. Different sub-groups within them have been lionised by successive governments and political rhetorics. Moreover, and on top of all this, they have a very particular geography. It is a geography of both concentration and privilege. Their distribution is quite highly focused in particular areas of the country, as previous chapters show (and although I am speaking here of the UK, the same is true of many if not most first world countries). And these are parts of the country which tend to be already privileged, whether that be the capital city, at a regional level the south eastern part of the country, or more locally the areas of perceived environmental attraction. Classically, they are to be found far less in areas dominated by blue-collar manufacturing, in the industrial areas of the north, in localities which are in decline. There is a two-sidedness to this distribution. Policy-makers often argue that the presence of such groups is a reason for the health of the areas in which they live; and the conclusion is drawn that attracting white-collar professionals into areas of decline would help them grow too. But while there is some truth in this as an observation the causal conclusions drawn are in an important sense the wrong way around. It is even more the case that these social groups abound in particular areas *because* they are healthy. The social power of these groups (for instance, their bargaining power within the labour market) gives them a power of choice of location, which may be fed through the *perception* of their preferences by the companies which seek their labour power. And they exercise that power overwhelmingly to avoid the physical and social environment of decline (perhaps the only exception, though it still replicates this pattern at a much smaller spatial scale, is that of gentrification). But what this means is that these groups use their social power to reinforce their privilege through location. And that in turn exacerbates the unevenness of uneven development.

[...]

Finally, conceptualising these social groups, and their spatial distributions, in terms of the social relations of class helps reformulate the questions which arise for the labour movement from their uneven geographies: it changes the political analysis. For these highly unequal geographies presuppose the stretching out over space of social relations which embody great power, of direction and control in the case of managerial hierarchies, and of strategic vision and extreme inequality in relation to the labour process, especially in the case of scientific/professional workers. These aspects are additional to the more immediately evident inequalities, of income for instance. What is at issue is both the spatiality of this form of power (and spatial form may be part of the construction of that power) and the construction of a power-filled space. But seeing things in this way changes the political questions which need to be confronted if serious progress is to be made towards more even development: 'The spatial inequality consists not so much in the uneven distribution of jobs of different social types (and thus in some way of geographical "equality of opportunity") but in the removal from some regions, and the concentration in others, of the more powerful, conceptual and strategic levels of control over production' (pp. 108–9). In relation to management hierarchies the same reformulation occurs of the old question of 'external control' (pp. 97–102) and in relation to scientific workers of the frequent clamour for more high-status, high-tech jobs (pp. 110–111).

Broadening the analysis

[...]

To begin with a clarification: there is much talk in the preceding chapters of the social relations which link phenomena together, and which construct them, as lying *behind, underneath,* or as being the *underlying* relations of, the distribution of jobs. It is a classic case of the use of spatial metaphor and, as so frequently, it may be interpreted in a variety of ways. What is meant by the formulation as used here is that 'underlying' relations have to be unearthed by intellectual labour. They are not, it is assumed, part of the immediately obvious way of looking at things. What is *not* intended is that these relations are ontologically beneath the distribution of jobs, lurking there beneath the surface waiting to be unearthed. Since these relations are what construct the jobs, or so I am arguing, they are in that sense 'on the same level'. What is at issue in this set of spatial metaphors is the process of intellectual work rather than the ontological structuring of the object of study. Moreover what that process of intellectual work yields is precisely an interpretation (not an absolute truth – and anyway how could we know?) – an interpretation deemed to be productive in terms of the questions being posed.

Further, it is important to emphasise that what is at issue in the preceding chapters is not just the social relations of production in space, or stretched over space, but the fact that those social relations themselves constitute social space. At a quite concrete level, this approach can influence the way in which place/locality/region is thought about. Not only are 'localities' the product of the articulation of social relations at a wide range of geographical scales, but they are constantly being formed and transformed (see, for instance, pp. 188–9 and 289). [...] As is said of the regional geography of the period as a whole 'even the shape of the map has been refashioned' (p. 288).

However, if this map is to be conceptualised in terms of social relations existing between economic functions/social groups which are mutually defining in relation to a division of labour, then some specification of the overall labour to be performed is necessary. In detail this will always be impossible. Since 'the total work to be performed' itself has to be defined socially, the system is almost by definition to some degree open. None the less, there are two important ways in which the empirical, and in one of the cases also the theoretical, analyses in *Spatial Divisions of Labour* can be extended here. Both of them are highlighted by current developments.

The first concerns unpaid labour. Wright's [1978] framework is typical of approaches to the analysis of class in that it deals exclusively with paid labour (indeed in some ways it has to be stretched to deal with all of that). And the preceding chapters, notwithstanding some clear recognition of the issue *(Elaborations,* p. 39), went along with that. Now, the concept of spatial division of labour was never meant, by myself at least, to encompass uneven development in every sphere of life. In that sense I have some reservations about attempts to extend it to include wide areas of civil society, for instance, and all the issues of what is sometimes called 'reproduction' (see, for instance, Warde, 1985) *although*, and this is an important caveat, any full understanding of the reasons for particular spatial structures/spatial divisions of labour for instance *must* inevitably look more widely – as the preceding chapters to some extent do at social relations and processes beyond the world of employment. So too, even more crucially, must any full analysis of class positions. None the less, the focus of concern of the concepts spatial structure/spatial division of labour is the space of paid work, and it is so quite deliberately.

However, there is a methodological problem with this restriction. For, given some broad notion of the labour to be performed in a society at any historical period, the boundary between that which is performed as paid work and that which is unpaid will not be determinate. It will vary between social classes, between regions, between different types of households (nuclear, single people, etc.) and crucially over time. In many countries over the last decade there has been a decisive shift, through cuts in public expenditure and public services, or structural adjustment programmes in third world countries for instance, of certain types of work from paid employment towards the unpaid sector. What this means is that the overall 'system' of paid work is undefined and that therefore the mutually-determining nature of the different elements within it is less secure. Thus the framework of spatial divisions of labour, the conceptualisation of jobs as mutually-defining interdependent functions, could importantly be extended to encompass those variable processes through which the paid/unpaid boundary is constructed and which will vary from the politico-economic activities of the State, the varying characteristics and demands (both material and symbolic) of different types of paid employment, inherited and changing formulations of femininity and masculinity to, for instance, negotiations within the household. Quite apart from all the many other reasons for studying this interface, this particular entry into the area underlines from yet another angle the interdependence of the paid and unpaid sectors of society.

There is a further way in which the formulation of elements of divisions of labour in preceding chapters has left the overall 'labour' underspecified. Here there is no tight exclusion, as there was of unpaid labour, but neither is there a clear specification. The focus of *Spatial Divisions of Labour* is on national (and first world, capitalist) economies, and again this was deliberately so: the concern was with intra-national divisions of labour. None the less, such economies are often very open in terms of trade. They are set in systems of production which go beyond them. They are, therefore, concomitantly embedded in divisions of labour and spatial structures of production which also go beyond them. This too could have been more developed in the preceding chapters [...] The results of such an extension would be twofold (at least). It would underline the relations of domination and subordination which the various parts of the UK's (or any other country's) economic structure and the various localities have with other parts of the world. And it would highlight the great differences which exist in these relations between geographical areas. This latter issue has become increasingly important, certainly in the UK, over the last decade. In many economies, regions are now clearly embedded in very different international spatial structures; in that sense there is an increased fracturing of national economies. [...]

There is a further issue raised by the generalisation of the concept of space as social relations, and which again reflects back on the argument of the preceding chapters. The strong, and still important, arguments of the seventies and eighties that space is socially constituted and that, conversely, the social necessarily has a spatial content/form had a tendency in much work to remain at the level of slogans. The precise ways in which these statements were true, and their implications, were less often ferreted out. *Spatial Divisions of Labour* spells out in some detail the nature of some of these relations and mechanisms, but it does so for only a limited range of the potential forms of social spatiality. In part this is simply because its remit is limited – it is concerned only with that limited bit of society engaged by industrial geography. But even within [industrial geography] its primary concern is with one kind of social relation over space; that of relatively ordered spatial structures within firms.

The point about ordered spatial structures within companies is that they represent only one kind of relationship between the social and the spatial. They are, in a sense, 'planned spaces'; their spatial arrangement is to one degree or another deliberate: it is part of the constitution of the structure itself. The relationship between a headquarters and a set of other locations (regional headquarters, production branch plants of various functions, etc.) is an element of what might be called ordered spatiality. Moreover, the nature of this joint social-spatial ordering has implications – the spatial form is precisely *meant* to have social effects, to increase profits by location according to differential criteria, to undermine workers' bargaining-power by multi-sourcing at a number of disparate places, and so forth (which is not to say that it does not have other, unforeseen, effects as well). This is one kind of way in which 'geography matters'.

However, there are other kinds of economic relations which contribute to the constitution of the spaces of industrial geography. Chief among these are market relations *between* firms, and these are far less considered in the preceding chapters. The nature of the connection between the social and the spatial in market relations can vary greatly. In some cases the nature of the firm and its location relative to others can be intimately linked: the two things may be planned together. In other cases, already-established firms may set up market relations *because of* a spatial propinquity which occurred for other reasons altogether. There are also cases, of course, where neither planned nor market relations exist. That is, there are activities and groups which are mutually indifferent in social terms, but which none the less necessarily exist in spatial relation to each other. Their relative locations are also part of what constructs social space. The point is that in each case the relation between the social and the spatial is different, and the impact of the one upon the other is correspondingly varied. In the case where contacts between companies occur only because of propinquity, spatial form can be seen to be influencing the form of social relations through its character of being in part unplanned. While it will be possible to explain the locations of company A and company B individually, their relative spatial location may not have a direct cause, the two locations having been arrived at independently. But such 'accidental' relative spatial locations may have effects, perhaps enabling/provoking contacts between the companies, for instance. Thus the accidental juxtapositions and distancings of social space may through their bringing together and separating of social phenomena have an effect on how those phenomena work. Such effects may be 'positive' or 'negative' (negative externalities are a clear case of the latter). The point is that social space has aspects both of 'order' and of 'chaos' (Massey, 1992), of the intended and unintended, the directly planned and the unplanned – and of attempts at negotiated stabilisations in between – which represent both different types of relations between 'the social' and 'the spatial' and different sources for the impact of the latter on the former. These contrasting aspects of spatiality highlight different aspects of the geography of power relations and indicate different sources of contradictions potentially existing in the spatiality of the social.

As has been said, *Spatial Divisions of Labour* concentrates firmly on only one aspect of these multifarious possibilities: spatial structures within firms. It must be stressed, for there has occasionally been some confusion, that spatial structures are not the same as spatial divisions of labour. While the former are intra-company concepts, the term spatial division of labour refers to a more overall form of uneven development, which will vary over time, and which is the product of all the spatial structures of production then in existence, but – it is hypothesised – most likely dominated by (in the sense of structured by, not of numerical dominance) one or a small group of spatial structures. An important question at issue therefore and which is not centrally addressed in the preceding chapters, is the nature of the relations (including non-relations) between spatial structures in constructing spatial divisions of labour.

Elaborating the investigation of spatial divisions of labour in this way opens analysis to the different degrees and natures of integration, or non-integration, of activities within local/regional economies, and the power relations through which this is constructed. Places/localities/regions will most frequently be embedded in a multitude of spatial structures, and part of their specificity comes from the articulation of these structures within them, and the emergent effects which result, as well as from the role of the place within its wider setting. Setting the analysis of spatial structures in a wider view of spatiality both enables analysis of this internal structure and opens the way to thinking more clearly about the structural potential of local economic strategies (see Lovering, 1986; Fincher, 1986). It opens it also to the power structures of inter-firm, as well as intra-firm, relations through which different places are articulated into an economy. [...]

The analysis of industrial districts could be enriched along similar lines, through a more rigorous conceptualisation of their spatiality. The content of social power which imbues the inter-firm linkages which criss-cross the districts, the social relations which locate (and thereby help construct) people in particular labour-market positions within them, the shifting flows of dominance and subordination in the wider relations which link these districts to the world economy, to their export markets, to multinational capital – a consideration of all these would greatly aid our understanding of industrial districts and our assessment of their potential future (see, for instance, Amin and Robins, 1990, and Amin, 1994). It would be possible to begin from locationally-concentrated spatial structures (see pp. 96–7), but go on to investigate further the social nature of the 'unequal market relations' (p. 97) which hold them together and link them into a wider economy. On the one hand the real social content of the relations which bind together the firms 'within' the districts could be elaborated to tease out the power relations which structure them internally. On the other hand the very different power relations which construct their connection to the world economy, linking these place-based constellations to internationalized spatial structures characterised by both spatial reach and great potential geographical flexibility emphasise the inherent vulnerability of some of these areas. [...] Extending the kind of analysis suggested in the preceding chapters for intra-firm relations to all the varied kinds of economic relations, especially including those between firms, would give a much fuller, and more complex and internally disintegrated and possibly contradictory, picture of spatial divisions of labour.
[...]

GENDER AND FEMINISM

Spatial Divisions of Labour, in its first edition, was not a book written within what was at that time defined as the field of feminist geography. That is to say, in the terms of the contemporary definition of that field (which is different from the way in which it would be defined today), it is neither particularly concerned with women nor centrally focused on gender relations. In terms of its subject matter it was, on the contrary, trying to address one of what Jane Jenson ironically calls 'the big questions tackled by the big boys' (Jenson,

1990, pp. 59 and 60). This is a formulation utterly lacking in any strict criteria of definition, and yet we know – or at least a good many of us know – exactly what she means. In the early 1980s, and perhaps still today, industrial geography and regional uneven development were precisely such questions.

This clearly does not mean, however, that the topic is immune to feminist treatment (indeed today my position would probably be that it is precisely some of the 'big-boys issues' that are most urgently in need of feminist critique). And there was constructive debate about the book's relationship to feminism in the years following its publication [...]

Recapitulation of themes

None the less, in *Spatial Divisions of Labour* I did attempt to tackle the issues as a feminist, though one who was in those days more politically engaged than theoretically sophisticated. Issues of 'gender', in one way or another, run through the book. These range in tone and content from ironic asides about the domestic incompetence, and therefore dependency, of young men from the south of Italy (Section 3.2, Some issues, p. 84) to more general political reflections on how racism and sexism, and the constructions of race and gender, divide the working class (Section 2.3, A framework, pp. 33–4) and how the sexism of male workers (that is, the cause of that division within the working class) can bring about their own and wider defeats (Section 6.3, Social and spatial restructuring in the working class, p. 284).

However, the ways in which issues of gender are most consistently woven into the argument are those which revolve around the book's core themes. Since in the preceding chapters these issues are embedded in particular analyses, it is perhaps again worth pulling out some of the main threads. Most clearly, there is a focus on divisions of labour, most particularly the division of labour in paid work, and their relationship to gender. Throughout, there is an insistence that none of these things is simply 'natural'. On the contrary, they are socially constructed. In particular, the social allocation of different social groups, in this case men and women, to particular places in the economic division of labour cannot be explained by the nature of the labour process, the requirements of technology, or any of the other production-deterministic variations which are so frequently called upon to play this role. Rather such social allocation (and the subsequent societal valuation of the jobs in question) is part and parcel of (that is to say, both an effect of and actively implicated in the process of) the social construction of gender [...]

Indeed, both theoretical and empirical research now indicate that the set of interlocking relations and processes is far more complex than is indicated in the preceding chapters. In particular, while *Spatial Divisions of Labour*

294

talks of the divisions of race and gender being 'constructed as much outside as within the workforce' (p. 34) it in fact places most of its reliance for the construction of gender on 'wider society' in various guises, and pays relatively little attention to the powerful forces for such construction which can equally be found within the workplace. Where it does, however, dwell on the ways in which paid work, and the social interpretations put upon it, can actively participate in the formation of particular gender categories/characteristics, it is perhaps more likely to talk about the construction of masculinity than femininity. Thus, the discussion of the definition of skills in the clothing industry reflects on the struggles of a particular group of men to preserve their threatened masculinity (Section 4.3, Spatial structures of big firms, p. 161); most obviously, the exploration of employment changes in mining areas points out how a central stake in what was at issue in those years was a specific (time-space specific) characterisation of masculinity formed very much in relation to a particular kind of work in a particular sector – the sexism which was integral in it, the bewilderment and even pain with which many men met the challenge to it, the self-defeating divisiveness which it represented within the working class. At least it makes the point that men and masculinity are – or should be – as much an issue for feminist, or gender-aware (better: gender-challenging), geography as are women and femininity.

Further, and moving beyond the constellation of issues around divisions of labour specifically, there is a concern to argue that, and to illustrate the variety of ways in which, the social relations of production and of gender (in another terminology, capitalism and patriarchy) articulate with and mutually inflect each other. The most obvious and sustained case here is the comparison in Chapter 5 between the coalfield areas and Cornwall. The comparison of 'the pre-existing structures' as well as of the subsequent 'combination of layers' in these very different areas is in part concerned to underscore how in each there is an articulation of spatial form, with the social relations of and around production, and with the constructed form of gender relations [...] A rather different instance is that of the variety of ways in which gender is a significant axis in the formation of spatial structures of production [...] What such cases do is to carry into this particular field the more general themes of (i) thinking in terms of articulation, and specifically (ii) articulation between class-related and other social relations in (iii) the production of (spatially) varied outcomes.

It is, moreover, precisely the fact that this really is articulation (and not the adding-in of some consideration from one arena to a story which is really about another) which enables a *mutual* influencing of the relations in play [...] In the overall story of the geography of the footwear industry, then, a whole set of social relations and social practices is involved: the nature of capital in the sector, technical change, the sexual division of labour outside of paid work, the nature of the relations of production, the sexual division of labour within work, the locational strategies of firms, and the impact of place and of the externally changing geography of social relations, especially the locational strategies of other sectors. Gender is implicated in this story throughout: its very definition and the organisation of gender relations within and beyond paid work are both moulded in relation to and have their own impact upon all the other elements in the unfolding story. Or again, a combination of prevailing ideologies of gender with the place in the economy of different sectors of production is argued to have been influential in the political determination of the geographical areas which would be assigned regional policy assistance (Section 4.1). [...]

In this sense then gender is essential to the empirical story told in the book. At a micro level, it is a crucial axis in the formation of spatial structures in a number of parts of industry. More broadly, it is an essential component in any serious understanding of the organisation and reorganisation of British economic space over the period in question. As economic policy and political strategy under Wilson enabled the emergence on to the labour market in Development Areas of a particular kind of female labour, itself constructed in a particular and locally-specific field of gender relations, so in some of the big cities, and most especially in London, a combination of increasing international competition (from the exploitation of women in the Third World) and the increasing demand for female workers in the growing service sectors meant that another group of women – young, usually childless – was coming to be in very short supply. Some of the companies squeezed in this pincer went 'north' to the coalfields, or to the West Country – moving from one changing labour market for women to another. Other companies went less far, sometimes shifting to areas like the East Midlands and thus disrupting yet another labour market highly structured on gender lines, and expelling existing employers to yet more 'peripheral' areas.

Both gender and geography, therefore, were integral to the recomposition of employment over this period, and gender was integral to the geographical reorganisation which took place. This was so in two ways. Both geographical differences in systems of gender relations and differences between distinct groups of women were important. The clearest example of the first, in this particular story, is the creation of potential labour-forces with particular characteristics, out of the gender relations of Cornwall and the coalfields. But the second aspect – differences among women, and their highly specific and distinct characteristics – is equally important in its articulation with the shifting economic geography of this period. The 'young girls' of the capital, not 'yet' married (labour market literature seems always to assume that marriage will be their fate) and certainly without children, left the dismal conditions of the footwear industry in droves – or, more likely, just didn't go into it on leaving school. Instead they took up their places – as secretaries, receptionists, clerks and typists – at the heart of the new emergence of London as a world city. Deprived of this labour force the footwear industry both shifted location and sought out a different group of women. This time the industry sought out women who were not cheap because they were assumed only to be in this job for a while, until they 'settled down', but cheap because now they were (assumed to be) married, with other functions and interests as their prime concern and pressing constraints on their ability to search a wider field for more remunerative employment. The women of the coalfields were different again, valued in the first place primarily for their supposed 'greenness'. Women as labour power, in this case as a result of the distinct modes of their insertion into (patriarchal) social relations, are a highly varied group.

Gillian Rose (1993) has recently suggested that 'marxists examine the uneven development of capitalist production, feminists focus on the relationship between production and reproduction as part of capitalist patriarchy' (p. 113). Whatever is actually the case, such a division of labour must weaken the arguments of both streams of thought. Not only are the categories (production/reproduction) themselves open to re-examination, but feminist (and marxist) analyses each have a contribution to make in a wider spectrum of fields than this. In particular, as the next section reflects and as Rose demonstrates, feminism has much to say in the sphere of modes of theorising and of conceptualisation. However, the reason Rose pulls out this contrast is to highlight a tendency within feminist geography to emphasise 'women's diverse experiences of production and women's shared experience of reproduction in the context of the Western City' (p. 116), to assume 'the similarity of women due to their shared experience of reproductive work and their diversity due to different experiences of uneven production relations' (pp. 121–2). This is an assumption which is unwarranted, as Rose points out. It underestimates the differences among women in the sphere of reproduction, most particularly along lines of sexuality and ethnicity, as well as of class. Moreover, there is a further point. For the differences among women in the sphere of production which are most often stressed are those of (sociological) class: middle class as opposed to working class, and so forth. What the analyses in the preceding chapters show, however, is that this is by no means the only form of differentiation among women in this sphere. Also important, not only in differentiating among women but also in setting them against each other in terms of immediate interests in the labour market and in relation to capital, are the more complex and multifarious aspects of what are called above their distinct modes of insertion into the social relations of patriarchy.

Finally, since much of what was going on between the sixties and the eighties was a shifting set of strategies on the part of British industry (and of the British government in relation to the British economy) to try to become more internationally competitive, so it can be understood that such strategies were actively *using* spatial differences in gender relations and between groups of women in their attempts to get out of what has become the seemingly perpetual weakness of the British economy.

A consciousness of this gender element in the story also influences any evaluation of the regional policy of the period. In the early days (and to an unfortunate extent still today) such evaluation was carried out through the correlation of the timing and size of the decentralisation of employment with the timing and geographical distribution of regional-policy incentives. It was a classic case of the 'correlation-between-maps' approach referred to in Chapter 2. When a high correlation was found between these two phenomena, it was deduced that they were causally related and moreover (though this was by no means shown by the statistics themselves) that regional policy was the cause of the decentralisation. On this reading, regional policy emerged as having been quite successful. The detailed, period-by-period analyses in Chapter 6 [...] present a range of both methodological and substantive arguments to demonstrate the inadequacy of this approach. Running through these arguments, and through the debate which took place over the period about the effectiveness of regional policy, was a thread of argument concerning gender.

The original, regression-based, evaluations had paid no attention to gender. But it was not long before complaints from the regions – from trade unionists and other spokesmen – made clear that the jobs which were arriving were not of the kind which had been expected: they were 'for women'. A revised evaluation of regional policy emerged, more muted in its claims for success. In its overtly sexist version this evaluation objected that the incoming jobs were not for the newly-unemployed, that they were 'only' for women. The more respectable version implicitly carried the same message arguing that the fact that the new jobs were for women was unfortunate in the sense that, because women's jobs tend to be less well paid, part-time, less skilled ... aggregate regional income would decline and everybody would suffer.

But, of course, not everyone would suffer. To begin with, the attractiveness to capital of this particular female workforce resulted precisely from the construction over the years of the specificity of the local gender culture. To the extent, therefore, that the men of the region were implicated in the construction of this culture, they only had themselves to blame. But further, a large part of the employment entering these regions over the period cannot be put down entirely to the operation of regional policy. Chapter 6 spells out some of the varied articulations of causes in which regional policy was to various degrees and in a variety of ways involved; but also involved was a shifting search by industry for new sources of female labour. So any claims for the success of regional policy have to take such complexities into account. Working in the opposite direction, however, is the fact that, while certainly much of the new employment was low paid, part-time, designated as low skilled, etc., it did none the less for the first time, and at the price of the double shift, bring some independent income for a significant number of women in these parts of the country. Moreover, as the very fact of the initial complaints itself indicates, it began to disrupt some of those old gender relations. On this score, then, although not on others, regional policy can be seen to have had some quite positive effects, but in a wholly different way from that claimed by those who performed the initial correlation-based evaluations.

Such reinterpretations are arrived at not just by looking at women, but by investigating geographical variations in the construction of masculinity and femininity, and the relations between the two. Moreover, the very focus on geographical variation insists on the fact that what is at issue here is not some essentialism of 'men' and 'women', but how people are (variously) constructed in relation to a distinction between masculinity and femininity.

A question of conceptual approach

These strands of thought concerning gender were written into *Spatial Divisions of Labour* from a position which was self-consciously feminist. Were I writing it today they would be treated differently and in more depth. Studying the book again now, however, another thread emerges. Jane Jenson (1990) has written about how, in her case, the form taken by her theoretical research, and particularly her invention of the concept of permeable Fordism, was made possible by her reading of feminist theoretical work. That is, although the concept was not designed as one within the field of gender studies or even feminist theory, its form was influenced by its originator's acquaintance with the latter body of work. Something similar may be the case with certain aspects of *Spatial Divisions of Labour*. It is perhaps worthwhile reflecting on some intellectual history in order to explore this point. But it must be stressed from the start that this is *not* an attempt retrospectively to claim *Spatial Divisions of Labour* for feminist geography. That is not the point, either way. Rather it seems valuable to reflect back on the book now, and most specifically on the nature of its theorising, from a feminist perspective.

Central to many of the arguments in *Spatial Divisions of Labour* is the notion of articulation. It is crucial to the idea of causality and causal structures, it is the basis of the postulated relation between the general and the

particular, it is the means of linking the global and the local (the wider relations of a spatial division of labour imbricated in the particularities of place),
it is the means of thinking of a particular form of employment (a job) at a
particular point in space-time as the product of sets of relations with other
parts of the employment structure, relations themselves also stretched out
to form that time-space.

It is difficult ever to be sure of where and why particular ideas come to
be important in one's mode of thinking. In the case of articulation, however,
it probably derived from, or was certainly underlined in significance by, my
early readings of works in and around Marxism. It was a combination of *The
German Ideology* and Louis Althusser which was the real spark. *The German
Ideology* was one of the first books I read within Marxism – this would be in
the late sixties – and it posed problems for me. The reason it did so was the
nature of its ruminations on the 'essential' difference between human beings
and other animals. It seemed to me to be a concern which was not only
unnecessary to a liberatory political project but one which was also likely to
hamper any such project by the potential essentialism of the way it was in
practice treated. For although Marx and Engels in this work are quite scru-
pulous in their theoretical injunctions against both spiritual and biological
essentialism (attacking these things is after all part of the point of the work)
their own implementation of this leaves some questions. Human beings are
said to produce themselves by 'labour', or at least this is the main emphasis,
rather than by activity, experience or, more generally, practice. There is a
reference to the 'large' historical component in human nature (my marginal
note of more than twenty-five years ago says 'total'). Moreover, the nature of
the residue implied in the text by the word 'large' (i.e. *not* total) becomes clear
as the analysis proceeds, and my marginal notes become more anguished.
There is reference to the 'first historical act' as being the production of the
means to satisfy the needs of eating, drinking, habitation and clothing. There
is the approach to the historical development of the division of labour, 'which
was originally nothing but the division of labour in the sexual act'. There are
the specifications of the division of society into 'families', and of the division
of labour within the family, as 'natural'. The point here is not to criticise the
work, which was written at a particular time and with a particular aim in
view (and indeed there are ambiguities even on the points mentioned above)
so much as to indicate the effect on me of a reading of it. There seemed to
be a division here between the large element of human nature which was
historical and a remainder which was read as being prior to, and thus even
more worryingly perhaps external to, history. Moreover, and this was the
point which exercised me most, if there was accepted to be in these spheres
something called the essential human being (i.e. in this formulation an aspect
prior to history) then any minute now there would be the essential woman.

To a young female at the time determined to escape many of the characteristics usually held up as female, together with much of what life reputedly
held in store – marriage, children, etc. – this was not easy reading. Far from
liberation, it seemed like a trap. It was Althusser, with his ideas of structured
causality (most especially 'Contradiction and Overdetermination') and his
famous dictum that 'there is no point of departure' (in other words, on my
reading, there is nothing which you have to accept as eternally pre-given,
which is not in itself a product of previous causal structures) who provided
a welcome way out. It is interesting, in this context, to note that Jane Jenson,
in tracing out her own trajectory, not only refers in particular to the work
of Nicos Poulantzas (p. 65), but also and most pointedly in this context she
argues that it was a political anti-essentialism and a derived need to tackle
the theoretical construction of gender relations, which lay at the heart of
her story. The springboard for launching into an exploration of these ways
of thinking, she argues, was the need to tackle 'the implications of one of the
oldest institutions of the women's movement, that "women are made, not
born"'. As she says 'A wide reading of this insight compels us to think not only
about the social construction of gender relations but also about the ways in
which *all* social relations are constructed' (p. 60, emphasis in original) and
further that 'If my feminism made impossible any assumptions that class was
the primary contradiction, my personal experience with the varieties of ways
of being a woman and a feminist ... made any resort to essentialism impossible. The only possible conclusion was that relations of difference must be a
social construction, and I began to wonder how social relations of difference,
reflecting inequities of power, came into existence' (p. 65).

This, evidently, is to refer to only one type of feminism: that developed at
a particular moment in specific social and theoretical contexts. By no means
all varieties of feminism are in this sense anti-essentialist and some recent
work has anyway problematised the distinction between essentialism and
(social) constructionism. Diana Fuss (1989), for instance, has demonstrated
the frequent mutual dependence of the two approaches, and argued in effect
that neither position can be entirely pure. None the less she remains, in terms
of the kind of argument advanced here, firmly of the anti-essentialist persua-
sion. [...] The point, then, is not that Jensen's was the only route to a feminist
position, nor indeed that it is the only possible position. Indeed, while my
own early experience shares much with Jenson's history it also differs from
it – mine was based more on the seventies' reading by many in the women's
movement in Britain of texts which were not themselves overtly feminist
but which we were reading as part of an attempt to develop a feminist theoretical perspective. Thus, my own particular feminist theoretical context, by
the early seventies, had been a long involvement in two women's movement
reading groups, one reading Marx's *Capital*, the other reading Althusser,

Poulantzas, Balibar, *et al.* As Jenson says 'I do not want to suggest that I am alone in experiencing this trajectory... Although I will tell this story from the perspective of my own biography, I do not think it is by any means exceptional' (p. 60).

Moreover, the insistence on the social construction of all social relations, and on the theorisation of this through concepts such as articulation, is a perspective which has subsequently been widely developed. It is important in Ernesto Laclau's *New reflections on the revolution of our times* (1990) where his unambiguous statement of the significance of articulation is the basis for both a critique of any form of deterministic Marxism and the possibility of holding open those windows of dislocation which alone make possible any real operation of agency or practice of politics. It is also a way of thinking which figures prominently in the closely related work of Chantal Mouffe (1988), most particularly on issues of identity.

What I think is significant is how this approach is related to that current strand of feminist thinking which argues in general for a mode of 'theorising in terms of relations'. The literature on this is now very considerable and its argument is that, whatever the facts and explanations of its empirical occurrence, it is in current circumstances a mode of thinking with particular liberatory potential. What is interesting, furthermore, is the way in which historically positions have been adopted for and against essentialism, as well as for its operational use in certain circumstances, largely on the basis of political requirements. The early feminist anti-essentialism (including my own) was based on a desire not to be stuck with any parameters of a supposed womanhood which we could not break down. Other women have argued, for different reasons, that there are characteristics which *are* essentially female. Spivak [1993] has argued a case for strategic essentialism, and Epstein has pointed out that 'people who base their claims to social rights on the basis of a group identity will not appreciate being told that that identity is just a social construct' (1987, p. 22).

But if, for me, what an anti-essentialist position (even if it cannot be a 'pure' one) has in the past represented is an optimism of ontological assumptions with particular reference to feminism, it has subsequently been invested with other advantages, most particularly the way in which, through the constant recognition of articulation, it enables an approach to the contingencies and uniquenesses, as well as the broad structures, of space-time.

Within geography the relational approach has been explicitly taken up by Susan Hanson (1992), and one of its clearest formulations is by the feminist writer Donna Haraway. Haraway (1991) argues for a politics of affinity rather than of identity (see, for instance, 'Reading Buchi Emecheta' and 'Manifesto for Cyborgs') and at the heart of her discussions is a rejection of a nature/culture dichotomy of a type which sees nature as merely a resource to be taken up by culture. Nature is in such formulations pre-given, a point of departure (to pick up on Althusser's formulation) and one of the forms in which it exists is as the body, and as sex in counterposition to (cultural) gender (see also Grimshaw, 1986). Haraway, as a natural scientist, a biologist, argues against such formulations – and, interestingly enough, sees *The German Ideology* as 'the major locus for Marx' and Engels' naturalisation of the sexual division of labour, in their assumption of a pre-social division of labour in the sex act (heterosexual intercourse), its supposed natural corollaries in the reproductive activities of men and women in the family, and the consequent inability to place women in their relations to men unambiguously on the side of history and of the fully social... The root difficulty was an inability to historicize sex itself; like nature, sex functioned analytically, as a prime matter or raw material for the work of history' ('"Gender" for a Marxist Dictionary', pp. 131–2). In formulating a way of knowing which can escape such debilitating limitations, she argues that 'Difference is theorized biologically *as situational, not intrinsic*, at every level from gene to foraging pattern' and that 'bodies as objects of knowledge are material-semiotic generative nodes. Their boundaries materialize in social interaction. Boundaries are drawn by mapping practices; "objects" do not pre-exist as such. Objects are boundary projects' ('Situated knowledges', pp. 200–1).

This, then, is not a view which does away with all distinction between natural processes and social processes, although they both have to be apprehended socially. What Haraway may be pointing to is the possibility of an anti-essentialist theorising of difference within the natural field as well as the social. It is the assumption that difference in nature is essentialist that she is attacking. The new debates in biology are exploding that old nature/ nurture dichotomy not (or not only) in the sense of arguing that the natural is also socially apprehended but also – and to my mind at least equally significantly – by demonstrating that environment (nurture) can have effects on organism (nature). In a passage which takes us back to the central theme, Ho (1988) has written 'Organism and environment engage in continual mutual transformation by virtue of an interconnectedness that reticulates in space and time' (p. 21).

There is then, here, in the similarities to ways of thinking developed in part in the context of the women's movement, a connection to the feminist theorising of the past decade. To take up again the article by Jenson ... 'women and men with a strong political and conceptual commitment to feminism are ... rethinking the received ways of doing political economy. This means they are doing more than "adding the women in". They are also doing something other than studying women, or theorizing patriarchy, or searching for the articulation of sex and class' (p. 60). The task at hand is re-thinking the way we think. Thinking in terms of relations may be one small aspect of that.

REFERENCES

Amin, A. (1994) The difficult transition from informal economy to Marshallian industrial district. *Area* 26 (1), 13–24.

Amin, A. & Robins, K. (1990) The re-emergence of regional economies? The mythical geography of flexible accumulation. *Environment and Planning D: Society and space* 8 (1), 7–34.

Chantal, M. (1988) Radical Democracy: Modern or Postmodern? In: Ross, A. (ed.) *Universal abandon? The politics of postmodernism.* University of Minnesota Press, Minneapolis, MN, pp. 31–45.

Epstein, S. (1987) Gay politics, ethnic identity: The limits of social constructionism. *Socialist Review* 17 (3/4), 134–159.

Fincher, R. (1986) Review of Spatial Divisions of Labour. *Professional Geographer* 38 (4).

Fuss, D. (1989) *Essentially speaking: Feminism, nature and difference.* Routledge, London.

Grimshaw, J. (1986) *Feminist philosophers: women's perspectives on philosophical traditions.* Wheatsheaf Books Brighton.

Gregory, D. (1989) The crisis of modernity? Human geography and critical social theory. In: Peet, R. and N. Thrift (eds.) *New models in gography: The political economy perspective,* volume II. Unwin Hyman, London, UK, pp. 348–385.

Hanson, S. (1992) Geography and feminism: worlds in collision? *Annals of the Association of American Geographers* 82 (4), 569–586.

Haraway, D. (1991) *Simians, cyborgs, and women. The reinvention of nature.* Free Association Books, London.

Ho, M.-W. (1991) Reanimating nature: the integration of science with human experience. *Leonardo* 24 (5), 607–615.

Jenson, J. (1990) Different but not exceptional: the feminism of permeable Fordism. *New Left Review* (184), 58–68.

Laclau, E. (1990) *New reflections on the revolution of our time.* Verso, London.

Massey, D. (1992) Politics and Space/Time. *New Left Review* (196), 65–84.

Rose, G. (1993) *Feminism and Geography.* Polity Press, Cambridge.

Sayer, A. (1984) *Method in Social Science.* Hutchinson, London.

Smith, M. P. (1993) Can you imagine? Transnational migration and the globalisation of grassroots politics, mimeo; Paper presented to the Conference on World Cities in a World System, Sterling, Virginia, April, 1993.

Spivak, G. C. (1993) *Outside in the Teaching Machine.* Routledge, New York and London.

Warde, A. (1985) Spatial change, politics and the division of labour. In: Gregory, D. & Urry, J. (eds.) *Social relations and spatial structures.* Macmillan, Basingstroke, UK, pp. 190–212.

Wright, E. O. (1978) Class, Crisis and the State. New Left Books, London.

CHAPTER 19

PHILOSOPHY AND POLITICS OF SPATIALITY: SOME CONSIDERATIONS (1999)

My overriding concern in this address is with how we might (in this day and age, and in the context of the debates in which we are currently engaged and the challenges which we face) think about space/spatiality. 'Space' is one of those most obvious of things which is mobilised as a term in a thousand different contexts, but whose potential meanings are all too rarely explicated or addressed. As Grossberg has written:

> "often the most 'obvious' features of our experience – e.g. the distinction between space and time – are the least examined philosophically". (Grossberg 1996. p. 171)

My particular interest [...] is to explore the connections between this question of how to conceptualise space on the one hand, and, on the other hand, first how social science theorising is conducted,[1] and second how both these things are related to what appear to be significant current shifts in political philosophy and political thinking more generally. The connection to theorising in the social sciences (the challenge of spatialising social theory) is taken up in the paper: 'Imagining globalisation: power-geometries of space-time' (Massey 1999a). The relationship to shifts in approaches to politics is the central focus of this current paper.

---

1 There are connections also to the natural sciences but these are mentioned only briefly here (for a detailed, if preliminary, exploration see Doreen Massey (1999)).

1. THREE PROPOSITIONS

To initiate the argument, then, the following are three propositions about how space could be conceptualised:[2]

i.   space is a product of interrelations. It is constituted through interactions, from the immensity of the global to the intimately tiny. This is a proposition which will come as no surprise at all to those who have been reading the recent Anglophone literature!;[3]
ii.   space is the sphere of the possibility of the existence of multiplicity: it is the sphere in which distinct trajectories coexist; it is the sphere of the possibility of the existence of more than one voice. Without space, no multiplicity: without multiplicity, no space. If space is indeed the product of interrelations, then it must be predicated upon the existence of plurality. Multiplicity and space are co-constitutive;
iii.   finally, and precisely *because* space is the product of relation-between, relations which are necessarily embedded material practices *which have to be carried out,* it is always in a process of becoming; it is always being made. It is never finished; never closed.

This last point is, perhaps, of particular significance. For it implies that there are always – at any moment 'in time' – connections yet to be made, juxtapositions yet to flower into interaction (or not, for not all potential connections have to be established), relations which may or may not be accomplished. On this way of imagining things then, space is indeed a product of relations (first proposition) and for that to be so there must be multiplicity (second proposition). However, these are absolutely *not* the relations of a coherent, closed system within which, as they say, 'everything is (already) related to everything else'. In this way of imagining it, space can never be that completed simultaneity in which all interconnections have been established, and in which everywhere is already linked with everywhere else.

2. CONNECTIONS TO A NEW POLITICS

Now, the argument here is that this approach to the conceptualisation of space/spatiality resonates with recent shifts in certain quarters in the way

---

2   This first part of the paper draws on "Spaces of politics" in Doreen Massey, John Allen and Philip Sarre 1999.
3   [...] On wider potential meanings of 'social', in which it can embrace interrelation more generally see Barbara Adam 1990; and particularly therein discussions of Mead, and of Luhmann.

in which 'progressive' politics can also be imagined. Although it would be incorrect, and too rigidly constraining, to propose any simple one-to-one mapping, it is nonetheless the case that each of the three propositions advanced above elucidates a slightly different aspect of this connection. Thus:

i.   imagining space as a product of interrelationships (proposition one) chimes well with the emergence over recent years of a politics which attempts to operate through a commitment to anti-essentialism. That is, in place of a kind of identity politics which takes those identities as already, and forever, constituted ('woman', 'homosexual') and argues for the rights of, or claims to equality for, those already-constituted identities, this anti-essentialist politics takes the constitution of the identities themselves to be one of the central stakes of the political. Rather than accepting and working with already-constituted identities, this anti-essentialist politics lays its stress on the *constructedness* of identities and things (including those things called political subjectivities and political constituencies). It is wary therefore about claims to authenticity based in notions of unchanging identity. Instead, it proposes a *relational* understanding of the world.

This politics of interrelations mirrors, then, the first proposition of this paper, that space too is a product of interrelations. Indeed more generally I would argue that identities/entities, the relations 'between' them, and the spatiality which is part of them are all co-constitutive (Massey 1995). Chantal Mouffe, in particular, has written very insightfully on how we might conceptualise the relational construction of political subjectivities (see especially Mouffe 1993 and 1995). For her, identity and interrelation are constituted together. What I am proposing here is that space is necessarily integral to and a product of that process of constitution. Not only, then, is there a parallel between the manner of conceptualising space and the manner of conceptualising entities/identities (such as political subjects) but also space is from the beginning integral to the constitution of those political subjectivities;

ii. further, imagining space as the sphere of the possibility of the existence of multiplicity (proposition two) accords with the greater emphasis which has over recent years in political discourses of the left been laid on 'difference' and multiplicity. Thus, in what has been perhaps the most evident form which this has taken, there has been a growing insistence that the story of the world can not be told (nor its geography elaborated) through the eyes of 'The West' alone (as had been so long the case) nor from the viewpoint of, for instance, that classic figure (ironically, frequently itself essentialised) of the white, heterosexual male. This approach insists upon a recognition that the understandings (through the eyes of the West, or the straight male) are themselves specific; quite particular local viewpoints, and not the universals which they have for so long proposed themselves to be. It is an approach which has been elaborated and fought for above all by feminists and those working within the framework of postcolonial studies.

The relationship between this aspect of a changing politics (and manner of doing social theory) and the second proposition about space is of a rather different nature from that in the case of the first proposition. In this case, the argument is that the very possibility of any serious recognition of multiplicity and difference itself depends on a recognition of spatiality. Quite often this recognition will be implicit (sometimes harmlessly so, sometimes with seriously detrimental effects); at others, particularly when spatiality is itself one of the dimensions of the construction of difference, it will be – must be – explicit. This argument will be taken up again later, but the essence of the case is that for there to be multiplicity (and by extension for there to be difference) there must be space;

iii. finally, imagining space as always in a process of becoming, as never a closed system (proposition three) resonates with an increasingly vocal insistence within political discourses on the genuine openness of the future. It is an insistence founded in an attempt to escape the inexorability which so frequently characterises the grand narratives related by Modernity. The frameworks of 'Progress', of 'Development' and of 'Modernisation', and the succession of modes of production elaborated within Marxism all propose scenarios in which the general directions of history, including the future, are known. However much it may be necessary to fight to bring them about, to engage in struggles for their achievement, there was always nonetheless a background conviction about the direction in which history was moving. Many theorists today reject such a formulation and argue instead for a radical openness of the future, whether they argue it through radical democracy (see especially Ernesto Laclau 1990), through notions of nomadism (Deleuze and Guattari 1984) or through certain approaches within queer theory (for instance William Haver 1997). Indeed, as Laclau in particular would most strongly argue, only if we conceive of the future as genuinely open can we seriously accept or engage in any genuine notion of politics.

Now, here again – as in the case of the first proposition – there is a parallel with the way in which I am urging that we conceptualise spatiality. Both space and history are 'open' – indeed, as the argument progresses, I hope it will become evident that these two opennesses are really two sides of the same coin, each essential to the other.[4] Conceptualising space as 'open, unfinished, always becoming', in other words, is an essential pre-requisite for history to be open; and thus, after the arguments of Laclau, a prerequisite for the possibility of politics.

3. CONTRASTING INTERPRETATIONS OF SPACE

It may be that on an initial reading these propositions about space/spatiality seem unexceptionable; that they seem reasonable and are quite quickly accepted. In a strange way (although of course I heartily want you – eventually – to agree with me) that might be for me a disappointing response. For I also want to argue that these elements of a revised imagination of space are new, that they in some cases flatly contradict and in other cases seriously challenge the customary ways in which we think about space. One aspect of this is, as already mentioned, that we often do *not* think about space – we use the word, in popular discourse or in academic, without being fully conscious of what we mean by it (see Lefebvre 1991). Another aspect of the way in which this proposed revision of our imagination of space is a challenge derives from the fact that there have been many conceptualisations which are startlingly different.

So, in this section, in order to underline what is different about the three propositions outlined above, I shall spend just a little time examining some ways in which space has been thought about, and thought about by very significant theorists and schools of theory, which are completely different from what is being proposed here. This elaboration of other views will enable a deepening of the argument about the present propositions.

First, there is a long and influential line of thinking within 'Continental philosophy' whose main concern was in fact, in this sphere, with the conceptualisation of time but in whose work this preoccupation with the temporal had as a by-product a highly particular understanding of space. This connection between conceptualisations of time and conceptualisations of space is not restricted to this group. As we shall see, it is integral to many of the positions which follow. It is also part of my own argument: that the two conceptualisations are (coherently or incoherently) related. In the present case, as has already been indicated, the argument is that any conceptualisation of time which is radically open requires as its partner a conceptualisation of space, too, as open. In this first line of thinking Henri Bergson is probably

---

4   There is a link here back to the first proposition. For many anti-essentialists, the real importance of their position [...] is that, precisely, it holds open the possibility of change [...]

the emblematic figure.[5] His influence remains powerful today, perhaps most especially in the work of Deleuze and Guattari. So this is not 'merely' a historical matter.

The second proposition of this paper is that it is space which is the sphere of the possibility of the existence of multiplicity. By extension space as a dimension is necessary to the existence of difference. This is diametrically opposed to Bergson. For Bergson, it was time which is the essential dimension of difference. The reason for this was that, for Bergson and others including many current theorists, 'difference' was itself imagined, not as a potential aspect of multiplicity as in this paper, but as change in time. The reasons for Bergson's position need not detain us here, though my own hunch is that they derived from the battle in which this strand of philosophy was engaged with Newtonian and Einsteinian science (Massey 1999b). The logic, insofar as conceptualisations of space were concerned, was devastating. If difference is defined as change (of one thing in time) (rather than as the simultaneous existence of a multiplicity of things), then time is the crucial dimension of difference *and* time becomes the crucial dimension, the sole vehicle, of creativity. Space, therefore, is excluded from any process of creativity (in other words the openness of the future: proposition three). Indeed for Bergson space was the dimension of representation, of fixity, of tying things down. It was the language of scientists rather than (he opposed the two) the life of the world. It was thus that he could write:

> "We must break out of the spatialization imposed by mind in order to regain contact with the core of the truly living, which subsists only in the time dimension".   (cited in Gross 1981-2)

Space, then, as the realm of stasis. Perhaps the most provocative statement by Bergson (1959, p. 1331) in this regard is the following:

> "What is the role of time? ... Time prevents everything from being given at once ... Is it not the vehicle of creativity and choice? Is not the existence of time the proof of indeterminism in nature?"

A whole host of points clamour for attention here. To begin with, it should be pointed out that 'indeterminism' in this quotation is meant to mean precisely that creativity and that possibility of politics – that genuine openness of the future (proposition three!) – for which this paper too is arguing. For Bergson, change implied real novelty, the production of the new, of things not already totally determined by the current arrangement of forces. Thus:

---

5   See particularly his works: "Time and free will", and "Matter and memory."

"To [Bergson] the future is *becoming* in a way that can never be a mere rearrangement of what has been". (Adam 1990. p. 24)

The first point to note, then, is that there is some coincidence of desires here. Both Bergson's project and the argument of the present paper push towards opening up our conceptualisations of temporality and the future.

The second point, however, highlights the divergences, and these concern our understandings of what is thus required of space and time. In the earlier quotation, Bergson writes that time is the vehicle of change. That much might be conceded. But being the vehicle is not the same as being the cause. Unless one takes a thoroughly essentialist position, time can not somehow unaided bootstrap itself into existence. That is to say, unless one holds to some notion of an immanent unfolding of an undifferentiated entity, only interaction can produce change (creativity) and therefore time. *However*, the possibility of interaction is dependent upon the prior existence of multiplicity (there must be more than one entity in order for interaction to be possible: the pure form of the argument is of course that the interaction itself is integral to the production of the entities). In other words:

• for there to be time there must be interaction
• for there to be interaction there must be multiplicity
• for there to be multiplicity there must be space.

In other words, and to modify the quotation from Bergson, time may indeed 'prevent everything from being given at once' (though it's a wonderfully curious way of putting it!), but *for* there to be time, at least more than one thing must be given at once. *For there to be time*, there must be space.

Second, the school of French structuralism also worked with a conceptualisation of space which is thoroughly at variance with the one being proposed here, and again their influence can still be detected strongly at work in the writings of their theoretical descendants – Ernesto Laclau, for instance, and Michel de Certeau among others, including Michel Foucault. Again, as in the case of Bergson, the initial stimuli for the approach taken by the structuralists were ones with which this paper would have considerable sympathy, and once again they were really – centrally – concerned with time. Within anthropology in particular one impetus towards a 'structuralist' conceptualisation of the world derived from a wariness about the implications of the then hegemonic notions of temporal narrative. Too often, they argued, such narrative (temporal) ways of conceptualising the world led to classifications of levels of development which relegated the societies they were studying to the status of 'primitive', as only existing as forerunners of our own 'developed' status. Structuralism argued for the coherence of such societies *in their own right.* In place of the dominance of temporal narrative they asserted the significance of internally coherent self-standing structures. So far so good.

The problems arose when this debate was translated (mis-translated, I would argue) into conceptualisations of (and dichotomies between) space and time. The structuralists were arguing against the dominance of temporality (in fact, a particular view of temporality). In their eagerness to do this, and in a leap of logic which may be understandable but which has absolutely no philosophical foundation, they equated their a-temporal structures with spatiality. The underlying assumption was that time and space were the opposite of each other, and that space was a lack of temporality. As with Bergson, then, the structuralists set time and space in opposition to each other (Bergson supporting time, the structuralists space) and as with Bergson the spatial was understood as the sphere of stasis and of fixity.

There was no need, even in the structuralists' project, for this to have happened. For the structures which they proposed, though they may have been lacking in temporality, were in no sense spatial. They were simply a-temporal (see also Peter Osborne 1995). They only came to be called spatial because of an over-easy assumption that a lack of time must mean one is dealing with space.

This vision of spatiality as stasis, moreover, was reinforced by their conceptualisation of the structures themselves. For these they imagined as totally interlocking systems of relations. 'Space', then, was understood not just as a synchrony but as a *closed* synchrony, and opposed to a diachrony. Certainly, then, this notion of spatiality accords with this paper's first proposition: that space is a product of interrelations. But it is in complete contradiction to the third proposition: that space is always in a process of becoming; that it is never a closed system. It was this stasis of their structures/space which led to all their well-known difficulties in mobilising these structures and to the unbridgeable oppositions between such pairs as 'langue' and 'parole'. And thus it is that de Certeau writes:

> "... the spatialization of scientific discourse ... scientific writing
> ceaselessly reduces time, that fugitive element, to the normality
> of an observable and readable system".   (de Certeau 1984, p. 89)

And thus it is that it is little wonder that Foucault can retrospectively ruminate about how we used to think of space as the dead, the fixed, the immobile.

Third, there is a more familiar manoeuvre, which is found in social sciences (including geography) and in a wide range of current popular discourses. It is that strategy which was termed, in the previous lecture (see Massey 1999a), convening space in 'temporal terms'.

312

When we use terms such as 'advanced', 'backward', 'developing', 'modern' in reference to different regions of the planet what is happening is that spatial differences are being imagined as temporal. Geographical differences are being reconvened in historical sequence. It is a manoeuvre which has interesting relations to the two other positions just presented. In a sense it is taking up a Bergsonian position. That difference is essentially temporal. It is, on the other hand, the kind of reading of spatiality to which the structuralists might be imagined to have objected.

This convening of space in temporal terms is a way of conceiving of difference which is typical of many of the great modernist understandings of the world. The stories of progress (from tradition to modernity), of development, of modernisation, the Marxist tale of evolution through modes of production (feudal, capitalist, socialist, communist), many of our current stories of 'globalisation' (Massey 1999a) ... all these share a geographical imagination which rearranges spatial differences into temporal sequence. The implication is that places are not genuinely different: rather they are just ahead or behind in the same story: their 'difference' consists only in their place in the historical queue.

In itself, this is not an argument original to this paper. Foucault in some ways recognised it, and there is a strong debate along similar lines in anthropology (Fabian 1983). But what has never really been highlighted is that this manoeuvre represses the real significance of spatiality. It obliterates, or at least reduces, the real import and the full measure of the differences which are at issue. The argument here, in the present paper, is that a real 'political' recognition of difference would understand it as more than place in a sequence; that a fuller recognition of difference would acknowledge the contemporaneity of difference; would acknowledge that actually-existing 'others' might not just be following us, but might have their own stories to tell. It would grant the other, the different, at least a degree of autonomy in that sense. It would grant the possibility of at least relatively autonomous trajectories. In other words, it would entertain the possibility of the co-existence of a multiplicity of histories.

However – and to wind the argument back again – in order for there to be co-existing, multiple, histories there must be space. In other words: a full understanding of spatiality entails the recognition that there is more than one story going on in the world and that these stories have, at least, a relative autonomy.

Fourth, there is one final approach to understanding space which it is necessary to escape. For, as part and parcel of that 'modernist' view of space as temporalised went something else: a particular way of understanding the relationship between 'space' and 'society'. Above all, geographical space was imagined as partitioned, as divided up into localities, places, regions... As Gupta and Ferguson have written:

313

> "Representations of space in the social sciences are remarkably dependent on images of break, rupture, and disjunction".
>
> (Gupta and Ferguson 1992, p. 6)

Moreover, this partitioned space was imagined in relation to a particular form of organisation of society: into nation states, local communities, the local tribes of the anthropologists, the regional cultures of the sociologists and geographers. There was, in other words, an assumption of an isomorphism between culture/society on the one hand and place on the other. Cultures had their own places.

There was, moreover, a further step. For the differences between these place-based cultures, and the identities of those cultures, were assumed to be internally generated and pre-constituted. First, it was imagined, the cultures (regional cultures, nations, etc.) came into existence and then they came into interaction. The characteristics of a place and its 'local culture' were assumed somehow to grow out of the very soil. It is a classically Newtonian, billiard-ball, view of places and of regions, and of the constitution of identities and difference. It is essentially essentialist, and individualist. And it is indeed a mode of understanding which can itself be subject to analysis [...]

In this paper, in contrast to this partitioned view of space, there is an imagination of space and of places, and of the identity of places, regions, nations, ..., as precisely in part a *product* of interaction. Moreover this case is argued both in principle (as a useful way of conceptualising space) and as a matter of historical understanding. That is to say, it is both a theoretical proposition about how we might best imagine places and regions (Allen/Massey/Cochrane 1998) and an argument that things were ever thus.

It is, for instance, not the case that places and nations existed in a state of self-enclosure until the current phase of globalisation [...] Eric Wolf (1982) in his book 'Europe and the People without History' convincingly argues the case for societies prior to 1492: there never were, he argues, 'cultural isolates' [...] Given this way of looking at things, then, we are presented with a question for today: how shall we characterise the identity of the new 'Europe'? Can we imagine it in a way which pays due recognition to how much 'Europeanness' owes to long centuries of relations with a wider world beyond?

4. INTERMEZZO

A brief recapitulation may be in order. The argument is that crucial to the conceptualisation of space/spatiality is the recognition of its essential relation to and constitution through coexisting difference(s) – multiplicity; of its enabling and incorporating the coexistence of relatively independent trajectories.

314

It is a proposal for recognising space as the sphere of the meeting up, or not, of those trajectories – where they coexist, affect each other, fight. Space, then, is the product of the intricacies and complexities, the intertwinings and the non-interlockings, of relations, from the unimaginably cosmic to the intimately tiny. Space, to repeat yet again, is the product of interrelations.

Moreover, as a result of that, and as already argued, space is always in the process of being made; it is always unfinished. There are always loose ends in space.

Now, all this leads to a further result. This relationality of space together with its openness means that space also always contains a degree of the unexpected, the unpredictable. As well as loose ends then, space also always contains an element of 'chaos' (of the not already prescribed by the system). It is a 'chaos' which results from those happenstance juxtapositions, those accidental separations, the often paradoxical character of geographical configurations in which, precisely, a number of distinct trajectories interweave and, sometimes, interact. Space, in other words, is inherently 'disrupted' (Massey 1997). Perhaps most startlingly of all, given hegemonic conceptualisations, *space is not a surface*.

Now, the reason for this recapitulation is to enable me to draw out two further points.

The first point is simply to stress that this disruptedness of space is important. It distinguishes the argument being made here about interrelationality from that which characterises the position of what one might call 'New Age holism'. The latter is that way of envisioning the world as constructed through interrelations but where, in a sense, all the interrelations are already established: where everything is already connected to everything else. In this formulation there is the danger of ending up with a totalising closure, the claustrophobia of the closed system, the closed coherence where there is no opening for anything new. To move from the 'individualist' view of space criticised earlier (space as a container for 'things') to this kind of relationality is to move straight through from the billiard-ball world of an essentialist Newtonianism to a closed holism which leaves no opening for an active politics.

This paper is not arguing for that move, therefore. Rather it is arguing for an open 'system' (though the term itself may no longer be appropriate) which contains existing, changing and future relations. It is a formation of *potential*. It contains, as an integral aspect, what has been called 'the productiveness of incoherence' (Levin 1989).

Moreover that productiveness of incoherence is key to the second point: a point which may indeed be sufficiently significant to warrant the status of 'fourth proposition'. This is that, precisely because it is the sphere of the potential juxtaposition of different narratives, of the potential forging of new relations, spatiality is also a source of the production of *new* trajectories, *new* stories. It is a source of the production of new spaces, new identities, new relations and differences. It is interesting, and significant, how the argument is constrained at this point by the non-availability of an adequate language. The implication is, returning to the earlier ruminations about Bergson (and again in dispute with Bergson) that time needs space to get itself going. Time and space are born together. It really is imperative that we conceptualise the world in terms of time-space.

[...]

The case for this interpretation of space

There is, however, a serious question which needs now to be raised, and addressed. Even if all the above is cheerfully accepted there is still the issue of *why* we should be imagining space in this way. There is one possible answer, which is increasingly popular these days, but of which I remain at least wary if not thoroughly unconvinced. This is the answer that 'physics tells us so'. One of the more amusing and puzzling aspects of much current writing under the sign of postmodernism is that, on the one hand, there is a deep suspicion of any form of claim to universal truths and yet, on the other hand, there is a liberal (and, I would argue, often lazy) recourse to references to the natural sciences. Quantum mechanics, chaos theory, fractals ... are frequently called upon to serve some (often rather unspecified) function in arguments which themselves are centrally concerned with the human world. Until we have had more serious debate about the status of these appeals they need to be treated with – at least – great care. Physicists argue amongst themselves at least as much as we do. It is not clear why 'hard' sciences (so-called) should be treated as a source of unimpugnable truth by those working in the field commonly called 'social' (Massey 1999b) [...]

[...] It is not that kind of strategy that I wish to deploy here. Rather, I wish to argue for this approach to the conceptualisation of space on a rather different basis: that particular understandings (for instance of space) become appropriate in specific moments of space-time and from particular (political) perspectives. Old ways of thinking can run into the ground, can become blockages to thought and action, can indeed be actively mobilized *as* blockages to change. On this ground, the reason for advancing this particular way of conceptualising space is not because of any claim to its eternal or objective truth or correctness. Rather, it is on the basis that it refuses the reactionary entrapments of previously hegemonic formulations and opens up the ground for new questions which – politically – I would argue need urgently to be posed. The final section of this address, therefore, takes up four ways in which

I believe this to be the case: how the world which we face in the approach to the new millennium demands of us new geographical imaginations.

The first of these is very general and very briefly stated. It is simply that this approach opens space/spatiality up to politics in a new way. Indeed it enables it to be made *integral to* the political. Space is no longer the realm of the dead (Bergson, the structuralists), not merely a cross-section through time, nor a dimension whose specificity is persistently occluded by being read in terms of temporality (many current versions of 'globalisation'). Rather, space is now rendered as part (a necessary part) of the generation, the production, of the new. In other words the issue here is not to stress only the production *of* space but space itself as integral *to* the production of society. Indeed, the argument is that if we want time (the future) to be open (as Bergson did and as so many are now arguing) then we *need* to conceptualise space in this way, as also itself thoroughly open and active.

The second reason for arguing for thinking of space in this way is more specific and relates to the particular question of conceptualising space in terms of relations. There are, I believe, very many routes into arguing for the significance of this approach, many of them put forward in recent years by those in queer studies, feminism and postcolonial studies. Rather than repeat their arguments I shall take an issue more particular to geography: the issue of identity, but in this case the issue particularly of the identity of place.[6] In this context, 'place' can refer to locality, region, nation state, a newly-emerging entity such as 'European Union', or any other such geographical entity. Such 'objects' have always been central to geographical thought, and there has been much debate about how best to define them. Though, I have to say, much of that debate was more concerned with technical definition than with conceptualisation: it was often assumed that the task was to draw a line around a space, and that the problem was simply where to draw it.

For me personally, the dramatic events of 1989 brought to a head a number of doubts which had been stirring in me over the years. That year saw, across Eurasia, the emergence to new heights of a series of nationalisms, of local parochialisms, of mutual antipathies between ethnicities which often defined themselves in geographical terms (and therefore claimed a geographical base). It was from this period that terms such as 'ethnic cleansing' began again to have currency on our continent. There was bloody violence in defence of local specificity. And it continues to this day, in many parts of the world. For me this generated an internal conflict. On the one hand I absolutely rejected the claims to local exclusivity and the terms on which they were being made. On the other hand I absolutely did not want to give up

---

6 This argument has been written up at greater length in Doreen Massey 1998 [...]

on the ability to appreciate local difference (it is one of the reasons I became, and remain, a geographer).

My response was to set about trying to re-imagine place (or, more generally, geographical specificity) in a way which was (i) not bounded (ii) not defined in terms of exclusivity (iii) not defined in terms of counterposition between an inside and an outside, and (iv) not dependent upon false notions of an internally-generated authenticity. It meant, in other words, precisely rejecting that conceptualisation in terms of Newtonian essentialism which I mentioned earlier. This way of conceptualising spatiality had become a blockage to thinking our way past the confrontation of geographical essentialisms. Instead of that, it meant beginning to argue for an understanding of the identity of place as constructed through relations with elsewhere: 'a global sense of place' (Massey 1991). It is this kind of approach, I believe, which may enable us to argue for a political position which allows both the appreciation of local specificity and the firm maintenance of an internationalist stance.

Thirdly, conceptualising 'identity' in this way – both identity in general and geographical specificity more particularly – enables new questions to be raised and new arguments made about the forms of possible politics. As intimated earlier, I believe our age demands what might be called 'a relational politics'. That is, not a politics of pre-constituted identities (not an 'identity politics' as in the USA) but a politics of exposing the maps of power *through which* identities are constructed. There is, of course, a real (and I believe reactionary) politics which depends precisely upon suppressing the recognition of the cartographies of power upon which identity-construction is necessarily based: so simple recognition is a step forward. Simple recognition alone, however, is not enough. As argued earlier, the proposition that 'we are all related' is insufficient. For all those relations are actively made (and some of them may never be made), and the fact that they are made (they are integrally social practices) in turn implies that they are full of social power. So, politically, what we have to do is recognise also the *form* of those relationships, their inevitable content of social power, the relations of dominance and subordination which they may entail, or (more positively) the enabling potential to which they may give rise.

Such a politics would, in other words, rather than claiming rights for a rapidly multiplying set of pre-constituted identities, take responsibility for, and – where appropriate – challenge, the form of the relationships through which those identities are formed – and indeed in which we are individually and collectively positioned and through which society more generally is constituted.

Fourthly and finally, this in turn connects with a further way in which we might think about politics. It has already been argued that many 'modernist' approaches to politics (whether liberal-progressive or Marxist) imagine the world very much in terms of historical sequences [...] What is (must be?) now on the agenda is a fuller appreciation of the fact that the future is genuinely open [...] Modernist organization of the world into a single grand narrative suppressed the existence of real difference. If there is only one narrative, one future towards which we are all marching (in the way in which we imagine the world) then we have suppressed the genuine and potential multiplicities of the spatial. The single linear history organises space into temporal sequence. A refusal to temporalise space, therefore, both opens up our stories to multiplicity and recognises that the future is not already written; that it is, to some small extent at least, within of course the constraints of circumstances not of our own choosing, ours to make.

REFERENCES

Adam, B. (1990) *Time and social theory*. Oxford: Polity Press.

Allen, J., Massey, D. and Cochrane, A. (1998) *Rethinking the region*. London: Routledge.

Bergson. H. (1959) *Oeuvres*. Paris: Presses Universitaires de France.

de Certeau, M. (1984) *The practice of everyday life*. Berkeley: The University of California Press.

Deleuze. G. and Guattari. F. (1984) *A thousand plateaus: capitalism and schizophrenia*. (English translation). London: The Athlone Press.

Fabian, J. (1983) *Time and the other: how anthropology makes its object*. New York: Columbia University Press.

Gross, D. (1981–82) Space, Time and Modern Culture. *Telos* 50, pp. 59–78.

Grossberg. L. (1996) The space of culture, the power of space. In Chambers and L. Curti (eds): *The postcolonial question: common skies, divided horizons*. London: Routledge. pp. 169–188.

Gupta. A. and Ferguson, J. (1992) Beyond 'culture': space, identity, and the politics of difference. *Cultural Anthropology* 7, pp. 6–23.

Haver, W. (1997) Queer research; or, how to practise invention to the brink of intelligibility. In S. Golding (ed): *The eight technologies of otherness*. London: Routledge, pp. 277–292.

Laclau, E. (1990) *New reflections on the revolution of our time*. London: Verso.

Lefebvre, H. (1991): *The production of space*. (English translation). Oxford: Blackwell.

Levin, Y. (1989): Dismantling the spectacle: the cinema of Guy Debord. In E. Sussmann (ed): *On the passage of a few people through a rather brief moment in time: the Situationist International, 1957-1972*. Cambridge, Mass.: MIT Press, pp. 72–123.

Massey, D. (1991) A global sense of place. *Marxism Today*. June, 24–29. Reprinted in Massey, D. (1994) *Space, place and gender*. Oxford: Polity Press, pp. 146–156.

Massey, D. (1995) Thinking radical democracy spatially. *Environment and Planning D: Society & Space*, 13, pp. 283–288.

Massey, D. (1997) Spatial disruptions. In S. Golding (ed): *The eight technologies of otherness*. London: Routledge, pp. 218–225.

Massey, D. (1998) 'Identity': some parallels between feminist debate and the identity of place. Berichte zur deutschen Landeskunde, 72, pp. 53–59.

Massey, D. (1999a) Imagining globalisation: power-geometries of space-time. In A. Brah, M. Hickman and M. Mac an Ghaill (eds): *Future worlds: migration, environment and globalization*. Basingstoke: Macmillan.

Massey, D. (1999b) Space-time, 'science' and the relationship between physical geography and human geography. *Transactions of the Institute of British Geographers*, vol 24, no 3, pp. 261–276.

Massey, D., Allen, J. and Sarre, P. (1999) *Human geography today*. Oxford: Polity Press.

Mouffe, C. (1993) *The return of the political*. London: Verso.

Mouffe, C. (1995) Post-Marxism: democracy and identity. *Environment and Planning D: Society & Space* 13, pp. 259–265.

Osborne. P. (1995) *The politics of time: modernity and avant-garde*. London: Verso.

Wolf. E. (1982) *Europe and the people without history*. London: University of California Press.

CHAPTER 20

CONCEPTS OF SPACE AND POWER IN THEORY AND IN POLITICAL PRACTICE (2009)

[...]

POWER-GEOMETRIES IN ACTION

In itself, the term power-geometry does not imply any specific form (any specific geometry). It is a concept through which to analyse the world, in order perhaps to highlight inequalities, or deficiencies in democracy. It is in this mode an instrument of potential critique. It may also, however, be an instrument through which to imagine, and maybe to begin to build, more equal and democratic societies. This point was brought strongly home to me in the spring and summer of 2007 when I received an invitation to visit Venezuela to participate in the processes of change underway as part of the Bolivarian project of building a socialism of the twenty-first century. After a resounding election victory in December 2006 this project, led by Hugo Chávez, had moved in a more explicitly socialist direction (its own characterisation) and in this context five motors had been set out to carry the revolution forward. The fourth of these motors is to build a new power-geometry (*la nueva geometría del poder*). Here, then, a geographical concept is being put to positive political use. Indeed, as will be seen, part of what lay behind the proposal was an impressive recognition of the existence and significance, within Venezuela, of highly unequal, and thus undemocratic, power-geometries.

In its particular form of the fourth motor, the new power-geometry referred to the need to reorganise the geopolitics of Venezuela, the geopolitical organisation of its territory. Importantly, however, this was recognised to refer both to the formal *geography* of its democracy and to the *form* of the power-relations that it entailed. Schematically, it is possible to spell out these aspects separately. Thus, on the more purely geographical side, the intent is

321

to distribute «power» and participation more evenly – to give more voice to the vast regions of the south of the country, that stretch away from the towns and populated areas of the coast towards the headwaters of the Amazon; to give more voice to smaller communities; and to give more voice to indigenous communities. On the other side, there was recognition of the need also to address the nature of the power within these power-geometries. By the time of Chávez's election in 1998, the formal state apparatus in Venezuela, including its mechanisms of representative democracy, were completely delegitimised. The long period of *puntofijismo*, the subsequent chaos and farce, the extremely high levels of corruption..., all of these things meant that it was not feasible simply to continue with the forms of state and democracy that had been inherited. The most important structural innovation here has been the introduction of participatory democracy from below.

The mechanisms for the implementation of these changes are more complex than can be elaborated here, but a few points can be made. One small and symbolic one is the proposal to call all basic-level settlements within the democratic structure «cities». The politics of this change revolved around the linguistic connection between city and citizenship (*ciudad y ciudadanía*) and the equality of rights and responsibilities, that inhere in citizenship, that had previously been lacking. In symbolic terms it proclaims that every geographical collectivity, however small and wherever it is in the country, has the same political status. As such, it is a small step in the building of a new power-geometry. It is also, as is much of the Bolivarian revolution, about the recognition and assertion of voice, and of a multiplicity of voices. It resonates in other words with the conceptualisation of space (as a multiplicity) [...]

Much bigger have been the changes wrought through the introduction of elements of participatory democracy. This has taken place through the initiation of a process of the formation of «communal councils» (*consejos comunales*). These are formed by people themselves (there are posters and leaflets and so forth detailing how to do it). Each communal council brings together about 400 households (this number can be adjusted in indigenous and rural areas to conform with local customs and conditions). There is then, in principle, a successive aggregation of these councils up to national level, forming a structure parallel to that of the elected state. Broadly speaking, the aims of these councils are on the one hand to take unto themselves the collective self-management of their neighbourhoods and on the other hand to maintain pressure on the elected state (the pressure of constituent power on constituted power). In terms of power-geometries some things are immediately evident. This is an attempt (again) to shift political voice towards those who previously did not have such a voice – the poor in the cities being the clearest example. Moreover this political voice exemplifies a different kind of power-relation. It is not about representative democracy and the individualism of voting; rather it is about *collective* organisation, decision-making, management and campaigning. Moreover, this very process of self-government, the very formation of communal councils, is one that, being new, has to be learned. It is thus in itself empowering. It is part of the process of formation of *popular* power (*poder popular*, or *poder protagónico*). It is possible to see here, in other words, how both the very nature of power-relations and the geography of those relations might be changed. Truly an attempt to shift the whole nature of the national, political, power-geometries.

Let us, then, reflect briefly on this mobilisation of the concept of power-geometry, primarily at this point from the point of view of political practice but bearing in mind also the conceptual arguments elaborated [elsewhere].

First, if power is relational then it is necessary to consider not just entities (such as, for instance, smaller settlements in rural areas, or communal councils) and their establishment and recognition, but also the wider relations of power within which they are set. Thus, in the case of communal councils, in any political evaluation it is necessary to take into account a host of questions such as: where is control over their recognition located? (communal councils have to be officially recognised in order to participate in the new structures) and where is control over the distribution of resources to and between communal councils located? Such considerations will influence greatly the reality of the project to distribute democratic participation more evenly. So too will the issue of resources and capabilities. If the aim is greater equality, if power is relational, and if the starting-point is gross inequality (which it is in Venezuela), then the establishment of structures and rights has to be supplemented by an expansion of resources and capabilities, human and physical, in those areas currently underendowed.

Second, there is the question of time and temporality. The intuitive image of a power-geometry might be as a kind of diagram, or map. It is essentially a spatial concept, and this map-like image of it would fit with those understandings of space that see it as a flat, finished, surface or network. As something already completed. As, indeed, dead. Yet as soon as that is said it is obviously incorrect. For a power-geometry is precisely a product of relations, and relations are social processes, and very much alive. In that sense power-geometries precisely exemplify the conceptualisation of space as always under construction. The spatial as imbued with temporality.

This is richly evident in the policy of power-geometries in Venezuela, and it raises reflections both political and conceptual. It is evident in a situation, as in Venezuela, where establishing a new power-geometry is part of politics, that power-geometries are *processes*. They are not diagrams on a page; they are the evolving outcome of processes of socio-political contestation. Thus, politically, what matters is not only the initiating policy statements and formal definitions, the declarations about communal councils and the delineation of territories, but the socio-political practices of their realisation. And these practices will reflect and depend on everything from the general political culture of the nation to the behaviour of individuals (the microphysics of power).

Furthermore, in building a new power-geometry it is necessary to take account of this essential dynamism and to make it part of the politics. In particular, it is necessary to grapple with the possibility that there may be more than one temporality within a power-geometry, *and* that there may be dislocations between them. There is a very clear case of this in Venezuela. Thus, one of the most frequent criticisms of the Bolivarian process is that it is producing a situation (a power-geometry) which is too focused on the centre, specifically in the figure of Chávez. One response to this is that this (acknowledged but perhaps inevitable) centralisation will be balanced by the development of popular forces through, for instance, the communal councils. Whether or not one thinks this is an adequate response, the point to be made here is that it is to attempt to balance two very different temporalities. On the one hand, the power-resources of the president can be established almost immediately, through the passage of laws. On the other hand, the power-resources of small communities in the south of the country, for instance, or in the poor barrios of the coastal cities, will take years to develop. From economic weight, to cultural resources, to the forming of collectivities, to the very confidence that one can raise one's political voice at all, all these things have been seriously lacking in such places and among such groups. Here the passing of legislation is merely an enabling act. The bringing to fruition of the aim will take many years and much hard work. Meanwhile, the imbalances within the emerging power-geometry are likely to persist.

A further reflection arises from the fact that in Venezuela the concept of power-geometry is being mobilised specifically in the sphere of politics. However, [...] there are geometries of power in all instances of society. Moreover they relate to each other and, if there is any general tendency, it is that they are likely to reinforce each other. For that reason the real functioning of a power-geometry within the political will depend also on that within the economic, that within the distribution of educational resources, that within the cultural sphere, and so on. In the Venezuelan con- text, one thing this means is that other motors of the revolution will be important contributors to the establishment of a new, more democratic and egalitarian, political power-geometry. One might, for instance, cite here the third motor (*moral y luces*) with its emphasis on popular education. Most particularly, this interdependence of power-geometries within different spheres highlights the importance of economic reform – the building of what is said to be a new productive economic model that is collective and cooperative. Such a process (also likely to be long and conflictual) would contribute greatly to the reality of a new geometry of power within the political sphere.

One final, brief, reflection – and one which relates closely to recent debates within geography – concerns the role of «place» in the building of this new power-geometry. The basic building-blocks of the new popular, participatory, forms of democracy are *places*. They are groups of households in which the grouping is through criteria of spatial contiguity (they form a neighbourhood, or settlement, etc.), and much of the task which they have been set concerns the forming of that place into a collective to address issues of local (within-place) self-management. This is typical of all such initiatives, and indeed representative democracy also typically functions through a territorial base. It does, however, raise reflections, again both political and conceptual.

In the constitutional proposals in Venezuela «communes» were defined as the social cells of the territory, each of which is to constitute the basic and indivisible nucleus of the state («serán las células sociales del territorio [...] cada una de las cuales constituirá el nucleo territorial básico e indivisible del Estado»). From the point of view of the concept of space advocated here, and from that of power-geometries, space is not simply an aggregation of territories; it is also a space of flows and relations. In its turn this implies that «places» are never homogeneous or closed. Each place is a node of relations, an internal complexity. And this in turn implies that «places» are the products of negotiation, conflict, competition, agreement, and so forth between different interests and positions. This is in no way to throw doubt upon the proposals. But it *is* to argue that these «basic nuclei» will, as political entities, be an evolving *result* of the process of building participatory democracy rather than a presumed already-existing coherence that one can take as an *input* to the process. (Once again, the political and the conceptual engage with each other in productive conversation.)

The political implications are significant. One aspect is, as already mentioned, that the process of building these nuclei into political entities (the consejos comunales) is a long, difficult, and potentially conflictual one. The existence of collectivities cannot be taken as given. On the other hand this very process is itself a learning process, and an empowering one. (It might be noted that this form of territorial base is thus in fact very different from that of representative democracy. In representative democracy the territorial base is effective only as the unit of aggregation of individuals. In participatory democracy and local self-management, however, the territorial base is required also to be effective as the scaffolding for the constitution of a collective voice. It is also different, moreover, from those autonomous communities that establish themselves, also in places, as demonstrations of the possibility of political alternatives, for in their case some kind of agreement,

325

or commitment to the project, is assumed from the start. This is important, for it means that there is no need to confront radical differences in interests or political position. In the places of the consejos comunales any such differences will have to be addressed, and this is important – and positive – politically.) Furthermore, there is some evidence, for instance in the detailed empirical investigations in Caracas by Miguel Lacabana and Cecilia Cariola, that this emerging place-based collectivity is beginning in itself to give people from the poorer barrios a confidence and, very interestingly, that this place-basis (anclaje territorial) has enabled people from these barrios to break out of their previous territorial enclosure (a romper el encierro territorial) and participate more widely in the public and institutional spaces of the city as a whole (Cariola and Lacabana, 2005).

Before turning to the final section, which will reflect some more on the engagement between the theoretical and the political, there is one further point to be made. This is that, although the only way that the concept power-geometry is mobilised consistently and explicitly in the Bolivarian project is in relation to the restructuring of politics and democracy in the internal political sphere, there are of course numerous other ways in which the project is having considerable effects on other geometries of power. This is especially the case at the global level where the insistence has been on the attempt to create a world that is more explicitly politically differentiated – multipolar as opposed to unipolar. This has taken many forms, including perhaps most importantly, the moves to create a more distinguishable voice within Latin America (from ALBA, to Telesur, to PetroCaribe, to the Banco del Sur, and so on). It also included [...] an equal exchange agreement between Caracas and London that clearly challenged the neoliberal mantras that all relations between places should be those of the market and that places must compete against each other. No, it said, they can cooperate. This was an explicit politics of relations (a politics *of* place *beyond* place, as I have called it) and quite clearly a very small, but symbolic, remodelling of the existing power-geometries of neoliberal globalisation. And, although indeed tiny, its potential symbolic significance was ironically confirmed when the incoming Conservative mayor cancelled the agreement almost immediately on taking office.

CONCEPTUAL LESSONS FROM POLITICAL PRACTICE

The previous section, then, presented one small story of the mobilisation of a geographical concept in political practice. A concept being employed to do real work. This kind of deployment raises a host of questions. One of these is the issue of one's responsibility, as it were, for and towards a concept when it is deployed politically, and especially when as in this case the concept has travelled from its place of origin to be deployed elsewhere. (This latter aspect raises particular questions for postcolonial geographies.) [...] Here what was fascinating was the way in which the concept was further moulded by the very fact of its engagement in political practice [...]

[...] Witnessing the active use of the idea of power-geometries enriched the concept in a variety of ways. Thinking about how it could relate to a whole range of different kinds of power-relations – popular, participatory, collective – and appreciating even apparently small things such as the intended symbolic force of calling all settlements «cities», gave the concept a richer, more qualitative sense. It elaborated still further, for me, the range of possibilities of what might be a «power-geometry».

REFERENCES

Cariola, C.; Lacabana, M. (2005). «Globalización y metropolización: tensiones, transiciones y cambios», in *CENDES-UCV: Venezuela visión plural: Una mirada desde el Cendes.* Caracas: Cendes.

SELECT BIBLIOGRAPHY OF DOREEN MASSEY

Allen, J. & D. Massey (eds) 1988. *Restructuring Britain: The Economy in Question*. London: Sage.

Allen, J., D. Massey & A. Cochrane 1998. *Rethinking the Region*. London: Routledge.

Amin, A., D. Massey & N. Thrift 2000. *Cities for the Many Not the Few*. Bristol: Policy Press.

Amin, A., D. Massey & N. Thrift 2003. *Decentering the Nation: A Radical Approach to Region Inequality*. London: Catalyst.

Cordey Hayes, M., T. A. Broadbent & D. Massey 1970. "Towards Operational Urban Development Models". Working Paper 60, Centre for Environmental Studies, London.

Hall, S. & D. Massey 2010. "Interpreting the Crisis". In R. Grayson & J. Rutherford (eds) *After the Crash: Re-inventing the Left in Britain*. London: Soundings, Social Liberal Forum and Compass, 37–46.

Hall, S. & D. Massey 2012. "Interpreting the Crisis". In S. Davison & K. Harris (eds) *The Neo-liberal Crisis*. London: Soundings, 55–69.

Hall, S., D. Massey & M. Rustin 1995. "Editorial: Uncomfortable Times". *Soundings* 1: 5–18.

Hall, S., D. Massey & M. Rustin (eds) 2012. *After Neoliberalism? The Kilburn Manifesto*. London: Lawrence and Wishart.

Hall, S., D. Massey & M. Rustin 2013. "After Neoliberalism: Analysing the Present". *Soundings* 53: 8–22.

Harrison, S., D. Massey & K. Richards 2006. "Complexity and Emergence (Another Conversation)". *Area* 38 (4): 465–71.

Harrison, S., D. Massey & K. Richards 2008. "Conversations across the Divide". *Geoforum* 39 (2): 549–51.

Harrison, S., D. Massey, K. Richards, *et al.* 2004. "Thinking across the Divide: Perspectives on the Conversations between Physical and Human Geography". *Area* 36 (4): 435–42.

Henry, N. & D. Massey 1995. "Competitive Time-Space in High Technology". *Geoforum* 26 (1): 49–64.

Lury, K. & D. Massey 1999. "Making Connections". *Screen* 40 (3): 229–38.

Martin, R., A. Markusen & D. Massey 1993. "Classics in Human Geography Revisited: Spatial Divisions of Labour". *Progress in Human Geography* 17 (1): 69–72.

Massey, D. 1968a. "Problems of Location: Linear Programming". *Working Paper* 14, Centre for Environmental Studies, London.

Massey, D. 1968b. "Problems of Location: Game Theory and Gaming Simulation". *Working Paper* 15, Centre for Environmental Studies, London.

Massey, D. 1969. "Some Simple Models for Distributing Changes in Employment within Regions". *Working Paper* 24, Centre for Environmental Studies, London.

Massey, D. 1971. "The Basic: Service Categorization in Planning". *Working Paper* 63, Centre for Environmental Studies, London.

Massey, D. 1973. "Towards a Critique of Industrial Location Theory". *Antipode* 5 (3): 33–9.

Massey, D. 1974. "Social Justice and the City: A Review". *Environment and Planning A* 6 (2): 229–35.

Massey, D. 1978. "Regionalism: Some Current Issues". *Capital and Class* 2 (3): 105–25.

Massey, D. 1979. "In What Sense a Regional Problem?" *Regional Studies* 13 (2): 233–43.

Massey, D. 1983a. "The Shape of Things to Come". *Marxism Today* April: 18–27.

Massey, D. 1983b. "The Contours of Victory – Dimensions of Defeat". *Marxism Today* July: 16–19.

Massey, D. 1983c. "Industrial Restructuring as Class Restructuring: Production Decentralization and Local Uniqueness". *Regional Studies* 17 (2): 73–89.

Massey, D. 1984a. "New Directions in Space". In J. Urry & D. Gregory (eds) *Social Relations and Spatial Structures*. London: Macmillan.

Massey, D. 1984b. *Spatial Divisions of Labour: Social Structures and the Geography of Production*. Basingstoke: Macmillan.

Massey, D. 1984c. "Introduction: Geography Matters". In D. Massey & J. Allen (eds) *Geography Matters! A Reader*. Cambridge: Cambridge University Press, 1–11.

Massey, D. 1985. "New Directions in Space". In D. Gregory & J. Urry (eds) *Social Relations and Spatial Structures*. London: Macmillan, 9–19.

Massey, D. 1986. "Nicaragua: Some Reflections on Socio-Spatial Issues in a Society in Transition". *Antipode* 18 (3): 322–31.

Massey, D. 1987a. *Nicaragua: Some Urban and Regional Issues in a Society in Transition.* Milton Keynes: Open University Press.

Massey, D. 1987b. "Spatial Labour Markets in an International Context". *Tijdschrift voor Economische en Sociale Geografie* 78 (5): 374–9.

Massey, D. 1988a. "A New Class of Geography". *Marxism Today* May: 12–17.

Massey, D. 1988b. "Uneven Development: Social Change and Spatial Divisions of Labour". In D. Massey & J. Allen (eds) *Uneven Re-development: Cities and Regions in Transition.* London: Hodder and Stoughton, 250–76.

Massey, D. 1991a. "A Global Sense of Place". *Marxism Today* June: 24–9.

Massey, D. 1991b. "Flexible Sexism". *Environment and Planning D: Society and Space* 9 (1): 31–57.

Massey, D. 1991c. "The Political Place of Locality Studies". *Environment and Planning A* 23 (2): 267–81.

Massey, D. 1992a. "A Place Called Home?" *New Formations* 17: 3–15. Massey, D. 1992b. "Politics and Space/Time". *New Left Review* 196: 65–84.

Massey, D. 1992c. "Space, Place and Gender". *London School of Economics Magazine* Spring: 32–4.

Massey, D. 1993a. "The Different Side of the 'Sixties'". *Environment and Planning A* Anniversary Issue: 10–13.

Massey, D. 1993b. "Power-Geometry and a Progressive Sense of Place". In J. Bird, B. Curtis, T. Putnam, G. Robertson & L. Tuckner (eds) *Mapping the Futures: Local Cultures, Global Chance*. Abingdon: Routledge, 59–69.

Massey, D. 1994. *Space, Place and Gender*. Cambridge: Polity Press.

Massey, D. 1995a. "Masculinity, Dualisms and High Technology". *Transactions of the Institute of British Geographers* 20 (4): 487–99.

Massey, D. 1995b. *Spatial Divisions of Labour: Social Structures and the Geography of Production*. 2nd edition. Basingstoke: Macmillan.

Massey, D. 1995c. "Thinking Radical Democracy Spatially". *Environment and Planning D: Society and Space* 13 (3): 283–8.

Massey, D. 1997a. "Editorial: Problems with Globalization". *Soundings* 7: 7–12.

Massey, D. 1997b. "Spatial Disruptions". In S. Golding (ed.) *Eight Technologies of Otherness*. London and New York: Routledge, 218–25.

Massey, D. 1999a. Curriculum Vitae. Papers of Doreen Massey.

Massey, D. 1999b. "Imagining Globalization: Power-Geometries of Time-Space". In A. Brah, M. J. Hickman & M. Mac an Ghaill (eds) *Global Futures: Migration, Environment and Globalization*. Basingstoke: Macmillan, 27–44.

Massey, D. 1999c. "Negotiating Disciplinary Boundaries". *Current Sociology* 47 (5): 5–12. Massey, D. 1999d. "Philosophy and Politics of Spatiality: Some Considerations". *Geographische Zeitschrift* 87 (1): 1–12.

Massey, D. 1999e. *Power-Geometries and the Politics of Space-Time: Hettner Lecture 1998*. Heidelberg: Department of Geography, University of Heidelberg.

Massey, D. 1999f. "Spaces for Co-Existence?" *Soundings* 12 (Summer): 7–11.

Massey, D. 1999g. "Space-Time, 'Science' and the Relationship between Physical Geography and Human Geography". *Transactions of the Institute of British Geographers* 24 (3): 261–76.

Massey, D. 2000a. "Bankside: International Local". In I. Blazwick (ed.) *Tate Modern: The Handbook*. London: Tate Publishing, 24–7.

Massey, D. 2000b. "Travelling Thoughts". In P. Gilroy, L. Grossberg & A. McRobbie (eds) *Without Guarantees: In Honour of Stuart Hall*. London: Verso, 225–32.

Massey, D. 2001a. "Geography on the Agenda". *Progress in Human Geography* 25: 5–17.

Massey, D. 2001b. "Living in Wythenshawe". In I. Borden, J. Kerr, J. Rendell & A. Pivaro (eds) *The Unknown City: Contesting Architecture and Social Space*. Cambridge, MA: MIT Press, 458–75.

Massey, D. 2001c. "Talking of Space-Time". *Transactions of the Institute of British Geographers* 26: 257–61.

Massey, D. 2002a. "Don't Let's Counterpose Place and Space". *Development* 45 (2): 24–5.

Massey, D. 2002b. "Globalisation: What Does It Mean for Geography? *Geography* 87 (4): 293–6.

Massey, D. 2002c. "Geography, Policy and Politics: A Response to Dorling and Shaw". *Progress in Human Geography* 26 (5): 645–6.

Massey, D. 2003a. "No More, No Less". *Building Design* July 25: 36.

Massey, D. 2003b. "Some Times of Space". In S. May (ed.) *Olafur Eliasson: The Weather Project*. London: Tate Publishing, 107–18.

Massey, D. 2004a. "Geographies of Responsibility". *Geografiska Annaler B: Human Geography* 86 (1): 5–18.

Massey, D. 2004b. "The Responsibilities of Place". *Local Economy* 19 (2): 97–101. Massey, D. 2005. *For Space*. London: Sage Publications.

Massey, D. 2006a. "Space, Time and Political Responsibility in the Midst of Global Inequality". *Erkunde* 60 (2): 89–95.

Massey, D. 2006b. "Landscape as a Provocation: Reflections on Moving Mountains". *Journal of Material Culture* 11 (1–2): 33–48.

Massey, D. 2006c. "London Inside-Out". *Soundings* 32: 62–71. Massey, D. 2007. *World City*. Cambridge: Polity.

Massey, D. 2008. "When Theory Meets Politics". *Antipode* 40 (3): 492–7.

Massey, D. 2009a. "Invention and Hard Work". In J. Pugh (ed.) *What is Radical Politics Today?* Basingstoke: Palgrave Macmillan, 136–42.

Massey, D. 2009b. "Concepts of Space and Power in Theory and in Political Practice". *Documents d'Anàlisi Geogràfica* 55: 15–26.

Massey, D. 2010. "The Political Struggle Ahead". *Soundings* 45: 6–18.

Massey, D. 2011a. "Ideology and Economics in the Present Moment". *Soundings* 48: 29–39. Massey, D. 2011b. "A Counterhegemonic Relationality of Place". In E. McCann & K. Ward (eds) *Mobile Urbanism: Cities and Policy Making in the Global Age*. Minneapolis: University of Minnesota Press, 1–14.

Massey, D. 2011c. "Espacio y Sociedad: Experimentos con la Espacialidad del Poder y de la Democracia". In A. G. González (ed.) *Latinoamérica: Laboratorio Mundial*. Madrid: La Oficina de Arte y Ediciones, 29–46.

Massey, D. 2011d. "Landscape/Space/Politics: An Essay". The Future of Landscape and the Moving Image Research Project website. https://thefutureoflandscape.wordpress. com/landscapespacepolitics-an-essay/ (accessed 17 December 2017).

Massey, D. 2012a. "Landscape/Space/Politics: An Essay". In R. Tyszczuk, J. Smith, N. Clark & M. Butcher (eds) *Atlas: Geography, Architecture and Change in an Interdependent World*. London: Black Dog Publishing, 90–5.

Massey, D. 2012b. "Learning from Latin America". *Soundings* 50: 131–41.

Massey, D. 2012c. "Los Significados de la Multiplicidad". *Debates y Combates* 27 March. www.youtube.com/watch?v=9wn4QphR4Yw (accessed 9 January 2018).

Massey, D. 2013a. "Vocabularies of the Economy". *Soundings* 54 (Summer): 9–22. Massey, D. 2013b. "Neoliberalism has Hijacked our Vocabulary". *The Guardian*, 11 June. www. theguardian.com/commentisfree/2013/jun/11/neoliberalism-hijacked-vocabulary (accessed 17 January 2018).

Massey, D. 2014. "The Kilburn Manifesto: After Neoliberalism?" *Environment and Planning A* 46 (9): 2034–41.

Massey, D. 2015a. "Globalización, Espacio y Poder". In CEPAL *Memoria del Primer Encuentro de Expertos Gubernamentales en Políticas de Desarrollo Territorial en América Latina y el Caribe*. Santiago de Chile: CEPAL, Naciones Unidas, 9–14.

Massey, D. 2015b. "Why the Corbyn Leadership is Still the Best Hope for Labour". *Soundings blog*, 18 November. www.lwbooks.co.uk/soundings/blog/why-corbyn-leadership-still-best-hope-labour (accessed 18 December 2017).

Massey, D. 2015c. "Vocabularies of the Economy". In S. Hall, D. Massey & M. Rustin (eds) *After Neoliberalism? The Kilburn Manifesto*. London: Lawrence & Wishart, 24–36.

Massey, D. & J. Allen (eds) 1984. *Geography Matters: A Reader*. Cambridge: Cambridge University Press.

Massey, D. & P. Batey 1977. "Introduction". In D. Massey & P. Batey (eds) *Alternative Frameworks for Analysis*. London: Pion, 1–5.

Massey, D., S. Bond & D. Featherstone 2009. "The Possibilities of a Politics of Place Beyond Place? A Conversation with Doreen Massey". *Scottish Geographical Journal* 125 (3–4): 401–20.

Massey, D. & A. Catalano 1978. *Capital and Land: Landownership by Capital in Great Britain*. London: Edward Arnold.

Massey, D. with the HGRG [Human Geography Research Group] 2009. "The Possibilities of a Politics of Place Beyond Place? A Conversation with Doreen Massey". *Scottish Geographical Journal* 125 (3–4): 401–20.

Massey, D. & J. Jacobs 2016. "Significant Geographies: Reflections from a Paper Age". Unpublished proposal. Papers of Jessica Jacobs.

Massey, D. & K. Livingstone 2007. "The World We're In: Interview with Ken Livingstone". *Soundings* 36: 11–25.

Massey, D. & R. Meegan 1978. "Industrial Restructuring versus the Cities". *Urban Studies* 15 (3): 273–88.

Massey, D. & R. Meegan 1979. "The Geography of Industrial Reorganisation: The Spatial Effects of the Restructuring of the Electrical Engineering Sector Under the Industrial Reorganisation Corporation". *Progress in Planning* 10 (3): 155–237.

Massey, D. & R. Meegan 1982. *The Anatomy of Job Loss: The How, Why and Where of Employment Decline*. London: Methuen.

Massey, D. & R. Meegan (eds) 1985. *Politics and Method: Contrasting Studies in Industrial Geography*. London: Methuen.

Massey, D. & N. Miles 1984. "Mapping Out the Unions". *Marxism Today* May: 19–22.

Massey, D., P. Quintas & D. Wield 1992. *High-Tech Fantasies: Science Parks in Society, Science and Space*. London: Routledge.

Massey, D. & M. Rustin 2015. "Displacing Neoliberalism". In S. Hall, D. Massey & M. Rustin (eds) *After Neoliberalism? The Kilburn Manifesto*. London: Lawrence & Wishart, 191–221.

Massey, D. & A. Stevens 2010. "The Future of Landscape: Doreen Massey: An Interview by Andrew Stevens". *3:AM Magazine* 29 September. www.3ammagazine.com/3am/the-future-of-landscape-doreen-massey (accessed 8 January 2018).

Massey, D. & H. Wainwright 1985. "Beyond the Coalfields: The Work of the Miners' Support Groups". In H. Beynon (ed.) *Digging Deeper: Issues in the Miners' Strike*. London: Verso, 149–68.

Massey, D. & N. Warburton 2013. "Doreen Massey on Space". *Social Science Bites* 8 May. www.youtube.com/watch?v=Quj4tjbTPxw (last accessed 8 January 2018).

McDowell, L. & D. Massey 1984. "A Woman's Place". In D. Massey & J. Allen (eds) *Geography Matters! A Reader*. Cambridge: Cambridge University Press, 128–47.

Peck, J., D. Massey, K. Gibson & V. Lawson 2014. "The Kilburn Manifesto: After Neoliberalism?" *Environment and Planning A* 46 (9): 2033–49.

CREDITS

The editors and the publisher are grateful to the publishers, co-authors and Estate of Doreen Massey for their permission to reproduce the following material. While every effort has been made to trace and acknowledge all copyright holders, we would welcome any information that enables us to rectify any inadvertent omission or error in subsequent editions.

Chapter 2 Doreen Massey, "Towards a Critique of Industrial Location Theory", *Antipode*. © John Wiley & Sons 1973.

Chapter 3 Doreen Massey, Richard Barras & Andrew Broadbent, "Labour Must Take Over Land", *Socialist Commentary* (1973).

Chapter 4 Doreen Massey, "The Analysis of Capitalist Landownership: An investigation of the case of Great Britain", *International Journal of Urban and Regional Research*. © John Wiley & Sons 1977.

Chapter 5 Doreen Massey, "Regionalism: Some Current Issues", *Capital & Class*. © Sage Publications, 1978.

Chapter 6 Linda McDowell & Doreen Massey, "A Woman's Place?", in *Geography Matters! A Reader*, edited by D. Massey and J. Allen, 1984, with permission from Cambridge University Press.

Chapter 7 Doreen Massey & Joe Painter, "The Changing Geography of Trade Unions", in *The Political Geography of Contemporary Britain*, edited by J. Mohan (1989), with permission from Palgrave Macmillan.

Chapter 8 Doreen Massey & Hilary Wainwright, "Beyond the Coalfields: The Work of the Miners' Support Groups" (1985), with permission from Verso.

Chapter 9 Doreen Massey, "Power-Geometry and a Progressive Sense of Place", in *Mapping the Futures: Local Cultures, Global Change*, edited by J. Bird, B. Burtis, T. Putnam, G. Robertson & L. Tickner (Routledge, 1993), with permission from Taylor & Francis.

Chapter 10 Doreen Massey, "A Place Called Home?", *New Formations* 1992, with permission from Lawrence & Wishart.

Chapter 11 Doreen Massey, "Masculinity, Dualisms and High Technology", *Transactions of the Royal Institute of British Geographers*, 1995, with permission from the Royal Geographical Society.

Chapter 12 Doreen Massey, "The Geography of Power", *Red Pepper* 2000, with permission.

Chapter 13 Doreen Massey, "Globalisation: what does it mean for geography?" Published in *Geography*, 2002, with permission from the Geographical Association.

Chapter 14 Doreen Massey, "New Directions in Space", in *Social Relations and Spatial Structures* edited by D. Gregory & J. Urry, Macmillan Education 1985, with permission from Palgrave Macmillan.

Chapter 15 Doreen Massey, "Flexible Sexism", *Environment and Planning D: Society and Space* 1991 (9) 31–67. © Sage Publications.

Chapter 16 Doreen Massey, "Reflections on Gender and Geography" in *Social Change and the Middle Classes*, edited by T. Butler & M. Savage, pp. 330–44, UCL Press 1995, with permission from Taylor & Francis.

Chapter 17 Doreen Massey, "Politics and Space/Time". © New Left Review, 1992.

Chapter 18 Doreen Massey, "Reflections on Debates over a Decade", *The Spatial Divisions of Labour*, second edition, Macmillan Education 1995, with permission from Palgrave Macmillan.

Chapter 19 Doreen Massey, "Philosophy and Politics of Spatiality: Some Considerations" (1999), Hettner Lecture in Human Geography, Heidelberg University, Germany, with permission.

Chapter 20 Doreen Massey, "Concepts of Space and Power in Theory and in Political Practice", Documents D'Analisi Geografica 2009, with permission.

INDEX